MW01506225

WHISKEROLOGY

WHISKEROLOGY

The CULTURE OF HAIR *in*
NINETEENTH-CENTURY AMERICA

SARAH GOLD McBRIDE

Harvard University Press

Cambridge, Massachusetts
London, England

2025

Publication of this book has been supported through the generous provisions
of the Maurice and Lula Bradley Smith Memorial Fund.

Library of Congress Cataloging-in-Publication Data

Names: Gold McBride, Sarah, author.
Title: Whiskerology : the culture of hair in nineteenth-century America /
Sarah Gold McBride.
Description: Cambridge, Massachusetts ; London, England : Harvard
    University Press, 2025. | Includes bibliographical references and index.
Identifiers: LCCN 2024035363 | ISBN 9780674249295 (cloth)
Subjects: LCSH: Hair—Social aspects—United States—History—19th
    century. | Hairstyles—United States—History—19th century. | Beards—
    Social aspects—United States—History—19th century. | Gender
    expression—United States—History—19th century. | United States—Social
    life and customs—19th century.
Classification: LCC GT2295.U5 G65 2025 | DDC 391.5—dc23/eng/20240902
LC record available at https://lccn.loc.gov/2024035363

for Louis and Rosalie

CONTENTS

INTRODUCTION

THE PASSAGE CAME FROM an obscure and unremarkable book published in Paris. *Les Secrets de la Beauté et du Corps De L'Homme et de la Femme* (Secrets of face and body beauty for men and women) (1855) offered, as its title laid plain, over a hundred beauty secrets—from the secret to perfectly clean hands to the secret for soothing cracked nipples after breast-feeding.[1] But there was one passage in particular, on the first page of chapter 9, "Des Cheveux" (The hair), that catapulted beyond the pages of this book. Plucked out of the text, translated into English, and sent across the Atlantic Ocean, it landed in American print media in the late 1860s; over the next forty years, this passage was republished—with slight tweaks, variations, and addendums—in more than fifty American newspapers and magazines. It appeared in newspapers from twenty-one states representing every region of the country, and in national magazines as varied in genre and audience as *Harper's Weekly* and *The Monthly Journal of the Brotherhood of Locomotive Engineers*.

In each of these periodicals, the passage—unmoored from its original context among other beauty secrets—offered a lengthy and extremely specific taxonomy of the connection between hair and character:

> Coarse, black hair and dark skin signify great power of character, with a tendency to sensuality. Fine black hair and dark skin indicate strength of character along with purity and goodness. Stiff, straight, black hair and beard, indicate a coarse, strong, rigid, straightforward character. Fine, dark-brown hair signifies the combination of exquisite sensibilities with great strength of character. Flat, clinging straight hair a melancholy but extremely constant character. Harsh,

upright hair is the sign of a reticent and sour spirit; a stubborn and harsh character. Coarse red hair and whiskers indicates powerful animal passions, together with a corresponding strength of character. Auburn hair with florid countenance denotes the highest order of sentiment and intensity of feeling, purity of character, with the highest capacity for enjoyment of suffering. Straight, even, smooth, and glossy hair denotes strength, harmony, and evenness of character, hearty affections, a clear head, and superior talents. Fine, silky, supple hair is the mark of a delicate and sensitive temperament, and it speaks in favor of the mind and character of the owner. Crisp, curly hair indicates a hasty, somewhat impetuous and rash character. White hair denotes a lymphatic and indolent constitution.[2]

Most of the American reprints ended with the same declaration: "The very way in which the hair flows is strongly indicative of the ruling passions and inclinations, and perhaps a clever person could give a shrewd guess at the manner of a man's or woman's disposition by only seeing the backs of their heads."[3]

Both this detailed taxonomy and its emphatic nation-wide circulation reflect a cultural narrative that began to emerge in the United States during the eighteenth century and became dominant during the nineteenth century: that hair had the power to reveal the truth about the person from whose body it grew. People from different regions, racial and ethnic groups, and class backgrounds shared an extraordinary faith in the revelatory and diagnostic power of hair. Hair was popularly understood to be capable of quickly and reliably conveying important information about a stranger's core identity—especially their gender (man or woman, masculine or feminine) or their race (African-, European-, or East Asian-descended, or indigenous to North America). Hair could illuminate intimate characteristics of their personality, such as whether they were courageous, ambitious, duplicitous, predatory, or criminally inclined. In some contexts, hair was even considered more reliable than other body parts at communicating meaningful information about the body from which it grew—more so even than those body parts that usually dominate the study of the body and identity in modern American history, such as facial profile, skull shape, and skin color. As an influential white supremacist wrote in 1853, there was "nothing that reveals the specific difference of race so unmistakably as the natural covering of the head"—the hair.[4]

To categorize hair alongside body parts like skulls and skin is intentional: hair was, indeed, conceptualized as a body part in the nineteenth century. Writers often used the word *appendage* to refer to hair, such as the Philadelphia hairstylist who described hair in 1841 as "the peculiar or necessary appendage of the human frame." Moreover, even though barbers and surgeons had long separated into distinct professions, a haircut might be deemed an *operation*, and frequent haircuts could mean having "hair that is constantly kept *bleeding* under the scissors of the barber."[5] Twentieth- and twenty-first-century scholars have largely overlooked this important nineteenth-century cultural belief because it is so different from our own. For the last century, hair has not generally been viewed as a body part: for most Americans, hair occupies a different mental category from legs or ears or even skin—parts whose skeletal or cartilage construction, whose connections to nerves and muscles, make them integral to the composition of a human body; hair, meanwhile, *grows from* the body, but is not *part of* the body.[6] In the nineteenth century, by contrast, hair was as essential to the body as any of its flesh-and-bone parts. Hair also continued to have significance and power even when it was detached from the body—preserved, perhaps, in a book or locket—because the strands of hair themselves functioned as a synecdoche for their owner. By taking these assumptions and beliefs about hair's relationship to the body seriously, this book reveals how nineteenth-century Americans came to understand their hair as a body part capable of indexing each person's race, gender, and national belonging.

The cultural function of hair in the nineteenth century was, at its core, a reflection of the profound economic, political, and social transformation the United States experienced during that century, when nearly every structural facet of the country changed. An agrarian economy became overwhelmingly capitalist. New forms of transportation and expanding transportation networks made the nation increasingly (though unevenly) connected, linking producers in the interior to national and international markets. Emergent forms of mass media—newspaper, magazines, national advertising campaigns, mail-order catalogs, even touring circuses and western shows—also made the nation more culturally connected. Industrialization changed how, when, and where people worked, moving hundreds of thousands of people from rural communities into the nation's growing cities.[7] Colonization of the western half of North America enlarged not only the geographic size of the United States, but also its demographic composition. Although the Civil War ended with the abolition of slavery in 1865, white Americans continued to politically disenfranchise and violently attack Black Americans into the twentieth century. Indigenous tribes, too, were the targets of white supremacist violence, as well as forcible institutional assimilation, particularly for Indigenous children. Immigration from Europe and Asia increased rapidly, only to be legally restricted according to race. Voting rights were extended first to all adult white men by the 1850s, then—thanks to abolitionist and feminist activists—to Black men in 1870, and, by 1920, to women; violence and coercion, however, limited Black men and women's ability to exercise their political rights until the Civil Rights Movement. Finally, new ways of understanding the world became increasingly prestigious—particularly science, which offered authoritative accounts for bodily and national difference, especially differences of gender and race.

Collectively, these changes affected virtually every major institution that shaped Americans' daily lives—*especially* institutions that had offered, for generations, ways of understanding and navigating observable differences between human societies, cultures, and bodies. Crucially, they also put Americans in contact with people they did not know far more frequently than had been the case in the seventeenth and eighteenth centuries. For the first time in English colonial or US history, interactions with strangers became a part of everyday life for hundreds of thousands of people: strangers riding on street cars, strangers sitting next to them in a theater or lecture hall, strangers buying goods from their shops, strangers trying to sell them a cure-all remedy, strangers coming through town on the train, strangers who did not look the same or work the same way or speak the same language. For many Americans, daily life in the nineteenth century felt like living in a world of strangers.[8]

While the anonymity of this world offered some Americans exciting new possibilities for mobility and even reinvention, others instead felt extremely, even existentially, concerned. Some Americans worried that all these changes—and all these strangers—undermined their ability to discern people's authentic identities. This was especially true of upper- and middle-class white men and women, particularly in the North—the Americans likeliest to live in cities, work and consume through the market economy, attend large cultural and commercial events, and thus have significant social and financial stakes in being deceived. The potential for encountering someone with a falsified identity felt ever greater in this mobile and modernizing world, and deception seemed to lurk around every corner—from the confidence men who haunted American cities, to patent medicines laced with arsenic or lead, to counterfeit currency issued by nonexistent banks, to the deceptive exhibits (often deemed *humbug*) peddled by showmen like P. T. Barnum. Furthermore, long-standing methods of verifying the identities of unknown people—such as the cultural norm in most communities that anyone who lodged a visitor in their home or business would inform local authorities—were largely incompatible with these changes, as people became more mobile, and the primary unit of community shifted from small towns to larger cities.[9]

As a result, many nineteenth-century Americans became interested in creating new methods for evaluating unfamiliar people quickly and reliably. The cultural authorities of the emergent middle class devised what historian Karen Halttunen has called a "cult of sincerity" in the 1830s—a response to the vexing challenge, faced by "the aspiring middle classes[,] to secure success among strangers without stooping to the confidence man's arts of manipulating appearance and conduct."[10] Conveying oneself as sincere became fundamental to identifying oneself as *part of* the middle class—until, in the 1850s, the performance of sincerity became, itself, insincere. Others tried solutions tailored more specifically to the fluidity of the market economy. For example, Lewis Tappan's Mercantile Agency—a prototype for the modern credit-rating agency—opened in New York in 1841, offering businessmen detailed financial and personal information to help them evaluate the creditworthiness of potential business partners (and thus avoid getting scammed).[11] Even commercial amusements that played with illusion, such as trompe l'oeil paintings and chess-playing automatons, helped train Americans of all classes to identify the signs of deception.[12]

Yet no methodology or category of evidence was as compelling to nineteenth-century Americans than the human body itself. In scientific tracts, medical journal articles, advice guidebooks, conduct manuals, and the pages of popular newspapers and magazines, nineteenth-century scientific and cultural authorities attempted to identify, measure, and classify parts of the body that were impossible to fake. Even the best confidence man's performance, they argued, could not obscure the truth that was evident in his physical form.[13] In a nineteenth-century context, *truth*—a person's *true* identity—was understood quite differently than its twenty-first-century usage. Instead of emphasizing a process of agency, self-discovery, and self-acceptance, the nineteenth-century search for embodied truth instead focused on *innate,* even *biological* truths visible in the human body itself. As historian Stephanie M. H. Camp put it, "By the nineteenth century, most Americans believed that they could know a great deal about a person simply by looking."[14] The body could reveal information about who a person *really was*—information about their inherent personality, behavior, race, and gender—regardless of how that person wished to be perceived. The body, in other words, was a tell.

The most well-known sciences that emerged from this search for authentic meaning in bodies were physiognomy and phrenology, which claimed that a careful examination of a person's facial features or head shape, respectively, would reveal qualities of their character with scientific precision.[15] Physiognomy and phrenology, both European sciences of the body that gained enormous popularity in the United States in the late eighteenth and early nineteenth centuries, were new and old at once: although both employed new empirical methodologies of natural science to posit direct connections between observable body parts and character traits, they were both also building on centuries of interest in the relationship between a body's visible exterior and its hidden interior.[16] Since the fourteenth century, Europeans had largely understood this relationship between body and character through the theory of humoralism: the belief that each body contained within it four fluids (blood, phlegm, yellow bile, and black bile) called humors, and that an individual's specific balance of these humors directly shaped not just their health, but also their behavior and the appearance of their body. So connected were the exterior and the interior that, as historian Sharon Block has written, as late as the eighteenth century "writers might interchangeably use 'complexion,' 'constitution,' and 'temperament' to explain the collection of humors that characterized all living creatures," even though these three terms are understood to be completely distinct today.[17] Thus, the contribution of the men who formalized physiognomy (Johann Lavater) and phrenology (Franz Josef Gall) was systematizing a broader humoral worldview about the connection between body and character, and giving it the prestige of modern science.[18]

What has not been sufficiently appreciated, however, is that the same systemic analysis of the exterior body's flesh-and-bone parts that fueled physiognomy and phrenology in the eighteenth and nineteenth centuries *also* extended to the hair. To be sure, even under the humoral system, hair could be used as evidence in diagnoses of the balance of fluids.[19] There is even residue of this perspective in the hair taxonomy with which this book opened, which included the assertion that white hair indicated a "lymphatic" body. (Lymphatic is analogous to humoralism's buildup of black bile.) Yet before the eighteenth century, Europeans—including the English people who colonized North America—did not conceptualize hair as an integral body part. Hair was, instead, discharge: like semen, breastmilk, vomit, and urine, hair was a form of waste matter excreted by the humoral body.[20] In fact, some seventeenth-century writers even used the word *excrement* to describe human hair. The English writer William Prynne, for example, referred to hair as "Hairie excrements" or just "their Excrements," and to periwigs—a style he loathed—with the colorful (and completely repulsive) phrase "powdred [*sic*] bushes of borrowed excrement."[21] That hair lay outside the boundaries of the human body was even more clearly emphasized in Welsh historian James Howell's 1645 travel memoir. Anticipating that his readers would not believe his claim that his hair had changed color during his travels away from England, Howell wrote, "but you will say that *Hair is but an excrementitious thing*, and makes not to this purpose."[22] Howell's seventeenth-century contemporaries, as subscribers to humoralism, likely *did* understand the human body to be vulnerable to change when one's environment changed; this environmental framework explained, for example, differences in skin color in different parts of the world: people who lived in hotter climates were presumed to have darker skin *because of* that climate.[23] However, because hair was not considered part of the body under humoralism, Howell's claim that environmental change also changed his hair would likely have been received with the very skepticism he anticipated.

For the first century of English colonization of North America, then, European-descended people largely understood hair to be beyond the body's boundaries. Hair *did* carry meaning, but in a different way than emerged in the eighteenth century. Seventeenth-century colonists believed that hairstyling—such as its ornamentation and its length—offered important evidence of a person's social identity. The way a person styled their hair could indicate their social status in their community, such as whether they were an elite. It could also indicate their religious identity: an English Puritan man who wore his hair long, for example, communicated to his fellow Puritans that his adherence to his faith had lapsed.[24] Yet, importantly, the fact that English colonists accorded significance to specific hair*styles* did not mean they defined the hair as a body part. The history of scalping demonstrates precisely this point. Scalping was a form of wartime trophy-taking practiced by some Indigenous tribes, who understood the hair (and attached skin) they collected to be a powerful body part—one that carried with it the scalped person's spirit. In the late seventeenth century, colonial New England's leaders appropriated scalping into their own legal codes in the form of bounties paid for the scalps of enemies. It is easy to assume that colonists' adoption of scalping meant that they, too, adopted the same kinds of bodily meanings attributed to the shorn hair. However, English scalp bounties made scalping purely transactional: they divorced an Indigenous practice (the act of removing the hair from the scalp) from its original meaning (that to remove the hair was to remove a part of the body). English scalping did not, in other words, undermine their understanding of the meaning of hair as beyond the boundaries of the body.[25]

The meaning of hair began to shift in English North America in the eighteenth century. As humoralism eroded and natural science emerged, hair was increasingly understood *not* as excrement, and *not* as meaningful only for its styling—instead, hair's biological nature and biological features became increasingly significant to the way European-descended people conceptualized hair. Firmly in place by the early nineteenth century was an understanding that hair was a *part of the body*, and with this sense of hair's corporeality came a growing emphasis on the significance of its biological qualities, such as color, texture, and thickness. These qualities, moreover, became increasingly significant as markers of gender and racial difference. The importance of hairstyles did not disappear from American culture, but even some hairstyles became increasingly subject to claims of biological inevitability: white women grew long hair *naturally*, and white men grew full beards *naturally*. Hair was increasingly believed to offer nineteenth-century Americans the same kind of empirical reliability and prestige as other forms of body science. For example, a New Orleans journalist named Dennis Corcoran asserted in 1843 that, "if properly and practically understood," a person's hair "would as unerringly indicate character as either physiognomy or phrenology." Corcoran outlined a taxonomy specifically for facial hair: "With large and naturally glossy black whiskers," he wrote, "we always associate honesty of mind and firmness of purpose," while "a moderately sized crescent-formed whisker" indicated "good nature and a tolerable share of self-esteem," and "a short, ill-shaped whisker, an inordinate love of riches and penuriousness." Corcoran told readers that this classification system could, in fact, be a new branch of natural science—a science he dubbed "*whiskerology*."[26] In Philadelphia, a lawyer and scientist named Peter Arrell Browne set out to develop just such a science, though he referred to his work as *trichology*, *trich-* derived from the Greek etymon for *hair*.[27] Using experimentation, precise measurement, and microscopic analysis, Browne argued that hair science had the power to reveal racial truths, *especially* when other bodily characteristics, such as skin color, were ambiguous: the shape of a single strand of hair would, he argued, reveal a person's authentic racial category, no matter how they presented in public.[28] To Corcoran, Browne, and many of their contemporaries, there was no body part more reliable than hair.

Although Americans generally understood hair to be part of the body during the nineteenth century, they also reckoned with the fact that hair is still different from other body parts in several important ways. Unlike the bones and soft tissues, hair can withstand extreme levels of manipulation; it can also be separated from the body painlessly, retaining the same color and texture it had when it was attached to the body, and usually resisting decay for decades or longer.[29] Nineteenth-century Americans saw, understood, and documented these differences. For example, when a girl named Margaret E. Smiley added some of her hair to her friend's hair album—a book for collecting locks of hair—she penned a poem alongside that began: "There is a lock from the giver[']s brow / Which will retain its usual hue / When she is absent from your face."[30] Mark Campbell, a hair-work artist from New York, took this sentiment even further when he claimed that hair had been "found on mummies, more than twenty centuries old, in a perfect and unaltered state."[31] Charles Ball experienced this type of arresting scene firsthand. In his narrative of his life while enslaved, Ball described entering a wealthy Maryland family's vault, where he saw "more than twenty human skeletons, each in the place where it had been deposited by the idle tenderness of surviving friends." One pair of skeletons in particular moved Ball the most: "a mother and her infant child," lying within a single coffin. His description of these two figures emphasized their decay: the mother wore gold rings "on the bones of the fingers," earrings "lay beneath where the ears had been," and a necklace "encircle[d] the ghastly and haggard vertebrae of a once beautiful neck"; even the coffin was "so much decayed that it could not be removed." Yet despite this overwhelming deterioration, the hair remained unspoiled. As Ball wrote, "the hair of the mother appeared strong and fresh. Even the silken locks of the infant were still preserved."[32] When the entire body and even the box intended to house the dead had withered away, the hair remained as "fresh" as it had been in life.

Nineteenth-century Americans did not simply notice hair's unusual properties. The unique materiality of hair, relative to the rest of the body, provided the very basis of its meaning. An 1855 issue of *Godey's Lady's Book*, the most popular women's magazine of the nineteenth century, captured precisely this significance:

> Hair is at once the most delicate and lasting of our materials, and survives us, like love. It is so light, so gentle, so escaping from the idea of death, that with a lock of hair belonging to a child or friend, we may almost look up to heaven and compare notes with the angelic nature—may almost say: "I have a piece of thee here, not unworthy of thy being now."[33]

This description echoes in the letter a New Jersey woman—sentenced to death for murdering her mother—sent to her husband from prison in 1812. Enclosed in the letter was a lock of her hair that she instructed her husband to save for their infant son; this lock, she wrote, was "a part of [the baby's] poor unfortunate mother," and thus "will stand as a living monument of my wishes, when worms are devouring my skin and flesh."[34] To this woman— and to the hundreds of thousands of other Americans who wrote about, talked about, and preserved locks of hair—hair was incomparable to any other part of the body.[35]

Hair's unusual properties made it particularly significant to nineteenth-century Americans anxious to find specific meaning in the physical body— the same drive for meaning that made body sciences like phrenology and physiognomy so popular in the same era. Phrenology even sometimes incorporated hair into its evaluations of the head, such as the explanation, in the popular *Illustrated Self-Instructor in Phrenology and Physiology* (1857), that "coarse-haired persons should never turn dentists or clerks, but should seek some out-door employment," whereas "dark and fine-haired persons may choose purely intellectual occupations, and become lecturers or writers with fair prospects of success."[36] (This dark-haired lecturer and writer has no comment.)

Yet hair is also different in one crucial way from the skulls that formed the evidentiary basis for phrenology, as well as other parts of the body that have historically carried racial meaning: it is *extremely* capable of change. Some phrenology enthusiasts—including many Black intellectuals at mid-century, who sought to use phrenology to challenge the rigid racial hierarchies of mainstream racial science—did argue that education and mental cultivation could change the shape of the brain. A new brain shape would, in turn, transform the shape of the head, thus altering a person's phrenological profile. But even those who believed that changing the shape of the head was possible admitted that it would be a slow and uncertain process without a predictable roadmap.[37] Hair, by contrast, could be changed in an instant. It has a unique capacity for easy and immediate manipulation—alterations that could be performed by almost anyone, on demand, and, in many cases, as easily enacted as reversed. These characteristics made hair's potential for destabilizing and ungovernable play greater than any other part of the body.

Hair's capability for change made it different from the body's flesh-and-bone features, but nineteenth-century Americans understood that hair was *also* different from the objects they used to cover or adorn their bodies. For all its malleability, hair is not entirely of the wearer's choosing, unlike clothing, hats, jewelry, and other accessories. Hair is, at once, neither completely rigid nor completely plastic. It is biological—as nineteenth-century Americans increasingly emphasized—but it is also cultural. This middle position between fixed and flexible made some Americans uncomfortable; it made others ambivalent about whether hair had any fixed meanings at all. Indeed, hair's meanings in American culture were not always stable, and people did not always agree on a universal taxonomy or code for what each specific color, type, or texture meant. But this capaciousness is precisely what gave hair its power: it could be a tool for marking the bodies of who was, or who had the potential to become, part of the American body politic—but, with a modification as simple as a haircut or a false mustache, it could also be a tool for subverting existing power structures or redirecting them in subversive ways.

By tracing both parts of this story—the regulations (and forms of violence) that tried to manage the hair on certain kinds of bodies, and the contexts in which Americans played with or took advantage of hair's malleability—this book demonstrates the important role that hair played in defining, policing, and contesting the borders of belonging in the nineteenth century. In an era of such rapid and enormous change, the characteristics that defined an American, an American body, and, therefore, American citizenship itself were unstable and uncertain. That there were racial and gender facets to American identity was obvious to most Americans by the early nineteenth century, but how to locate those facets in the body was not.[38] Hair was uniquely powerful because it could do two things at once: it could offer certainty to those who wanted certainty, and it could offer transformation to those who wanted transformation. Bodies of all kinds sought access to, and challenged each other's claims to, American citizenship—and hair became a lightning rod for all of it.

Recentering the Culture of Hair in Nineteenth-Century America

Thanks to its near ubiquity in the human population, as well as the significant role it has played in many world cultures and religions, hair has been the subject of substantial research and study by humanists, social scientists, and scientists. Psychologists, anthropologists, and sociologists in particular have analyzed hair frequently since the mid-twentieth century. Perhaps the earliest modern example of a psychoanalytical theoretical analysis of hair is Sigmund Freud's essay "Medusa's Head" (1922), which connected Medusa's hair to men's castration anxiety.[39] Many influential scholars have asserted that hair has universal or even evolutionary symbolic connections to sexuality or political power. Others have focused their anthropological analyses more narrowly on a particular group or community, such as women in Samoa or the Kuttantavar cult in India.[40]

Studies that approach hair historically—which are less common than anthropological accounts—have documented hair's social meanings and functions in different times and places. Many of these books are popular histories about historic hairstyles, which also describe hair-care technologies, hair labor (such as barbering and hairdressing), and legal or cultural hair regulations. Despite the usefulness of the stories they capture, these histories tend to focus primarily on cataloging hairstyles over time, an approach that generally obscures the social significance of hair in favor of the putatively random whims of fashion; other histories assert the social, political, or personal significance of hair in an ahistorical sense, without attention to hair's culturally specific meanings or changes over time.[41] Less common are books and articles by historians and other scholars intent on contextualizing hair as historical—an approach that can help us understand what hair reveals about, for example, race, gender, class, the body, and power in a specific time and place, from Europe during the Middle Ages to American high schools in the 1960s and 1970s.[42] More recently, the emergent field of hair studies has examined the meaning of hair in historical and contemporary culture, especially popular culture and media.[43]

The cultural meaning of hair in Black communities has been an especially important focus of the study of hair in the United States over the last thirty years. Black feminist scholars have written extensively about Black women's hair, hair's role in constructing racialized gender, and how hair has informed Black women's sense of both their racial and gender identities and also their understandings of beauty, intimacy, and community. As anthropologist Ingrid Banks explained, "hair is a means by which one can understand broader cultural issues. If cultural theorists want to understand how black women and girls view their worlds, it is essential to understand why hair matters to them."[44] Hair's empirical and lived meanings—as opposed to the more abstract theoretical preoccupations of earlier hair scholars—are central to Black feminist hair scholarship and shape its methodology; many scholars draw on interviews, focus groups, and personal reflections, usually in combination with historical context, theoretical frameworks, and media or visual analysis.[45] So, too, do these methodologies shape the time period of focus, which is usually the twentieth and twenty-first centuries in which the authors and their interviewees live.

Central to this body of Black feminist scholarship on hair is the idea of beauty: the significance of hair to white conceptions of beauty in the United States, to Black women's perceptions and treatment of their own hair, and as a medium for contesting beauty ideals in a white supremacist culture. The texture of Black Americans' hair has been central to evaluations of beauty and even, as chapter 3 examines, evaluations of race. Some scholars have focused on how the hair texture that is common (though not ubiquitous) among African-descended people—what scholar Jasmine Nichole Cobb calls "Afro-textured hair"—has changed over time from being a source of pride in many African cultures, to later becoming a source of denigration and a crucial element of racial hierarchies of the body.[46]

Texture is also central to another topic that looms large in Black feminist hair scholarship: the hair-care industry. This industry presents coun-

tervailing cultural forces: on the one hand, hair labor has provided an op-
portunity for Black entrepreneurs—from nineteenth-century barbers, to,
most famously, Madam C. J. Walker—to become wealthy and successful
members of the Black middle class.[47] On the other hand, the hair-care industry, now largely controlled by multinational corporations, has also sold
millions of dollars of hair-care products to Black women that are specifically designed and marketed to straighten Afro-textured hair, such as hot
combs and chemical relaxants. Indeed, the straightening of Black women's
hair is central to many scholars' works. Some scholars interpret hair straightening as a regrettable imitation of white hair texture—a body care practice
that can cause psychological and physical harm, but that some Black women
find necessary for survival within the structure of white supremacist capitalism. Other scholars see hair straightening as a meaningful ritual at the
heart of Black women's intimate culture. As bell hooks writes, the Saturday
morning hair-straightening sessions of her childhood were "not connected
in my mind with the effort to look white"; instead, they were "connected
solely with rites of initiation into womanhood. . . . There are no white people
in our intimate world. It is a sign of our desire to be women."[48] At the same
time, because the broader context of Black women's hair-straightening practice is a white beauty standard that prizes straight hair, the act of straightening Afro-textured hair appears to signal self-hatred or internalized racism.
Ultimately, scholars conclude, for Black American women hair straightening
is neither solely oppressive nor solely communal—it is both.[49]

Hair's cultural meaning is fundamentally intersectional, and Black feminist scholars have demonstrated how conceptions of *beautiful* hair, *professional* hair, *appropriate* hair, and, of course, *good* hair are different for Black
women and white women, and for Black women and Black men. White
women's hair can be neutral—*just hair*—whereas, as Banks writes, "black
hair and hairstyling practices can never escape political readings. The motivation of the person sporting the hairdo is irrelevant. Black hair and hairstyling practices are politicized. Just ask Angela Davis."[50] Indeed, an important theme of Black feminist scholarship is Black hair as a vehicle of
and symbol for Black freedom. Cobb writes that "learning to accept and
appreciate features characterized as inherently Black, such as textured hair,
became central to a visual culture interested in denouncing white supremacy."[51] Cobb's emphasis on the tactility and beauty of Afro-textured
hair pushes back against narratives of Black women's hair as a "problem we
must solve," as hooks put it—as the "part of our black female body that

must be controlled." For hooks, "true liberation of my hair came when I stopped trying to control it in any state and just accepted it as it is."[52] Together, these scholars have examined the many ways that Black women's hair has been fundamental to individual, communal, and political conceptions of their identities as women, as Black women, and as Black American women, all at once—to both the labor and the *power* that hair can hold. This book is indebted to their important work.[53]

Cumulatively, this collection of anthropological, historical, and Black feminist hair scholarship provides useful models for thinking about hair culturally, historically, and materially. It demonstrates that hair has been fraught with personal, cultural, economic, and political significance to many groups of people in the past as in the present. *Whiskerology* builds on this work by bringing greater historic specificity to the study of hair in nineteenth-century America—an era that has featured less prominently in existing scholarship. Indeed, one of the few well-documented hair stories from this century is the cultural practice of collecting, exchanging, and displaying cut locks of hair.[54] Jewelry made from hair is the most familiar form of hair collecting, perhaps because so many of these pieces have been preserved. However, the most characteristic feature of nineteenth-century hair collecting was its flexibility: cut pieces of hair became jewelry, artwork, embroidery, and buttons; they were also sent by mail, preserved in albums, sewed into valentines, tucked between the pages of books, and hidden away in storage chests for generations. (As chapter 3 will demonstrate, locks of hair even became media for scientific experimentation.)

Archives, museums, and historic homes across the United States include in their collections hair objects from people both famous and ordinary— from a ring that encloses Alexander Hamilton's hair at the New-York Historical Society, to a hair album that was handmade by a fourteen-year-old girl from Philadelphia named Ellen P. Gilbert to house twenty-five locks of perfectly preserved hair, which is archived by the American Antiquarian Society in Massachusetts.[55] Less amenable to archival preservation are stories of locks of hair exchanged in idiosyncratic, ad hoc, or intimate ways, such as the story of the recently emancipated father who wrote a letter to his wife, Laura, begging her to send him locks of their children's hair, since Laura and the children had been sold before the Civil War.[56] However, outside of hair-work objects and hair collecting practices—which are perhaps so fascinating to twentieth- and twenty-first-century Americans as to overshadow the other hair stories happening in concert—the nineteenth-century United States has been underrepresented in hair studies. Indeed, even hair collecting is too often siloed from its relationship to the meanings Americans assigned to human hair *in general* during the nineteenth century, especially the hair still attached to the body. This book, therefore, places the culture of hair firmly in its nineteenth-century American context in order to understand what hair meant, how its meanings and functions changed over time, and how it shaped the way people understood race, gender, and national belonging.

Hair and American Political Identity

The relationship between the body—especially the gendered and racialized body—and political identity in the nineteenth-century United States has been the subject of ample scholarship, especially over the last twenty years. Many scholars have explored how the body was central to the elaboration and contestation of gender ideals, including both normative femininity and normative masculinity.[57] Likewise, a rich historiography has identified how the body functioned as a site for the production of racial knowledge.[58] Other scholars have probed the borders of nineteenth-century citizenship along lines of disability, especially the ways in which ability—though less often surfaced than race or gender—was significant to the construction of the ideal political citizen.[59] In nineteenth-century America, particular kinds of bodies (or specific embodied senses) became a vehicle for elaborating ideas about identity, power, and place: much has been written, for example, about how Americans' relationship to (and even, in a medical context, access to) the bodies of the dead shaped mourning practices, medical authority, and even the reconciliation between the North and the South in the decades after the Civil War.[60] Bodies also became sites of activism and reform. While some nineteenth-century movements—including vegetarianism and anti-masturbation—took the body itself as the object of reform, historians have become increasingly interested in reform movements that instrumentalized the body as a site or symbol of a movement's values, such as abolitionism.[61] Reformers' efforts to create more perfect bodies, more perfect people, and thus a more perfect nation also resonate with another well-studied facet of the body's relationship to political citizenship: the ways in which the body functioned as a metaphor for the United States, linking individual bodies to the body politic.[62]

This large and vital collection of scholarship has been foundational to my conceptualization of the relationship between the body and American identity in the nineteenth century; this book would not be possible without it.[63] At the same time, hair remains curiously missing from these stories about the body and American identity. The very volume and variety of this scholarship shows us quite clearly that the body was important to nineteenth-century Americans—and from a nineteenth-century perspective, that body included the hair. Yet twenty-first-century understandings of the body's boundaries have too often clouded scholars' ability to see the contours of the body in nineteenth-century terms. It is this limitation that this book seeks to begin correcting.

Hair became a flashpoint for many of the nineteenth century's most important questions about the contours and constitutive components of political subjecthood in the United States—in other words, what an American body looked like and what it meant to *have* an American body. The fact that hair has not previously been part of the story of the American body and body politic in the nineteenth century has not merely left a gap in our understanding. Its absence has rendered important parts of this story untold: that people who claimed expertise in biological hair knowledge also gained access to certain kinds of police powers; and that hair's physical properties (an immediate and easily achieved malleability not shared with skin color or head shape) made it possible for people who lay outside of political and cultural power structures to turn these coercive powers upside down.

Expertise is, indeed, at the heart of this story. Nineteenth-century hair discourse was frequently drafted into concurrent cultural conversations about the creation and reliability of expert knowledge. Many occupations in the category once called *the professions*—including scientist, physician, lawyer, and even my own occupation, university teacher—claimed authority by professionalizing over the course of the nineteenth century. Professionalization included many components: establishing training standards and educational qualifications (and, for some professions, licensing requirements); founding specialized schools and universities; starting professional journals that published and circulated new research; and forming membership societies open only to practitioners of the profession. For example, the American Medical Association was founded in 1847, the American Association for the Advancement of Science in 1848, the American Bar Association in 1878, and the American Historical Association in 1884—all professional societies that oversee these professions to this day.[64]

This emergent (but growing) apparatus specified and promoted certain practitioners as *experts*—and, by extension, framed practitioners who fell afoul of these standards as dangerously unorthodox or, worse, charlatans. If we reframe hair as part of the body—as nineteenth-century Americans saw it—we can see why scientific and medical experts became increasingly essential not just for understanding hair's biology better, but for understanding hair's relationship to political identity better, too. Indeed, scientific and medical experts frequently weighed in on matters of hair and identity during the nineteenth century, from the ethnologists who deemed the beard a unique feature of the white male body to the criminologists who claimed privileged access to the ability to read criminality in a person's hair. Access to an expert's specialized tools reinforced their claims to hair expertise, such as the hair scientists who touted their use of microscopes.

These affirmations of experts' privileged knowledge also conferred upon them the power to weaponize their hair knowledge in order to police and control people they considered deviant, unruly, or even unamerican. Hair knowledge and hair evidence even entered the judicial system: as biological evidence of racial identity in racial determination cases, or as a signal of criminal intent (or criminal activity) in crowded American cities. For people and institutions of power, hair's supposed biological meaning (and thus its reliability) could be martialed to shore up the boundaries of race, gender, and nation—the lines along which the most threatening errant behavior fell. Indeed, nineteenth-century Americans were acutely interested in specifying the boundaries between different kinds of bodies—between white people and people who (according to the amorphous and unstable standards of the period) lay outside of whiteness, between men and women, and between people who were or could become American and those who could not. It is thus no accident that cultural conversations about hair attached to these three nodes of identity, too.

Hair discourse, moreover, highlighted just how overlapping, entangled, and intersectional these three sets of supposed binaries really were. For example, both long hair and facial hair were not just gendered but also racialized—two processes that reinforced each other. Evaluations of Chinese men's long braids (or, queues) as effeminate became fundamental to the way white Californians perceived both their race and their fitness for naturalized citizenship. Hair scientists' efforts to identify definitive correspondences between hair strand shape and racial categories were predicated on claims of rigid racial boundaries—but stories of racial (and gender) passing demonstrate just how fragile and labile these boundaries truly were. Even the boundary between humans and animals was unsettled (and thus captivating) during the nineteenth century, especially after copies of Charles Darwin's *On the Origin of Species* arrived in the United States in 1859. When freak shows presented hairy dark-skinned women as "The Missing Link" between humans and animals, or when hair scientists tried to taxonomize *hair* and *wool*, they were echoing this larger fascination.[65]

Yet expert knowledge and hair expertise were always in dialogue with the everyday wisdom of ordinary Americans, whose judgments about hair sometimes corroborated—and sometimes contradicted—experts' claims. (Hair was, indeed, something that ordinary people were allowed and expected to care for themselves.) For example, while Peter Browne's research affirmed folk wisdom that kinky texture was a tell for African descent, visitors to freak shows did not always agree with physicians' assertions of a Bearded Lady's gender, and sometimes preferred instead to decide bodily truths for themselves. Moreover, while hair experts could use their hair knowledge to police and shore up boundaries of race, gender, and nation, people without institutional power could also manipulate their hair to avoid such policing. Indeed, people fleeing enslavement frequently used hair disguises to help them pass as free—a process that frequently involved transgressions across racial lines, gender lines, or both. It was the easy, immediate, no-expertise-required malleability of hair as a physical medium—a quality not shared with the other body parts imbued with scientific meaning in the nineteenth century, such as skin color and head shape—that offered the possibility (if not the promise) of reinvention.

Sources and Methods

To tell this story of hair and the American body in the nineteenth century, *Whiskerology* does not rely on traditional archival methods. While historians have employed such methods for over a century to examine the lives of people from the past, it is extraordinarily difficult to find the story of hair in physical archival repositories—not because hair evidence is not *in archives,* but because it is rarely archived *accessibly.* With the exception of

objects made from or with strands of hair—like hair jewelry or hair albums—finding aids do not usually include "Makes reference to hair" when
describing manuscript documents like letters and diaries, even though letters and diaries are *replete* with such references. Although my research took
me to look at materials in archives, including the Bancroft Library at the
University of California, Berkeley, the special collections libraries at UCLA,
the American Antiquarian Society, and the Academy of Natural Sciences of
Drexel University, there is simply no central "hair archive" in the United
States.

Hair stories live in the ephemera of everyday life: in those letters and
diaries, but also in advertisements published in newspapers and on broad-
sides; penny newspapers and popular magazines; novels, biographies, and
personal narratives; religious tracts and scientific pamphlets; conduct manuals and etiquette guides; daguerreotypes and photographs; sheet music and
joke books; political cartoons and *cartes de visite*, and the everyday objects
Americans left behind. These are all the kinds of primary sources that social
and cultural historians have drawn on for decades. As long as I have been
researching this project, I have found breadcrumbs of hair history in other
historians' writing: an amusing anecdote in the introduction, a passing reference in the middle of a chapter, or a cartoon used as illustration in the
appendix. (Indeed, a few of the stories in this book are familiar tales recounted in many historians' books—here reinterpreted and recontextual-
ized through the lens of hair.) My friends and colleagues have noticed these
breadcrumbs, too, and have sent me so many fantastic hair stories they
found among the other subjects they were researching. It turns out that,
once you start looking for hair in the historical record, it is everywhere—
although rarely in the indexes of history monographs.

These breadcrumbs provided a valuable starting point. However, of even
greater significance are the innovations in archival digitization that have
occurred since the early 1990s—especially Optical Character Recognition
(OCR) and digital databases with keyword searchability—which allowed me
to uncover hundreds of stories that would otherwise have remained elusive.[66]
I relied heavily on digital databases and online archives available to the
public and those to which my university library provided access, including
Chronicling America, Hathi Trust, The Internet Archive, Project Gutenberg,
Documenting the American South, ProQuest, Making of America, Harp-
Week, North American Women's Letters and Diaries, Calisphere, Online

Archive of California, and the many books and periodicals hosted by Google Books. (Thanks to these online repositories, this book is able to draw, for example, on writing and advertising from over 150 different periodicals published in small towns and big cities across the United States.)

Digitization is, of course, imperfect and incomplete. Countless times I have gotten a hit when searching *hair* only to find the word in question was *heir* or *fair*; moreover, digital archives still suffer from many of the same biases and limitations of historical archives in general.[67] Still, digitization has completely transformed our ability to take hair seriously as a subject of scholarly historical inquiry. Quite simply, this book would not have been possible without it. Digitized sources allowed me to build a connected web of hair stories from the nineteenth century, turning hair history from a mere collection of anecdotes to a powerful narrative about how ordinary Americans interpreted and made meaning of their bodies and thus their world.

Finally, I want to briefly pause on one type of hair that—while central to conversations about hair today—is not discussed in this book: body hair. With very few exceptions, hair that grew below the neck was not displayed in public spaces in the United States during the nineteenth century. The clothing most men wore in public covered their bodies from wrists to ankles, and it wasn't until the 1920s that women's clothing began to reveal more of their arms and legs. Contexts in which the hair on the limbs, torso, or both might be visible in public were limited and infrequent: dancers and performers in theatrical, freak show, and other popular entertainment spaces; the bodies of people examined by physicians, scientists, and anthropologists and then described in (or photographed for) specialized professional journals; or, by the end of the century, on a beach vacation to a seaside resort like Coney Island. Because these kinds of bodily displays occurred rarely, in rarified spaces, and for narrowly defined audiences, they were thus marginal to the daily experiences of ordinary Americans in which they came to understand (and, sometimes, to shape) hair's social meaning.[68] Indeed, it is precisely those daily experiences that this book seeks to understand. The story of hair's significance in the nineteenth century was not confined to the university, the beach, or the stage, and it traveled far beyond the barber shops, beauty parlors, and wigmakers' workshops of the hair-care industry. It was made, remade, reinforced, and contested every day, on the bodies of millions of ordinary people.[69]

IN ORDER TO UNCOVER the meaning of hair in the nineteenth century, this book will examine four debates within hair discourse where hair's relationship to gender, race, and nation were particularly fraught: long hair, facial hair, the scientific study of hair, and hair's ability to facilitate a fraudulent disguise. These accounts make no claims to comprehensiveness. Indeed, the ubiquity of hair in human life (and on human bodies) would make such an endeavor impossible. Instead, by demonstrating the significance of hair and its function as a social signifier in many places and for many people, this book suggests that the cultural narrative of hair legibility was also pervasive and widespread, spanning social groups and discursive contexts.[70] These four narratives will also range in scale, some focusing on a widespread grooming practice, others on a narrow intellectual pursuit. This varied scope underscores the fact that the meaning and function of hair derived from both the conscious and unconscious production of knowledge. The scientific claim that strands of hair could be racial evidence, for example, was largely developed by one enthusiastic hair scientist, while the significance of facial hair for American masculinity is in large part the consequence of its adoption by so many white men.

What these four chapters have in common is that they each demonstrate how hair discourse mapped onto broader conversations about who was an American—and what it meant to *be* an American—during the nineteenth century. Hair's function as a legible external signifier of intrinsic internal identity made it a potent site for elaborating, performing, contesting, regulating, and policing the contours of such identifiers with particular significance in the United States, such as masculinity, whiteness, and American citizenship. It allowed elites to weaponize hair's legibility toward regulatory or even carceral ends, like the police detective who clocked false hair as the badge of a criminal, but it also enabled people marginalized from cultural and political power to mobilize its reliability toward destabilizing or liberatory ends, like the boy who prepared to escape enslavement by shaving his head.

Just as hair grows on virtually all human bodies, so too is *Whiskerology* a story about all different kind of bodies: racialized bodies, gendered bodies, children's bodies and adult bodies, incarcerated and enslaved bodies, prized bodies and enfreaked bodies.[71] Hair became a flashpoint for bodies of all kinds, even while different cultural conversations activated, categorized, and classified these bodies in different ways at different times. Indeed, across these four chapters we will sometimes see women's bodies, sometimes men's bodies, and sometimes the bodies of people who lived outside a gender binary. Sometimes we will examine racial taxonomies that singled out European-descended bodies as distinct from all others, while other taxonomies racialized African-descended bodies distinctly; sometimes white Americans grouped East Asian and Indigenous bodies together, but other times they defined them separately. The story of hair in nineteenth-century America is nuanced and complex; it resists simplification or a grand unifying theory. But what it *does* show is that hair's unique material form—its middle position between biology and style—gave it the power to help shape social and political citizenship unlike any other part of the body.

In the twenty-first century, long after nineteenth-century narratives of hair legibility—the kind captured by the taxonomy that opened this book— had largely faded from American culture, sociologist Rose Weitz characterized hair's cultural work as resting on a different kind of legibility. Weitz wrote that hair's "remarkable malleability . . . allows us to tell others who we are by 'writing' messages with our hair."[72] The decline in a shared understanding of hair as a body part since the early twentieth century—and with it, some of the meanings once attached to hair's biological qualities— has allowed hairstyling to more frequently stand alone as a signifier in ways it did not in the nineteenth century. Today, American culture mostly conceptualizes hair as a medium for self-expression through which a person can convey their sense of identity to the public in whatever way they desire. However, in the nineteenth century, most Americans believed something quite different: that hair was not only a *part of* the body, but also the inverse of Weitz's legibility: that *the body itself* revealed its intrinsic, authentic truth through the hair. Hair's biological qualities seemed to offer scientific reliability and accuracy. Yet while its "remarkable malleability" imbued it with meaning—both for Americans anxious to read those meanings, and those driven to defy them—it also opened up the potential for turning hair's power toward unanticipated ends.

CHAPTER 1

LONG HAIR

AS THE FRENCH SCULPTOR FRÉDÉRIC-AUGUSTE Bartholdi and his team worked to construct the Statue of Liberty in the early 1880s, a brash illustrated newspaper thousands of miles away envisioned what the equivalent statue might look like if it were located in the bay of San Francisco instead. This design, published on *The San Francisco Illustrated Wasp*'s back cover in 1881 (see fig. 1.1), shared some features with Bartholdi's final design; both featured a single figure standing on top of a tall pedestal, draped in layers of loose fabric, with one arm aloft. There was, however, one major difference: *Wasp* cartoonist Thomas Keller fashioned his central figure not as an allegorical female symbolic of liberty, but as a Chinese male.

The most distinctive feature of the figure at the center of Keller's design is his hair, which unfurls high above his left shoulder, curving through the air like a snake through sand. This is a queue: the long, braided, black ponytail that had been mandated by China's Qing government for men of Han ethnicity since the seventeenth century.[1] During the nineteenth century, most Chinese immigrants to the United States were Han men who wore queues. By the time this cartoon appeared in the *Wasp*, the queue had become the subject of white Americans' fascination, disgust, and even regulation: for example, an 1876 San Francisco law, which required all men sent to the county jail to have their hair shorn to a length of one inch, was later overturned by a federal circuit court because, despite its purportedly race-neutral language, it so transparently targeted Chinese men that, the court ruled, it violated the equal protection clause of the Fourteenth Amendment to the Constitution.[2] By the 1880s, the queue had become not just synonymous with Chinese people in America, but—like the Statue of Liberty herself—symbolic of broader conversations about American citizenship and belonging.

A STATUE FOR *OUR* HARBOR.

1.1 "A Statue for Our Harbor," chromolithograph by George Frederick Keller, *The Wasp*, November 11, 1881. In this illustration, the beams of light emanating from behind the statue's head read, from right to left, "FILTH, IMMORALITY, DISEASES, RUIN TO WHITE LABOR." The statue holds an opium pipe in his left hand.

CREDIT: Reproduced from *Wasp* (San Francisco, CA), f F850 .W18, v. 7, July–December 1881, No. 276, The Bancroft Library, University of California, Berkeley.

What was it about the queue that made it not merely a curiosity but also a body part capable of carrying such significant political meaning? It wasn't the queue's color or styling that mattered to white Americans: it was its length. In fact, when Keller drew a statue for the *Wasp* with hair so long that it stretched more than half the length of his body, Keller was building on a two-hundred-fifty-year tradition of European-descended religious leaders, political elites, government officials, scientists, labor organizers, newspaper editors, and other cultural authorities being baffled, bedeviled, impassioned, and enraged by long hair on men—including both the hair that grew from their heads and false hairpieces worn on top, especially periwigs.[3] (For the sake of clarity, I use *periwig* to refer to the stylized, long, curled, white or gray wigs worn in England and its North American colonies in the seventeenth and eighteenth centuries; and *wig* to refer to hairpieces intended to avoid detection and imitate a natural head of hair, such as those worn by bald men.)

During the first century of English colonization of North America, English colonists' perspective on long hair was grounded in a worldview, informed by humoralism, in which hairstyles were the most important evidence of a person's identity in their community. Many European-descended, African-descended, and Indigenous men (and most women) wore their hair long past their ears or shoulders in the seventeenth and eighteenth centuries. However, colonial elites, especially New England's Puritan leadership, condemned men who wore this hairstyle because they believed it communicated their indifference or even hostility to Christian faith; citing Biblical mandates that categorized long hair as a sign of women's subjugation to men, Puritan leaders criticized men whose hairstyles suggested unmanly subjugation. Starting in the eighteenth century, hair's *biological* qualities—such as texture and color—started to become very important to the way European-descended people understood the meaning of hair, and *especially* hair's role as an index of racial and gender difference.

Indeed, this growing emphasis on hair's biology was central to a broader shift in the cultural and scientific understanding of hair as an integral part of the human body. Increasingly, Americans understood their hair to be a body part—not the excrement of the humoral body, as it had been understood in European culture for centuries. Even though hair length—whether one's hair was cut frequently to maintain its short length, or whether it was left to grow long—was a hair *style*, by the early nineteenth century many scientific authorities pulled this style into the realm of biology, too, naturalizing long and short hair as biologically inevitable along lines of both gender and race. Claims that women's hair *naturally* grew long, while men's hair *naturally* stayed short, were implicitly (and sometimes explicitly) restricted to European-descended women alone, excluding African-descended women from what cultural authorities believed constituted inherent feminine beauty. These profound shifts in the definition and cultural meaning of hair were slow, piecemeal, and contested during the eighteenth century, yet by the first decades of the nineteenth century, hair's biological significance had become a broadly shared cultural narrative.

As European-descended colonists (and later, white Americans) conceptualized the gender and racial borders of American citizenship in the late eighteenth and early nineteenth centuries, hair length rhetoric both shaped and was shaped by questions about who could be (or become) a political citizen of this new nation. Conversations about hair length became conversations about American identity: what did it *mean* for an English man to wear his own hair instead of a periwig, or to shift from his own hair worn long to his own hair cut short? Why did it *matter* that European-descended women but not African-descended women innately grew longer hair than men? Why did it *matter* that Chinese men wore long hair, too? Hair length became a kind of visual shorthand: short hair signaled white masculine political power and social citizenship, while long hair signaled their absence: it was the style of Indigenous people resistant to assimilation, women too subjugated to men to be fit to vote, and immigrants ineligible for citizenship. Hair length thus became central to two kinds of American ideals at once: to emergent ideals of American political subjecthood, and to idealized American manhood—a manhood that was racialized as white (in tension with, and often defined in opposition to, not just African-descended men but also Indigenous and East Asian men) from its very conception.[4]

Long Hair and Periwigs in English North America

For the first 150 years of colonization in English North America, many European-descended, African-descended, and Indigenous men wore their hair long. There is no simple technological or demographic explanation for this hairstyle: it was not, for example, the unavoidable consequence of a lack of proper trimming tools or an insufficient number of barbers in colonial North

America.[5] Moreover, men from many different Indigenous North American tribes traditionally wore their hair long and assigned cultural and spiritual significance to their long hair.[6] Long hairstyles were simply some of the many different styles available to men in the English colonies and their environs throughout the late eighteenth century. Some of these men wore their own hair long, but many instead wore periwigs.

Periwigs—false hairpieces, usually made from human hair, that were long, curled, and often covered in white or gray hair powder—were common among young and old men across social classes through the eighteenth century.[7] Colonists began wearing periwigs within fifty years of the establishment of the first permanent English settlements in North America. Like most aspects of colonial culture, periwigs came originally from Europe. They first became fashionable for men in France in the 1640s under King Louis XIV, then spread to the members of King Charles II's court in England. By the 1660s, men on both sides of the Atlantic donned periwigs in public.[8] The long periwigs worn in the North American colonies—which were usually crafted (and often maintained) by professional wigmakers, with additional maintenance and powdering performed by a valet or servant—could be styled in many ways.[9] The full-bottom wig, which peaked in popularity around 1700, was composed entirely of curls. Later in the century, periwigs with queues—a column of long hair gathered at the nape, tied with a ribbon or encased in a drawstring pouch, and hung down the upper back—became the predominant aesthetic.[10] Some men even mixed false hairpieces with their natural hair rather than wear full periwigs; for example, false queues could be attached to the back of the head and worn with natural front hair.[11] Long periwigs were so popular, and have become so culturally identified with the English colonies, that an image of a white man in a long white periwig is perhaps the most iconic emblem of revolutionary visual culture (see fig. 1.2).

Since their adoption in English North America, periwigs were associated with the gentility of colonial elites. Seventeenth-century periwig wearers included many prominent men of church and state, such as John Wilson, Josiah Winslow, and Cotton Mather.[12] Such associations continued into the eighteenth century; as Reverend Devereux Jarratt described in his personal narrative, as a child growing up in 1730s Virginia "we were accustomed to look upon what were called *gentle folks* as being of a superior order," and "a periwig, in those days, was a distinguishing badge of gentle folk."[13] Indeed,

1.2 *George Washington*, painting by Gilbert Stuart, 1796–1803, oil on canvas. This portrait of the first president suggests the appearance of a periwig; in fact, Washington wears his own long hair styled and powdered to achieve a similar aesthetic to a periwig.

CREDIT: Image courtesy Clark Art Institute, clarkart.edu.

records from a Virginia wigmaker indicate that Thomas Jefferson purchased both wigs and false queues, as well as three pounds of hair powder, in the late 1760s and early 1770s. The more expensive and elaborate the wig, the higher onlookers would presume the wearer's social status to be.[14]

Yet periwigs were also worn by some middling and working people. Some sailors wore periwigs, as did some servants to wealthy families and some enslaved people. For enslaved men, wig wearing was most common among those with class or occupational status, such as enslaved people who worked inside colonists' homes, people enslaved by very wealthy families, skilled enslaved tradesmen, and enslaved seamen.[15] Even an inexpensive or used periwig—enslaved people often wore wigs cast aside by their enslavers— had the power to confer some social status on the enslaved, the enslaver, or both.[16] Advertisements for escaped indentured servants and prisoners some-times referenced wigs, too. A 1750 advertisement in *The Pennsylvania Ga-zette* noted that James Wilson, "a prisoner for debt" who had escaped from jail, typically wore a periwig and was wearing one when he escaped.[17]

The wigs worn by men of fewer means might be the less expensive scratch wig (partial periwig) style; they might be left unpowdered (and thus easier to maintain), or they might be constructed from lower-quality and less ex-pensive materials like wool or horse hair, rather than from real human hair. A poor man might even wear a hand-me-down wig from a wealthier man. Reverend Jarratt himself wore one such hand-me-down: when he was hired to be the schoolmaster of a distant town in the late 1740s, he attempted to transcend his humble upbringing and make himself "appear something more than common in a strange place" by acquiring "an old wig which, perhaps being cast off by the master, had become the property of his slave, and from the slave it was conveyed to me."[18] Thus, while periwigs were a class-marked accessory, they were also fairly accessible and could be found on the heads of men from varying class backgrounds.

The prevalence of periwigs in English North America—and the expec-tation that any long hairstyle on a man *could* be a periwig—is illustrated by the frequency with which colonial observers pointed out men who were *not* wearing wigs. For example, a 1750 advertisement for a stolen horse in Penn-sylvania described the alleged thief as "a tall slender fellow, about five feet ten inches high, [who] wears *his own* black hair."[19] In his 1774 travel journal, Dr. Alexander Hamilton—no relation to the more famous man with the same name—expressed surprise at seeing "two great hulking fellows, with long black beards, [and] having their own hair" at an inn he stayed in near Brookhaven, New York. (Their beards, too, marked these men as unusual in the 1770s, as chapter 2 will demonstrate.)[20]

Indeed, wearing one's own hair long was popular for men of both Euro-pean and African descent in the eighteenth century. In fact, some men who are widely remembered as wearing long white periwigs, most famously

President George Washington, were actually wearing their *own hair* styled and powdered to look like a periwig; Gilbert Stuart's famous portrait of the first president (see fig. 1.2) captures precisely this style.[21] Many enslaved men wore their hair long, too, as advertisements for enslaved runaways demonstrate. For example, Harry, who ran away in New York in 1773, had "straight black hair which he generally wears tied behind," and Jack, who ran away in New York in 1783, had "long black hair."[22] Like George Washington, many enslaved men styled their hair to look like a periwig. For example, Benjamin Latrobe's 1797 watercolor of a man named Alic from Virginia standing at a washbowl shows the combination of short hair and long hair in Alic's chosen hairstyle, which mirrors the aesthetics of the periwig: shaven along the hairline, short and puffed on the crown, and plaited into a queue in the back (see fig. 1.3).[23]

Whether styled to mimic a periwig or not, long hair was one of many different hairstyles that could be found on enslaved men's heads during the colonial era. Mirroring the wide variety of hairstyles worn by their African ancestors, enslaved men in the English North American colonies wore their hair long past the ears, cut short, shaved off in part or completely, short on top and long in the back, long in front and short on the crown, tied back into a queue, and combed and parted, among many other styles.[24] Indeed, as historians Shane White and Graham White have argued, hairstyling was "one notable slippage in a normally tight system of slaveholder control."[25] Despite their very limited access to the time and tools their ancestors used to craft elaborate designs in their hair (especially wide-toothed combs), enslaved people could enact a degree of agency over themselves and their bodies by caring for and styling their hair—a practice sometimes performed communally and often on Sundays.[26] White and White posit that mimicking the forms of the periwigs so popular among European-descended people may have also served as a form of subversive parody, since "African Americans' hair, being black, was the 'wrong color'" for a periwig, contrasted with the fashionable norm of white or very light brown. By making their own hair "resemble fashionable wigs, [enslaved people] may well have been contesting the idea of how a slave ought to look."[27]

For both European- and African-descended women, wig wearing was far less common during the colonial period than it was for men—even though, in Europe, the fashion actually originated with women. In the second half of the sixteenth century, wigs became fashionable for women in England,

1.3 *Alic, a faithful and humorous old servant belonging to Mr. Bathurst Jones of Hanover*, watercolor by Benjamin Henry Latrobe, 1797. In this watercolor, Alic wears his own long hair in a style similar to the appearance of a periwig.

France, and Italy. Both Queen Elizabeth I and Mary, Queen of Scots, had extensive wig collections, though each woman preferred a slightly different style and shape. Men's adoption of the style began in the seventeenth century, and the style lingered on their heads for decades longer than on women's.[28] As periwig wearing declined among English women in the seventeenth century, fashionable women began augmenting the hair that grew from their heads with false hairpieces instead: a braid, chignon (coil of hair worn at the nape of the neck), or cascade of curls affixed to the head with a pin or comb. False hair allowed English women to create intricate, elaborate, sometimes dizzyingly tall structures. Following a decline in popularity in the first half of the eighteenth century, some women in both England and English North America wore false hairpieces in that century's second half—a practice that only expanded in the United States in the late nineteenth century.[29] Thus, in the colonial era and early republic, some European-descended women (and perhaps African-descended women, though evidence is scarce) augmented their hair with false hairpieces—but periwigs were generally worn by men alone.[30]

Periwig or otherwise, by the eighteenth century long hair on men was so common and unremarkable that a person with long hair could successfully present as masculine, even if their other bodily gender signifiers might suggest they were a woman. Long hair worn in public spaces could even *strengthen* a masculine gender presentation, a fact most strikingly exemplified in the colonial period by the Public Universal Friend, an evangelist prophet who gained a substantial following in New England in the last quarter of the eighteenth century. Born Jemima Wilkinson in Rhode Island, the Friend emerged in 1776, when, as the Friend told it, Wilkinson died from a major illness; miraculously, God reanimated her physical form and placed within it a divine and otherworldly spirit named the Public Universal Friend.[31] The Friend's subsequent itinerant preaching led to hundreds of converts and significant public notoriety. However, for those outside of the Society of Universal Friends—the religious group that coalesced around the Friend—the spiritual content of the Friend's preaching was of little interest. As historian Paul B. Moyer has written, "those who commented on the Public Universal Friend were more interested in the messenger than his message."[32]

Central to the Friend's self-presentation was the separation of gender expression (masculine or feminine) from gender identity (man or woman)— and the Friend's long hair was crucial to this process. Contemporary sources

1.4 Portrait of the Publick Universal Friend. In this painted portrait, the
Friend's dark hair is worn in loose ringlets around the shoulders, a style
worn by many European-descended men in the late eighteenth century.
CREDIT: Image courtesy of the Yates County History Center.

were clear that the Friend was "neither man nor woman," as *The Freeman's
Journal* wrote in 1787; at the same time, the Friend presented very explicitly
and deliberately as masculine. From 1776 until the Friend's death in 1819,
the Friend presented both publicly and among members of the Society as a
"masculine spirit," dressing in items of clothing associated with men in the
late eighteenth century: a cravat, a waistcoat, and a hat with a low crown
and broad brim. Members of the Society honored this presentation by
using the pronouns he/him to refer to the Friend.[33] By contrast, people

outside the Society dwelled at length on the bodily features they thought indicated the Friend was a woman—especially what they saw as the feminine beauty of the Friend's mouth and shining black eyes—and often used she/her pronouns to refer to the Friend. However, when they *did* acknowledge that the Friend wanted to be perceived as masculine, the feature they focused on was the Friend's hair (see fig. 1.4). The Friend's dark ringlets were long and loose, not bound up or covered with a close-fitting cap as was typical for adult women in public spaces in the eighteenth century. To onlookers—even those outside of the Society who were not inclined to generous interpretations of the Friend's gender identity—this long hairstyle was unambiguously masculine. For example, a Philadelphian named Jacob Hiltzeimer, who heard the Friend preach on multiple occasions, recorded in his diary in 1783 that the Friend "looks more like a man than a woman," and in a later entry explained that the Friend's "hair was dressed like that of a man."[34] Ultimately, the Friend could not change Jemima Wilkinson's eye color or the shape of her mouth, but the Friend *could* uncover Jemima's hair—and, in so doing, change the way this body's gender was perceived. Long hair thus became a crucial way that the Friend publicly signaled masculinity and a masculine spirit.

Colonial Critiques of Long Hairstyles on Men

Despite the popularity of men in the English colonies either wearing their own hair long or sporting long periwigs, long hair was also subject to critique and censure. Like periwigs themselves, this, too, is a familiar story in colonial American historiography: many scholars have noted that some colonists, especially the Puritan political and religious leaders of seventeenth-century New England, criticized the practice of wearing periwigs.[35] However, what this scholarship frequently overlooks is that these critiques were not narrowly focused on the periwig as an object—they were, instead, broad denunciations of long hair on men's heads, regardless of whether that hair was a man's own or not. Moreover, the basis for criticism of long hair on men was not uniform throughout the colonial era: in the seventeenth century, condemnation of men's long hair treated hair length as a *hairstyle choice*— one that demonstrated the person's Christian observance or lack thereof. Starting in piecemeal (and contested) ways in the eighteenth century, as hair's *biological* qualities grew increasingly important, condemnations of

men who wore long hair or long periwigs increasingly grounded their response to hair length in an understanding of hair as a body part.

Puritan leaders' criticism of long hair on men was rooted in biblical mandates about hair length for men and women. The passage most frequently
cited was 1 Corinthians 11. For example, in a 1628 pamphlet that railed
against long hair on men, the English Puritan William Prynne reminded
readers "that Saint Paul did expressely note, and taxe the Corinthians, for
suffering their Haire to grow long."[36] Puritan leaders in the Massachusetts
Bay Colony followed suit: when Revered Michael Wigglesworth preached
against long hair on men in 1669, he told his congregants that the "length
of hair which is womanish and savo^{r}s of effeminacy, is unlawfull. The scp^t
[scripture] gives you an express rule for this in I Cor. 11 14. 15."[37]

In the part of 1 Corinthians these Protestant authorities so frequently
referenced, Paul explains to the Corinthians the rules they are required to
follow when they worship. The very first rule Paul lists is predicated on fundamental differences between men and women: "Christ is the head of every
man and the man is the woman's head"; in other words, men are women's
superiors, and women are subjugated to men. This hierarchical relationship manifested in mandates for different worship practices for men and
for women; as Paul explains, while "every man praying or prophesying
having anything on his head, dishonoreth his head, . . . every woman that
prayeth or prophesieth bareheaded, dishonoreth her head." Although colonial women did cover their heads with accessories like caps or kerchiefs, 1
Corinthians was emphatic that it was actually *long hair itself* that provided
the best and most appropriate cover for women's heads. Indeed, according
to this passage, the very reason God gave women long hair was for natural
head covering. As Paul tells the Corinthians, women's inferior position to
men is both obvious and natural because it manifests itself on women's
bodies: "Doth not nature itself teach you, that if a man have long hair, it is
a shame unto him? But if a woman have long hair, it is a praise unto her:
for her hair is given her for a covering."[38] According to this theology, long
hair was thus God's way of indicating women's submission to men—which
is why it was so important to Puritan leaders like Prynne and Wigglesworth
that men wear short hair instead.

For the particularly vehement, merely citing biblical prohibitions in their
sermons to congregants was insufficient to stem what many leaders viewed
as a religiously and socially dangerous transgression against gender norms.
Legislation was necessary. For example, in 1649 the Massachusetts Bay

Colony's governor, John Endecott, joined with the colony's magistrates to write a proclamation condemning men in the colony for wearing long hair. The proclamation denounced the hairstyle as inappropriate for a good Christian man; it was a style for "Ruffians and barbarous Indians," not Christians, and for women, not men. Christian men who wore their hair this way, they wrote, thus "deforme[d] themselves."[39] The proclamation empowered local leaders to "manifest their zeal against it [i.e., long hair] in their publike administration, and to take care that the members of their respective churches be not defiled therewith"—thus authorizing, if not legally requiring, local leaders to police their community members' hairstyling practices.[40] Six years later, Harvard College incorporated Endecott's proclamation into their dress code, which, like other hair regulations of the seventeenth century, treated hair *styling* as the site of its meaning: Harvard's Rule 7 forbid its all-male student body from wearing immodest clothing, gold or silver ornaments, as well as "long hair, locks, or foretops," "and from curling, crispeing, parteing or powdering theire haire."[41] To some seventeenth-century administrators, long hair on European-descended men was not just unacceptable, but an issue that necessitated community concern and control.

It was precisely this type of control that Puritan leaders also tried to exert over the Indigenous men they wanted to convert to Christianity. As English colonists documented when they first arrived in North America in the early seventeenth century, Indigenous men wore a wide variety of hairstyles: long, well-cared-for hair was prized for both men and women, so many men wore their hair long, or wore it long on one side and cut it short on the other. Men's hair could be shaved or plucked except for a strip of hair from forehead to nape or circular patch on the crown; hair could be braided, tied in a knot on the back of the head, or decorated with jewelry, fur, feathers, animal fat, or paint.[42] Yet to Puritan leaders, the only acceptable haircut for a Christian man—Indigenous or not—was short. Indeed, missionaries believed that the first step to turning Indigenous men into Christians was to change the way they looked, which is why the first legal codes created for praying towns included among their mandates that Christian Natives "weare their *haire* comely, as the *English* do"—which meant short hair for men.[43] (That many English men wore long hair during the colonial period made this mandate more like legislative magical thinking than an accurate description of reality.)

Clothing, shoes, and hairstyles were such important bodily signals in the colonial period that, as historian James Axtell has written, "an Indian's degree of acculturation could almost be read in his appearance."[44] Yet no other external signifier of Christian conversion—such as wearing English clothing, sporting hard-soled shoes, or even speaking English—was as powerful or consequential as a short haircut. Writes Axtell, "an Indian could change his clothes and even his moccasins for foreign articles and still retain his essential character; his bearing and his profile would still proclaim him an Indian. But a willingness to cut his long black hair signaled his desire to kill the Indian in himself and to assume a new persona." Short hair thus became the single most important visual index of an Indigenous man's allegiance and Christian identity.[45]

Consider the case of Monequassun, the Algonquin schoolmaster in the praying town of Natick, established by missionary John Eliot in the mid-seventeenth century. In October 1652, when Eliot convened a group of local religious and political leaders to hear public professions of faith from some of the Algonquin converts at Natick, Monequassun was one of five converts who spoke. His conversion narrative began with a conventional confession: according to Eliot's translation, Monequassun said, "I Confess my sins before the Lord, and before men this day." He then described the series of difficult and often heartbreaking experiences that led up to this moment: his initial encounter with (and rejection of) Christianity, his forcible movement into the praying town, rampant illness in his community, and the death of his wife and one of his children. Fearing that all of these tragedies were caused by his continued unwillingness to follow the Christian God, Monequassun "prayed [to] Christ, Oh! turn me from my sin, and teach me to hear thy Word; and I prayed to my Father in Heaven: and after this, I beleeved in Christ for pardon."[46] Finally, the narrative concluded with one final lesson:

> Afterward I heard that Word, That it is a shame for a man to wear long hair, and that there was no such custom in the Churches: at first I thought I loved not long hair, but I did, and found it very hard to cut it off; and then I prayed to God to pardon that sin also: Afterward I thought my heart cared not for the Word of God: but then I thought I would give myself up unto the Lord, to do all his Word. . . . then I thought my hair had been a stumbling to me, therefore I cut it off, and grieved for this sin, and prayed for pardon.[47]

That Monequassun's conversion narrative culminated in a protracted internal debate about whether to cut his long hair may seem, at first, surprising;

it occupies slightly more space in the narrative than his description of the sickness that killed his wife and child, and even scholars have remarked on this structure as "odd."[48] Hair was, indeed, deeply significant to many North American Indigenous tribes, as the practice of scalping demonstrates: although not all tribes incorporated scalping into their warfare tactics, those that did—including the Algonquin—treated the hair and skin they collected as powerful objects capable of transmitting to the scalper "the spiritual strength and courage of the vanquished," as historian Mairin Odle has written.[49] Yet the sheer volume of space dedicated to Monequassun's explanation of his decision to cut his hair may instead reflect the work of his translator, John Eliot, and Eliot's personal obsession with the importance of Christian men wearing short hair.

John Eliot *detested* long hair on men, both hair grown from their own heads and periwigs, and he hated long hair worn by Indigenous men and European-descended men alike. Eliot referred to the penchant of some fellow male colonists for wearing long hair as a "feminine protexity." Although the meaning of *protexity* is unclear—Eliot appears to be its only recorded user—the other word's denotation is plain: Eliot objected to men who wore their hair like women in violation of the gendered hair mandates of the Bible.[50] Eliot hated long hair on men so much that he even blamed colonists' conflicts with Indigenous people on unchristian hairstyling among the colony's men.[51] The connection Eliot envisioned between men's long hair and an attack by his Indigenous neighbors becomes more legible in the context of a 1675 order passed by the Massachusetts Bay Colony's General Court. Just five months after King Phillip's War began in New England, the General Court printed an anxious exhortation to colonists, ordering them to stop engaging in twelve types of bad behavior, including poor church attendance, price gauging, and excessive drinking. These behaviors had angered God so much, the Court wrote, that God had "heightened our calamity, and given comission to the barbarous heathen to rise up against us." King Philip's War, in other words, was the direct result of the colonists provoking God with their inappropriate personal behavior; without reform, the General Court worried, the community had little hope for survival.[52]

The first item on the court's list of bad behavior was poor church attendance, but the second was the inappropriate ways that men and women had been wearing their hair. The fact that hair ranked so highly on this list suggests that the Court considered these transgressions particularly important.

The Court denounced men in the community who were "openly appearing amongst us in that long haire, like weomens haire"—"either their oune [own] or others haire made into perewiggs"; women who wore false hair-pieces called borders (which augmented their natural locks) were also con-demned. The Court declared these "ill custome[s] as offencive to them, and divers sober christians amongst us, and therefore doe [do] hereby ex-hort and advise all persons to use moderation in this respect." Furthermore, like Endecott's 1649 proclamation, the Court empowered local officials to prosecute colonists who refused to change their hairstyling practices, "ei-ther by admonition, fine, or correction, according to theire good discre-tion."[53] Even though this order castigated both men and women for their hair practices, the objectionable behaviors represented different sins de-pending on gender. For women, wearing borders and curling the hair was a sin of excessive pride; this was the same sin referenced in the third item on the twelve-point list, which ordered colonists to stop wearing clothing that was too vain and that showed off "naked breasts and armes." Yet for men, the sin was not merely pride, but also, crucially, gender transgression: their hair was a problem because they were wearing it "like weomens haire."[54] It was the men's hair*styling* that was a problem.

Like Eliot, Reverend Nicholas Noyes was also opposed to periwigs be-cause their long length was inappropriately feminine when worn by men. Noyes stated quite plainly that "it is a Shame for a Man to wear long hair; [and] Perriwigs are usually long hair."[55] Like his seventeenth-century pre-decessors, he also referred to 1 Corinthians directly, writing that periwigs "removeth one notable visible Distinction of Sex: for so is Hair, as is evi-dent by 1 Cor. 11. 6, 7, 14, 15."[56] However, Noyes took this gendered cri-tique a step further: he condemned periwigs because they were typically con-structed from human hair that once grew on a woman's head. This specific issue was so central to Noyes's objections that he titled his 1700 anti-periwig essay "Reasons against Wearing of Periwiggs; especially, *Against Mens wearing of Periwiggs made of Womens hair*, as the custom now is, deduced from Scrip-ture and Reason."[57] While most discussions of periwigs took for granted that the severed strands of human hair used in periwig production were merely a commodified raw material—anonymized from the body that had grown it—Noyes argued that women's hair was *forever* women's hair, even when worn on a man's head.[58] Periwigs were thus a problem, Noyes argued, because they violated not only 1 Corinthians, but also 22 Deuteronomy,

which prohibited cross-dressing. To Noyes, periwigs worn by men represented a "transmutation of the visible tokens and distinctions of sex," and
thus it "is not lawfull; as is undeniably proved by Det. 22. 5." If a man was
forbidden from wearing a "Womans Habit[,] much less might he wear a
Womans hair."[59] (Contemplating the opposite inversion was beyond the
pale: "What a mad World would it be, if women should take the same affection to wearing of Men's beards; as Men do to Women's hair?"[60]) Noyes
posed a question to his readers: "Why should it not be accounted Effeminacy in Men, to covet Women's hair; which is a token of Women's Subjection, when they wear it themselves for a Covering[?] . . . Women's hair, when
on their own heads, is a token of Subjection: How come it to cease to be a
token of Subjection, when Men wear it?"[61] Noyes thus objected to periwigs
because, like women's clothing or women's head coverings, they were objects for women's use only—and, crucially, objects that reinforced women's
fundamental subjugation to men.

For nearly one hundred years, Puritan leaders like Endecott, Eliot, and
Noyes castigated long hairstyles that they believed were evidence of the men's
lack of Christian devotion. Yet, starting in the eighteenth century, religious
leaders' responses to men's long hair began to reflect an emergent significance of hair's *biological* qualities, and a growing understanding of hair as a
part of the body. This transition was gradual, piecemeal, and often contested, as English colonists grappled with and disagreed with each other about
what hair meant and, therefore, what a man should or should not do with
his hair. One story, frequently recounted by scholars of early New England,
demonstrates the contested nature of this transition: in 1701, Massachusetts
Bay Colony minister Samuel Sewall visited Josiah Willard, the nineteen-year-
old son of local Reverend Samuel Willard, to interrogate the young man
for shaving off all his hair and replacing it with a periwig.[62] Sewall asked
Willard why he had sacrificed such a "full head of hair"; although Willard
could not answer Sewall's question, the young man did not think he had
done anything wrong. Sewall, of course, disagreed, and encouraged Willard to read a chapter in John Calvin's *Institutes of the Christian Religion*,
which exhorted Christians to live their earthly lives with a balance between
intemperance and austerity: although Christians were encouraged to enjoy
the delicious food and beautiful clothing that God had created for humans'
use, it was not acceptable to allow that enjoyment to balloon to the point
of excess.[63] Willard wanted to become a minister like his father, so Sewall

reminded him that "your calling is to teach men self Denial." This message, he implied, would be difficult for Willard to convey persuasively if he was wearing a periwig, which he considered an excessive adornment.[64]

Sewall and Willard's conflict was not merely theological or generational—they were, instead, negotiating two different perspectives about the meaning of human hair in the eighteenth century. Willard (ironically, the younger man) represented the older perspective, informed by humoralism, that focused on hairstyle; Sewall represented the emergent perspective that instead prioritized hair's biological qualities and understood the hair to be a part of the body. Indeed, it is not accidental that Sewall's message to Willard about his future ministerial career focused on how the young man treated his hair, and not, for example, his moderate consumption of indulgent cuisine or appropriate selection of jackets and pants. Sewall's focus on hair is significant because it demonstrates that Sewall viewed hair as different from food or clothing, which are put *in* or *on* the body. In contrast, Sewall saw hair as *part of* the body. By assigning Calvin's teachings, Sewall hoped that Willard would realize the very reason God had given humans their head hair was as a test of their self-discipline—their ability to honor God by effectively achieving a middle-ground between excessive vanity and excessive piety. Sewall himself believed as much, telling Willard, "God seems to have ordain'd our Hair as a Test, to see whether we would be our own Carvers, Lords, and come no more at Him. If [we] disliked our Skins, or Nails; 't is no Thanks to us, that for all that, we cut them not off: Pain and danger restrain us."[65]

The unique physical properties that made hair different from other parts of the body also made it an exceptionally valuable indicator of an individual's essential qualities: the fact that the hair on the head *could* be completely shaved off without pain and danger made it all the more valuable as a test of man's deference to God that he *not* shave it off. No other part of the body could, or did, have the same function—not the skin, or nails, or anything else. Hair was, to Sewall— and to growing numbers of eighteenth-century people in English North America—a special kind of body part.[66]

White American Manhood and the Shift to Short Hair

After 150 years of men wearing long hair (and religious authorities critiquing long hair on men), European- and African-descended men's hair underwent a substantial transition starting in the 1780s: from periwigs to natural hair, and from long hair to short. (While some Indigenous men who lived in white communities also cut their hair short, sometimes earning the derisive nickname "cut-hairs" from men who resisted assimilation, most men in Indigenous communities retained the long-standing practice of wearing their hair long.[67]) With the exception of some lawyers, clergymen, and the very elderly, virtually no men wore periwigs by the 1820s.[68] President James Monroe, for example, who held office from 1817 to 1825, was the last American president to wear a periwig.[69] His successor, John Quincy Adams, wore his own hair short. Indeed, the change from long hair to short is, in many ways, the more profound shift than the doffing of periwigs. Not all men wore periwigs, so the transition from false to natural hair was moot for those who had always worn their own hair—but virtually *all* white men began to wear their hair short.[70]

Although extant sources are sparser for Black men's hair, advertisements for enslaved runaways strongly suggest a decline in long hair and a rise in short hair for Black men, too, in the nineteenth century. The frequent references to "long hair" and "large bushy head[s] of hair" found in eighteenth-century advertisements largely disappeared, replaced with terse mention of "rather short" hair or, frequently, no description of hair at all.[71] Moreover, illustrations produced as frontispieces for narratives of enslaved people's escapes, as well as early photographic portraits of Black men produced in the 1850s, also confirm that, at least by midcentury, Black men—like white men—had overwhelmingly adopted short hair.[72]

To be sure, these twin transitions—from long and bewigged to short and unwigged—were neither smooth nor swift, and sometimes contested. For example, at the turn of the nineteenth century, a colonel and Revolutionary War veteran named Thomas Butler was court-martialed twice because he refused to cut his long hair. In 1801, the new commanding general of the Army, James Wilkinson, issued an order that prohibited all US soldiers from growing their hair past the bottom of their ears.[73] Butler asked Wilkinson for an exemption and for two years it was granted, but when his waiver was suddenly withdrawn and Butler still refused to cut his hair short, he was court-martialed. At the trial, Butler's lawyer argued that hair length was personal—beyond the pale of what the military could rightfully regulate. Although the judges were sympathetic, they found him guilty of violating the haircut order, but owing to his long tenure of service and his good character, the judges sentenced Butler to merely an official reprimand.[74]

Yet, the matter of Butler's long hair, which he still refused to cut, was not yet settled, and in 1804 he was court-martialed again—the charge now elevated to "Wilful, obstinate and continued disobedience," as well as "Mutinous Conduct" because he took command of troops while insubordinate. At his second trial, the judge found Butler guilty on both counts and sentenced him much more harshly than before: one-year suspension without pay.[75] Butler would never fulfill this punishment: he died of yellow fever less than two months later. But he took his protest all the way to the grave, telling friends that he wanted them to "bore a hole through the bottom of my coffin right under my head and let my queue hang through it."[76] His deathbed dissent echoed something Butler said shortly before his first court-martial: he did not want to acquiesce to the haircut order because he believed his hair was "the gift of nature *and an appendage to my person.*"[77]

Butler's characterization of his hair as an "appendage" is extremely important. Even though he deployed it in support of *long* hair, this descriptor is why Butler's story actually captures the core significance of the uniform shift to *short* hair for men in the two decades following his death. And considering how uniform that transition was, it is curiously absent from many scholars' examinations of early America. Scholarship that has historicized this sudden embrace of short hair by American men focuses almost exclusively on the rejection of periwigs, not on changes to hair grown from men's own scalps—a focus that would, for example, omit Butler's story altogether. Typical arguments suggest that the disappearance of the periwig is merely one example of some broader political or cultural shift, such as the declining veneration for elderly men that occurred in the late eighteenth century. However, the most common explanation is that the periwig's disappearance was simply a material byproduct of the American Revolution, and of newly American citizens' desire to rid themselves of an object so associated with England.[78] It is indeed true that the fight for independence shaped American culture, consumption, and clothing significantly, and that part of the revolutionary era's embrace of a distinctly American identity included the rejection of English aesthetics and consumer goods. For example, in 1774 the Continental Association demanded that colonists stop engaging in forms of entertainment the Association deemed either aristocratic extravagance or too reminiscent of the English gentry, including balls, horse racing, and cock fighting.[79] Periwigs have largely been read as belonging to this category of newly odious English culture and consumer goods, especially because they disappeared from American men's heads around the same time as English tea disappeared from their tables.[80]

However, because these accounts analyze the periwig in isolation from patterns in men's natural hair, they miss the fact that changes to both occurred at precisely the same time—and, moreover, that their meanings were intertwined. We can only understand the waning popularity of periwigs and long hair among American men if we analyze them *together*, as two parts of the same process: the reconceptualization of the hair as an essential part of the body. Moreover, the growing emphasis on hair's biological qualities— especially as markers of racial and gender difference—offered a new kind of significance to short hair on men's heads: it could become an embodied index of idealized white masculinity in the new American republic.

In the United States' first decades, white men were clearly defined as the new nation's ideal political citizens, yet the characteristics that comprised the ideal American man were not self-evident. The traditional patriarch— an adult male who governed all the members of his household, including his wife, children, servants, apprentices, and enslaved people—was the dominant masculine ideal throughout the colonial period in both England and its colonies. However, its dominance was not absolute in the late eighteenth-century United States, where Republican political ideals clashed with absolute authority and early industrialization wrought changes to where and how people worked, undermining, in incomplete but important ways, the patriarch's real and idealized authority.[81] Alternative potential ideals for American manhood competed with the traditional patriarch—ideals that valued, for example, economic self-sufficiency coupled with civic-mindedness, or the unchecked individualist pursuit of material gain.[82] Despite their differences, all of these potential ideals shared one important quality in common: they emphasized self-mastery. The ideal man was, these varying ideals agreed, in control of himself—of his authority in the home, of his vote, and of his financial well-being. This emphasis on self-mastery also helps explain the relative unpopularity in the Early Republic of masculine ideals that emphasized genteel sensibilities, aesthetics, and consumer habits, which privileged fidelity to fashion over manly self-mastery.[83]

Although hair is not usually considered in relation to the formation of ideals of early American manhood, the shift to short hair in the late eighteenth century—just as these ideals were in formation—testifies to the significance of self-mastery in this broader discourse about American masculinity and the values of the ideal American subject. Increasingly naturalized as biological evidence of white male supremacy, wearing one's own short hair thus came to serve as an index of American men's self-mastery. Unlike a periwig, which obstructed American men's "open, manly, independent foreheads, which have freely sweat for the toil of freedom"—as one particularly vehement periwig opponent from Connecticut argued in 1796—short hair was unornamented, unadorned, and thus easy to care for. Long hair, by contrast, required lots of time to maintain.[84] In 1783, for example, Chief Justice of the Supreme Court John Jay—who wore his own hair long—wrote to John Adams that he had missed an appointment because a valet was combing and preparing his hair. Jay complained, "Thus does tyrant custom hold us by a hair," since "ridiculous fashions make us dependent on valets and the Lord knows who."[85] So, too, did wearing long periwigs threaten men's independence by yoking their finances to the dictates of fashion—"this shackle of slavery," the periwig's Connecticut opponent sneeringly called it.[86] Long hair, including long periwigs, threatened to enslave white men to fashion, to the cost of hair-care products, and to the laborers—sometimes themselves enslaved—who helped maintain their hair.[87]

The growing uniformity of short hair for men at the turn of the nineteenth century seemed to cement a sequence of racialized and gendered binaries: short hair is unornamented, and white men wear short hair because idealized American masculinity prioritizes unornamented body care; and long hair is an ornament, so white women wear long hair because idealized American femininity prioritizes ornamentation. Long hair, early-nineteenth-century writers repeated again and again, was "that crowning glory and charm of female beauty . . . without which all other attractions lose half their power."[88] Short hair thus came to epitomize a central feature of emergent early American white masculinity: the elimination of ornament from men's appearance; and the growing associations of decorativeness with femininity, effeminacy, and powerlessness—a powerlessness that could, crucially, also be read onto the bodies of non-white men whose wore their hair long. Short un-periwigged hair was, by contrast, powerful: it demonstrated white men's self-mastery, their self-discipline, and their rejection of decorativeness and of enslavement, all at once.

Long Hair, Beauty, and Racialized Womanhood

In the seventeenth century, Protestant leaders like John Eliot and Nicholas Noyes repeatedly reminded English colonists that women's subjugation to men was manifested in their long hair, citing 1 Corinthians to naturalize long hair for women as based in scripture.[89] However, at the turn of the nineteenth century, it was *political* subjugation, rather than religious, that took primacy in cultural conversations about hair—conversations that also increasingly included far more voices than just religious leaders. Yet although white political, scientific, and cultural authorities increasingly supported the same gender bifurcations for hair length as Eliot and Noyes, they did so not because it was scripturally ordained, but because it was natural in the secular sense: ordained, as it were, by nature. Women, they argued, were biologically predisposed to grow long hair and to be more decorative and beautiful than men—and their bodies testified to both of these biological facts. Almost always left unsaid, however, were the racial boundaries of these claims: it was white women, not Black women, whom these authorities meant when they spoke of women's inherent decorativeness and beauty. Because hair's biological qualities were, by the nineteenth century, understood to be reliable markers of both racial and gender identity, hair was far more capable than other body parts at carrying all the intersectional meanings of beauty at once.[90]

By the second quarter of the nineteenth century, white Americans had largely naturalized a gender binary for hair length: men's hair was *naturally* short, and women's hair was *naturally* long. This transformation of a stylistic choice into a biological fact bridged the bodily logics of both humoral medicine (in its decline) and empirical medicine (in its ascent). Hairdresser Thomas Bogue's 1841 scientific treatise on hair exemplifies the former. "The beauty of long hair," he wrote, "has, *from time immemorial*, been viewed as a highly prized ornament"; this ornament belonged almost exclusively to women because "the length of the hair is greatly increased by the abundance of the phlegmatic matter with which it is continually supplied, and causes it to augment to a great degree; there is more of this moisture predominant in women than men."[91] Twelve years later, the most respected hair scientist of the mid-nineteenth century, Peter A. Browne—whose work (while racially motivated) employed many of the hallmarks of empiricism, such as data collection and repeated experimentation—proclaimed, with matter-of-fact certainty, that in humans "the longest hair is upon the scalp, and females have generally longer hair upon their heads than males, as if it were to compensate for the comparative deficiency of it upon their bodies."[92] *Godey's Lady's Book* echoed Browne's sentiment, explaining, in the introduction to its six-month series of articles about the hair, that "in the female it grows longest, waving over the neck and shoulders . . . in the softer sex, the hair of the head usually reaches to the waist, and frequently, when suffered to grow, much longer."[93]

Long hair became so naturalized that even scientific authorities who prescribed short hair for its valuable health benefits still discouraged long-haired women from following suit. For example, an 1830 article in a journal for physicians claimed that one of hair's primary biological functions was to eliminate "accidental impurities" from the scalp; short hairstyles were healthier because short strands were less likely to have this function blocked or impeded as compared to long strands, which could become "entangled and matted together." The journal thus recommended that hair be cut frequently and "kept short"—but it did not extend this recommendation to women: "We admit that fine *flowing* tresses are among the most attractive ornaments of female beauty, and would therefore be the last to recommend their proscription."[94] The hairdresser Bogue gave similar advice to parents of young children, advising "every parent to be careful that their children's hair be frequently cut"—every month, he suggested—to keep their hair healthy and ensure they would always "possess a head of luxuriant hair." This advice was "essential for the benefit of children of either sex, to have the hair always kept short"—yet once again, the author assured the reader, this advice did not apply to adult women, who could rest assured that, for them, long hair was not "injurious to the general health as productive of debility."[95] Even women authors gave similar advice to their women readers, such as a female-authored beauty guidebook that asserted a short haircut was "equally hurtful to the health of females, as it is contrary to their beauty to wear their hair cut à la Brutus, Titus, or Caracalla. A luxuriant head of hair is the most beautiful ornament a female can possess."[96] For women, beauty—and thus decorativeness—should take precedence over physical health; for men and children, the opposite was true.

The notion that long hair on women was inherently decorative was so pervasive by midcentury that the utopian Oneida community—which prided itself on being freethinking, particularly when it came to women's social roles—presupposed that this was actually the *intention* of the 1 Corinthian mandate. As its first annual report from 1849 described, the community had to reexamine the Bible to learn 1 Corinthian's true intent:

> The ordinary practice of leaving the hair to grow indefinitely, and laboring upon it by the hour daily, merely for the sake of winding it up into a ball and sticking it on the top or back of the head, had become burdensome and distasteful to several of the women. Indeed there was a general feeling in the Association that any fashion which requires women to devote considerable time to hair-dressing, is a degradation and a nuisance. The idea of wearing the hair short and leaving it to fall around the neck, as young girls often do, occurred frequently, but Paul's theory of the natural propriety of long hair for women (1 Cor. 11) seemed to stand in the way. At length a careful examination of this theory was instituted, and the discovery was made that Paul's language expressly points out the object for which women should wear long hair, *and that object is not ornament, but "for a covering."*[97]

Unlike the religious leaders of the seventeenth century, who knew reflexively that 1 Corinthians mandated long hair for women as a covering to signal their subjugation to men, the Oneida of the mid-nineteenth century knew that 1 Corinthians said women were supposed to have long hair, but they weren't exactly sure *why*. Their assumption, based on the broader cultural meaning of long hair for white women that had become so pervasive by the mid-nineteenth century, was that 1 Corinthians mandated women have long hair because it was an ornament to their feminine beauty. It was only upon rereading the scripture that they learned its actual intent. (Satisfied by the "natural and scriptural propriety" of a short haircut as long as the hair covered part of the neck, Oneida women began cutting their hair to chin length.)[98]

Thoroughly naturalized by midcentury, decorative long hair's connection to womanhood was also continually reinforced by scientific and cultural authorities in the second half of the century.[99] For example, a late 1860s article on how to manage the hair—which circulated in multiple women's magazines, including *Godey's*—explained that "the greatest ornament to the 'human form divine' is, unquestionable, a fine, luxuriant, healthy growth of hair." The article clarified, crucially, that a good head of hair conveyed different meanings on men and women: "It is to beauty of woman the chief auxiliary, and to manhood the warrant of strength and dignity."[100] Similar assertions appeared in scientific texts. In his 1875 medical guidebook for women, Dr. Seth Pancoast described women's long hair as an "ornament" and "a special adornment of woman." This point was so important that, just two pages later, Dr. Pancoast reminded his readers of it again: "We repeat, to women, long hair is an ornament, and adorning."[101]

Dr. Pancoast also affirmed earlier writers' claims about the inherent gender differences in hair length. He argued that, even when "left uncut," a man's hair "will not grow to the same length" as a woman's hair because "a woman's back hair [i.e., the hair on the back of her head, not the back of her torso] is an appurtenance entirely and naturally feminine."[102] Indeed, he continued, "the hair of woman actually grows longer than that of man, which fact proves that flowing tresses are intended for some *especial* purpose in the economy of Nature."[103] Whether credit was due to the Christian God or the secular Nature, nineteenth-century authors agreed: decorative long hair was for women alone.

Moreover, hair length's gender binary is also evident in the nonchalant way nineteenth-century authors talked about the time, attention, and money required to maintain women's long hair, particularly since adult women wore their hair up in a styled arrangement when in public spaces.[104] For example, an 1869 etiquette guide explained that "the arrangement of the hair in men . . . should be as simple and as natural as possible"; short hair was the best choice for men because long hair would "demand an amount of time and attention *which is unworthy of a man*." Women's long hair, by contrast, naturally required extensive time and attention: the guidebook instructed that "a lady's hair should, in ordinary life, be dressed twice a day, even if she does not vary the mode. To keep it cool and glossy, it requires being completely taken down in the middle of the day, or in the evening, according to the dinner-hours."[105] While some personal care guidebooks and women's magazines suggested that women ignore hairstyling trends and instead style their long hair in whichever way best suited their face, other sources shrugged at the inevitability of women chasing every latest trend.[106] An 1892 article in *Scientific American*, for example, explained that, in the United States, "fashion is a law to the poor as well as to the rich," one that ensnared "factory and shop girls, and others of slender means, [who] vie with their wealthier sisters in the adornment . . . of their heads."[107] Inverting the turn-of-the-century arguments that made short hair a powerful way for white men to demonstrate their self-mastery, midcentury authors treated women's enslavement to hair maintenance as unavoidable, even self-evident. Yet unlike white men, for whom an enslavement to their hair would threaten their masculine independence, women were *not* understood as socially, politically, or economically independent. Both their naturally long hair and their enslavement to its maintenance reinforced the ways in which their exclusion from political participation hardened at the turn of the nineteenth century.

White women lay outside of political subjecthood in the nineteenth century, yet Black women were marginal both to political subjecthood *and* to white writers' mental imaginaries about the inherent beauty of women's hair. Indeed, when white writers waxed poetic about, as a local Connecticut newspaper put it, how hairdressing was "the chiefest of the decorative arts, inasmuch as its function is to adorn the most perfect of nature's works, the beauty of woman," it was implicitly a white woman's coiffed hair that they envisioned.[108] Decorative long hair was thus not merely gendered as womanly—it was also racialized as white. Black feminist scholars have explored the many ways that whiteness and beauty have been fused in the white Euro-American artistic, cultural, and scientific imagination for centuries. The eighteenth-century art historian and archaeologist Johann Joachim Winckelman, for example, elevated ancient Greek art—mistakenly believed to be carved from unpainted white marble—to be the paragon of human beauty; pale skin, he argued, was inherently more beautiful, too.[109] Yet by the early nineteenth century, race and beauty had fused together—no longer "merely coincidental to categories of racial difference," as historian Stephanie M. H. Camp writes, but determinative: "perceptions of physical beauty and ugliness became a measure of racial superiority and inferiority."[110]

Black community leaders, especially abolitionists, recognized and pushed back against such white supremacist beauty standards. For example, in the New York–based Black abolitionist periodical *Anglo-African Magazine*, Martin H. Freeman wrote in 1859 that crucial to Black Americans overcoming not just "the chattel bondage of the South, but every form of social, civil, and political oppression" was to develop in Black children a firm sense of self-respect—one that included a rejection of white supremacist beauty standards. In addition to the need for more examples of Black wealth, influence, and political office, Freeman urged Black parents to make sure they were not teaching their children that they were "pretty, just in proportion as the features approximate to the Anglo-Saxon standard." Such messaging at home—even *before* the pernicious influence of "out-door teachings and influences"—caused some Black parents to try to change Black children's kinky hair, "subject[ing] [it] to a straightening process—oiled, and pulled, twisted up, tied down, sleeked over and pressed under, or cut off so short that it can't curl." Instead, Freeman implored, parents must "cultivate in the mind of the child a respect for its own individuality" by refusing to make a "disparaging remark in regards to hair or features or colors," which are "just so many demons let loose to destroy our children."[111]

In a speech in Boston just one year earlier, reprinted in the local abolitionist newspaper *The Liberator*, abolitionist and physician Dr. John Stewart Rock did not just call on Black Americans to reject white beauty standards for hair, but praised what he believed to be the superior beauty of the Black body and Black hair texture. Dr. Rock told his audience, gathered on a Friday evening to commemorate the anniversary of the Boston Massacre and honor the memory of Black sailor Crispus Attucks, that white men's prejudice "against my color gives me no pain" because "he lacks good taste." Although admitting that he "admire[d] the talents and noble characteristics of many white men," Dr. Rock confided that he did not find white people to be beautiful: "When I contrast the fine tough muscular system, the beautiful, rich color, the full broad features, and the gracefully frizzled hair of the negro, with the delicate physical organization, wan color, sharp features and lank hair of the Caucassian [*sic*], I am inclined to believe that when the white man was created, nature was pretty well exhausted—but determined to keep up appearances, she pinched up his features, and did the best she could under the circumstances. (Great laughter.)"[112] Dr. Rock did not just "love my race"—he also loved "my color. . . . My friends, we can never become elevated until we are true to ourselves."[113]

Black women, too, rejected white efforts to exclude them from the feminine beauty found in women's hair, whether they wore their hair long or not. Since the seventeenth century, enslaved women put as much time and labor into caring for their hair as possible within the confines of the institution of slavery—often in community with other women, and often on Sundays. Such diligent care was particularly important because the curly and kinky textures so common among African-descended people are more vulnerable than straight hair to damage from the sun, sweat, and water. Styled into braids, cornrows, or Afros, or wrapped with cloth, twine, or string (which had the effect of straightening or relaxing Afro-textured hair), enslaved women's hairstyles were designed to be both protective and beautiful.[114] Sundays were also the day that many Black women combed out and styled hair that might be, during the rest of the working week, covered with a bandanna or scarf. Arranging one's hair into a beautiful hairstyle for church— often in styles that combined inspiration from African, Indigenous, and European fashions—was one way Black women could publicly proclaim the beauty of their hair.[115] By the mid-nineteenth century, free Black men and women in major cities like Philadelphia and Boston often wore hairstyles that mirrored contemporary fashions among their fellow white urbanites—though this could also draw white mockery: many of Edward W. Clay's famous caricatured illustrations of Black Philadelphians from the 1820s and 1830s show Black women with elaborate textured hairstyles that feature round puffs, coiled topknots, or cornrows (usually topped with hair ribbons, decorative headpieces, or large hats).[116]

As scholars like Jasmine Nichole Cobb and Ashton Gonzalez have demonstrated, since the early nineteenth century Black Americans have used visual culture as a kind of counterprogramming to images like Clay's that mocked and denigrated their appearance. Photography, an artistic and scientific medium that most nineteenth-century Americans believed produced authentic depictions of the human and natural world, offered an especially powerful format for self-possession and self-making.[117] Sitting for a photographic portrait *also* offered a platform for alternate visions of beauty found in the Black body and in Afro-textured hair, especially when the photographers, too, were Black. Photographers Alexander Thomas and Thomas Ball operated a photography studio in Cincinnati in the mid-nineteenth century, where they took many portraits of local Black men, women, and children; in the 1860s and 1870s, inexpensive *cartes de visite* made it possible for even more people to have their portrait taken and circulate prints to loved ones.[118] A portrait of Mattie Allen (see fig. 1.5), taken by Ball and Thomas's studio in the mid-1870s, is a vivid example of how portrait photography allowed Black women to proclaim the beauty of long Afro-textured hair. Allen is posed in three-quarter profile. Although this is a common portrait convention of the era, the pose also allows the viewer a clear perspective of her hair, its long length twisted into a coiled bun on top of her head (and decorated with a small white bow), while the short hairs above her forehead (and baby hairs along her hairline) display a kinky texture. Allen's hair is long, decorative, and textured, and its graceful styling amplifies the way

1.5 Portrait of Mattie Allen, ca. 1874–1877. In this photographic
portrait, Mattie Allen has textured hair and baby hairs above
her forehead and along her hairline, while the rest of her long
hair is coiled on top of her head.

CREDIT: "*Mattie Allen [albumen print, Carte de Visite], c. 1874–1877*";
SC#17—J. P. Ball and A. S. Thomas Photograph Collection [SC#17-005].
Image courtesy of Cincinnati Museum Center.

Allen—and the photographer who took her portrait—performs her femininity and her beauty.[119]

Yet it was not women like Mattie Allen that white writers had in mind when they rhapsodized about women's beautiful hair. Even though most white writers did not explicitly name the whiteness of the women they praised, this was merely a signal of the limits of their aesthetic imaginations—their praise was, indeed, implicitly in praise of white womanhood. An 1850 scientific hair treatise's discussion of hair and beauty is representative of this approach. Underneath the bolded phrase, "THE FIRST TRAIT OF BEAUTY IS A FINE HEAD OF HAIR," the author explained that "in every age and country, a fine head of hair has been considered the most distinguished ornament of the human frame, and indispensably necessary to personal beauty." Some beauty, however, could be found only in particular *kinds* of hair: "There is nothing in the wide world that contributes more to comeliness and beauty than a profusion of soft, flowing ringlets, or auburn tresses." Words like *soft* and *flowing* were racially coded as white, but so, too, was *auburn*: as the white supremacist polemicist John Van Evrie explained, "the hair of the Caucasian is a graceful ornament, and varies in color from black to *auburn*, giving variety and beauty to that species. In the negro it is always black . . . such a being as a light-haired, or flaxen hair negro was never known."[120]

Indeed, Van Evrie was an author who did not merely *imply* that the beauty of long hair on women was confined to white woman alone—he relished it. Van Evrie began his 1868 defense of white supremacy with a lengthy rumination on the beauty of white women's hair:

> The hair of the Caucasian is a graceful and imposing feature or quality, of course in perfect harmony with everything else, but sometimes, and especially in the case of females, it is an attribute of physical beauty more striking and attractive than any other. Its color, golden or sunny brown, and the dazzling hues of black, purple, and auburn tresses, has been the theme of poets from time immemorial, while its luxuriance, and silky softness, and graceful length, will continue to be the pride of one sex and the admiration of the other as long as the perception of beauty remains. . . . There is in fact no mere physical quality of the female so attractive, or that is capable of being rendered so charming, as the hair, and the elaborate dressings, the

time and labor spent on its decoration, proceed as much perhaps from that delicate perception of the beautiful innate in woman as it does from female vanity or the love of display.[121]

Even the lengthy time spent caring for the hair, making it as decorative and beautiful as possible, was a beloved trait in a white woman. By contrast, he continued, Black women's hair was not beautiful at all: "But with this 'wealth of beauty' of the Caucasian woman, what an immeasurable interval separates her from the negress!" Van Evrie presupposed that Black women's hair was not even *capable* of being long—further proof of its biological inferiority: "Is it possible for any who sees the latter, with her short, stiff, uncombable fleece of seeming wool, to endow her with the attribute of beauty or comeliness? . . . Can the sentiment of beauty, grace or dignity, or indeed any idea whatever—except as a necessary provision of nature for covering the negro head—attach to the hair of the negro?"[122] (As chapter 3 will demonstrate, Van Evrie's use of *wool* was also deeply racially coded.)

Van Evrie claimed that Black women's hair was fundamentally unattractive, owing to both its texture and what he believed to be its inherently short length. Yet the history of American slavery is replete with examples of enslaved women with long, beautiful hair—women whose hair made them the target of violence, including, tellingly, the violent forcible shaving or cutting of their hair. Harriet Jacobs described this type of violence in her autobiographical narrative *Incidents in the Life of a Slave Girl* (1861). Her enslaver, furious with her for rejecting his sexual predation and then becoming pregnant after choosing to have sex with a different man, cut off all of Harriet's hair: "I had a fine head of hair; and he often railed about my pride of arranging it nicely. He cut every hair close to my head, storming and swearing all the time." As historian Tiya Miles points out, this forcible hair removal had a dual function: it allowed her master "to exert control and deface her allure"—her beautiful hair.[123]

Even more common were hair punishments levied by white women against the Black women they enslaved, *especially* Black women whose long and beautiful hair, white women assumed, would attract sexual advances from white men. (The bodies of Black women and girls with long straight hair were also, of course, sometimes evidence of the history of white men's sexual predation.)[124] When James Brittan was interviewed by the Federal Writers' project in the 1930s, he recalled a story about his grandmother, an enslaved woman born in Africa, whose hair was "fine as silk and hung down below her waist." When her mistress became jealous that the "Old Master" paid her too much attention, the mistress forced her head to be shaved and to remain shaved "from that day on."[125]

James Brittan's grandmother gave the lie to the claim, made by Van Evrie and others, that only white women could grow beautiful long hair. Yet the violence she and other Black women experienced because of their long hair testified to many white people's desire to reserve this "proudest ornament of female beauty," as *Godey's* put it in 1855, for white women alone.[126] Indeed, although the beauty of long hair was already associated with white womanhood in the colonial period (especially thanks to 1 Corinthians), it was during the nineteenth century that white women's long hair became firmly naturalized as evidence of their political subjugation, too—proof that they lacked the kind of self-mastery necessary to be a political subject in the new United States. Scientific and popular media proclaimed that white women's value lay, instead, in their beauty. That these same media also denounced Black women's Afro-textured hair as ugly not only communicated Black women's distance from political subjecthood; it also reinforced a vision of womanhood that was racialized, solely, as white.

Chinese Immigrants, the Queue, and the Boundaries of Political Citizenship

By the mid-nineteenth century, a hair length binary that mandated long hair for women and short hair for men was firmly established in American culture. This binary was also racialized, with many white writers implicitly or explicitly defining the beauty of women's long hair as exclusive to white women alone. This gendered and racialized binary had also been naturalized: it had become evidence of the supposedly natural differences between men and women—and between white women and Black women—and, consequently, a visual indicator of white men's sole claim to political citizenship. Yet while a hair length binary that tied short hair to both manhood and political belonging largely held fast for white bodies, for non-white Americans it was not so straightforward. Short hair on a Black man's body, for example, did not automatically grant him political participation.

When Chinese immigrants began arriving in the United States in the late 1840s, with men wearing their hair in long queues, hair length's gender binary was tested in a major way. Of all the new immigrants who began arriving in the United States in the mid-nineteenth century, when immigration rates spiked for the first time in the nation's history, Chinese people received the most virulently xenophobic treatment—and, already forbidden from naturalized citizenship, became subject to the country's first-ever laws restricting immigration along racial lines: the Page Act of 1875 and the Chinese Exclusion Act of 1882.[127] Proponents of restrictive legislation cited Chinese laborers' supposed extraordinary productivity (and the threat it posed to white labor) as justification for their exclusion—yet at the same time, Chinese men were also derided for their supposed deficient masculinity. The feature that could hold, at once, these contradictory characterizations was the queue—and it is the queue that also shows how hair's legibility as an index of the racial and gender borders of belonging could also be deeply unsettled.

The first Chinese immigrants came to California, like many other immigrants and migrants, after the discovery of gold in 1848. Once gold mining declined after 1853, many Chinese workers were recruited to construct the transcontinental railroad, and following its 1869 completion, most settled in San Francisco and sought work in the city's industries.[128] Chinese people never made up more than 10 percent of the city's population during the nineteenth century, but because of their unusual demographics—most Chinese immigrants were adult men, with few women and fewer children—virtually all Chinese people who lived in San Francisco were de facto competitors with job-seeking white men.[129] With four times as many men in California as there were jobs available, white men perceived Chinese laborers as a particularly visible embodiment of that threat. Moreover, in spite of their small numbers, Chinese laborers *were* dominant in some industries: in 1871, for example, Chinese workers produced 50 percent of the state's boots and shoes.[130]

More than just the threat they posed in the labor market, however, white critics in the popular press claimed that Chinese men were at odds with norms of white American masculinity—and, therefore, worthy of condemnation and eventually exclusion—for many reasons: they largely immigrated to the United States as bachelors and did not create families, as adult men should; they performed feminine-coded labor in laundries, restaurants, and domestic service (no matter that state labor laws and threats of local violence made these jobs the only possibilities for many Chinese laborers); and, by supporting the immigration of Chinese women sex workers—far more a moral panic than a demographically significant number of women—they threatened American women and womanhood.[131] Chinese men's bodies, critics argued, testified to their supposedly inferior masculinity. While some critics denigrated Chinese men with gendered wisecracks about their clothing—for example, "that garment of his which passes for his 'pants'"—racialized critiques of Chinese men's masculinity primarily focused on their hair.[132]

Few records of nineteenth-century America better illustrate contemporary white attitudes toward Chinese immigrants—and the centrality of their long hair to this perception—than the *San Francisco Wasp*, an illustrated weekly newspaper published from 1876 to 1941 that featured colorful, often satirical illustrations on its front cover, back cover, and two-page centerfolds. At its peak in the 1880s, *The Wasp* was the most widely read newspaper on the West Coast. It was also in this decade that, under editor Ambrose G. Bierce, the *Wasp*'s signature cartoons became singularly, even obsessively focused on a single subject: opposition to Chinese immigration and hostility toward Chinese immigrants.[133]

The *Wasp*'s illustrations were fundamental to its function as an organ of public opinion, particularly on the issue of Chinese immigration. Indeed, the newspaper's editorial staff firmly believed that its full-page and centerfold cartoons were not merely supplemental to its articles or illustrative of its text—they were the newspaper's central purpose and its strongest vehicle for communicating its values. As one 1878 issue put it, "Our double-page illustration this week requires but little explanation. . . . Our artist condenses the whole Chinese question into a picture, and does it in such a manner that everybody can understand it at sight."[134] This was precisely the value of an illustrated newspaper: it condensed entire situations into bold, graphic images that could be comprehended even by people who did not (or could not) read its text.

Through these illustrations, *The Wasp* visually racialized and gendered Chinese men's bodies with an almost mind-numbing repetition. While the newspaper used detailed lifelike illustration techniques to depict famous contemporary figures like railroad magnates Charles Crocker and Leland Stanford, its illustrations of Chinese people relied instead on stereotype.[135] Rarely, if ever, did a specific Chinese individual appear in a *Wasp* cartoon. Instead, a standard caricature of Chinese men populated the newspaper's pages, signaled by three visual signs: loose clothing, thick-soled shoes, and a queue, as an 1881 cartoon demonstrates (see fig. 1.6). Thanks to their near-weakly repetition, these signs became so conflated with Chinese identity that they could even be used satirically as a form of racial drag—to suggest, as one 1882 cartoon did, that President Chester A. Arthur and his cabinet were too sympathetic to Chinese interests because Arthur had vetoed the first version of the Chinese Exclusion Act (see fig. 1.7). (He eagerly signed its second version just one month later.)[136]

More so than the other signs of Chinese identity, however, it was the queue that the *Wasp*'s cartoonists illustrated most often and by which they were the most obsessed and perplexed. This preoccupation is consistent with the way white Californians more broadly received the queue. As historian Erica Lee has argued, white Californians viewed the queue as a "cultural anomaly that is both sexually and racially ambiguous."[137] Indeed, its long length seemed to white Americans like evidence of Chinese emasculation or even gender inversion. Moreover, Chinese laboring men were dogged by accusations of economic dependency—and thus a lack of self-mastery—because white Americans assumed that all Chinese workers were indentured unfree "coolies." The century's most influential hair scientist, Peter A. Browne (who is the subject of chapter 3), even suggested that Chinese men were biologically predisposed to grow long hair—the same claim so many scientific and popular sources made about white women's hair, too.[138] Against a backdrop of white American manhood that, by the time the first Chinese men immigrated to the United States, deemed short hair a crucial index of political subjecthood, queues might have seemed like unambiguous evidence that Chinese men lay outside that boundary.

And yet: the queue was, instead, a destabilizing challenge to a system built on interlocking binaries: long versus short, feminine versus masculine, decorative versus plain, weak versus powerful. Queues behaved differently in the pages of *The Wasp* than the other visual markers of Chinese identity like clothing or shoes. Queues could curl, spiral, fly, or float (see fig. 1.1); they extended backward and stood up from the body completely erect, seeming to defy gravity (see fig. 1.7). What *The Wasp*'s illustrations so vividly capture is the queue's conflicting valences: it was vulnerable to being grabbed, yanked, or pulled; yet at the same time, it was also remarkably, almost unbelievably strong—strong enough, in some illustrations, to support an entire man's body weight. These qualities—weak and strong, vulnerable

THE COMING MAN.
Allee sammee 'Melican Man Monopoleeee.

1.6 "The Coming Man: Allee sammee 'Melican Man Monopoleeee,"
chromolithograph by George Frederick Keller, *The Wasp*, May 21, 1881. The
Chinese figure in this illustration holds a hand labeled "MONOPOLY" over
objects labeled to indicate six economies: "clothing factories," "shirt manufac.,"
"box factory," "Havana Cuba" (cigars), "underwear," and "laundries."

CREDIT: Reproduced from *Wasp* (San Francisco, CA), f F850 .W18, v. 6, Jan.–June 1881, No. 251,
The Bancroft Library, University of California, Berkeley.

1.7 "Our New Cabinet at Washington," chromolithograph by George Frederick Keller, *The Wasp*, April 28, 1882. In addition to drawing the bodies of President Chester Arthur and his cabinet wearing the style of clothing, shoes, fans, and hair associated with Chinese men in 1880s San Francisco, cartoonist Keller also rendered their names in a mocking fashion. President Arthur, for example, is labeled "Ah Ling Arthur."

CREDIT: Reproduced from *Wasp* (San Francisco, CA), f F850 .W18, v. 8, Jan.—June 1882, No. 300:265–266, The Bancroft Library, University of California, Berkeley.

and powerful—may seem irreconcilable, but they actually embody the same tensions evident in the way white Americans perceived Chinese immigrants during the nineteenth century.

These tensions are evident, for example, in a cartoon *The Wasp* published in 1882, as Congress was debating the Chinese Exclusion Act (see fig. 1.8). In this centerfold cartoon, a Chinese figure is rendered as a kind of human octopus, his many arms performing sewing, ironing, cigar rolling, painting, and construction labor simultaneously—while another arm prepares a large bag of money to be sent back to China. A group of out-of-work white men stand and sit idly outside; a police officer even drags one of the idle men in the direction of the infamous California prison, San Quentin. All the while, the Chinese man's queue curves and floats gracefully through the air behind him. White Americans agreed that Chinese

1.8 "What Shall We Do with Our Boys?," chromolithograph by George Frederick
Keller, *The Wasp*, March 3, 1882. Many of the Chinese figure's eleven arms perform
the same kinds of labor identified in fig. 1.6, published ten months earlier,
including cigar rolling, sewing, and box manufacturing.

CREDIT: Reproduced from *Wasp* (San Francisco, CA), f F850 .W18, v. 8, Jan.—June 1882,
No. 292:136–137, The Bancroft Library, University of California, Berkeley.

men were, at the same time, too feminized to be eligible for American political citizenship, *and also* so hardworking that they threatened to deprive
white American men of their livelihoods. They were insufficiently masculine men *and also* a kind of hypermasculine superman—the apotheosis of
the productive working body that American industrial capitalism would
increasingly demand. The queue was the one body part flexible enough to
encompass both of these claims.[139] In so doing, it suggested there might be
some cracks in the gendered hair length binary that had naturalized white
men's political supremacy for decades.

IN ENGLISH NORTH AMERICA, scriptural mandates about gendered
hairstyles shaped the way English colonial leaders responded to the hair
worn by both English colonists and Indigenous people because, informed

by humoralism's definition of hair as external to the body, hairstyling was the most important evidence of a person's identity in their community. Whether a person's hair was long or short reflected their location along a set of social identities: man or woman, heathen or Christian, friend or foe. Within this framework, religious leaders proclaimed that long hair on men was unchristian and unmanly, but European- and African-descended men alike often ignored these denunciations, choosing to grow their hair long and style it with powders and ribbon, or to wear a long periwig on top of their heads. Yet colonial leaders maintained that hair was a matter of community concern—and, frequently, control—because the group and the individual were so profoundly *intertwined*: it only took a few colonists styling their hair in a prideful manner for God to send a band of Indigenous people to attack their entire community.

By the beginning of the nineteenth century, the meaning of hair had changed profoundly. As hair became increasingly understood as a part of the body and its biological qualities became increasingly significant, its capacity to carry social meaning became unmoored from its spiritual foundations. Hair began to speak more to a person's *inherent* and *individual* character, not merely if the person was comporting themself with Christian virtue in service of their community; moreover, the meaning of hair also grafted onto contemporary conversations about the racialized and gendered dimensions of American political citizenship. Short hair indicated the self-mastery of a white male citizen of the new republic, while long hair indicated someone who lacked the independence to be included as a political subject. Yet the long hair worn by tens of thousands of Chinese men in the second half of the nineteenth century unsettled many of the core assumptions that undergirded this gendered hair length divide.

Ultimately, the short hair / long hair binary was always about more than hair alone. The body on which the long or short hair grew—whether that person was a man or women, but also their racial and ethnic identity, even their immigration or legal citizenship status—also mattered, long into the twentieth century. So, too, did the body matter in respect to the most gendered kind of hair of all: facial hair.

CHAPTER 2

FACIAL HAIR

IT WAS AN ORDINARY SUNDAY in March 1926 when the *New York Times* declared that the beard was dead. About seventy-five years earlier, after two centuries of near-total barefacedness in English North America, American men began growing out their facial hair. In the second half of the nineteenth century, tens of millions of men both ordinary and powerful wore beards. (Indeed, the word *beard* had a much broader meaning in that era than it does today, encompassing not just the ear-to-ear chin-covering style that we know as a *beard*, but also mustaches, side-whiskers, or anything in between; if it grew on the face, it could be called a beard.[1]) Evidence of beard wearing abounds in late nineteenth-century culture. From the beginning of Abraham Lincoln's term in 1861 through the end of William Howard Taft's term in 1913, all but two presidents sported some kind of beard or mustache (or both). Before 1861, and since 1913, no president wore a beard or mustache of any kind.[2] Indeed, presidential facial hair testifies to the powerful but brief reign of the beard in the second half of the nineteenth century: by the end of the 1890s, beards were on the decline, receding both in popularity and in extent (mustaches stayed in favor for a few more years) until they were shaved off almost unilaterally in the early twentieth century.[3]

By 1926, it was clear that the beard was decidedly passé. Acknowledging that "perhaps there is no hope" for beard wearing to return, *New York Times* author Hollister Noble announced that "it is time to salute an honored relic, to console the memory" of the bearded days of the past. Noble wistfully listed famous people known for their beards: "Barbarossa, Solomon, the Smith Brothers, Concord intellectuals, Philadelphia politicians, Mohammed, Brigham Young, Judas, Southern Colonels, Bluebeard, Blackbeard, the Lombard or Long Beards, Buffalo Bill, Santa Claus, and Barnum's Bearded Lady—all of them sported yards of unexcelled hirsutage."[4] At the end of the list, as the tongue-in-cheek culmination of a list of famous men, was a single woman: Madame Clofullia, popularly known as "Barnum's Bearded Lady," the first bearded woman exhibited on an American freak show stage.[5] (To distinguish between lived experience and performance contexts, I use the capitalized *Bearded Lady* to refer to the character portrayed by many different women, and *bearded women* to refer to individual women who had facial hair.)

As nineteenth-century Americans accorded increasing biological significance to the length of the hair that grew from the head, the lower half of the face offered an even more obvious site for grappling with the relationship between gender, race, and nation. In the second half of the century—starting at nearly the precise moment Madame Clofullia made her US debut—beards did not merely become suddenly popular in the United States; they also became fundamental to American men's performance of masculinity.[6] Moreover, for American men both powerful and ordinary, facial hair became a marker of American citizenship. For white men, the right kind of facial hair—a beard (in the twenty-first-century sense of chin-covering) that was thick and full but neither too overgrown nor too scanty—affirmed, even naturalized, white men's social and political power. On bodies that did not present as white and male, however, the same kind of facial hair signified not power but a threat: a destabilizing challenge to the social order.

As scholars like Londa Schiebinger have noted, beards have been a sign of masculine power in many different cultures for thousands of years, yet not uniformly so. For example, while ancient Egyptians portrayed *all* their monarchs, even women like Hatshepsut, wearing beards, ancient Romans believed only criminals wore beards. In the early modern period, humoralism naturalized the beard's role in a gender binary: while the body processed women's excess bodily fluids into menstrual blood, men's excess fluids were excreted, as Schiebinger writes, as "sweat, semen, and beards." There was also nascent evidence of the beard's racialization: in the late seventeenth and eighteenth centuries, European naturalists turned facial hair into evidence for rudimentary racial classification systems.[7] By the eighteenth century, then, the beard's symbolic power was fairly well established in Western Europe, yet virtually all men on both sides of the Atlantic removed their facial hair assiduously, usually by visiting a barber multiple times a week.[8]

Indeed, in his exhaustive study of hairstyles from the ancient world to the twentieth century, Richard Corson described the eighteenth century as a rare moment in history when "almost total beardlessness" was the norm in Western Europe and English North America.[9] This norm changed dramatically when, in the nineteenth century, men started growing beards in overwhelming numbers.

The process of crystallizing the beard's role as an index of white male power in the nineteenth century, however, required more than millions of hairy faces—it also required a story. White scientific and cultural authorities took an old story about the masculine beard and imbued it with renewed cultural gravity and political urgency, framing it clearly as an indicator of which bodies fit within the bounds of political citizenship. This story had four parts: a robust (though ad hoc) beard canon that explained the many reasons why men (implicitly, white men) should grow beards; the elevation of bearded male heroes; the delineation of what kinds of facial hair fell outside of the racialized standard, thus locating non-white men outside of political power; and the enfreakment of women with facial hair—white Bearded Ladies and hairy women of color featured in American freak shows, and, by metaphorical extension, suffragists pushing for women's rights.

Together, these four processes reinforced the broader cultural meaning of hair in the nineteenth century as a reliable external signal of the bearer's intrinsic internal self, as well as the nineteenth century's growing emphasis on hair's biological qualities—an emphasis that framed even specific hairstyles, like beards, as biologically determined. Facial hair, like the hair on the head, was considered an essential part of the body in the nineteenth century—one with the power to reflect the intrinsic character and identity of the person from whose face it grew. The choice to wear a beard offered white American men—even ordinary men far removed from financial or electoral authority—a hyper visible symbol of not merely their *own* masculine power, but of the patriarchal white supremacy from which they benefited. Meanwhile, critiques of facial hair on other kinds of bodies became a powerful tool for condemning social changes that threatened that power—such as the abolition of slavery, the political changes posed by Reconstruction, and the voting rights expansion sought by the women's suffrage movement.

Indeed, for people who fell outside white masculinity's bodily norms, access to both the beard's symbol of masculinity and to the power it conferred was far more fraught. White observers' claims about the inherent beardlessness of East Asian, Indigenous, and African-descended men framed these men of color as possessing an insufficient masculinity that made them too distant from white manhood to make persuasive claims for political subjecthood. Meanwhile, white women with facial hair—paradigmatically, the freak show's Bearded Ladies—were insufficiently feminine and thus too close to white masculinity. This rhetoric, too, reinforced the naturalness of white masculine political power by categorizing white women's pursuit of that power as inherently freakish. Finally, East Asian and Indigenous women with facial hair—who performed in freak shows not as Bearded Ladies but as "missing links" or "animal people"—were framed as so distant from political subjecthood as to render their very humanity unstable.[10]

The Rise of the American Beard

Beards were virtually unseen in English North America during the eighteenth century. None of the men who signed the Constitution, for example, wore beards, and an American Quaker named Joshua Evans was prohibited from traveling for the ministry simply because he wore a beard.[11] A major shift occurred in the nineteenth century, when facial hair began to enjoy unprecedented popularity first in western Europe and quickly thereafter in the United States.

Facial hair's nineteenth-century progression occurred piecemeal: side-whiskers became popular first, becoming common in Europe by 1810. Indeed, the only facial hair to be found on the faces of American presidents before Abraham Lincoln are side-whiskers, such as those worn by James Monroe and John Quincy Adams. Yet a full ear-to-ear beard remained, at first, unusual. For example, in 1832 the Prophet Matthias was arrested by New York City police officers and forcibly shaved of his large greying beard. Although Matthias's beard was not the cause of his arrest—accusations of fraud were—in an era of mostly bare faces, onlookers saw such a large beard as evidence of a man who was antisocial or even unwell.[12] Even military men were not exempt from such censure: two years before Matthias's arrest, a bearded veteran named Joseph Palmer moved from his isolated farm to the town of Fitchburg, Massachusetts, where residents found his beard so unusual and upsetting that they smashed Palmer's windows, threw rocks at him in the street, and refused to grant him communion at church. Palmer believed he had a right to wear a beard if he so chose, but his conviction afforded him no protection: when four men armed with soap and a razor attacked Palmer and tried to forcibly shave him, Palmer's attempts to hold off the assault resulted in his arrest, and he was sent to prison for one year. When Palmer died in 1875—by which point beards were exceedingly popular among American men—his tombstone was inscribed with the words, "Persecuted for wearing the beard."[13]

Matthias's and Palmer's beards predated beard wearing's popularity in the United States by two decades, but in Europe the popularity of beards began to rise in the 1830s. Because none of the kings who ruled France during the first half of the nineteenth century wore a beard, young French romantics and revolutionaries adopted beards as a way to rebel against dominant tastes; beards worn by prominent European socialists such as Karl Marx—and by radical reformers like vegetarians—only bolstered the connection between radicalism and beardedness.[14] By contrast, for much of Western history up to that point, the popularity of beards was tied to the whims of kings: if a king had a beard, his royal court and then his subjects were likely to grow beards, too, and a beardless king would likewise inspire his subjects to shave.[15] Even contemporary observers noted this unexpected shift from a prevailing history of monarchical beards to their embrace by radicals. An 1854 article in the *Westminster Review* recalled how the beard had once functioned as a "symbol of patriarch and king," but had now become one of "revolution, democracy, and dissatisfaction with existing institutions."[16] Such a description is fitting for a contemporary American radical who wore a beard, too: John Brown. By the time he led the raid on Harpers Ferry, Brown had grown the iconic long, white beard that fellow abolitionist and painter Thomas Hovenden captured in *The Last Moments of John Brown* (1882–1884), which depicts Brown descending the courthouse staircase on the way to his execution.[17]

The popularity of the fully beard quickly spread beyond radicals. From the early 1850s through the mid-1860s, chin-covering beards became mainstream first in France, then in England, and then in the United States.[18] The reason for their sudden ubiquity in these countries is difficult to reconstruct and has therefore been the subject of debate. Many popular sources claim that the beards of veterans returning home from the Crimean War inspired Englishmen to let their beards grow too, but historian Christopher Oldstone-Moore points out that English beard wearing started in 1850— four years before the war even began.[19] Some scholars suggest that, across the Atlantic, Hungarian revolutionary Lajos Kossuth may have inspired American men to grow beards when he toured the country in 1851.[20] It is also possible that the international men's fashion press, published in France and England and reprinted in US tailors' magazines, inspired trends in facial hair as well as clothing.[21] Historian Sean Trainor argues that in the United States, a growing sense of unease toward and mistrust of Black barbers—who had long dominated the barbering industry—was extremely important to many white men's decisions to start growing their beards. Between 1800 and 1850, white men increasingly saw barber shops, especially those owned by free Black men, as spaces that unsettled racial hierarchy and white supremacy, especially since barbering offered some Black men access to wealth and local power in an era when both were scarce.[22] With shaving tools like razors and soaps more readily available in the emergent market economy, home shaving seemed like an attractive alternative to submitting to a Black barber. However, many men quickly discovered that home shaving was not nearly as easy or painless as they had assumed. Growing a beard, Trainor argues, became an attractive alternative.[23]

In truth, the beard's popularity in the United States by the 1850s likely owes to a combination of these origin stories. Some men probably followed French fashion, some mimicked soldiers or Kossuth, and others ditched both the barber shop and their home shaving routines. The cumulative effect of these individual and group decisions was staggering: in the span of just a few decades, the overwhelming beardlessness of the preceding two centuries had been completely transformed.[24]

With all these newly bearded faces also came a clear and consistent message about what it meant for men to wear the beard: beards signified masculinity and power. Wearing a beard allowed men to physically distinguish themselves from women, who, thanks to urbanization, industrialization, and the women's suffrage movement, were becoming increasingly present in public spaces and central to public discourse.[25] White men in Western Europe and the United States had long written, even in times of overwhelming beardlessness, about how beards marked the male members of the human race—or, in some texts, the male members of the *white* race, specifically—as strong, wise, and powerful. However, it was only once the homosocial spaces long reserved for white men were threatened—including theaters, colleges, and, if activists had their way, ballot boxes—that a codified facial hair uniform became an appealing option. It was then, in the mid-nineteenth century, that white American men started to cultivate the very beards they had publicly admired (but personally shunned) for generations.[26]

Men's Beards, Masculinity, and Political Citizenship

In the 1850s, American men did not just start wearing more beards—contemporary writers also began to write about beards *constantly*, publishing dozens of amateur beard histories, philosophical treatises on the beard, and other kinds of pro-beard essays and pamphlets. These writers—most of whom were white men, like their intended readers—recycled facial hair folklore, cheered for bearded heroes, and proclaimed the enormous health benefits and time savings that would accrue to those who eschewed the razor.

The 1850s were not the first time Euro-American print culture celebrated the beard. Even when shaving was the cultural norm—when, as amateur beard historian Jacques Antoine Dulaure wrote in 1786, the beard was "an object of ridicule"—French and English writers praised the beard as a "mark of manhood" that is "natural only to man, is the mark of his virility, and gives him precedency among his species."[27] But the explosion of beard media in the mid-1850s was unique because it began *after* beard wearing started to become popular among Anglo-Americans. These writers did not intend their works to make the beard more popular, but to cement the beard's cultural connotations: although the beard had a long global history as a symbol of masculinity, that history was also contingent and inconsistent, in some eras associated with rugged masculinity, in others with eccentric antisociality or even effeminacy.[28] Pro-beard writers tried to ensure *all* Americans understood that *the beard* as a concept—as well as actual beards on white men's faces—was an index of not just individual manhood, but of a *collective* sense of white masculine power.

The ad hoc beard canon that began in the mid-1850s claimed that beards made men's lives better in a material or physiological way, that beards conveyed masculine authority and power (and bare faces an unmasculine or emasculated *lack* of power), and that beards were reserved for men because of the inherent hierarchy between men and women that was evident in their bodies. Yet while few pro-beard writers said so explicitly, their hierarchy of the body was not just gendered—it was also fundamentally racialized. In these pro-beard texts—as well as ethnological and medical writing produced by some of the era's most lauded experts—the relative beardedness of East Asian, Indigenous, and African-descended men also carried vital significance. The masculine power of the beard, these authors claimed, was only activated on the right kinds of bodies; even if they grew some hair on their faces, men of color still could not access the cultural signifier that was *the beard*.

What Beards Meant to White Men in the Nineteenth Century

Many authors in the ad hoc beard canon of the 1850s praised the beard for its money-saving, health-giving, and spirituality-enhancing powers. The cost and time saved by no longer visiting the barber—a chore nineteenth-century men undertook between two and six times per week—was the reason many pro-beard articles cited for growing beards. Some authors attempted to quantify this savings over a lifetime, with sums ranging from $350 to $1,000—or, as one local newspaper put it, more than four thousand hours of time not shaving that could instead be spent reading books.[29] Many pro-beard writers also praised the health benefits of growing a beard. John Shoebridge Williams, a Spiritualist medium and beard advocate, explained that a beard "protects the throat and chin from the effects of damp and cold atmospheres, and thus the bronchial tubes from inflammation, both winter and spring. . . . The grown beard supplies necessary fluids to the head, and thus keeps it, as well as the throat, cool in summer, by covering the face it protects it from cold in the winter."[30] A local newspaper in Texas even suggested that facial hair and eye health were directly linked, proclaiming that "there was no use for spectacles when beards were worn."[31]

Overall, these varied authors agreed, the beard was "a preservative of health" denied to men who shaved. It was a "statement of fact," one author proclaimed, that "a man of 50 years will on average have cut off eight feet of beard," and "shaving the beard [has] on this account, been deprecated by many physiologists, as tending to weaken the strength by the general drain of blood; [and] to diminish the reproductive power by an unknown sympathy."[32] Indeed, pro-beard writers frequently linked the beard and virility, perhaps reflecting cultural residue of the humoral human body that categorized facial hair as an outgrowth of the same internal heat that produced semen; thus, the larger the beard, the more virile the man.[33]

Some writers even analogized shaving-induced weakening of individual men's bodies to a weakening of the American body politic—demonstrating the connection between hair and nation in the nineteenth century.

Particularly vehement on this point was a Massachusetts medical practitioner named Dr. E. Sanborn, who wrote a lengthy explanation of the deleterious effects of shaving for the *Boston Medical and Surgical Journal* in 1854; his arguments reached an even wider public through summaries and responses printed in local newspapers across the country.[34] Dr. Sanborn, himself a beard wearer, argued that in cultures where beard wearing was ubiquitous, such as Jewish communities, physical health was stronger than in communities where most men shaved, and incidence of diseases located in the head or neck—scrofula (infections of the lymph nodes), bronchial infection, and coughs—were lower.[35] Quoting a well-traveled medical colleague, Sanborn explained the high stakes for a Protestant nation like the United States that envisioned itself as a vanguard of modernity: "Who shall say that this chosen people, this most heavily bearded of all races, is not by their religious devotion to the laws of health, destined to stand upon the earth and fill it with unabridged, unadulterated manliness, when other nations of greater boasted light and knowledge shall, by their fool-hardy violations of nature, have consumed themselves and passed away?"[36] To remove the hair from a man's face was, Dr. Sanborn argued, a violation of natural law.

Even as a man of science—and even with his admiration for the health of Jewish men abroad—Dr. Sanborn also explained how growing the beard could help strengthen American men's Christianity. To shave every day "not only destroys the germs of their future physical health" but also "wastes away . . . confidence in the wisdom of their Creator. Neither the image of God nor any of his works remain sacred in their sight."[37] As a spiritualist medium, Williams felt similarly: "It seems to us," he wrote, "that an all-wise Creator could not have placed the beard of the male man on his face, without some wise end to be obtained by it growing there." Williams worried that "to practice shaving is a continual exertion on the part of man to destroy the works of God, and unnatural, because the Creator is in the continual endeavor to reproduce and establish a beard." The beard, to Williams and his mid-nineteenth-century contemporaries across the United States, was a part of the body; for Williams, then, its removal was an insult to God himself.[38]

The beard offered men stronger finances, health, and connection to God—but it also offered, according to writers in the mid-1850s, a sense of power. Although most of the pro-beard writers acknowledged that there had been eras in human history when beard wearing was uncommon, the beard's connection to male power, authority, wisdom, and strength repeated across their pages. Many 1850s beard histories asserted that monarchs of past centuries were generally "distinguishable by their handsome beards," as an anonymous British beard historian who called himself Trichocosmos wrote in the 1850s.[39] A beard was so important to the monarchy in the Middle Ages, Trichocosmos claimed, that the enclosure of three hairs from a king's beard in the seal of a letter was considered by his contemporaries to be "the most solemn pledge a king could give."[40] Some authors also praised facial hair worn by historical, cultural, and intellectual leaders. For example, some texts mentioned that both Plato and Socrates were given the "most honorable title" of "*Magister Barbatus*," or *Beard Master*, because of their wisdom.[41] Fully convinced of the power of the beard, pro-beard amateur historians consistently associated beardless faces and forcible shaving with male servitude, weakness, and shame—with enslaved men, incarcerated men, and other groups of men without access to power. Many of their narratives pointed to cultures that used bare chins to indicate servitude and cultures in which enslaved people were forbidden from wearing beards; one author explained that "slaves among the Turks are deprived of their beards; to shave them off *voluntarily* subjects the offender to total exclusion from society."[42]

Whether they focused their pro-beard boosterism on physical health, spiritual well-being, or king-like power, the writers of the ad hoc beard canon made clear that the beard was, most importantly, "the naturall ensigne of *manhood.*" The word *manhood* carried three simultaneous valences: of being an adult, a man, and, crucially, *manly* (in contrast to feminized or effeminate).[43] John Shoebridge Williams, for example, emphasized that beards marked manhood as distinct from boyhood: "It has been told to this medium, from the spiritual world . . . that man, by removing the beard from his face, destroys the distinction that God has wisely placed there to show that he is a man, and not a boy."[44] So, too, was "the presence or absence of the beard," an 1854 newspaper article explained, "the most marked and distinctive peculiarity between the countenances of the two sexes."[45] To shave the beard, as an 1858 magazine article put it, "detracts from the manliness of a countenance"; it was "the caprice of fashion" alone that compelled men to "shave off those appendages which give to the male countenance that true masculine character, indicative of energy, bold daring, and decision."[46] By the 1850s, facial hair had become so tied to manhood in the popular imagination that even feminist activist Helena Marie Weber admitted in

1851 that the beard was "intended solely to man" and was "the natural token of the sex."[47]

Indeed: pro-beard writers stated explicitly that beards were important for men to wear, but they also held very strong opinions about why women were *not* supposed to wear them. Perhaps the most passionate argument against female beard wearing came from Horace Bushnell, a prominent theologian and preacher who, in 1869, published a vehement tract entitled *Women's Suffrage: The Reform Against Nature.* Although suffrage activists argued both that women were equal to men *and* that women were different from men—a tactical duality that provided activists with a possible counterargument for every opposition to their cause—Bushnell presumed that suffragists desired only the former: equality.[48] No claim of gender equality could be valid, Bushnell argued, because men and women's bodies are so different: "In physical strength the man is greatly superior, and the base in his voice *and the shag on his face*, and the wing and sway of his shoulders, represent a personality in him that has some attribute of thunder. But there is no look of thunder in the woman. Her skin is too finely woven, too wonderfully delicate to be the rugged housing of thunder. . . . Glancing thus upon man, his look says, Force, Authority, Decision, Self-asserting Counsel, Victory."[49] For Bushnell, the beard was a symbol of masculine authority; only a man could have a beard, and thus only a man could wield authority. This gendered ideal, imbued with innate power, persisted in the thought of Bushnell's contemporaries.

Bearded American Heroes

The ad hoc beard canon grew in response to the growing frequency of beards on American men's faces, especially the faces of male authority figures. Many of the mid-nineteenth century's most famous white political, intellectual, and military heroes wore a beard, including Henry David Thoreau, Walt Whitman, John C. Frémont, Ulysses S. Grant, Robert E. Lee, and Jefferson Davis. Perhaps the most famous political leader to grow a beard in this era was Abraham Lincoln, the president who inaugurated fifty years of virtually uninterrupted presidential facial hair. The story of why Lincoln decided to grow a beard during his 1860 presidential campaign has reached the status of American folklore: a girl named Grace Bedell wrote to Lincoln suggesting that he "let [his] whiskers grow" because it would improve the look of his thin face (and perhaps earn him more votes); Lincoln responded to her letter with uncertainty, but by January 1861 he indeed began growing a beard. After winning the election, Lincoln met with Bedell and told her that he had taken her advice.[50]

Even symbolic and allegorical male authority figures gained new (or newly robust) beards during the mid-nineteenth century. Jesus's facial hair, for example, became the subject of concern for proponents of muscular Christianity, who worried about the then-common artistic convention of painting Jesus with a small, thin beard; if visual depictions instead showed Jesus with a full beard, muscular Christians believed, he would become the kind of masculine leader that would inspire men and women alike to re-commit to their faith.[51] Yet the connection between American political citizenship and symbolic male beardedness is perhaps best illustrated by Uncle Sam, who became bearded for the first time in the 1860s.

Although the term "Uncle Sam" had been used since the War of 1812, the first known visual depiction of the character appeared in 1852 when cartoonist Frank Bellew personified Sam for the New York comic newspaper *The Lantern*. Bellew drew Uncle Sam without a beard, and this is how he appeared for the next decade. In the 1860s, the important political cartoonist Thomas Nast gave Sam his canonical look, including his now-ubiquitous beard. (Tellingly, Nast is also credited with creating the modern American image of a bearded Santa Claus.)[52] This new version of Uncle Sam became canonical in American nationalistic and imperialistic imagery, especially in political cartoons found in the growing number of lithographed and chro-molithographed newspapers published in the final decades of the nineteenth century. In these cartoons, Uncle Sam—with his prominent beard—fre-quently symbolized the United States and American values. One vivid ex-ample is the imperialist cartoon "School Begins," published in the illustrated weekly *Puck* in 1899 (see fig. 2.1). In this cartoon, a bearded and bespectacled Uncle Sam teaches what the caption calls "his new class in Civilization" to a classroom full of students of color, each of whom represents a Western state (*California, Arizona, Alaska*); overseas island (*Hawaii, Porto Rico, Cuba*); or colonized racial minority (a Black child cleans the windows; an Indige-nous child reads a book upside down on the far edge of the classroom; a Chinese child stands at the classroom's threshold).[53]

Uncle Sam's symbolic power as a metonym for American imperial ambi-tion—a quality most directly embodied by his beard—even became a vehicle for critiquing the politics of real-life political leaders. This was especially

2.1 "School Begins," chromolithograph by Louis Dalrymple, *Puck* v. 44 no. 1142 (January 25, 1899). Illustrator Dalrymple captioned this centerfold illustration with an imagined instruction from the bearded Uncle Sam to the children in the front row, who represent colonized island territories: "Now, children, you've got to learn these lessons whether you want to or not! But just take a look at the class ahead of you"—a reference to the western states—"and remember that, in a little while, you will feel as glad to be here as they are!"

CREDIT: Library of Congress, Prints & Photographs Division, LC-DIG-ppmsca-28668.

true in the 1890s, amid the increasing popularity of a new version of American masculinity that prized self-assertion and even aggression—including imperial aggression—in contrast to the self-restraint characteristic of early American masculinity.[54] In response to political leaders whose masculinity the public doubted, a bearded Uncle Sam represented vigorous, imperialistically aggressive masculine political authority. For example, an 1898 cartoon published in *The Chicago Chronicle* critiqued then–President William McKinley—the only president elected during the era of presidential facial hair who had no facial hair of his own—for not being aggressive enough in declaring war on Spain. Uncle Sam towers over the barefaced McKinley as he shoves a rifle down the back of McKinley's coat, declaring, "All that you need is backbone" (see fig. 2.2).[55] Historian Kristin L. Hoganson has pointed out how this cartoon's depiction of the rifle "exploit[s] less than subtle phallic imagery."[56] But significantly, this phallic symbolism extends even to Uncle Sam's beard, which is drawn as a thick, straight cylinder far more akin to a penis than realistic human facial hair; were it not for Sam's strategically placed left hand, the reader can easily envision the head of a penis capping the end of this beard. In popularly circulated images like these, Uncle Sam's beard became synonymous with his—and, therefore, the United States'— masculine political and imperial power.

Racializing Men's Beards

By the second half of the nineteenth century, white American men had made clear what it meant for a white man to have a beard: it improved his health, gave him power and authority, and allowed him to demonstrate his superior masculinity. But if a full beard marked white men as the natural seat of social and political power, *too much* or *too little* facial hair on a man's face signaled his distance from that power. Young white boys, of course, were one such group, both too young to grow facial hair and too young to fully embrace their birthright as political citizens. But of far greater significance were the men with racialized identities who, relative to the norms set by and for white men, grew too much or too little hair on their faces. Their aberrant beards, or lack thereof, marked their bodies as outside both the gender *and* racial boundaries of American political citizenship, and visually reinforced claims that they were unfit for full participation within it.

In their catalogs of human natural history, American ethnological, medical, and scientific authorities often remarked that some groups of non-European men were especially hairy. For example, in *Types of Mankind* (1854), an influential 700-page tome of human natural history, ethnologists Josiah C. Nott and George Gliddon emphasized high levels of hairiness as characteristic of non-white men in particular, such as Aboriginal Australians. Although, Nott and Gliddon argued, skeletal evidence suggested that Aboriginals were similar to African-descended people, the feature that proved Aboriginals were not African-descended was their hair. Quoting the observations of US Navy Lieutenant Charles Wilkes, whom Congress had authorized to survey the Pacific Ocean in 1846, Nott and Gliddon explained how "[Aboriginals'] most striking distinction is their hair, which is like that of dark-haired Europeans, although more silky. It is fine, disposed to curl,

UNCLE SAM—"All that you need is backbone."
—*Chicago Chronicle.*

2.2 Cartoon from the *Chicago Chronicle*. This cartoon's critique of President McKinley's policy toward Spain contrasts the president's body with Uncle Sam's body in stature, body shape, and facial hair.

CREDIT: Reproduced from *Cartoons of the War of 1899 with Spain from Leader Foreign and American Papers.* Chicago: Belford, Middlebrook & Co., 1898.

and gives them a totally different aspect from the African, and also from the Malay and American Indian." Crucial to this distinctive hair was their facial hair: "Most of them have thick beards and whiskers, and they are more hairy than the whites."[57] In their later publication, *Indigenous Races of the Earth* (1857), Nott and Gliddon included similar observations of an Indigenous Japanese community called the Ainu—notorious in the western world for their "hairy endowments." The Ainu's

> beard is bushy . . . [and] generally black, but often brownish, and seldom exceeds five or six inches in length. I only saw one case where it reached more than half-way to the waist; and here the owner was evidently proud of its great length, as he had it twisted into innumerable small ringlets, well greased, and kept in something like order. . . . Their beard, which grows well up under the rather retreating eye, their bushy brows, and generally wild appearance and expression of countenance, give them a most savage look.[58]

As this description of the Ainu makes clear, too much facial hair—when located, crucially, on a non-white body—meant too uncivilized, too primitive, and too close to non-human animals.

But even more common than descriptions of non-white men with very large beards was documentation of the relative beard*less*ness of men of color from many parts of the globe. Indeed, since at least the seventeenth century, European and American writers had noted with curiosity and arrogance that Indigenous men from Asia, Africa, and the Americas—men they considered to be their racial inferiors—had less facial hair than European-descended men. For example, John Smith wrote in 1624 of the Indigenous people he met in North America that "few have any beards."[59] Over 160 years later, Thomas Jefferson gestured to observations like Smith's when he wrote, "it has been said, that Indians have less hair than the whites," yet he clarified that this may be a product of hair removal practices: "With them it is disgraceful to be hairy on the body," and so "they therefore pluck the hair as fast as it appears."[60]

Nineteenth-century racial scientists added scientific ballast to claims like Smith's and Jefferson's. In *Crania Americana* (1839)—probably the most important American racial science text of the nineteenth century—scientist Samuel George Morton described facial hair as intrinsically deficient in two of what he recognized as the five human races: "Mongolian" (East and

Southeast Asian) and "American" (Indigenous North American). Bela C. Perry, a Black barber from Massachusetts who wrote a scientific treatise on the hair, also claimed that "the Chinese make the most of the small beards furnished them by nature, and hugely envy those Europeans who have been in that respect more bounteously endowed."[61] Nott and Gliddon's work also included many descriptions of different groups of Asian men who, unlike the extraordinary Ainu, had thin beards. Of the men who lived on the Indo-Chinese Peninsula, "the beard is remarkably scanty, consisting only of a few straggling hairs," and among residents of India, "the beard [was] very thin."[62] Most revealing is the language they used to describe male residents of what is now Thailand (to the nineteenth-century reader, Siam), who possessed only "a few scattering of hairs, *which scarcely merit the name of beard*, grow[ing] upon the chin and upper lip."[63] This framing—written in 1854, amid the broader explosion of pro-beard writing in the United States—starkly illustrates that *the beard* was more than a collection of hair on the face. The beard was, to midcentury white American men, an ideological object as much as a style of facial hair. It was the elevated, rarefied paragon of facial hair perfection—the *only* true symbol of inherent masculine power, and one reserved for white men alone.

Nott and Gliddon's emphasis on the inadequacy of Asian men's beards also echoed in contemporary scientists' discussions of Indigenous North American men. Morton, for example, asserted that "the beard is very deficient among the Americans generally, and the little that nature gives them they assiduously eradicate from early manhood."[64] To not be able to grow the beards that white men so prized was problem enough, but to electively remove the hairs that *did* grow on the face only reinforced the message Indigenous men's facial hair conveyed: both biologically and culturally, Indigenous men were inferior to white men. (At the same time, as the United States' repeated efforts to assimilate Indigenous people by forcibly changing their cultural practices suggest, it also left open the possibility for Americanization—a subject to which the Conclusion will return.) In his polemic against shaving for the *Boston Medical and Surgical Journal*, Dr. Sanborn even argued that Indigenous men's decision to "wag[e] war unceasingly against nature" by "resist[ing] her kindly efforts to mantle their faces with manly beards" was the very reason for what he and many of his white contemporaries believed was their imminent extinction: each "generation [grew] more and more effeminate, became an easy prey to their enemies, and now, like the beard which they so obstinately uprooted from their faces, they are themselves uprooted from the face of the earth."[65]

Some naturalists and other men of science took these racialized facial hair claims one step further, making the beard not just one of many racialized bodily traits, but instead the most important body part that distinguished European-descended men from everyone else. For example, English naturalist Charles Hamilton Smith—whose book *The Natural History of the Human Species* (1848) was reprinted in Boston three years later—posited three racial groups that he named according to their hair: "The Woolly-Haired Tropic Type" from Africa; "The Hyperborean, Beardless, or Mongolic Type" from Asia; and, finally, the "Bearded, Intermediate, or Caucasian Type." Smith opened his chapter on the Bearded Type by explaining that it is "so named, because neither of the two other typical forms is distinguished by a well-grown beard." "Intermediate," he explained, was an allusion to geographic position: it was a "reference to the boreal and tropical positions of the other types."[66] Yet intermediacy—in the sense of the highest position on a bell curve sloped downward on either side—is also evident in the way Smith positioned the Bearded Type as a superior middle position between oppositional binaries: hair that was neither too lank nor too kinky, and facial hair that was neither too much nor too little. The facial hair of the Bearded Type was, in true Goldilocks fashion, just right: "The beard is neither villous [i.e., composed of long thin hairs] nor woolly, but spreading over the lips, chin, and the whole of the nether jaw. It fringes the sides of the face up to the temples, and is crisp, curly, or undulating, but never quite straight or lank, as in the Mongolian. . . . Man of the bearded type attains the highest standard." All of this physical perfection equipped the Bearded Type to "endure the greatest vicissitudes of temperature in all climates," and, therefore, to conquer: "to emigrate, colonize, and multiply in them."[67]

Smith's description of the white Bearded Type emphasized its distinction not just from the beardlessness of Asian men, but also from what he deemed the sparse and thus deficient facial hair of African-descended men. Black men's facial hair, he claimed, was "scanty on the upper lip, generally confined to the point of the chin, [and] without any at the sides of the face."[68] It was this claim of Black men's deficient facial hair—their supposed inability to grow the full beard that marked white men's bodies for full political citizenship—that defined the work of the most vocal and most influential advocate for the white supremacy of the beard: John Van Evrie, a Canadian-born physician who became, in the words of scholar Donald Yacovone, the United States' "first professional racist." Van Evrie was also, crucially, a newspaper and book publisher with an "unprecedented genius for marketing."[69] Indeed, Van Evrie's tremendous influence in, and thus his significance to, the story of scientific racism lies not in the originality of his ideas. Instead, he took the intellectual work of major ethnologists like Nott and Gliddon and Louis Agassiz—whose dense tomes of four hundred to seven hundred pages were filled with specialized scientific language, which limited their reach to fellow men of science—and translated it for a broader audience.[70] By writing short, accessible pamphlets designed to be sold to the widest audience possible, Van Evrie repackaged scientific racism's most pernicious ideas for a popular audience.[71]

In a series of pamphlets and short books that he published himself in New York City in the 1850s and 1860s, Van Evrie argued that no bodily feature more clearly signaled both male supremacy *and* white supremacy than the beard. "The Caucasian is the only bearded race," he announced in his first major pamphlet on the subject, *Negroes and Negro "Slavery": The First an Inferior Race; The Latter Its Normal Condition*, which was published as a pamphlet in 1853 and later expanded into a book in 1861. White men were characterized by a "full, flowing, and majestic beard," whereas the facial hair found on the faces of men of color was merely a pale imitation—"nothing that can be confounded with a beard." Black men's facial hair growth was "the furthest removed of all" from "the full, flowing, and majestic beard of the Caucasian:" it was, instead, a mere "little tuft on the chin and sometimes on the upper lip"—the same facial landscape Charles Hamilton Smith described.[72] Crucially, Van Evrie made clear that there is a fundamental difference between *facial hair* and *the beard*: although the former could sometimes be found on men's faces across racial and ethnic boundaries—though, he and many of his contemporaries argued, it was often thin and sparse—the latter was reserved for white men alone.

Van Evrie's writing differed from that of most of the ethnologists and natural scientists who preceded him in its overwhelming preoccupation with the facial hair of Black men and comparatively minimal interest in Asian or Indigenous men. The reason for this imbalance becomes clear when his work is considered in context: when he was writing these pamphlets in the 1860s, both during and after the Civil War, the most pressing racial issue of

the moment was slavery and its abolition—and, crucially, what would become of formerly enslaved people. Would Black Americans become full-
fledged members of the United States' body politic and fully integrated
into white social and cultural institutions? As a proud northern Democrat
antagonistic to Reconstruction, Van Evrie desperately wanted the answer
to be *no* on all accounts, which is why he worked so hard to reach not just
a popular audience but also the nation's most influential political leaders in
Congress and even the White House.[73]

The publication that most acutely demonstrates what Van Evrie saw as
the immediate and grave stakes of his writing was also the one published in
the war's immediate aftermath: *The Six Species of Men* (1866). *The Six Species of Men* posited a racial hierarchy that "begins with the negro, the lowest
and simplest in its organism," and stretched upward "until the highest and
most complete of all God's wonderful works, the Caucasian, completes the
whole."[74] The remaining four groups sat in between these poles: just below
the Caucasian was the Mongolian (Chinese), then the Malay, the American
Indian, and the Esquimaux (now spelled Eskimo). Van Evrie's descriptions
of "a typical man of each species" included hair among a list of bodily characteristics: the Mongolian, for example, had "hair black and straight"; the
Malay's hair was "black, lank, coarse, and abundant"; the American Indian's "long, black, and straight"; and the Esquimaux's "long, straight, coal-
black." The sparse repetitiveness of these descriptors echoes in Van Evrie's
descriptions of the facial hair for these four non-white and non-Black groups:
the Malay and Esquimaux descriptions bear no mention of facial hair, while
the Mongolian ("face beardless") and American Indian ("no beard") are passed
by in just two words each.

Such brevity lies in stark contrast to the lengthy passages Van Evrie spends
praising white men for their "flowing beard[s]" and excoriating Black men
for their "absence of beard."[75] Van Evrie saw Asian and Indigenous men as
so irrelevant to 1860s conversations about the racial boundaries of American political citizenship—so marginal, in other words, to the American body
politic—that their facial hair inferiority was barely worthy of comment.
The Esquimaux, for example, "is least known of all" the racial groups thanks
to their distant location, and "is of but little importance either in a general
or anthropological point of view"—yet Van Evrie still proclaimed with
confidence that "it is superior to the negro in the scale of creation." Even
more telling is Van Evrie's indifferent dismissal of the American Indian:

"This race or *Species* of men is more or less familiar to all Americans. No one can mistake an Indian for a white man, however much he may fancy a negro to be one."[76] Here it was, laid bare for the reader in stark terms: because Van Evrie believed that the stakes of Black men's political rights, their masculinity, and their very bodies were so much higher in the 1860s than those of Asian or Indigenous men, Black men's facial hair demanded extensive, detailed commentary to prove, without question, what Van Evrie deemed their fundamental inferiority.

Crucially, moreover, Van Evrie argued that it was in the hair—and *especially* the facial hair—that Black inferiority was most evident. While skin color may have drawn the greatest attention as a visual marker of racial difference, Van Evrie argued that "[skin] color is only one, and in fact *not the greatest distinction* between the races or Species of men." It was instead hair and facial hair that were the "specific differences [most] palpable" on Black bodies.[77] To Van Evrie, Black men's minimal facial hair—"a little tuft on the chin, and sometimes on the upper lip"—was the most important bodily metaphor for the impossibility of Black equality:

> A negro with the flowing, dignified, and majestic beard of the Caucasian, would indeed be a curiosity, and about as amusing a specimen of humanity as it is possible to conceive of. If Sumner & Co. expect to make anything of Sambo, they must strike for "equal beard" for him as well as for "equal education," or "equal voting." When they have endowed the negro with the full and flowing beard of the Caucasian, there will be some prospect of the success of their efforts in "reconstructing" the race.[78]

By describing a scenario of impossible absurdity, Van Evrie categorized the very project of Reconstruction—the very concept of Black equality and political citizenship—as absurd, too.

Van Evrie believed that "the Caucasian is really the only bearded race, and this is the most striking mark of its supremacy over all others." Yet the core of this claim—that white men grew beards and Black men did not—was simply not true. Even during what Richard Corson deemed "the beardless eighteenth century," many enslaved men wore beards.[79] Evidence of bearded African-descended men can be found repeatedly in advertisements for enslaved runaways. Examples abound in Virginia alone: Tony from Caroline County escaped in 1739 "with a large Beard," London escaped in 1755 with a "full Beard," and Peres ran away from a plantation in Fairfax County in 1761 sporting "a full black Beard." When Harry from Westover escaped in 1767, his enslaver indicated that Harry "generally wears his beard long." Similar language appears in the 1796 advertisement for a twenty-seven-year-old man named Africa, from Princess Anne County, whose enslaver described how Africa "generally wears his beard very long."[80] Beards became even more commonplace on Black men's faces in the mid-nineteenth century, just as they were for white men. In the wake of the Civil War, the very moment that beard wearing reached its cultural zenith, wearing a beard also became a way for Black American men to publicly proclaim their place in the body politic. Crucially, when Black men wore facial hair, they were claiming *for themselves* the beard's powerful symbolic meanings. To wear a beard was thus one way to visibly embody and enact one's freedom.

The cover of a November 1867 issue of *Harper's Weekly* made this connection explicit (see fig. 2.3). In an illustration captioned "The First Vote," a group of Black men stand in line to cast their ballots on Election Day. The first man in line—both the eponymous first voter and, as a newly enfranchised citizen, casting his first vote—wears a striking full white beard. This older working man—his work signaled by the mallet in his coat pocket—stands at the center of the illustration as he drops his ticket in the glass ballot jar. His face is encircled by an Afro-textured white beard and a head of white hair, both of which flow seamlessly into each other. The first voter's beard mirrors the white beard of the white election official on the illustration's left edge, their faces nearly lined up in perfect parallel. That these two men share not only their connection to electoral politics—one as the government official, the other as the voter—but also their full beards reinforce the hopeful vision of this early stage of Reconstruction: that Black men, too, now have the manhood rights of political citizenship.[81]

Some Black intellectual, political, and civil rights leaders wore facial hair too, often sporting the very same styles that were contemporaneously popular for white men in similar leadership roles. Scholar and activist W. E. B. DuBois and inventor and engineer Norbert Rillieux both wore trim goatees and mustaches in adulthood, and physician and abolitionist Dr. John Stewart Rock wore a full beard. Many of the pioneering Black men elected to national political office during Reconstruction wore facial hair, too, such as P. B. S. Pinchback, the nation's first Black governor, who led Louisiana from December 1872 to January 1873. Indeed, as "The First Vote" illustrates,

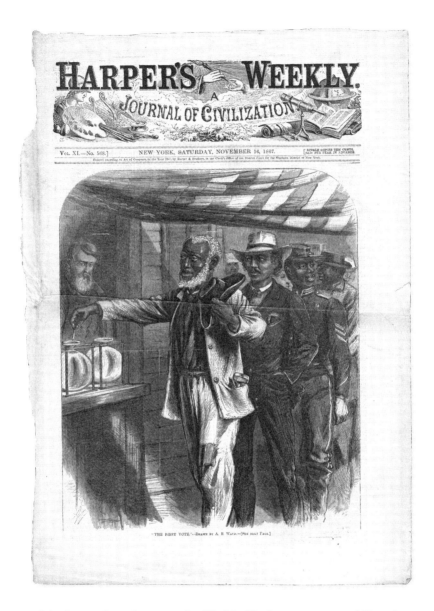

2.3 "The first vote," wood engraving by Alfred R. Waud, magazine cover of *Harper's Weekly* v. 11, no. 568 (November 16, 1867). The hats and clothing worn by the first three Black men in line to vote in this illustration imply that they each have a distinct profession: a working man, a businessman, and a soldier. All but the soldier also sport facial hair.

CREDIT: Library of Congress, Prints & Photographs Division, LC-DIG-ppmsca-31598.

facial hair features prominently in postbellum Black visual culture, especially in prints and photographs that depicted political participation and leadership. For example, an 1872 lithograph by popular printers Currier & Ives entitled "The First Colored Senator and Representatives" depicted a group portrait of the seven Black men who served in the 41st and 42nd sessions of Congress: Robert C. De Large of South Carolina; Jefferson Franklin Long of Georgia; Hiram Revels of Mississippi (the first Black member of the Senate); Benjamin S. Turner of Alabama; Josiah T. Walls of Florida; Joseph H. Rainey of South Carolina; and Robert Brown Elliot of South Carolina (see fig. 2.4). All seven men wear prominent facial hair of some kind, with styles ranging from a trim mustache to lengthy sideburns to a full mustache and beard.[82]

Another popular print entitled "Heroes of the Colored Race" (1881) featured four full-color scenes of recent Black history—enslavement, military service, "Receiving the News of the Emancipation," and "Studying the Lesson" in a schoolhouse—alongside ten portraits of political leaders who supported Black civil rights (see fig. 2.5). Located at the print's center and anchoring its four corners, portraits of Revels and Rainey are joined by other bearded Black leaders: Blanche K. Bruce, Senator from Mississippi, is in the print's center with Revels; and House Representatives John R. Lynch, Robert Smalls, and Charles E. Nash join Rainey in its corners. These seven portraits are joined by smaller portraits of four white political leaders who, too, were known for their facial hair: Abraham Lincoln, James A. Garfield, Ulysses S. Grant, and John Brown. Significantly, the facial hair styling on the white men's faces mirrors the Black leaders' own: all ten men wear sidewhiskers, mustaches, or full beards.[83] The overall effect is one of parallel strength, political leadership, and patriotic heroism—shared by Black and white men alike.

Yet perhaps no nineteenth-century Black American's beard is more famous than the one worn by the man featured at the very center of this print: Frederick Douglass. Douglass is, of course, best remembered as an abolitionist, newspaper publisher, public speaker, and the author of autobiographies of his escape from enslavement, including *Narrative of the Life of Frederick Douglass, an American Slave* (1845). Douglass was also, crucially, obsessed with photography. From the 1840s until his death in 1895, Douglass wrote essays about photography, gave talks on photography, and, most importantly, visited photographers' studios over a hundred times,

2.4 "The first colored senator and representatives—in the 41st and 42nd Congress of the United States," lithograph by Currier & Ives, 1872. The seven Black Congressmen depicted in this print represented five of eleven states that composed the Confederacy during the Civil War. These men represent many popular permutations of facial hair worn by Black and white men in the 1860s and 1870s.
CREDIT: Library of Congress, Prints & Photographs Division, LC-DIG-ppmsca-17564.

making him the most-photographed person in the United States during the nineteenth century. Scholars and archivists have identified 160 distinct photographic images of Douglass—more than any other nineteenth-century American.[84] Douglass also worked hard to make sure his photographic portraits circulated as widely as possible: he gave prints to family members, friends, and fans; advertised prints in his newspapers; and sold prints as a fundraiser for abolitionist and educational causes. Truly *mass* reproduction of photographic prints was limited by available technologies: to reproduce a photograph in a book or newspaper required an engraver to create a reproduction of the photograph, and Douglass was very wary of the possibility—even likelihood—that a white engraver would allow anti-Black racism

2.5 "Heroes of the colored race," published by Joseph Hoover, chromolithograph, ca. 1883. This full-color print combined detailed portraits of Black and white political leaders of the 1860s and 1870s (all of whom wear facial hair) with illustrations of ordinary Black men, women, and children working, serving in the military, celebrating emancipation, and learning inside a classroom.

CREDIT: Library of Congress, Prints & Photographs Division, LC-DIG-pga-01619.

to mar the verisimilitude of his engravings. As he wrote in his newspaper *The North Star* in 1849, after discovering an inaccurate rendering of his portrait in a British abolitionist text, "Negroes can never have impartial portraits at the hands of white artists."[85]

Douglass understood photography to be a democratic art—a technology that allowed *everyone* to create and exchange images of themselves and loved ones, not just those who could afford to sit for a painted portrait. In a lecture in Boston in 1861, Douglass praised Louis Daguerre (of the eponymous daguerreotype) because "what was once the special and exclusive luxury of the rich and great is now the privilege of all."[86] Douglass saw in photography the power to counteract the racist stereotypical imagery that circulated in contemporary popular culture, print media, and scientific literature.[87] By creating a vast body of photographic images of his *own* free body,

Douglass tried to reframe the way white Americans perceived Black people, and to claim for Black men their right to political citizenship.

Douglass took his appearance seriously when he sat for a portrait. He set his facial features in a focused and unsmiling expression and chose clothing that reinforced a sense of respectability: in virtually every extant portrait, Douglass dons a dark suit coat (sometimes paired with a vest), a white collared shirt, and a cravat or tie.[88] But another consistent—and arguably even more significant—element of Douglass's self-presentation as a Black man worthy of political citizenship was his hair. The hair on his head, always worn textured, ranged from ear-length in the 1840s through the late 1860s to collar-length from the 1870s onward.[89] Yet it was the hair on his face that, in the context of contemporary philosophies about the meaning of the beard, carried the most symbolic weight.

Although he did not begin wearing the iconic full white beard seen in "Heroes of the Colored Race" until the 1870s, facial hair was part of Douglass's photographed body from the very beginning. In his first extant portrait, a daguerreotype from around 1841, the short curls of an under-the-chin beard are visible in sharp relief against the crisp whiteness of his shirt collar; a similar beard is visible in Douglass's second daguerreotype portrait from 1843. Douglass appears to have shaved prior to some of his early portraits; the frontispiece to his 1845 autobiography, for example, showed Douglass barefaced.[90] However, starting with an 1852 daguerreotype taken in Akron, Ohio, in which Douglass wore a goatee-style beard on his chin, Douglass was never photographed without facial hair again.[91]

Douglass's facial hairstyle varied as he aged: from the mid-1850s to 1863 most portraits show him with a trimmed beard and mustache, such as an 1856 portrait that is now part of the National Portrait Gallery (see fig. 2.6a). In portraits dated from 1864 to March 1873 he wears a neatly trimmed mustache that curves around his lips. And, from September 1873 onward—for the final twenty-two years of his life—Douglass wore a full beard, mustache, and side-whiskers in every portrait.[92] A representative portrait from this last, lengthy bearded era was taken by photographer Lydia Cadwell in January 1875 (see fig. 2.6b). In this portrait, Douglass gazes out in three-quarter profile, his white hair flowing away from his face and long enough to cover his ears. On his face is a neatly trimmed full beard, mustache, and side-whiskers. His beard is at virtually the precise center of the frame, and its black-and-white textured strands appear more crisply rendered than almost any other detail.

2.6 *(Left)* "Frederick Douglass," ambrotype, 1856. *(Right)* "Portrait of
Frederick Douglass," cabinet photograph by Lydia J. Caldwell, 1875.
These two photographic portraits represent a small fraction of the
160 known photographic images of Frederick Douglass. Douglass
wore facial hair in every photograph after 1852.

CREDIT: Left: National Portrait Gallery, Smithsonian, acquired through
the generosity of an anonymous donor. Right: Chicago History Museum,
ICHi-010140; Gentile, photographer.

DOUGLASS, FREDERICK

Gentile   CHICAGO.

Douglass did not just wear a beard on his face—he also directly took on John Van Evrie's assertions about Black men's beards, underlining the fact that Douglass understood the beard to be an important emblem of manhood for Black men just as it was for white men. In the 1850s, Douglass and Van Evrie traded insults and taunts in the newspapers they published. Van Evrie sneered at Douglass's protestations against Black people's poor treatment in the United States, taunting, "either you must go from us, or melt away as the Indians have."[93] Douglass, in turn, cast Van Evrie as an immoral and unintelligent man whose claims were so baseless that he regularly contradicted himself. For example, Van Evrie argued in *The Six Species of Men* that Black men's beards were merely evidence of their having white ancestry, yet he claimed elsewhere that such a scenario was impossible. As Douglass wrote, "[Van Evrie] reveals his ignorance by declaring, in proof of the utter dissimilarity of the races, that the two cannot amalgamate. Did you ever!"[94] Douglass also rejected Van Evrie's assertion that abolitionists believed Black people were actually white: "We have never, as a race, professed to be white people. God forbid! We profess to be *men*, endowed with the same natural conformation as any other people, and which only needs the same favorable circumstances, for a similar development."[95]

Douglass's emphasis on Black men's desire for access to the same manhood rights as white men echoed in his 1856 response to Van Evrie's claim that Black men cannot grow beards. Van Evrie, "the Editor of the New York *Day Book*," Douglass groaned, is "growing weary of his *unprofitable* twaddle about the negro's brain," and "endeavoring to relieve the dull monotony, by learned disquisitions upon the beard of the negro. He has discovered that the Black man, the *real,* unadulterated negro, has no beard. His next attempt will be, perhaps, to prove that the brainless, and beardless negro has no *soul*."[96] It was obvious to Douglass—his own face bearded by this time—that Black men and white men both grew beards because *both were men*. To claim that Black men were beardless was as absurd and as dehumanizing as claiming that Black people had no souls. Douglass's scathing critiques did not explicitly refer to his own face, but it easy to imagine that Douglass saw his own visage and its many photographic prints as counterprogramming for the white supremacist vision of American political citizenship that work like Van Evrie's propped up.

In the mid-nineteenth century, white supremacists like Van Evrie tried to claim for white men privileged access to the beard, arguing that nonwhite men either grew too much facial hair (like the Ainu) or, more often, too little. However, the cultural significance of the beard as a marker of American manhood also became a way for Black men to visually and publicly proclaim their place in the body politic. Yet the political upheaval of the mid-nineteenth century, including the growing agitation by activist groups to expand who had access to political rights, was not limited to racial identity alone. Black and white women, too, were increasingly insistent that women deserved the right to vote—and here, too, the beard became a symbolic battleground for delineating the boundaries of political citizenship.

Women's Facial Hair and the Boundaries of Citizenship

The pro-beard canon that emerged in the mid-1850s focused its attention on hair that grew (or didn't) on men's faces. But the mid-1850s were also the moment when women's hairy faces gained a more prominent place in both American popular culture and in its cultural imagination than ever before. While critics like Horace Bushnell claimed the beard grew on men's faces alone, some women have grown terminal hairs on their faces throughout human history.[97] To be sure, some women did try to remove the hair from their faces. Nineteenth-century physiognomic manuals pointed out, for example, that excess hair growth on the forehead or temples could cause the appearance of a low forehead. Women who wished to remove hair from their faces used homemade recipes or, by midcentury, premade depilatories available for purchase. For example, one widely circulated midwifery book said that a mixture of lime, arsenic, and water, soaked and boiled, would soften hairs on a woman's foreheads and temples enough to be easily removed. Yet both homemade and purchased compounds could cause skin irritation, vomiting, and even deadly poisoning; by the second half of the century, concern about the toxicity of chemical depilatories led physicians to push for federal regulation.[98]

At the same time, for a woman to choose *not* to remove her facial hair was also rather unremarkable. In 1872, for example, an article in Philadelphia's *Transatlantic Magazine* casually mentioned that, "as for 'women with beards descending to their breasts,' there is nothing very remarkable about them, and plenty of instances have been known."[99] Physicians George M. Gould and Walter L. Pyle affirmed this claim in their influential medical encyclopedia *Anomalies and Curiosities of Medicine* (1896): women with beards were not, they wrote, anomalous—they were actually "not at all infrequent."[100]

Common, too, was the Bearded Lady character on the late-nineteenth- and early-twentieth-century American freak show stage. Freak shows were an extremely widespread form of popular entertainment from the 1830s through the 1920s.[101] American men, women, and children from all social classes paid an admission fee to view groups of performers deemed "human curiosities" who stood together on large, raised platforms or stages. These performers included a wide range of people with unusual bodies, faraway homelands, and surprising talents, such as sword swallowing or snake charming. Freak shows were a flexible mode of popular entertainment: they could be staged in small or large venues, in fixed locations or as part of a traveling show, and could be part of circus sideshows, dime museums, amusement parks, carnivals, seaside resorts, world's fair exhibitions, and even film.[102]

By the mid-nineteenth century, freak shows had become a widespread popular cultural phenomenon. It wasn't just that huge crowds attended performances—the freak show also had broader cultural resonance outside of entertainment spaces. Indeed, the freak show as an institution (and its most famous archetypes and stars) appeared often in popular novels, news coverage, and other popular media on totally unrelated topics, even becoming legible points of reference for humor and critique.[103] Thus, both inside the sideshow tent and on the pages of the popular press, the freak show became a form of public pedagogy: a site that taught people not just how to discern truth from falsehood (real exhibits from fakes), but also how to think about and interpret human difference. By displaying people with bodies and, often, cultural backgrounds that were different from the audiences' own, the freak show seemed to both justify and explain hierarches of race, gender, and nation.

Some freak show performers relied on unusual hair as part of their appeal, such as the Seven Sutherland Sisters' floor-length locks or the soft afros worn by Circassian Beauties.[104] But no hair-based archetype was as widespread as the Bearded Lady. In the decades following Madame Clofullia's 1853 debut, the Bearded Lady—a white adult woman with long well-styled hair, a fashionable dress, an honorific title, and a large beard and mustache—became one of the most popular and ubiquitous freak show archetypes in the United States. These performers entertained large audiences in venues across the country; countless more Americans learned about these women, thanks to a growing American print culture that made cheap pamphlets, newspaper articles, and magazine interviews accessible to a national audience. By the end of the nineteenth century, the Bearded Lady archetype had become so popular in freak show spaces that, according to Dr. Gould and Dr. Pyle, there was a Bearded Lady to be found in "every circus sideshow."[105]

If facial hair on women is not particularly rare, why, then, did it make sense to nineteenth-century Americans that a woman with a beard should be on a freak show stage at all—especially standing alongside actual statistically anomalous bodies like conjoined twins?[106] Moreover, why did the Bearded Lady character start to become a freak show mainstay in the 1850s, specifically? Some scholars have suggested that the Bearded Lady's appeal was simply the same as that of many popular freak show archetypes: she intrigued audiences because her body transgressed the boundaries of an established binary. In other words, just as African-descended performers with albinism troubled the border between Black and white, Bearded Ladies disrupted the gender binary with what sociologist Robert Bogdan called their "incongruity of whiskers and femininity."[107] Yet this interpretation minimizes both the historic particularity of the Bearded Lady archetype *and* the way this archetype is part of the larger story of hair in nineteenth-century America. If the Bearded Lady's attraction was owed simply to her mix of femininity and masculinity, why was there no male counterpart—such as an "Effeminate Man," for example—in the nineteenth-century freak show? To explain why this *particular* type of gender transgression was so enormously popular as to become a commonplace archetype—and why the Bearded Lady character was portrayed almost exclusively by white women—we must look beyond the freak show stage.

It is not a coincidence that in the same midcentury moment when facial hair on men became associated with inherent white male power, facial hair on women became enfreaked. These two cultural narratives were instead two sides of the same coin: both the supremacy of white bearded man and the freakery of the bearded woman reinforced the message that white patriarchal supremacy was natural and intrinsic. Yet the cultural meaning of beards on women, just like men, was also racialized. The manner in which freak shows presented—and the popular press wrote about—bearded women was distinct for white women and women of color. White women who violated prescriptions for white femininity—whether because they proudly showcased their facial hair in freak shows, or because they advocated for women's political rights—traveled so close to white masculinity that they reinforced the naturalness of men's beards (and men's power) and the unnaturalness of their own. On the other hand, freak shows framed East Asian and Indigenous women with facial hair as marginal to American political subjecthood—and even humanity itself—by twining racial inferiority and gender inversion together.

Enfreaking the Bearded Lady

When the popular journalist Fanny Fern visited Barnum's American Museum in New York City in 1854, during the freak show's heyday, it was indeed Madame Clofullia, the Bearded Lady, who caught her attention first.

Fern described Clofullia as "one of the most curious curiosities ever pre-sented."[108] Clofullia was not only fascinating but also lucrative; according to writer Frederick Drimmer, she was one of Barnum's most successful ex-hibitions in his long and varied career.[109] It is fitting that Barnum would be responsible for bringing the Bearded Lady to the American public's atten-tion, for he was undoubtably the most successful, innovative, and durable showman of his era. He had a greater impact on nineteenth-century popular culture than any other individual, and many of his most famous exhibits were replicated by other showmen hoping to cash in on his success.[110] When Barnum arranged for Madame Clofullia to appear in his American Mu-seum, he was doing what he did best: discovering the next exciting, never-before-seen exhibit to present to the American public.[111]

What began in 1853 as a unique exhibition by the most entrepreneurial of nineteenth-century showmen became, by the end of the century, a stan-dard archetype that could be found on virtually every freak show stage in America. In the freak show's waning days in the 1930s, the manager for the Congress of Strange People at the Ringling Brothers and Barnum & Bailey circus admitted that Bearded Ladies were "not particularly sensational," but they were such a "traditional" component of the freak show that "people feel there's something lacking" if a sideshow did not have a Bearded Lady on display. The Bearded Lady was as requisite in the freak show as the clown in a circus.[112] While it is impossible to know exactly how many women worked as Bearded Ladies from the 1850s through the 1930s, three of the most famous performers—Madame Clofullia, Madame Viola, and Lady Olga—left biographies and gave interviews to journalists.[113] These sources, placed alongside contemporary accounts by the many physicians who ex-amined these women, provide some sense of what it meant to be a Bearded Lady, how these bearded women were presented to the public, and how the hallmarks of this archetype constructed her gender *and* her race in tandem.

The first bearded woman to be exhibited in the United States with the appellation *Bearded Lady* was Madame Clofullia, who began her tenure at the American Museum in 1853.[114] Madame Clofullia was born Josephine Boisdechêne in Switzerland in 1829. Her promotional biography claimed that her face and body were "covered with a slight down" at birth; by age eight she had grown a beard "fully two inches in length," and by fourteen the beard was five inches long.[115] She began performing in cities across France when she was seventeen years old, which is where she met and married her husband, Fortune Clofullia, Jr. In 1851, to coincide with the Great Exhibition held in the city that year, the newly christened Madame Clofullia traveled to London, where she performed for huge crowds; her biography boasts that "upwards of 800,000 persons" came to this exhibition, including "all the dignitaries of this immense city."[116] Clofullia also became a mother in London, giving birth to a daughter named Zelea (who died in infancy) and a son named Albert. Although baby Zelea did not grow facial hair, Albert quickly became as hairy as his mother had been as a child; London physicians declared him to be "as decided a singularity and freak of nature as his mother."[117] In late spring 1853, an American man arrived in London and gave Clofullia "a very advantageous offer" to come to the United States. After a brief engagement at Boston's Armory Hall, Clofullia met P. T. Barnum for the first time, and accepted his proposal to exhibit herself at his American Museum. Clofullia continued to exhibit both at the American Museum and with the touring freak show Colonel Wood's Grand Museum of Living Wonders until 1863, when she appears to have stopped performing before the public.[118]

One year after Madame Clofullia's American debut, the woman who would later perform as Madame Viola Meyers—her birth name is not known—was born in Buena Vista, Pennsylvania. Her biography and experiences mirrored Clofullia's in many ways: she was born with a light covering of hair on her body that grew in "the manner of whiskers" by age three.[119] When she was seventeen, she married Amos Meyers, and later gave birth to two children, though both died in childhood. In September 1876— midway through Philadelphia's Centennial Exposition, the United States' first World's Fair—Meyers began performing as a Bearded Lady for the first time; as a freak show performer, Meyers shared the stage in Philadelphia with both animals (a six-legged cow, a 140-pound snake) and humans (an armless man, an albino woman).[120] Meyers continued performing through the 1880s at least, including daily performances at the Globe Dime Museum and Professor C. W. McGlennen's European Museum, both in New York City—less than one mile from Barnum's American Museum.[121]

One of the last bearded women to perform in the United States was born just a few years before Madame Viola's first performance began: Jane Barnell, known professionally as Princess Olga, then Madame Olga, and finally (and most famously) Lady Olga. Barnell was the longest-performing woman in the American freak show, as well as the only Bearded Lady to give a detailed, personal interview to a reporter: the writer Joseph Mitchell's profile on Barnell was published in the *New Yorker* in 1940, when she was sixty-nine years old.[122] Barnell was born in Wilmington, North Carolina, in 1871, to a Russian Jewish father and a mother with Irish and Indigenous Catawba ancestry. Like Clofullia and Meyers before her, Barnell was hairy from birth and grew a beard before she turned two.[123] When Barnell was four, her mother, who believed her daughter was cursed, gave Barnell to a traveling circus that came through their town; Barnell never knew if she had been sold or simply abandoned.

Barnell traveled with the Great Orient Family Circus and Menagerie through the United States and into Europe before her father, who was out of town when her mother gave her away, rescued Barnell, and brought her back to North Carolina. Barnell began exhibiting her beard voluntarily when she was twenty-one, and as she told Mitchell, her beard had "been my meal ticket" ever since.[124] Barnell spent the majority of her career performing in circuses, carnivals, and dime museums, including six years as part of the Congress of Strange People in the Ringling Brothers and Barnum & Bailey Circus; the Congress's manager told Mitchell in 1940 that Barnell was "the only real, old-fashioned bearded lady left in the country."[125] Barnell also had one foray into the film industry: in 1932, she performed the role of the Bearded Lady in MGM's *Freaks*, a horror film about the sideshow with a cast of real-life freak show performers. She told Mitchell that she regretted taking the job because she felt that the movie "was an insult to all freaks everywhere."[126] Barnell, who was married four times and whose two children died in infancy, died in Manhattan in 1945 at the age of seventy-five.[127]

Madame Clofullia, Madame Viola, and Lady Olga each had their own paths to freak show stardom, but once they stepped into the Bearded Lady character, they shared many common experiences. One such experience was a medical examination. To be sure, part of what drew audiences to freak shows was the thrill of figuring out for themselves if what they were seeing was authentic or fraudulent—a *humbug*.[128] Yet physicians were also significant voices of authority in declaring that a Bearded Lady was, indeed, a woman. As the first Bearded Lady in the United States, Madame Clofullia was subject to many medical examinations, spurred by curious (and sometimes suspicious) physicians and audience members. Her first London performance also occasioned her first documented medical authentication: she was inspected and authenticated by medical professionals before she could start performing at London's Linwood Gallery in 1851. Dr. W. D. Chowne delivered a lengthy report on his examination to medical students, and subsequently published the account in the prestigious London medical journal *The Lancet*. After the examination, Dr. Chowne signed an affidavit declaring that she was an authentic woman, and Clofullia began her London exhibition; both affidavits were also reprinted in the biography about her sold in the United States. (Years later, the births of Clofullia's children were also both certified by physicians' affidavit and reprinted in her biography.)[129]

Clofullia was examined repeatedly once she arrived in the United States, too, including an 1854 evaluation published in the *Boston Medical and Surgical Journal*, in which the physician affirmed that she "possesses a full beard and masculine conformation of face, though [is] unmistakably of the feminine sex."[130] In a stunt that Barnum likely arranged himself to drum up audiences, an accusation of fraud soon after Clofullia began appearing at Barnum's museum occasioned another medical examination and another confirmation that she was indeed a woman. When a visitor claimed to have discovered that "the Bearded Lady [was], in his opinion, a male, and an impostor on the public," he demanded that Barnum be arrested for fraud. Barnum scheduled another medical examination, which was performed by three different doctors, and the case was dismissed—but the "crowds poured in for a closer look." Barnum's trick had succeeded.[131] Two years later, a physician for the *Southern Medical and Surgical Journal* examined both Clofullia and her son, Albert, while they were performaning in Georgia, recording that "with the exception of the upper lip, she has as strong a beard as we usually see in man."[132] Madame Viola was also evaluated by physicians, including the prestigious dermatologist Louis A. Duhring at the University of Pennsylvania's hospital, who reported his examination in extensive detail in the medical journal *Archives of Dermatology* in 1877. Dr. Duhring confirmed that Viola was a woman. Indeed, he expressed with surprise, "the most interesting feature, however, is the complete absence of all assigns of masculinity"—but for, of course, her beard.[133]

Medical examinations were an important way that the Bearded Ladies affirmed their femininity to the public. These exams also served other important functions. Pragmatically, a doctor's certification assured both the paying audience and the broader public that the performer was not a gaff (freak show terminology for *fake* or manufactured). Medical authentication preempted accusations of fraud—yet, as Clofullia's engagement at the

American Museum demonstrated, showmen like Barnum also knew that such accusations could be profitable, too, since they caused spectators to flock to the exhibit to decide for *themselves* whether the performer was real or not.[134] Legally, medical exams also legitimized what could otherwise be, in many jurisdictions, an illegal act of cross-dressing. During the second half of the nineteenth century, thirty-four cities across twenty-one states criminalized cross-dressing. Dr. Chowne alluded to these laws in his examination of Madame Clofullia: he described how, when Clofullia traveled to strange towns, she covered her beard with a handkerchief when off-stage, "lest the police should regard her as a man disguised in woman's apparel."[135]

The final function of these medical examinations, however, was the cultural work they performed in concert with contemporaneous promotional, scientific, and popular media coverage of the Bearded Ladies, even their own biographies—all of which emphasized, with unwavering confidence, the Bearded Ladies' normative femininity. Scientific journals, for example, detailed the women's "small and feminine" hands and feet, arms and legs that were "slender" and "feminine in shape," normal menstruation, and "strictly womanly" characters and domestic tastes.[136] Madame Clofullia's biography cataloged her "large and fair" breasts, and emphasized that even as a young girl she "excelled particularly in those works adapted to her sex, such as embroideries, lace, network, and all kinds of needle-work."[137] When interviewed by Joseph Mitchell for the *New Yorker* profile, the manager for Lady Olga's longtime employer, the Congress of Strange People, praised her womanliness foremost: unlike most women with beards, who "look like men, Lady Olga is a woman, and she looks like a woman."[138]

Aesthetics were, indeed, key. In an 1853 portrait by photographer Thomas M. Easterly, Clofullia wore her hair in a style that was extremely common among contemporary white American women: parted in the center, looped to cover the ears, flat at the crown, and puffed on the sides (see fig. 2.7).[139] In other visual materials, Bearded Ladies were posed in middle-class parlors standing next to their husbands or children, both of which telegraphed the normative femininity nineteenth-century Americans assigned to heterosexuality and motherhood. For example, in her 1856 biography, Madame Clofullia appeared in one print posed next to her husband, Fortune, and in another print with her children (see fig. 2.8).[140] The overall effect of this presentation style was an emphasis on the Bearded Lady's femininity—with the obvious exception of her beard.[141]

2.7 "Josephine Clofullia. [Madame Clofullia, P.T. Barnum's "Bearded Lady of Geneva"], daguerreotype by Thomas M. Easterly, 1853. The brooch Clofullia wears along the neckline of her dress in this photographic portrait contains a daguerreotype portrait of her husband, Fortune Clofullia. Visual and textual reminders of Bearded Ladies' heterosexual marriages were frequent in publicity material, which reinforced the message of normative white femininity communicated by their presentation style.

CREDIT: Image courtesy of the Missouri Historical Society, N17387.

MADAME CLOFULLIA AND CHILDREN.

2.8 Illustration of Madame Clofullia with her two children. Madame
Clofullia's promotional biography included illustrations of her
with her father, her husband, and her children, Zelea and Albert.
This is an imagined portrait: Zelea died as a baby, six weeks
before Albert was born. Clofullia's biography includes testimony
from London physicians who affirmed that Zelea "showed no
symptoms of beard" while Albert's face was "fully surrounded
with whiskers" as a toddler, as this illustration captures.

CREDIT: Reproduced from Josephine Boisdechene Clofullia Ghio, *Life of the
Celebrated Bearded Lady, Madame Clofullia and Her Infant Esau* (New York:
Courrier des États-Unis, 1856).

When medical examiners wrote about the Bearded Ladies' breasts, their facial and body hair, their heterosexual marriages, their children, their "feminine demeanor," and even their aptitude in feminine-coded tasks like needlepoint, they were imbuing gender signifiers with the weight of sex determination.[142] Genitalia mattered very little to these assessments of gender and, therefore, of sex: an evaluation of more than a dozen accounts of medical examinations of Bearded Ladies' bodies—all of which affirmed they were women—revealed no references to a genital exam.[143] By contrast, a genital exam was a common experience for many women of color who performed in the freak show, particularly when the nature of their bodily curiosity involved gendered parts of the body, such as the conjoined pelvis of sisters Millie-Christine McKoy.[144] That Bearded Ladies avoided a genital exam is simply further evidence of the whiteness of this archetype.

Bearded Ladies and the Women's Suffrage Movement

The women who performed as Bearded Ladies in the nineteenth and early twentieth centuries were not simply figures for the amusement of American families. Their popularity, ubiquitous inclusion in freak show lineups, and public visibility also gave them symbolic currency for many contemporary writers. Most observers, scientists and laymen alike, believed that, even if facial hair growing on a woman's face was not particularly unusual, women who actually *cultivated their facial hair*—instead of endeavoring, often painstakingly, to remove it—were unnatural, even threatening, because they were refusing to properly perform their gender.

It was this problem of gender performativity that caused many American men to connect the Bearded Lady to another group of American women who gained a new level of visibility in the second half of the nineteenth century: suffragists. Starting the very first year Madame Clofullia appeared on an American stage, many journalists, scientists, and theologians drew on the cultural resonance of the freak show—and the Bearded Lady in particular—as they turned the Bearded Lady into a metonym for suffragists. The freakishness of the on-stage Bearded Lady, they hoped, might in turn enfreak women's rights activists—whose agitation, they feared, threatened to undermine white men's political and cultural power. Moreover, even though Black women were at the forefront of the women's suffrage movement, critics who linked the Bearded Lady to women activists focused on white activists alone—further evidence of both the Bearded Lady's whiteness *and* how even the white leaders of the women's suffrage movement (let alone their critics) consigned Black women to the movement's margins.[145]

Comparisons between the women's suffrage movement and the Bearded Lady often functioned as a condemnation of suffragists, with the Bearded Lady serving as a hyperbolized symbol of women attempting to violate what white men believed to be the natural dissimilarity (and hierarchy) between men and women. For example, a profile of Madame Clofullia published in Boston's *Gleason's Pictorial Drawing-Room Companion* began by announcing her arrival in the city before abruptly changing topics: "Can we well get through with penning this article," the author mused, "and not refer this matter to the woman's rights society? Here is a member of their sex, who out-Herods Herod; not content with claiming the right to vote, and laying siege to our nether garments (*a la* bloomer), our beards are actually in jeopardy! Heaven forbid!"[146] The author identified bearded women from history, from a bearded woman named Phaetusa described by Hippocrates, to a ballet dancer at the 1726 Carnival in Venice. Such a history of bearded women would seem to contradict the urgency conveyed by the preceding passage, which made it seem as though the bearded woman was as contemporary a phenomenon as "the woman's rights society." The article's final line, however, revealed the distinction: notwithstanding the unusual examples the author had detailed, "the art of suppressing the growth of hair on the female face, has been pursued with great pains-taking" throughout human history.[147] This sentence made clear the difference between the contemporary Bearded Lady and these other historical examples of bearded women: while her hairy predecessors had gone to great lengths to remove all evidence of their facial hair, Madame Clofullia wore her beard on a stage for the whole world to see.

An 1853 article in the *New York Times* similarly critiqued what its author believed were the mistakes of another women-led activist movement, the temperance movement, by comparing its villainous "masculine women"— whom the author believed undermined "the respectability of [their] cause"— to Madame Clofullia:

> They profess to be acting on behalf of their sex; and their special object is to assert for women all the rights and all the faculties of men. They go about the country, therefore, for the purpose of showing in their own persons how little difference there is after all between the

two sexes,—and how nearly they can succeed in discharging functions which it is commonly supposed nature, and propriety[,] have assigned to individuals of the opposite gender. . . . And yet they are only women after all;—and cease to be respectable as such, just in proportion as they try to be something else. The case is not essentially different with their sisters who take so much delight in parading their masculine faculties before the public eye. They draw large audiences, of course. BARNUM'S *bearded* lady is visited by great numbers of those who have a curiosity for all these instances of the confusion of genders.[148]

Comparing Clofullia's beard to "the masculine gifts of Messrs. Stone and Brown," the author used the masculine honorific "Messrs." (an abbreviation for "Misters" or "Masters") to suggest that activists Lucy Stone and Antoinette Brown were similarly confused about their gender. Even Fanny Fern, whose high-paying success as a newspaper writer might have similarly enraged the *New York Times* writer, jokingly pondered asking Clofullia, "Who shaves first in the morning—you, or your husband? Do you use a Woman's Rights razor?"[149] Writers like these thus used the Bearded Lady as an absurd symbol for the activists involved with the women's suffrage movement.[150]

Horace Bushnell's 1869 tract against women's suffrage also used the supposed absurdity of female beards to support his argument that political rights for women were completely unnatural. Bushnell argued that "men and women are . . . [so] unlike in kind" so as "forbid any such inference of right for women because that right is accorded to men." Suffragists' argument that women should be allowed to participate in the political process was so extreme, Bushnell argued, that "the claim of a beard would not be a more radical revolt against nature." As Bushnell had already established earlier in the text, a beard conferred power and authority on a man. Women were subordinate "by their nature itself," and attempting to subvert the natural rules of authority was precisely the same as trying to grow a beard.[151]

Later in the century, writers began to accuse suffragists and the Bearded Lady—rhetorically collapsed into one entity—of trying to steal white men's natural authority by laying claim to *the beard*. The 1878 biographical pamphlet for Madame Viola quotes an onlooker who, upon seeing Viola perform, was inspired to muse about how "the women want to vote, and want to preach, and to sit in the hall of legislation, to be at the head of our post offices and city governments, to teach our schools, to fight our battles, to regulate our code of laws, and take a general supervision of poor, uncertain mankind, and now, lo and behold, we have a lady with a beard, come to astonish the world, with a truly wonderful hirsute appendage."[152] Another onlooker wondered, "isn't that an infringement on the rights of man?" While normally, this onlooker argued, men wore beards as a "badge of superiority," Madame Viola presented a situation where "things are reversed," for a woman had "assume[d] the supremacy of a beard." Although Viola's biography generally described its subject sympathetically, this passage (attributed to "onlookers" rather than the pamphlet's compassionate author) expressed quite explicitly how a woman with a beard threatened the perceived rights of men.[153]

The comic reversal in Madame Viola's biography echoed into the early twentieth century, amid increased agitation for women's suffrage. In a 1911 cartoon for *Life* magazine, for example, a woman identified as "Suffragette" leans over to a Bearded Lady and asks her, "How did you manage it?" (see fig. 2.9).[154] The implication of this image is that the suffragette wishes she, too, could overcome her womanhood and grow a beard—the same critique of the *New York Times* writer who accused all suffragists of wanting to *become* men. (In this way, the critique was similar to that other hair-based phrase that sometimes dogged women activists: "short-haired women and long-haired men.")[155] The way the suffragette character is drawn in this cartoon only amplified this message: her shirt collar, necktie, cane, facial features, and tall height mirror those of the man standing next to her. In this cartoon, the Bearded Lady became the comic ideal for which the suffrage movement strove. Indeed, in the 1920s, in the aftermath of both the Nineteenth Amendment (which gave women the right to vote) and the beard's fall from fashion, some writers linked feminists to the most famous "feminine barber," Delilah, accusing her of stripping men of both their political supremacy *and* their beards. This connection was particularly strong in the 1926 *New York Times* article that mourned the passing of the beard. Author Hollister Noble, who pointedly entitled his paean to bearded faces "Beardless Man is Facing a Dreary Existence," blamed women for the waning popularity of facial hair, "for it is the ancestors and descendants of that greatest of feminine barbers, Delilah, who have de-whiskered the flower of the human race. The rise of feminism has always abolished beards and destroyed mustaches."[156] By the twentieth century, when facial hair had fallen out of fashion,

Suffragette: HOW DID YOU MANAGE IT?

2.9 Untitled cartoon by A. S. Daggy. Although only the Bearded Lady is identified with a written placard on the wall, this illustrated freak show also features two other archetypical characters played by women: the Snake Charmer and the Fat Lady.

CREDIT: Reproduced from *Life*, v. 57 (1911).

suffragists were not simply accused of claiming the right to wear a beard, but also of forcing men to stop wearing their beards—a double assault on white men's supposedly natural authority.

The very same journalists and theologians who decried beards on women as unnatural—and drafted the Bearded Lady archetype into critiques of women's rights—also frequently admitted that bearded women were not at all uncommon. How, then, did it make sense to nineteenth-century showmen, journalists, and other cultural authorities to take the kind of woman they might meet every day and place her on the freak show stage? To these men, what was ultimately unnatural about the bearded women who performed on stage was not that they *had* beards, but that they did not try to *remove* their beards. Nineteenth-century physicians believed a key component of womanhood to be a woman's desire to *appear* feminine and her willingness to actively enact her femininity; as gender studies scholar Rebecca Herzig has shown, getting rid of facial hair was a crucial part of this enactment.[157] For example, Dr. Duhring's description of Madame Viola ended by addressing this possibility directly: "In regard to the question which was asked to me by the patient, whether the growth of the face could be successfully and permanently removed (*and I need not add that it is to her the source of intense mortification and distress*), I would say that the only justifiable means at our command is palliative, consisting in either the daily use of the razor or in the employment of a depilatory powder."[158] Similarly, Dr. George Henry Fox's 1882 article on electrolysis for hair removal explained that while "in nearly every 'museum of living curiosities' a bearded woman figures as one of the chief attractions, and it is quite probable that but a small proportion of bearded women are willing to advertise their misfortune for pecuniary gain." While there were currently "at least a half-dozen" Bearded Ladies on display in New York City, where he lived and worked, Fox declared confidently that he had "no doubt that there are hundreds" of "ladies in private life who endeavor, by articles of various kinds, to conceal the unpleasant fact that they have or might have a beard."[159] Centering the significance of hair removal to the performance of feminine gender presentation allows us to reconcile two seemingly contradictory statements contemporary observers often made: that women with facial hair were naturally common, *and also* that the Bearded Lady was unnatural.

When the Bearded Lady was enshrined as a freak show character in the nineteenth century, what was really being canonized as freakish was not her facial hair, but her attitude toward her facial hair—and, by implication, her attitude toward the proper place of women. What linked the Bearded Ladies to suffragists, therefore, was their shared attitude—one that did not conform to what was expected of contemporary women. This is precisely what the 1853 article in *Gleason's Pictorial Drawing-Room Companion* had identified in Madame Clofullia, and this is exactly what made the Bearded Lady worthy of her enfreakment. Just like the ubiquity of men with beards, Bearded Ladies who posed on freak show stages conveyed a very clear message to white women: white men are the ones who wear the beards, white men are the ones who have the power, and anything to the contrary is unnatural, freakish, and should be ridiculed and rejected.

The Bearded Lady's Racial Boundaries

One way in which Madame Clofullia's influence can clearly be seen in the Bearded Lady archetype was in her name: almost without exception, Bearded Ladies who performed in the century after Clofullia's debut also included aggrandized titles in their stage names. In addition to Madame Viola and Lady Olga, American Bearded Lady performers included Madame Devere, Madam Squires, Princess Gracie, and "Miss Annie Jones, the Bearded Princess."[160] Bearded Ladies were, indeed, *ladies*: middle- or upper-class women whose image was respectable, refined, and genteel.

However, the Bearded Lady's femininity was not just classed—it was also racialized. In order to portray the Bearded Lady character, a performer needed to be publicly perceived as white. Indeed, that Josephine Boisdechene's Swiss heritage was central to her transformation into Madame Clofullia was not a mere coincidence. Yet ancestry was not destiny: as scholar Erin Naomi Burrows argued in her biography of Jane Barnell (the woman who performed as Lady Olga), Barnell was only able to gain access to the category of whiteness—despite her Russian Jewish, Irish, and Catawba ancestry—*because* she participated in the freak show. When Barnell stepped into the role of the Bearded Lady, adopting the title *Lady* and the other aesthetic trappings of the archetype, the audience perceived her as white.[161] However, hairy women freak show performers who could not be pass as white were rarely referred to as Bearded Ladies, but were instead displayed as more bestial archetypes that toed the line between human and animal.[162] The freak show displays of Julia Pastrana and Krao—both bearded women of color—visually reinforced the fact that non-white women's bodies placed them at the margins of American political citizenship—and even suggested they might be at the margins of humanity itself.

One of the first examples of a hairy non-white woman to perform in the mode of animal-woman began performing the very same year that Madame Clofullia debuted the Bearded Lady archetype. Julia Pastrana was an Indigenous Mexican woman with a hairy face and body who was exhibited across the United States in the 1850s under titles like "The Bear Woman," "Baboon Lady," "Ape Woman," or even "The Ugliest Woman in the World"—the latter title emphasizing the pernicious connections between beauty and whiteness. (Other displays emphasized Pastrana's liminal status *between* animal and woman, or her body's resistance to classification altogether, by titling her "Marvelous Hybrid," "Misnomer," or "The Nondescript.")[163]

The American press's coverage of Pastrana was similarly uncertain about how to characterize her, vacillating between awe and disgust. Articles in local newspapers described Pastrana as "the greatest and most wonderful curiosity in the world," "the greatest natural curiosity we have ever seen in the shape of a human or semi-human being," "a most repulsive looking person," "most revolting, hideous, baboonish female," and a "beastly exhibition and villainous imposition on the public."[164] Pastrana's career as a freak show sensation was but brief: after debuting in New York City in 1854, she performed for the next three years across the United States in large cities and small towns, from South Carolina to Illinois to Washington, DC. In 1857, she began performing in Europe, and did so until her death in Moscow in 1860. (The chilling postmortem story of her embalmed body's public display in Europe as late as the 1970s—and her eventual repatriation and reburial in Mexico in 2013—has become the subject of film, theater, and art.)[165]

That American newspapers' death announcements rarely failed to mentioned that Pastrana's death was because of complications from childbirth echoes the way contemporary sources lingered on Madame Clofullia's children as evidence of her womanhood. Indeed, there are a few similarities in the way these two contemporaries were portrayed and received in the 1850s. For example, promotional lithographs for Pastrana's London performance signaled her femininity through her clothing, jewelry, accessories, and hairstyle—stylishly pinned and adorned with flowers (see fig. 2.10). Also like Clofullia (as well as the other women who later performed as Bearded Ladies), Pastrana was subject to medical examination by physicians. For example, in 1857 the British physician Dr. John Zachariah Laurence wrote a brief description of his evaluation of Pastrana for the London medical journal *The Lancet*. Dr. Laurence described Pastrana's "large tuft of hair depending [i.e., descending] from the chin—a *beard*, continuous with smaller growth of hair on the upper lip and cheeks—moustache and whiskers." While the hair on her face and body made her body similar, "in an exaggerated degree, with what is not very uncommonly observed in the male sex," the rest of her body "agrees with the female:" her breasts were "remarkably full and well-developed," she "menstruates regularly," and her voice "is that of a female, as is especially brought out in her higher notes when she sings."[166] This description echoes the way medical journals described Clofullia, cataloging

2.10 "Julia Pastrana, "the nondescript," advertised for exhibition,"
lithograph, [1857]. This illustration advertised Pastrana's 1857
exhibition at London's Regent Gallery.
CREDIT: Wellcome Collection (CC BY 4.0).

both her "main peculiarity" (as Dr. Laurence called Pastrana's hairiness) and other corporeal signifiers of gender.

However, there is one revealing difference in the way the medical journals wrote about these two women: while the articles in the *Boston Medical and Surgical Journal, Southern Medical and Surgical Journal,* and *The Lancet* referred to Clofullia by name (Madame Clofullia, Mrs. Clofullia, Mrs. C., or "Josephine B——") and as "a bearded woman" and "Swiss woman," Dr. Laurence never refers to Pastrana by name, calling her only, repeatedly, "a female."[167] That his article is about Pastrana at all is only legible thanks to context clues: other corroborating sources that confirm she was indeed on display at the Regent Gallery in July 1857, as Dr. Laurence indicated.[168] By referring to Pastrana only by the clinical *female,* this medical evaluation rendered Pastrana more scientific object than human. Although articles and advertisements for Pastrana's American performances sometimes used the honorific "Miss" when naming her, the American popular press was at pains to distinguish the differences between Pastrana and Clofullia. For example, a local newspaper from Indiana noted in 1855 that "her face is covered with short, thick hair, not unlike the Bearded Swiss Lady," but owing to what the writer classified as Pastrana's animallike features—"her jaws project like a baboon's"; "a monkey's phrenological display would equal hers"; "any thing in human shape, that possessed less of human nature, we never saw"—Pastrana was too marginal to whiteness to perform as the Bearded Lady character.[169]

Twenty years after Pastrana's death, another hairy woman of color, Krao, became enormously popular in American freak shows, performing with an animalistic aesthetic. Krao was just seven years old in 1883 when she was "caught . . . in the forest near Laos"—kidnapped is likely more accurate—by the Canadian showman Signor Guillermo Antonio Farini (the stage name of William Leonard Hunt), who exhibited the girl as "the missing link" between animals and humans.[170] American newspapers buzzed so frequently about this exciting new freak show performer that Krao even became a legible cultural reference—the nineteenth-century version of a meme. For example, when John S. Gray, the California State Secretary of Harbor Commissioners, was arrested in 1883 after embezzling state funds and then fleeing to Guaymas, Mexico, the *San Francisco Illustrated Wasp* briefly paused its anti-Chinese criticism (as chapter 1 examined) to poke fun at Gray—and it did so using a widely circulated photograph of Krao and Farini from earlier that year. In the photograph (see fig. 2.11a), a besuited Farini balances Krao, who is naked, on his left arm, her arms wrapped around his neck and her left leg straight across his chest. This photograph was so recognizable that it was this precise pose to which the *Wasp* alluded when poking fun at Gray, in the role of Krao—naked and hairy, with handcuffs on one of the wrists around the neck of his captor, Alexander Willard, US Consul at Guaymas (see fig. 2.11b). The *Wasp* made the allusion even more explicit with its caption: "Gray-O, The Missing Link. Captured in the Wilds of Guaymas, and Now on His Way to the Museum at San Quentin."[171]

In this famous photograph, Krao's body is posed to maximize the traits that a white audience would read as primitive, even bordering animalistic: she is naked (in stark contrast to Farini's besuited body), and the photographic processing has rendered every dark hair on her face, arms, back, and legs in sharp relief. As historian Kimberly A. Hamlin has demonstrated, Farini convinced the Laotian government that "his kidnapping served a higher purpose" by arguing that "she was the long-sought intermediate step between apes and humans."[172] Indeed, in the years since Pastrana's 1860 death, the publication of Charles Darwin's research on human evolution had aroused great public curiosity. To capitalize on that curiosity, hairy people, including Krao, were now advertised, as one 1892 advertisement put it, as "The Living Proof of the Darwinian Theory" (see fig. 2.12).[173] Krao was, these advertisements proclaimed, "not a freak of nature! But a genuine descendant, in a regular way, of a race of people inhabiting the Northern portion of Siam, possessing the attributes of the Man and the Ape in equal proportion, proving the truth of the Darwinian Theory; showing the half-way point in the evolution of Man from the Ape."[174] Such promotional material even took Darwin's conclusions one step further by suggesting that the process of evolution could occur not across millennia, but within a single human lifespan. Since Krao's "rescue from her semi-barbarous surroundings," she "has developed into a human being, just as mankind developed originally."[175] Indeed, as Krao aged, her presentation style shifted in reflection of this evolutionary logic: photographs of Krao as a teenager and adult show her clothed, with long dark hair and a dark mustache and beard. In her performances, Krao displayed a sense of civility and intelligence that surprised audiences. She was well read in many different subjects, played the piano, and could even speak five languages.[176] And yet, Krao's *bodily* differences remained the focus of the public's fascination and the reason for her decades-long freak show

"KRAO."
FARINI'S MISSING LINK

W. & D. DOWNEY
PHOTOGRAPHERS

57 & 61 EBURY STREET
LONDON S.W.

COPYRIGHT

2.11 *(Left)* W. & D. Downey, "Krao, Farini's Missing Link."
ca. 1883. *(Right)* "Gray-O, The Missing Link," *The Wasp*,
April 14, 1883. The popular circulation of this
photographic portrait of Krao in the first months of 1883
is evident in its parody on this cover of San Francisco's
illustrated weekly newspaper, *The Wasp*. The bracelet Krao
wore on her left wrist is replaced with Gray's handcuffs.
CREDIT: Left: TCS 8. Houghton Library, Harvard University. Right:
Reproduced from *Wasp* (San Francisco, CA), f F850 .W18, v. 10,
Jan.—June 1883, No. 350, The Bancroft Library, University of
California, Berkeley.

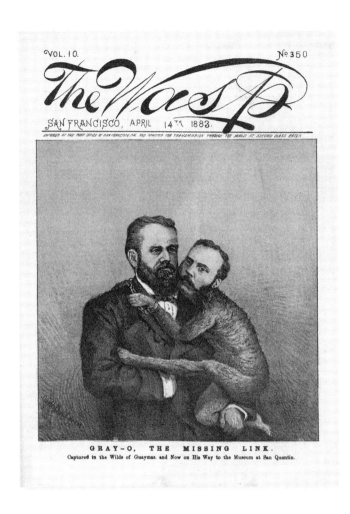

VOL. 10.   № 350

The Wasp

SAN FRANCISCO, APRIL 14ᵀᴴ 1883.

GRAY-O, THE MISSING LINK.
Captured in the Wilds of Guaymas. and Now on His Way to the Museum at San Quentin.

career; at the time of her death of influenza, in 1926, Krao was still performing as "the 'Missing Link'" in the Ringling Brothers and Barnum & Bailey Circus. Because of her facial hair, Krao was, and would always be, an "exotic domestic pet."[177]

Just as the meaning of white bearded men and white Bearded Ladies reinforced the same cultural narrative—that beards signal the naturalness of white male power—so too was the cultural work of hairy Indigenous and East Asian women like Julia Pastrana and Krao complementary to that

HARRY DAVIS'
FIFTH AVENUE MUSEUM
AND
FAMILY THEATER.

WEEK COMMENCING **MAR. 7.**

THE SEASON'S TRIUMPH!

FOR ONE WEEK ONLY,

LIONINE,
THE LION-FACED WOMAN.

In All the World There Is None Like Her—Human and Beast Combined. Her Body That of a Perfectly Formed Woman, Yet She Has the Head and Face of the King of Beasts.

SEE HER! SEE HER!

The Triple-Jointed Wonder,

ZAMORA,
And Many Other Curios.

THEATER.

First Appearance in Ten Years of the King of Laugh-Makers and famous Minstrel Man,

COOL BURGESS
And the Renowned

MONUMENTAL SPECIALTY CO.
Composed of the Greatest Vaudeville Stars of the

Theatrical Firmament.

ADMISSION, 10 CENTS.

Doors open from 1 to 10 P. M.

WORLD'S MUSEUM-THEATRE
GEO. CONNOR MANAGER. EDW. KEENAN BUSINESS MANAGER.

The Leading Amusement Resort for Ladies and Children.

COMMENCING MONDAY, MARCH 7.
CURIO HALL:
The Living Proof of the Darwinian Theory,

"KRAO!"
THE MISSING LINK.

HALF GIRL! FATHER KRAOS MOTHER **HALF MONKEY!**

NOT A FREAK OF NATURE!
BUT A GENUINE DESCENDANT,

In a regular way, of a race of people inhabiting the Northern portion of Siam, possessing the attributes of the Man and the Ape in equal proportions, proving the truth of the Darwinian Theory; showing the half-way point in the evolution of Man from the Ape. A rather bright girl who, since her rescue from her semi-barbarous surroundings, has developed into a human being, just as mankind developed originally. THE WONDER OF ANTHROPOLOGISTS.

A large list of other attractions also.

THEATER: THE GREAT CAUCASIAN ETHIOPIAN SPECIALTY COMPANY.

ADMISSION, - 10 CENTS.

Next Week—Frank E. McNish and his Own Specialty Company.

mh6-100

of the supposedly hairless Indigenous and East Asian men. Claims of the intrinsic hairlessness of men from the Americas and most Asian cultures reinforced racial hierarchies of the body by suggesting that the inability to grow a full European-style beard testified to their distance from both American manhood and American political citizenship. Enfreaking hairy women from those same cultures suggested that gender inversion—the barefaced men and bearded women—was yet more proof that Indigenous and East Asian people were biologically unfit for the American body politic. Indeed, it was these two racial groups that would remain ineligible for American citizenship until decades into the twentieth century. The nineteenth-century's cultural narratives of hair thus offered repeated visual reminders, in both ordinary and extraordinary contexts, of the biological foundation for the racial and gendered boundaries of political subjecthood.

IN THE FIRST TWO DECADES of the twentieth century, when Hollister Nobel penned his ode to the majesty of that "honored relic," the beard's place in American culture shifted once more.[178] Beards lost their rarefied place on men's faces, as younger men increasingly embraced their razors— the technology now far cheaper, easier to use, and safer thanks to innovations in razor technology, especially King Gillette's disposable safety razor.[179] Indeed, popular advertising began to depict the ideal white male body as smooth, clean, and youthful—a stark contrast to the idealized older and bearded body of the nineteenth century. By 1920, beards were very uncommon in the United States and remained so for decades.[180] Hair's changing

2.12 Advertisement for World's Museum–Theatre, *Pittsburgh Dispatch*. March 6, 1892. This advertisement for Krao's performance in Pittsburgh characterized Krao as "the missing link" between humans and animals—a "half girl" and "half monkey" who embodied Darwinian evolution. The broad appeal of such animal-people archetypes in the late nineteenth-century freak show—and the way that facial hair facilitated the enfreakment of some women's bodies—is visible in the advertisement that ran directly to the left for "Lionine, The Lion-Faced Woman," who was pitched as "Human and Beast Combined."
CREDIT: Library of Congress, Chronicling America, sn84024546.

cultural meaning helps explain this shift: as the shared understanding of hair as a body part faded from American culture in the early twentieth century, white supremacist narratives of the beard's biological qualities—that white men grew beards *naturally*, for example—faded away, too.

Crucially, moreover, new biological understandings of the body at the turn of the twentieth century gained an urgency that, in piecemeal ways, eroded the beard's role as a cultural signifier of male political subjecthood. When, for example, American physicians responded to the mounting evidence of the germ theory of disease by adopting strict cleanliness protocols, one important way young doctors signaled that they were modern practitioners was by shaving off the full beards that had long been popular among American doctors. As alternative medicine practitioner Edwin F. Bowers wrote in *McClure's Magazine* in 1916, "There is no way of computing the number of bacteria and noxious germs that may lurk in the Amazonian jungles of a well-whiskered face. . . . Today a bushy-whiskered American surgeon is almost as rare as a dodo."[181] It was the growing significance of hair's biological qualities in the mid-nineteenth century that cemented facial hair's cultural meaning as an index of white male power, and in the end, it was biology, too, that changed the beard's meaning once more: The cultural meaning of hair was, indeed, deeply rooted in science.

CHAPTER 3

HAIR SCIENCE

IN 1857, AN ENSLAVED FIFTEEN-YEAR-OLD named Alexina Morrison ran away from her enslaver, a Louisiana man named James White. Morrison—who had blond hair and blue eyes—surrendered herself at the local jail in Jefferson Parish, claiming that she was actually a white woman from Arkansas who had been kidnapped and forced into slavery. She found an unlikely ally in her jailer, a white man named William Dennison, who allowed Morrison to live with his family and helped her file a suit against White for her freedom. This case, *Morrison v. White*, was tried three different times between 1858 and 1861, twice reaching the Supreme Court of Louisiana on appeal; the first trial ended in a hung jury, the second ruled unanimously in favor of Morrison, and the third ruled again for Morrison, 10–2.[1] At the heart of each of these trials was a single question: was Morrison white, and thus free, or was she Black, and thus enslaved?[2]

Morrison v. White was one of nearly seventy cases tried in state supreme courts in the nineteenth-century South known as racial determination cases: cases in which the outcome hinged on legally determining a person's race.[3] In the case of whether Alexina Morrison was white or Black, James White's lawyers relied on evidence that came directly from Morrison's enslavers: five of Morrison's former owners, as well as official documentation such as bills of sale, testified to Morrison's lifetime of servitude. By contrast, Morrison's legal team relied almost entirely on testimonies about her physical appearance. In a typical testimony, a witness declared that, in his judgment, Morrison was white, and that he knew she was white because of her physical features; the specific physical feature or features each witness referenced as their evidence varied, but frequently included the color of her eyes, the prominence of her cheek bones, or the shape of her nose. In the first trial, which ended in a hung jury, none of Morrison's witnesses cited her hair as evidence for her whiteness. However, in the second and third trials—the trials that Morrison won—no body part was cited more frequently than her hair.[4]

Most witnesses who examined Morrison's hair in the second and third trials did so at a distance and solely with their eyes, relying on the impression left by its light color and straight texture. But one expert witness, Dr. John Leonard Riddell—a New Orleans physician with considerable scientific authority in the local community[5]—testified to a completely different kind of investigation:

> Witness [Dr. Riddell] made an examination of the Hair of plff [plaintiff], witness himself cut off a piece of her hair and compared the same with some of her hair that the Counsel said was plaintiff's, [and] he did not find any trace in this hair that would indicate that the girl had negro blood in her. Peter A. Brown[e,] a distinguished Savant of Philadelphia[,] says that there is peculiar difference in the hair[—] its texture & c[—] of a person of African descent from that of a white person. Witness himself has made some observations, which served to verify what Mr Brown[e] has asserted[.] In the hair of the caucassian [*sic*] race the cross section of the hair is an oval, a moderate oval in which the long diameter would be five [and] the short diameter about three, in the negro hair the cross section shows a greater difference in diameter and has a more elongated oval, the long diameter being greater than the short diameter. Negro hair approaches the character of wool. Witness prepared a careful examination of the hair of this girl with a proper apparatus, he prepared with the proper apparatus the cross sections of the hair of the Girl and then examining it with a microscope he discovered it to be of the moderate oval characteristic of the caucassian or white race.[6]

Dr. Riddell's testimony hinged on the scientific research of a man named Peter Arrell Browne, a lawyer and self-trained scientist from Philadelphia. By 1860—the eve of both his death and the outbreak of the Civil War— Browne had become the most influential hair scientist (or, practitioner of what Browne deemed *trichology*, the science of hair) in the United States. He was also the scientific community's foremost expert on the relationship between hair and race. At the heart of Browne's research lay three powerful assertions: first, that hair's most important meanings were located within individual strands; second, that these important meanings were only accessible to experts—such as himself—because they required specialized scientific knowledge and technology, including microscopes; and third, that the evidence experts could obtain in these investigations was an extraordinarily reliable confirmation of a person's race.

Between 1848 and 1853, Browne collected hair from hundreds of humans and animals; conducted extensive experiments on these hair samples; and wrote articles, speeches, and books on the science of hair. He presented his research to fellow scientists at conferences held by the era's most important professional societies, such as the American Association for the Advancement of Science, and was frequently called to serve as an expert witness in court cases. Browne's work was widely circulated, read, and reprinted across the American scientific community, making him the single most important expert of his era on the science of hair.[7] It was Browne, for example, that white supremacist John Van Evrie cited for his "microscopic observations" of hair's "elementary structure."[8] For these reasons, Browne's hair research provides unparalleled insight into contemporary perspectives on the scientific meaning of human hair and, crucially, the racial truths scientists asserted hair could reveal.

In the second quarter of the nineteenth century, American scientists began to claim for themselves a privileged expertise about the meanings embedded in hair. By 1840, hair's ability to reveal the intrinsic truth about the person from whose body it grew was well established, but in the 1840s and 1850s these assessments of hair's meaning also began to bear the weight of scientific authority. The centerpiece of scientists' claims of expertise was their unit of analysis: the single strand of hair. The strand of hair, they argued, was the site of hair's essential biological features: its thickness, its color, its texture, and its strength (and thus whether it could grow long or not). Hair strands were also a reliable scientific material because their dimensions were constant, and because they could be measured using tools like microscopes. Indeed, by the 1840s microscopy had become such a trusted technology that simply *using* a microscope validated the data it produced.[9] (It was no coincidence that the most important ethnological tome of the era, *Types of Mankind,* explicitly couched Browne's expertise in his "microscopic experiments.") But when it came to identifying hair's racial meanings, many hair scientists turned away from their microscopes and relied, just like lay people did every day, on their eyes: they looked at the overall color, thickness, or texture of a full head of hair, positing that "woolly knots" indicated African ancestry, or dark-colored hair indicated Spanish or Italian heritage.[10]

What set Peter Browne apart from his scientific peers—and what likely made his research so persuasive in the racial science community—was that Browne located racial meaning in the strand, too. Using not just the microscope but also specialized tools made specifically for hair science, Browne argued that definitive evidence of racial identity could be found in the shape of a cross section cut from a single piece of hair: strands with a cylindrical shape came from Indigenous people, strands with an oval shape came from white people, and strands with what Browne called an "eccentrically elliptical" shape came from Black people—a perfect and unerring correspondence between strand shape and race.[11] Browne claimed that his knowledge about hair's racial meaning down to the strand level gave him more truthful and dependable information about hair than other ways of studying it; this privileged knowledge was also what made Browne's three-part racial classification system so persuasive to so many of his peers. To understand the strand, Browne argued, was to understand the fundamental truth about the person from whose body it grew. Moreover, this knowledge formed a kind of synecdochical chain: the strand revealed the full head of hair, which revealed the full person, which revealed the racial group into which that person could be classified. For Browne, hair offered clarity on racial identity where other parts of the body—such as skin color—had proven unreliable. Browne's singular focus on strand shape thus represented the pinnacle of the nineteenth century's growing emphasis on hair's biological qualities: it was his attempt to locate hair's racial meaning in its *most* biological quality— one visible only to the scientist and his tools.

As the country's leading hair scientist, Browne's research became part of one of the biggest scientific debates of the first half of the nineteenth century: whether human beings were all part of a single race (known as *monogenesis*) or whether each racial group was its own distinct race (*polygenesis*). Browne thought that his research on human hair's racial meanings had the potential to settle this debate because he believed hair strand evidence offered the proof that no other body part could. Those were the stakes of Browne's trichology: to make hair *the* definitive index of racial identity in the United States.

Racial Science and Hair Science in the Early Nineteenth Century

By the mid-nineteenth century, the American life sciences community—including ethnologists, anatomists, paleontologists, and physicians—had a single overwhelming preoccupation: race. Scientists from Europe and its colonies had been surveying the human body in pursuit of classification criteria since Swedish botanist Carl Linnaeus first applied the principles of natural science to human classification in *Systema Naturae* (1735). In the one hundred years that followed, scholars from England and the United States examined and classified humans into their own taxonomies, some concurring with Linnaeus's four racial groups and some departing from it. For example, Johann Friedrich Blumenbach, the German naturalist who originated the term *Caucasian* as synonymous for white, posted five racial groups in his famous treatise *On the Natural Variety of Mankind* (1775): Caucasian, Mongolian, Malay, American, and Ethiopian.[12] Other scientists proposed their own taxonomies ranging from three to sixteen groups.[13] Even when they disagreed on the correct number of racial groupings, most nineteenth-century scientists searched for evidence of racial classification in the human body's flesh and bone.[14] Racial science publications from the nineteenth century are replete with dense, detailed descriptions of many parts of the body that might, singularly or in combination, carry racial meaning. Different authors prioritized different features, but the list included features as wide-ranging as the shape of the forehead, nose, lips, cheekbones, or chin; the size of the eyes, ears, earlobe, or tongue; the length of the arms of legs; or the body's overall height or size.

Samuel George Morton, the most influential American racial scientist of the nineteenth century, took the narrative description favored by the scientists who came before him and added a new precedent that gave his research a sense of systematic rigor: measurement. Morton's preferred body part was the skull. By 1849, Morton had amassed a collection of eight hundred skulls from across the globe. Although he initially gathered these skulls for use as a teaching collection, he ultimately argued that precise measurements—especially the measurement of cranial capacity: the size, in square inches, of the skulls' interiors—aligned with racial identity.[15] In *Crania Americana* (1839), Morton paired illustrations of each skull with precise measurements of over a dozen dimensions, including "Longitudinal diameter,"

"Facial angle," and, most importantly to Morton, three measurements of cranial capacity.[16] To Morton, these measurements offered the possibility for not just classification, but also evaluations of intelligence. Morton drew a direct line from the cranial capacity to the size of the brain to intelligence: the larger the cranial capacity, the more intelligent the person.[17] Although Morton himself did not explicitly use these evaluations of intelligence to argue for a racial hierarchy, as historian Samuel Redman has written, "he did little to prevent his readers from making the small mental leap to that conclusion."[18]

Morton's skull collection seemed like powerful evidence of the possibilities that quantification and measurement offered to scientists' search for reliable evidence of racial classification. But it was also limited by his preferred medium: despite having hundreds of skulls in his collection, that was still simply not enough. In the preface to *Crania Americana*, Morton admitted that "I do not even now consider my task as wholly complete"; he felt the work was particularly lacking in evidence about people from Mexico, "owing to the extreme difficulty of obtaining *authentic* crania of those people." He closed the preface with a plea: "The author therefore respectfully solicits the further aid of gentlemen interested in the cause of science, in procuring the *skulls of all nations*, and forwarding them to his address in this city" of Philadelphia.[19] This was, indeed, the problem with skeletal evidence: it was limited by access to the objects *and* by the limitations of (and potential for fraud in) establishing the skeletons' provenance accurately. A racial taxonomy would be impossible without confidence that a skull was, in fact, from a Seminole and not, for example, Peruvian (the origin of many of Morton's skulls).

Other bodily characteristics did not face these limitations. Some white phrenologists and physiognomists, for example, used insights gleaned from their evaluations of head and facial shape to justify racial hierarchy.[20] Skin color was even more commonly linked to racial identity. However, as racial evidence, both the shape of the head and *especially* the color of the skin had two problems that, by the mid-nineteenth century, felt dire to white scientists and laypeople alike. For one, skin color could not be easily simplified into a binary or ternary (nor could head shape, for that matter, which instead elicited broad conclusions about individual faces from phrenologists).[21] Moreover, as the *Morrison* case showed so starkly, skin color did not map consistently onto racial identity; even people with very pale skin could be legally enslaved if they had African ancestry. Hair offered solutions to both of these problems.

Although scientists since Linnaeus often listed skin color as one piece of their racial identification puzzle, hair itself was rarely the subject of in-depth and sustained scientific or medical inquiry before the nineteenth century. However, a modest boom in scientific writing about hair began to emerge in the United States in the 1830s. With names like *Treatise on the Human Hair; A Treatise on the Human Hair;* and *Treatise on the Structure, Color, and Preservation of the Human Hair*, these books and pamphlets varied nearly as little in their content as they did in their titles. Each text described the physical structure of hair strands; explored the functions hair provided for the body; outlined variations in hair color, texture, and length; discussed hair diseases and disorders; and surveyed hair practices across different cultures.[22] The backbone of every text, moreover, was its claim of privileged knowledge: the assertion that an accurate understanding of hair could only come from an evidence-based scientific investigation performed by an expert.

Authors from a range of backgrounds—and with a range of medical, scientific, or vocational credentials—claimed this expertise for themselves as they produced scientific writing about hair. This writing came in two waves: the first group, published from late 1830s through the 1850s, were written by hair-care professionals, including hairdressers, barbers, and wigmakers, and were almost always intended to advertise a product: a patent medicine for the hair, usually referred to as a *specific*, that would solve every possible malady that could plague a head of hair. For example, one of the earliest known scientific hair texts published in the United States—probably published between 1838 and 1842—was written by a Manhattan hairdresser and wigmaker named Vair Clirehugh, who advertised a product called "Tricopherous" as "the only Effectual Remedy ever discovered to prevent Baldness and Grey Hair, to restore the Hair where it has fallen off, and to eradicate Scurf and Dandriff [*sic*]."[23]

After 1860, trained physicians—increasingly professionalized with the formation of the American Medical Association (AMA)—began contributing to the genre. For example, Dr. C. Henri Leonard, author of *The Hair: Its Growth, Care, Diseases, and Treatment* (1879), was a professor of medical and surgical diseases of women and of clinical gynecology at the Detroit College of Medicine and a member of the AMA. Other authors tried to gain access to the growing prestige of medical training by falsely claiming such titles for themselves: the self-proclaimed "Professor Alexander C. Barry" was actually a wigmaker with no evidence of a doctoral degree; and Bela C. Perry, a Black barber and hairdresser from Massachusetts who wrote at least two hair treatises, referred to himself as a "practical dermatologist" in the preface to his 1865 book *Human Hair, and the Cutaneous Diseases Which Affect It.*[24] Still others had pedigrees that are less possible to corroborate, such as Sarah A. Chevalier, who referred to herself as "Dr. Chevalier, M.D." in her 1868 treatise on hair.[25]

Regardless of whether they were professionally trained physicians or simply pretenders, what this group of authors shared was their appeal to the authority and prestige of science in order to establish their own credibility. Some authors used specialized medical vocabulary or tools to demonstrate their expert knowledge of the human body, such as H. T. Lovet, who wrote in *Treatise on the Human Hair* that he offered "microscopic examinations of the hair (gratis) *daily*, from 2 to 5 P.M." at his office in Manhattan. (Dr. Chevalier, too, offered to meet potential customers for free at her Manhattan office: "Dr. C. can be consulted gratuitously, at No. 1,123 Broadway, where information in regard to the treatment of the Head and Hair will be *clearly explained.*"[26]) For those without their own credentials, drafting on the authority of medical professionals could be just as powerful. Perry, for example, listed by name seventeen "medical gentlemen of high standing" as the references he relied on when he composed his "Scientific Treatise," *A Treatise on the Human Hair, and Its Diseases* (1859); he even dedicated the book to "The Physicians of New Bedford, Mass.," for their "unqualified approval" of the "New System of treatment for Capillary Diseases" that his book proposed.[27] Once established, this scientific credibility became a powerful tool for those authors endeavoring to sell a hair specific. For example, Barry's pamphlet *A Treatise on the Human Hair*—which advertised the most famous nineteenth-century hair specific, Barry's Tricopherous—appealed to readers' scientific interests by describing the process of creating and testing Tricopherous as an "investigation" into the compound's scientific properties. This investigation, he wrote, included running a "course of experiments" with "hundreds" of subjects.[28]

Dr. Chevalier emphasized her stellar reputation among reliable scientific peers to promote her own specific, Dr. S. A. Chevalier's Life for the Hair: "In justice to myself, I may add, that I submit for your perusal the testimony of the best scientific skill, the testimony of persons whose honor is unimpeachable, whose opinions command universal respect, and who would not, on any consideration, compromise their honor by any false recommendations."[29] (An 1878 investigation would find, however, that her specific contained 1 gram of lead per fluid ounce.[30]) Even using the word *specific* was a nod toward a scientific pedigree: contemporary editions of Webster's *American English Dictionary* defined the noun as, "in *medicine*, a remedy that certainly cures a particular disease."[31] In this respect, this group of authors can be considered *scientific* not because they collected data or ran controlled experiments—though a few, like Browne, did—but because they appealed to their readers' desire for empirical (as opposed to spiritual or supernatural) knowledge about the natural world.[32]

Whether they were wigmakers or trained physicians, this group of authors attributed their scientific conclusions to their knowledge of one particular feature: the physical structure of individual strands of human hair. In this way, this motley crew of hair science writers mirrored shifting norms in the medical profession more broadly: as historian Michael Sappol has demonstrated, by the time Vair Clirehugh wrote his treatise on the hair, "the connection between anatomical expertise and healing authority had been firmly established throughout the spectrum of medical belief, among both the laity and professionals."[33] Clirehugh—who, like many of his peers, offered a specific for sale—asserted in the preface that his *Treatise* was more accurate and useful than his competitors' because "not one of the many who pretend to the discovery of a specific for the growth of the human hair, has ever studied, or in fact possesses any knowledge either of its organization or structure." For this reason, he argued, "it may be reasonably inferred, that little or no faith is to be placed in the use of any of these Oils, Balms, Compositions, &c., which are foisted upon the public by ignorant empirics."[34]

Similarly, the first two images in Thomas Bogue's *Treatise on the Structure, Color, and Preservation of the Human Hair* (1841) were prints of "an exact representation" of human hairs and their roots, as "viewed from a solar microscope."[35] This passage by Dr. Seth Pancoast—whose book *The Ladies' Medical Guide* (1875) contained two lengthy chapters on the hair—is typical of the genre in the way it explains, in almost excruciating detail, the structure of a strand of hair:

> Hair consists of a *shaft*, covered or enveloped by a distinct structure, called the *corticle* substance, and may be compared to the outer bark

of a tree. . . . The root of hair is first developed. It consists of two parts, *sheath* and *bulb*. The bulb is two or three times the diameter of the hair, and consists of granular cells. The cells form at the bottom of this follicle and gradually enlarge as they mount in the soft bulb, which owes its enlargement to the increase in the size of the cells. (*Fig.* 81.). The color of the hair is also developed in the bulb, which is diffused with the hair cells giving it color. . . . The shaft is usually divided into the corticle, medullary, and fibrous portions. The corticle, as before remarked, consists of a layer of cells like the tiles upon the roof of a house. The fibrous portion consists of the aggregation of cells as they are formed in the bulb. It is colored with pigment, in young and healthy hairs. The medullary canal will be found in the centre of the hair, (*Fig.* 81, e.) as is generally filled with coloring matter. In old and grey hairs the canal is nearly empty.[36]

These descriptions managed to do two things at once: they used extensive technical language to establish the authors' credentials, while also incorporating metaphors and explanations designed to make the discussion legible to ordinary readers. For example, Dr. Pancoast compared layered cells to "the tiles upon the roof of a house" and hair's corticole substance to "the outer bark of a tree."[37] Some authors were explicit about their desire to make this scientific information broadly accessible. As Bogue wrote, "My object also has been to produce a work, in some degree instructive to the scholar and man of taste, and also interesting to general readers."[38] Although microscopy was not a new technology, during the 1830s and 1840s scientists made enormous advancements in microscopic instrumentation and methodology, which conferred a new authority on microscopic images.[39] Publications like Bogue's *Treatise* participated in the mass dissemination of these microscopic images to the public while retaining the *use* of microscopy for experts alone.

Lengthy descriptions of hair's physical structure at the microscopic level were not, however, included merely for the sake of intellectual or anatomical enrichment. Physical structure also became the basis for hair scientists' claims about racial identity—the quality that they, like the broader racial scientific community, believed to be the body's most significant category of difference. For example, one 1872 encyclopedia's entry for *hair* wrote blithely that the differences in human hair "depending on situation, age, and sex, are so obvious that we shall pass them over without notice"—and then proceeded to devote a lengthy paragraph to explaining "the most important differences dependent on race."[40] In their books and pamphlets, scientific writers used hair to explain and naturalize racial difference. Some authors focused on racial differences evident in hair's thickness, volume, and texture. For example, Bogue wrote in 1841 that "the hair presents well marked varieties in the different races of men," contrasting "the short woolly knots on the head of the Negro" with "the coarse, straight and thin hair of a Mongolian, together with their beardless faces" and "the ample growth of fine and undulated locks, and the full beard which so gracefully adorn the head and face of the Caucasian race."[41] Others found racial fault lines in hair color, such as Dr. Pancoast, who posited that "it would seem that race determines the color of the hair."[42]

However, when he tried to divide the globe along latitudinal lines according to hair color—a schema that anticipated Madison Grant's famous three-part geographic racial hierarchy by a few decades—Pancoast discovered that his system had too many exceptions to actually function as a taxonomy. He began with a confident description of his taxonomy, declaring that "the fair-haired inhabitants of the earth are found north of the parallel of 48°" and "between the parallels of 48° and 45° . . . are found the genuine dark-haired races." Yet exceptions surfaced immediately: "The exceptions to this gradation," he admitted, "are the dark tribes still lingering in England, the Celtic majority of the Irish, while even the modern Normans are included among the black-haired"; furthermore, Venice, "which is in a southern latitude, has always been famed for the golden beauty of the hair of the people, beloved so of Titian and his school."[43] Hair color, Pancoast realized, was simply too varied to make broad geographic generalizations.

Bogue, Pancoast, and others discovered another problem when they tried to taxonomize the human population according to hair color or appearance: human intervention. It was simply too easy for people to braid, straighten, or artificially color their hair—all of which threatened to complicate and thus compromise the scientific reliability of those features. Moreover, crucially, evaluations of the hair that relied on the eye alone were, to nineteenth-century scientists, not sufficiently reliable or rigorous.[44] However, hair had another physical feature that not only lay beyond the scope of human intervention, but that offered solutions to the problems similar taxonomies of skin color faced, too: the lateral shape and dimensions of a cross-sectioned strand of hair. It was this feature that obsessed Peter Browne.

Peter A. Browne's Trichology

Peter Arrell Browne (1782–1860) was a white lawyer and amateur scientist from Philadelphia. Although he is not a well-known figure today, during his lifetime Browne was a well-regarded intellectual, one of the most influential American ethnologists, and the most famous practitioner of trichology in the United States.[45] He was an elected member of many learned societies, including the Pennsylvania Society for the Encouragement of Manufactures and the Useful Arts (for which he served as Secretary), the Academy of Natural Sciences in Philadelphia, and the Franklin Institute, which was founded in Philadelphia in 1824 to promote science, technology, invention, and engineering. (Browne's hometown of Philadelphia was, indeed, a hub of science—and especially racial science—in the middle of the nineteenth century.) He wrote for distinguished publications like *Transactions of the American Philosophical Society*, the journal of the United States' first learned society that counted George Washington, Benjamin Franklin, and physician Benjamin Rush among its members. His research was also cited in scientific, professional, and literary periodicals published in both the North and South, such as the *United States Magazine and Democratic Review* and *Southern Quarterly Review*.[46] In 1834, for example, the inaugural issue of the *Southern Literary Messenger*—the most important literary periodical published in the South during the nineteenth century—listed Browne as one of the six endorsements it had received from "eminent literary men."[47]

Browne began his career as a lawyer and practiced law locally in Philadelphia.[48] However, as he grew older, Browne's interests increasingly gravitated away from the law and toward the sciences, even as he continued to be credited in his numerous publications as "Peter A. Browne, Esq." Moreover, his reputation as an expert worth listening to was rooted largely in his scientific work; for example, in its inaugural issue the *Southern Literary Messenger*'s editor praised Browne as "an able proficient in the science," boasting that the magazine's "scientific readers" would enjoy his "communications."[49] As his reputation grew, Browne—the scientist, not the lawyer—was frequently called as an expert witness in court cases, controversies, and mysteries related to ambiguous identity: was Warder Cresson, the US diplomat to Jerusalem, actually suffering from insanity as his wife and son claimed, or he had just converted to Judaism? Was Eleazar Williams actually the "Lost Dauphin" from France and thus the heir to the French throne?

Were the bodies found inside huge earthen burial mounds actually ancient relatives of Native Americans? (According to Browne, the answers were no, no, and yes, respectively.)[50] Browne even boasted to the jury in Cresson's case that he was frequently called to the South to serve as an expert witness in determining the race of potential witnesses. Because many Southern states forbid Black people from testifying against white people in court, an accurate identification of a witness's race could be critical in shaping a case's outcome.[51]

Browne was also a prolific writer. Over the course of his career, he published more than thirty articles, pamphlets, and books—a wide range of publications that illustrate his broad interest in many branches of human and natural sciences. In addition to formal legal publications, Browne wrote about hydrology, steam engines, minerals, corn, veterinarians, meteors, geology, weights and measures, the Oregon territory, animal hibernation, anti-Catholicism, and federal citizenship laws. Indeed, his interest in human hair was likely an outgrowth of his prior research on agriculture, especially animal husbandry; his first publication about hair was actually not about humans at all, but armadillos, and he routinely analogized back and forth between humans and animals in his writing.[52] In the late 1840s, however, the diversity of his early pursuits narrowed in on the subject that would preoccupy the remainder of his career: hair. With very few exceptions, every publication Browne wrote from 1848 until his death in 1860 focused on hair, wool, and other types of what he referred to as "tegumentary appendages."[53]

Browne's career as a published trichology expert began with his 1848 book *Trichographia Mammalium.* Browne coauthored this short twenty-page book with Philadelphia physician and archaeologist Montroville W. Dickeson. (Henceforth Browne labored on his hair work alone: *Trichographia Mammalium* is the only one of his extant hair studies to have a coauthor.[54]) In an advertisement printed on the book's final page, Browne and Dickeson announced that *Trichographia Mammalium* was but the first publication of many: the authors planned—but, available evidence suggests, never executed—a major hair series that readers could purchase by subscription for 62½ cents per issue. Wearing their legal and medical credentials proudly, the authors declared their intention to revolutionize this corner of natural history:

> The reader may, perhaps, be inclined to imagine that these tegumentary appendages have already undergone severe scrutiny, and that their

organic structure has been completely displayed; but we assure him that much remains yet to be developed. Having discovered that a great deal that has been published is incorrect, we have commenced our labours with the firm determination to take nothing for granted, but to examine each hair, and to put down nothing of which we are not morally certain. . . . To the scientific natural historian we offer no apology for entering upon his arena, determined, if possible, to make ourselves welcome guests.[55]

For the next few years, Browne pursued this project with his usual level of energetic productivity: He delivered papers about his hair research for scientific organizations such as the American Ethnological Society and American Association for the Advancement of Society, and published articles on Rocky Mountain goats' wool and swine's bristle in the farmers' magazine *The Plough, the Loom, and the Anvil*.[56] Browne's hair research culminated five years after it began with his magnum opus, *Trichologia Mammalium* (1853). This book, he wrote, "brought our examinations [of hair] to a tolerably successful termination."[57] *Trichologia Mammalium* is a tome indeed: Its nine chapters stretch nearly two hundred pages and are filled with dozens of data tables, illustrated plates, citations to other scientists, and exhaustive descriptions of every imaginable facet and feature of the hair, horns, whiskers, and wool of creatures from across the animal kingdom.

Whereas in 1848 Browne anticipated that his readers might assume a vast preexisting literature on hair, by the time he wrote *Trichologia Mammalium* he had realized that the opposite was true: readers were skeptical that the subject was worth studying at all.[58] Browne nevertheless maintained that his research was justified. As he wrote in the book's preface, "If the Deity had not deemed it beneath *His* dignity to *create* an object, surely it would be presumptive in man to consider it too insignificant for *his* study. Then let no one marvel that we have devoted so much time to ascertain the organization, properties and uses of hair and wool. To the unreflecting, this department of knowledge may, at first view, appear to be trifling; but, with each successive advance, it will acquire more importance."[59] Despite this appeal to the reader's spiritual beliefs, Browne did not rely on religious conviction to legitimize the area of research that would define his career. Instead, he sought scientific legitimacy in two ways: through his use of technology and data; and through the implication that his results could be reproduced by other scientists—a key tenet of the scientific method. Indeed, he ended the preface of *Trichologia Mammalium* with reference not to God but to machines: "We have made use of none but superior instruments, and some of these are entirely new—either in themselves or their application to this study."[60]

Browne's Scientific Method

Browne's trichological writing represented the findings of his own scientific inquiry into hair's physical properties. One way he sought to establish the legitimacy of this research—and, implicitly, his own legitimacy as a scientist, despite his degree in law—was by emphasizing his use of scientific instruments. This strategy is evident starting with Browne's first publication on hair, which included a reference to technology in its full title: *Trichographia Mammalium; or, Descriptions and Drawings of the Hairs of the Mammalia, Made with the Aid of the Microscope*.[61] The book's title page also included a quote from a book on microscopes by Dr. Louis Mandl, one of the first people to use the device in anatomical research. Translated into English, the quote read, "The microscope, this powerful means of investigation without the help of which we can not speak of any body, without feeling justified timidity."[62] Browne continued to reference the microscopic nature of his research in later publications. However, what distinguished his hair research from that of his contemporaries were the two new instruments designed specifically for hair research that he had added to his toolkit by 1852: the *discotome*, which cut transverse sections of individual hair strands; and the *trichometer*, which measured hair's "Ductility, Elasticity and Tenacity"—its pliability, how able it was to return to its original shape after being stretched, and its resistance to breakage, respectively. These three measurements, along with flexibility, constituted what Browne called the "*essential properties*" of hair.[63]

Browne designed the trichometer himself, and probably the discotome, too. In an 1851 letter to Samuel Morton, who was then president of Philadelphia's Academy of Natural Sciences, Browne summarized "the discoveries I have made, by means of the Microscope . . . & trichometer"—adding, in the margin, that the trichomter was "an instrument invented by myself to determine the ductility elasticity & tenacity of the filaments."[64] One year later, in the first published reference to the discotome, Browne implied that it was his original design, writing, "the forms or shapes of pile [i.e., hair] are seen best, and are measured with the greatest accuracy in these transverse sections, which we cut with an instrument called by us a *Discotome* (from *discos*, a disk; and *tenuo*, to cut)."[65]

Browne's use of the trichometer and the discotome were crucial to his research—and, likely, to the authority it offered to the scientists, lawyers, and others who relied on his work. Browne believed that these tools offered a corrective to what he saw as the problems of previous research, in which "hairs have been misrepresented in regard to shape" because of "the way they have hitherto been examined. A hair is placed horizontally between two pieces of glass and examined under a microscope; but it is exceedingly difficult, if not impossible, to determine whether it is cylindrical or oval." By contrast, Browne assured his readers, "We have a machine with which we cut transverse sections or disks of pile, thereby completely obviating the difficulty." Browne boasted that he "made use of none but superior instruments," some of which were "entirely new—either in themselves or their application to this study."[66] Browne believed that his use of technology—the microscope, the trichometer, and especially the discotome—made his hair research superior to that which had come before. In a field of study that, Browne acknowledged, many people might disregard, careful use of the most up-to-date technology provided a sense of scientific legitimacy.

In addition to employing specialized tools, Browne also sought to establish his credibility by using the scientific method: collecting hundreds of hair samples, conducting controlled experiments on those specimens, analyzing the results, and then drawing conclusions from those results. Throughout his career as a trichology expert, Browne amassed a vast personal collection of hair specimens—almost certainly the largest collection of hair in the world at the time.[67] Browne's collection included both hair samples he had obtained himself and those he received as donations from fellow scientifically inclined citizens, each one mounted on a piece of custom-printed paper that was decorated with an ornate border and titled, "P. A. Browne's Collection of Pile."[68] For example, after learning about an eight-year-old boy in Washington, DC, who had premature pubic hair, Browne "wrote for a specimen, and the [boy's] Doctor kindly sent me a lock, accompanied by one of the boy's head."[69] Indeed, Browne was particularly interested in hair from extraordinary bodies, which is likely why his collection included hair from Julia Pastrana, the hairy woman discussed in chapter 2.[70] In an advertisement on the last page of *Trichographia Mammalium*, Browne and Dickeson called on the public to send them "specimens of human hair"— just as Morton had done with skulls—so that they could properly study and understand these objects in their full range and diversity: "if ancient, from mummies; if recent, from foreigners, or our own Indians, either pure, or crossed by whites or negroes; hairs that have been produced in unusual places, or have been developed under peculiar circumstances; hairs of Albinos, idiots, lunatics, fœtal monsters, or of persons laboring under diseases of the hair or diseases of the skin likely to affect the hair."[71] The twelve-volume collection that resulted comprised hundreds of hair samples from across the globe—eight volumes of human hair, and four volumes of fur, hair, and wool from animals like monkeys, dogs, squirrels, bears, and sheep.

Contained within Browne's eight volumes of human hair was a lock of hair from each president of the United States, from George Washington to Zachary Taylor, often sent by members of the former presidents' immediate families.[72] These presidential hair samples differed from the sterile microscopy slide that might be expected of a scientific specimen. Aesthetically, they shared many features in common with the locks of hair preserved in hair albums and baby books—objects that many nineteenth-century Americans created and cherished as testaments to relationships of love, friendship, and family.[73] In George Washington's sample, for example, the lock is tied with a blue ribbon, mounted below a print of Washington's portrait (and above four lines of poetry about his death), and surrounded by an ornate gold and blue border (see fig. 3.1)—a more elaborate and decorative backdrop than even the custom-printed paper he used for much of his collection. Browne's sample of John Adams's hair was mounted in a similar fashion: the lock of hair tied with blue ribbon, a print of Adams's portrait, and a handwritten notation: "His Excellency. John Adams. President of the U.S."[74] Despite the reverent manner in which Browne preserved these particular presidential hair samples, they, too, became raw material for his investigations.

After amassing such a large collection of hair samples from humans and animals alike, Browne used these samples as the scientific media on which he conducted precise and elaborate experiments. His texts are peppered with minute, detailed measurements of data points from this experimentation, such as hair strands' size, weight, tensile strength, and elasticity. For example, in *Trichologia Mammalium* Browne included a data table with measurements

3.1 Peter Browne's hair sample from George Washington. The clippings that accompany the hair are an engraved copy of Gilbert Stuart's portrait (see fig. 1.2) and a short poem: "Fame spread her wings and with her trumpet blew, / Great WASHINGTON is come, what praise is due— / What titles shall he have? She paus'd and said, / Not one—his *name alone* strikes every title dead." The inclusion of the portrait may have been intended to convey physiognomic evidence that would complement the meaning revealed by the strands of hair; however, physiognomic portraits were usually taken in profile, not in the three-quarter view, so its function may have been more aesthetic than scientific.

CREDIT: Photograph of George Washington's hair from the collections of the Academy of Natural Sciences of Drexel University by Rosamond Purcell, first published in *Specimens of Hair: The Curious Collection of Peter A. Browne* by Robert M. Peck, published by Blast Books, used with permission.

of the "ductility, elasticity, and tenacity" of twenty-eight hair samples from different kinds of mammals. The first ten entries read:

> Hair of the head of a lady, which had laid 32 years in a grave,
> Hair of the Sloth,
> Mummy hair, from Thebes,
> Ancient hair, from Pisco, Peru,
>   "   "   "   Mexico,
> President Madison's, (fallen out,)
> Hair from the stomach of a Ruminant,
> President Jackson's, (cut after death,)
> Hair of a compound Hybrid, (Hilton,)
> Hair of the Hon. Jno. Sergeant.[75]

As this table demonstrates, Browne frequently fused discussions of humans and nonhuman animals so completely that it seems as though he saw no distinction between them. Unlike the ordinary people who collected hair from friends and family during the nineteenth century—who revered each lock or braid as a unique synecdoche for a beloved individual—Browne treated his experimental samples as interchangeable scientific media, flattening the differences between Andrew Jackson and an anonymous sloth.

In addition to conducting experiments on individual hair strands, Browne also employed more descriptive research methods. In *Trichologia Mammalium*, the aforementioned numerical data sets were accompanied by detailed descriptions of skulls from Browne's collection. These descriptions included a specialized and technical vocabulary that was intended to signal Browne's scientific credentials to his readers. For example, the "*Examination and Description of hair and a portion of scalp from the skull of a young American Indian, supposed to be a female of about ten years old*" began with "General Appearance":

> Of the scalp, that of old tanned sheep-skin. The hair has a dead, dry appearance. Length, (natural,) about 2 inches; shape, cylindrical; diameter, 1/364 of an inch; color, dark brown; no lustre; direction, straight; inclination, at an acute angle with the epidermis; ductility, with 370 grains one inch stretched 3/90 of an inch; elasticity, entire; tenacity, broke with 520 grains; fracture, the fibres drawn out of the cortex; button [bulb], when free, spindle-shaped, and split at the

posterior extremity; sheath, none; follicle, none; the posterior termination of the hair in the scalp, club-shaped and black; length, 1/212;
diameter, 1/364; while the diameter of the shaft is 1/500 of an inch;
shaft, brown color; no lustre; colored matter, apparently in the cortex,
in lines; intermediate fibres, white; diameter of one, 1/1572 of an inch;
apex, mostly pointed; some few abrupt; no furcations; disk, of one
uniform color.[76]

Browne's use of the scientific method and his transparency about his data
illustrate how seriously he took his hair research and the significance he attributed to his findings. At the same time, they also demonstrate how desperately he sought the legitimacy and respectability of scientific research.

Browne did not, however, confine himself to simply describing the strands
in his collection and their physical properties. The reason for amassing all
these measurements—from the precise weight in grams of a hair from a
Choctaw to the ductility of a grizzly bear's hair to 1/100th of an inch—was
that Browne believed trichology had the power to reveal truths about mammals that were otherwise difficult (or even impossible) to ascertain. Hair,
Browne argued, provided irrefutable evidence by which species both human
and nonhuman could be sorted, classified, and named—and placed in hierarchical relation to each other.

Classifying *Hair* and *Wool*

One classification question that preoccupied Browne was an issue of hair
terminology: whether the word *hair* or *wool* was the correct scientific term
to classify the hair of African-descended people. Browne was far from the
first person to engage in this debate. The word *wool* was not even new to
the mid-nineteenth century; European-descended and African-descended
people alike had long used *wool* when describing Afro-textured hair. For
example, some advertisements for enslaved runaways used *wool* or *woolly* to
describe the enslaved people's hair, such as a 1776 ad from Pennsylvania for
a twenty-year-old woman named Sarah, who "had remarkable long wool
on her head for a Negro."[77] At the same time, *wool* and African ancestry
were not necessarily synonymous in the eighteenth and early nineteenth
centuries; the first editions of Webster's dictionary, for example, did not
include any reference to African ancestry in its definition for *wool*, which
read simply, "short, thick hair."[78]

However, by the mid-nineteenth century, *wool* had become to many white Americans a shorthand for African ancestry. For example, John Campbell, an Irish immigrant and book publisher from Philadelphia, conflated *wool* and Black identity repeatedly in his book *Negro-Mania* (1851), a nearly six-hundred-page refutation of what he decried as "the falsely assumed equality of the various races of men." "Negroes," he wrote, were "men with woolly heads, flat noses, thick and protruding lips."[79] Later, he sneered at claims of Black intellectual potential through a series of rhetorical questions that reveled in the supposed historical absence of Black leaders and thinkers:

> What woolly-headed Homers, Virgils, Dantes, Molieres, or Shakspeares ever inscribed their names upon the pillar of fame, by the numbers of immortal song? . . . What woolly-headed Xenophons, Tacituses, Gibbons, Voltaires, Humes and Bancrofts. . . . What woolly-headed Epaminondases, Cæsars, Alexanders, Washingtons, Napoleons and Wellingstons. . . . What woolly-headed Solons, or Numas, or Alfreds, or Jeffersons. . . . What woolly-headed Demostheneses, or Ciceros, or Mirabeaus, or Sheridans, or Calhouns, or Bentons, or Clays. . . . What woolly-headed Euclids, or Archimedeses, or Laplaces, or Gallileos, or Herschels, or Newtons. . . . What woolly-headed Watses, Arkwrights, or Fultons. . . . What woolly-headed Columbuses, or Hudsons, or Drakes. . . . In fine, have the woolly-headed races of men ever produced one, even only one man famous as either a lawgiver, statesman, poet, priest, painter, historian, orator, architect, musician, soldier, sailor, engineer, navigator, astronomer, linguist, mathematician, anatomist, chemist, physician, naturalist, or philosopher[?][80]

For Campbell, *woolly-headed* was so synonymous with *African* that he felt no need to include the latter word at all. Indeed, by the nineteenth century *wool* was so definitional to white Americans' perceptions of African identity that it could even be used as metaphor. In 1860, Mormon apostle Wilford Woodruff wrote in his diary that, although the Mormon Church had thought about trying to get a charter from the Masons' Grand Lodge in England (in an effort to challenge the perceived power of Masons in the United States), such a move would require too much "ming[ling] with our enemies to the injury of this people"—or, as Woodruff put it, be like "mix[ing] hair and wool."[81]

In these examples, *wool* was not a scientific word; it was merely an adjective useful to describe the hair of some people of African heritage. In some cases, *wool* was value-neutral, too, devoid of judgment about the caliber, quality, or meaning of the hair in question. Yet in other settings, *wool* carried a clear pejorative tint; *wool* was the less beautiful, more bestial, and therefore fundamentally inferior version of hair—a logic that illustrates the racialized power of beauty discussed in chapter 1. An 1854 article in the *Southern Quarterly Review*, the most ardently pro-slavery publication of the antebellum South, described Africans' hair as *wool* and *wooly* in an article about the "wretched condition" of "that peculiar people."[82] Combining portraits of specific communities with generalizations about the entire African continent, the article conflated assessments of beauty, intellect, and civilization as it reinforced a degraded and uncivilized portrait of African people; in one passage, for example, the author claimed that "blood, as wine with us, is their favourite and most honoured drink."[83] In the Congo, the article announced, people had "thick lips, flat nose, [and] woolly hair," a combination of features that "deny to them all beauty, and suggest little hope of the exercise of intellectual energy or further development."[84] In the middle of a detailed discussion about African language and polygamy practices, a single non sequitur captured the article's contention that the African continent was an inherently and irredeemably backward place: "In this country the men have *wool* and the sheep *hair*."[85]

At the same time *wool* became synonymous with African descent, the linguistic distinction between *hair* and *wool* also increasingly became the subject of scientific inquiry. In scientific contexts, however, *wool* was no longer merely a descriptive term. Instead, starting in the 1850s, writers with varying professional credentials started to specify and define the differences between *hair* and *wool* along scientific lines, using scientific terminology, methods, and tools to do so. Browne's research was central to this process. As the era's most influential and deeply studied scientific hair expert, his work lent scientific credibility to the claim that African-descended people grew wool, not hair, on their heads. Even nonscientific publications began to cite Browne's trichological research when they referred to Black people's hair as *wool*. For example, a lengthy article in the *Southern Quarterly Review* from October 1854 evaluated five recent publications that argued for a long history of racial difference using linguistic, historical, and scientific evidence. Although Browne's publications were not among those reviewed, he was nevertheless present in a key way: when the author described Black people's hair as "a true *wool*, cospidate [*sic*], [which means] having a multitude of projecting points, so that it can be and has been, *felted*," and specified that "in shape it is eccentrically elliptical, the diameters being respectively about 1-312 and 1-970 of an inch, while the hair of the European is oval (about 1-273 by 1-364) and that of the American Indian cylindrical in shape"—it was Browne's hair strand shape data cited in the footnote.[86]

Browne, had, indeed, published a detailed taxonomy to distinguish between *hair* and *wool* four years earlier in *The Classification of Mankind*:

> 1st. Hair is, in shape, either cylindrical or oval; but wool is eccentrically elliptical or flat; and the covering of the negro's head is eccentrically elliptical or flat.
>
> 2d. The direction of hair is either straight, flowing or curled; but wool is crisped or frizzled, and sometimes spirally twisted; and the covering of the negro's head is crisped or frizzled, and sometimes spirally twisted.
>
> 3d. Hair issues out of the epidermis at an acute angle, but wool emerges at a right angle; and the covering of a negro's head issues out of the epidermis at a right angle.[87]

Crucially, moreover, Browne was intent on drawing explicit connections between the wool grown by animals and what he referred to as "human wool." In the eleventh volume of his hair collection—a volume otherwise devoted to sheep—Browne included four human hair samples and instructed the future user of the volume that "these Specimens should be studied before those of Sheep of different countries are examined." The specimens in question were mounted on two pages: on the first page, two long locks of dark brown hair, which stretched nearly the full length of the page, were labeled "Straight, lank, cylindrical hair" and "Curling oval hair," respectively. On the second page, two piles of tight curls carried very different labels: "Coarse African *human wool* from a negro's head born in Africa" and "Fine, African *human wool* from the Coast of Africa."[88]

By the 1850s, Browne had become the go-to reference for scientific information about human hair—*especially* hair's capacity to reveal racial truths. By calling explicit attention to what he saw as similarities between sheep's wool and the hair grown by African-descended people, Browne was not just drawing racial lines—he was muddling the boundary between animals and humans.

Browne's "Three Species of Mankind"

One of the most revealing sentences in Browne's extensive bibliography opens the third chapter of *Trichologia Mammalium*. Under the subheader "Of a Perfect Hair," Browne wrote that Dr. Burkard Eble, a German physician, was "of opinion that the most perfect *hair* is the *whisker* of some of the lower animals, such as the seal, the lion, the rabbit, &c.; but we (considering these whiskers as organs of touch) place the hair of the scalp of the white man, as regards perfection, at the head of the list of piles."[89] After considering the entirety of the animal kingdom, Browne had nominated white men's hair as the most perfect specimen to ever exist. He provided no explanation for why white men's hair was perfect or what qualities comprised its perfection; after this opening sentence, the chapter turned its attention to outlining the characteristics of human hair without returning to the subject of perfection again. Though seemingly out of place, this single sentence betrays precisely the underlying motive of Browne's years-long inquiry into the science of hair. Browne claimed that his experiments and investigations were objective and his arguments arose from the natural conclusion to be drawn from the results. But there was, in fact, nothing inevitable or evidence-based about his claims. Instead, Browne's research presupposed a racial hierarchy—a hierarchy that had long existed in the United States, but one that had gained more urgency as antislavery northerners developed an intellectual infrastructure to critique slavery and the slave society so thoroughly entrenched in the American South by the 1840s and 1850s.[90] Like the ethnologists who proclaimed the white supremacy of the beard in the 1850s, Browne had simply leveraged his expertise in the science of hair to participate in a larger discussion of racial hierarchy and racial purity.[91]

The concept for which Browne would become most famous, most respected, and most influential in midcentury racial science was his three-part taxonomy of hair strand shapes. Browne first explained this taxonomy in *The Classification of Mankind* (1850) and elaborated on it in *Trichologia Mammalium* (1853). After measuring the dimensions of every single hair in his collection to 1/100th of an inch using the microscope and discotome,

Browne arranged his findings into a three-part taxonomy of hair strand shapes: Class I, the cylindrical strand, had the shape of a circle (with both diameters being equal) when cut transversely; Class II, the oval strand, had one diameter that was one-third greater than the other; and Class III, the eccentrically elliptical strand, had one diameter that was two-thirds greater than the other (see fig. 3.2). These three classes, Browne argued, corresponded precisely and exactly to three racial categories: Class I hairs came from the group Browne called "American Indians," Class II from white people, and Class III from Black people. These were, according to Browne, "the three species of men." Browne used the word *species* quite deliberately: indeed, in his 1851 letter to Morton, Browne initially referred to these groupings as "classes of man," but then crossed off the word *classes* and wrote *species* in its place.[92]

Browne was confident in the correctness of his tripartite racial taxonomy, writing that, in all his research, he had "never witnessed a single deviation from this law."[93] Yet to posit just three races set Browne apart from many of his racial science contemporaries, most of whom suggested four, five, or more racial categories. For example, Johann Gottfried von Blumenbach—who originated the word *Caucasian*—posited five races: Caucasian, Mongolian,

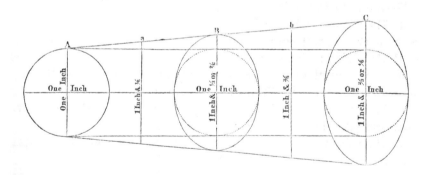

3.2 Peter Browne's hair strand shape classification system. In this figure, published in Browne's book *The Classification of Mankind*, the circle marked "A" represents cylindrical Class I hairs, "B" represents oval Class II hairs, and "C" represents eccentrically elliptical Class III hairs.

CREDIT: Reproduced from P[eter] A. Browne, *The Classification of Mankind, by the Hair and Wool of Their Heads, with The Nomenclature of Human Hybrids*. Philadelphia: J. H. Jones, 1852.

Malay, Ethiopian, and American (the category that Browne instead called "American Indian").[94] Indeed, to arrive at just a three-part classification system, Browne engaged in some creative categorization: he classified Chinese people as American Indians. Although ten of the eleven hair samples listed under Class I came from Indigenous people from North or South America, the eleventh sample came from a Chinese person identified as Tsou Chaoong.[95] Moreover, *Trichologia Mammalium* also included a short section entitled "On Chinese Pile," in which Browne asserted his "determination that this numerous people"—the Chinese—"belong to the cylindrical-haired species." Browne did not comment on the correct categorization for people from other parts of Asia.[96]

Browne came to a monumental conclusion about the result of this research on the shape of hair strands: "The three species of man . . . may be identified by the pile." Browne emphasized the significance of hair strand shape in *Trichologia Mammalium* by repeatedly treating strand shape and racial identity as synonymous—even interchangable. For example, the book's frontispiece depicted three illustrated heads in profile to represent "The Three Species of Mankind" Browne posited in that book. Yet each head was labeled not with its racial category name but with its hair strand shape: "The Cylindrical Piled," "The Oval Piled," and "The Eccentrically-Elliptical Piled" (see fig. 3.3). Similar conflations of race and strand shape appear throughout the book, such as when, about halfway through the text, Browne reminds the reader that "by *white*, we mean the oval-haired species; by *Black*, the eccentrically elliptical-piled species; and by 'Indian,' the cylindrical-haired species."[97] With these claims, Browne was arguing that the *most essential* distinction between these three groups of people could be found not in language, cultural practice, or even other bodily evidence like skin color— but in the shape of each strand of hair, cut with a discotome and viewed under a microscope.

Browne's conviction that hair was the most reliable evidence of racial identity was further cemented by his study of people with albinism. Albinism had long puzzled scientists because it seemed to defy the connection between skin color and racial classification. Linneaus, for example, thought that people with albinism might belong to the subcategory of *Homo sapiens* that he called *Troglodytes* or *Homo nocturnus*: nocturnal humans who lived in caves.[98] James Cowles Prichard, an English physician and ethnologist whom Browne considered one of his main antagonists, asserted in *Researches into*

REPRESENTING THE THREE SPECIES OF MANKIND.

Fig. 61.

THE CYLINDRICAL PILED.

Fig. 61 a.

THE OVAL PILED.

Fig. 61 b.

THE ECCENTRICALLY-ELLIPTICAL PILED.

3.3 Frontispiece to *Trichologia Mammalium*. The frontispiece of Browne's magnum opus paired illustrated portraits rendered in profile (likely to convey physiognomic evidence about each of the three racial categories represented) with an identification of each group by the shape of the strands of hair on their heads.

CREDIT: Reproduced from Peter A. Browne, *Trichologia Mammalium; or, A Treatise on the Organization, Properties, and Uses of Hair and Wool; Together with an Essay upon the Raising and Breeding of Sheep*. Philadelphia: J. H. Jones, 1853.

the Physical History of Man (1813) that "the colour of the skin is always the same with that of the hair," leading him to conclude that people with albinism constituted a separate race of their own.[99]

Unlike his predecessors, Browne was not puzzled at all by the seemingly contradictory corporeal evidence that albinism presented. In an 1850 paper delivered at the American Association for the Advancement of Science's annual conference, Browne sneered at what he saw as Prichard's obvious mistake. Although mathematician John Howard Van Amringe had calculated that no more than "one in a million of the inhabitants of this earth" had albinism, "Dr. Prichard treats them as a *distinct race*," categorizing humans into three groups based on hair color: "He divides the human family into the Melanic, or black-haired race; the Xanthous, or yellow haired; and the Albino, or white-haired."[100] Browne argued that because Prichard had relied merely on one of hair's *visible* characteristics, its color, he had come to the wrong conclusion about racial categorization. Browne, on the other hand, used his trio of machines to *microscopically* examine hair from people with albinism. Browne had four hair samples from people with albinism in his collection, two from people with white parents and two from people with Black parents.[101] After examining these samples and measuring nine characteristics—including shape, color, elasticity, and tenacity—Browne concluded that "there is no ground for treating the Albino as a distinct race, as Dr. Prichard has done." Instead, each person with albinism belonged to the same racial category as their parents: "That specimens No. 1 and 2 [i.e., the people with white parents], by their oval shape and other qualities . . . entitle the individuals upon whom they grew, respectively, to be ranked with the oval haired species of men," and "that specimens No. 3 and 4 [i.e., the people with Black parents], by their eccentrically elliptical shape and other qualities . . . entitle the individuals upon whom they grew, respectively, to be ranked with the eccentrically elliptical haired species or negro."[102] Browne's findings provided powerful evidence for the profound importance of hair's physical structure to the determination of racial identity: even when skin color suggested a person might be white, microscopic evidence in their hair betrayed their Blackness.

Browne argued that his claims about the relationship between hair and race were the obvious conclusions *any* scientist would draw from this hair strand data. However, Browne's racial biases were embedded throughout his process—starting with his data collection. The way he acquired and wrote about that data revealed the racial belief system that permeated and therefore compromised his research.[103] For example, in every one of his publications that included his strand shape taxonomy, all of the hair samples from a white man's head referred to its donor by an honorific, such as "his excellency," "Esq.," "Hon.," or "Count"; the paradigmatic example of oval hair printed in the first edition of *The Classification of Mankind* (1850) was from none other than "his Excellency, General George Washington." These titles conveyed the superiority of the white hair donors relative to their Indigenous and Black counterparts, whose own paradigmatic examples in *Classification* are labeled simply "a full-blood Choctaw Indian" and "a pure negro."[104] Notably, Browne did not include hair from any ordinary white man (or any women at all).

Unlike the honorific titles of the white hair samples, only three of the eleven Indigenous hair samples were even from named individuals; the rest were listed anonymously with titles like "a Choctaw American Indian" or "a mummy found in Mexico," suggesting that Indigenous people were homogenous, interchangeable, and lacking in individual identity. Unlike the Indigenous samples, the two Black hair samples Browne used in this experimentation did come from named individuals. However, Browne acquired both samples via white middlemen whose relationship to the Black men in question was rooted in either slavery or imperialism: Colonel S. B. Davis of Delaware gave Browne a sample of hair from a man he formerly enslaved named Congo Billy, and a Philadelphia professor named C. Meigs gave Browne "the wool of the Bushman Bay [Boy]," who had been brought to the United States "from the Cape of Good Hope by the American Consul, M. Chase."[105]

Despite Browne's evident feelings of racial antipathy, in much of his writing about what he called "the three distinct species of men" Browne did not place the three hair types into a racial hierarchy.[106] Most of his ethnographic peers had no hesitation about drawing such conclusions; for example, Josiah Nott wrote in an 1849 speech that "the same God who had permitted Slavery to exist by His *Word*, had stamped the Negro Race with *permanent inferiority*."[107] Yet at times Browne betrayed his otherwise measured exterior and revealed that he did indeed believe that the oval strands characteristic of white people's hair were inherently superior to the strands grown by Black and Indigenous people.

Although Browne referenced history, art, and poetry to explain why white people's hair was the most perfect type of hair, it was his scientific explanation that was most significant. Browne's microscopic research on hair strands yielded, he wrote, a significant distinction between the physical structure of oval strands from white people and the eccentrically elliptical strands from Black people. (Notably, Browne never mentioned Indigenous people's hair in these discussions of perfection, despite Native Americans representing one of the three racial categories in his tripartite taxonomy. The Black-white binary clearly held greater significance in his mind, and thus in his research.) He first explained this distinction, and its connection to perfection, in an 1849 speech for the American Ethnological Society, which was later published as *The Classification of Mankind*:

> The head of the hair of the white man, besides its cortex and inter-mediate fibres, has a *central canal*, in which this coloring matter, when the hair has any [e.g., before greying occurred in old age], flows; when this hair is *colorless*, the central canal is still found, but it is then *vacant*. But the wool of the negro has *no central canal*; the coloring matter, when present, is disseminated throughout the cortex, or is in the cortex and intermediate fibres. . . . This variation in the disposition of the coloring matter is, as regards classification of pile, a more important feature than at first strikes the mind; for, according to the rules of science, one organ is considered *more perfect* than another, if it employs a greater variety of apparatus in the performance of its functions. Now, *here* we find the hair of the head of the white man possessing an apparatus, viz. a canal for the conveyance of its coloring matter, which, in the wool of the negro, is *entirely wanting*. . . . The inference is irresistible. The hair of the white man is *more perfect* than the hair of the negro[.][108]

It is easy to critique Browne's definition of scientific perfection as illogical. But even the very *factual legitimacy* of his claim—that human hair should have a central canal—was subject to contemporary scrutiny. An undated review of Browne's work from around 1850 criticized his claim that "perfect" human hairs contained a central canal, sneering that Browne "would have saved himself from the laughter of the scientific world by avoiding the re-assertion of the exploded idea that any '*human hair has a central canal.*' The Quarterly Journal of Microscopical Science, Vol. I., p. 136, where M. Morin is immolated for a similar statement, may be profitably consulted by our learned LL. D."[109] Despite these shaky observational foundations,

Browne nevertheless asserted the perfection of white people's hair, and thus the superiority of white people.

Browne's belief in a racial hierarchy that placed white men at its apex were well documented long before he began researching hair. For example, in his 1843 book in support of the United States' acquisition of the Oregon Territory, Browne blithely denigrated Indigenous North Americans as "barbarous nations," claiming that "it appears to be a law of nature, that *civilized* man shall gradually succeed to the *un*civilized."[110] The natural fate of the Indigenous people was to wither away: "As the buffalo retires before the footsteps of civilization, so will the Comanches; leaving behind them, (like Gog and Magog, to whom they have been likened,) nothing but an empty name."[111] Browne also criticized what he believed were the hypocrisies and inconsistencies of American abolitionism—a movement that was very active in his hometown of Philadelphia. In an 1851 review of the kidnapping conviction of Browne's legal client George F. Alberti, who was notorious among Philadelphia abolitionists for kidnapping both runaway enslaved people and free people of color, Browne sneered that "a citizen of Philadelphia is confined in the Eastern Penitentiary . . . for a term of ten years. Had his skin been *black*, considerable sympathy would have been excited in a certain portion of this community; but he is a *white* man, and very few, comparatively, appear to evince an interest in his fate."[112]

Browne also supported federal fugitive slave laws, declaring that "the mistaken notion that colored persons are to be *protected* from [these laws,] . . . when we know the country is overrun with runaway slaves, has been the cause of much evil."[113] (Browne may have been drawing on personal experience with this critique: in 1802, he placed an advertisement in a local newspaper offering a six cents reward for recovery of a child he referred to as "an indented [indentured] black servant boy about eleven years of age named JOHN MORRIS" who had run away from him one week prior. He ended the advertisement with a warning: "All persons are warned against harboring or trusting him."[114]) By the 1850s, Brown viewed abolitionism as an "infection." Foreseeing the political upheaval that division over slavery would cause in the future, he wrote that "ultra abolitionism, . . . if allowed to pass unreduced," might ultimately "end in a dissolution of our glorious Union."[115]

Yet abolitionism was not the threat to the United States that most preoccupied Browne in his trichological texts—it was what he referred to with disdain as *amalgamation:* animals bred across species, and humans of mixed-race ancestry. Browne was obsessed with species purity. He dedicated many pages in *Trichologia Mammalium* to mammals he called "hybrids": "an animal whose parents, respectively, belong to a different *species*." Browne immediately analogized hybridity in animals to humans: "And if we have succeeded in showing that in the human family there are three distinct *species*, it follows that, by the union of any two or more of them, a hybrid will be produced."[116] People with a mixed-race ancestry did not undermine Browne's tripartite classification system: Browne explained that "human hybrids" simply grew many different strands with different shapes, "perfect filaments which resemble that of the one parent, and other perfect filaments which resemble that of the other parent; for example, the progeny of a white and a black will have some oval hairs, and some perfect eccentrically elliptical wool; so the progeny of a white and an Indian will have some perfect oval hairs and some perfect cylindrical hairs." Moreover, he wrote, "one who has in his veins the blood of all these species will generally have in his head pile belonging to all three."[117] Browne's thesis about the simultaneous presence of different strand shapes on a single head of hair even became part of some of his expert testimony. For example, in the case of Eleazar Williams, who claimed to be the long-lost heir to the French throne, Browne examined strands of Williams's hair and announced that "some are oval, some cylindrical—therefore he is a cross of Indian and white—consequently he is not the Dauphin."[118]

Browne believed that mixed breeding weakened mammals because "hybrids" were always weaker and sicker than mammals from a single species. "Mulattoes," Browne argued, were "doomed" to "premature decay and demolition" because they were "*natural deformities*"—perverse variations on the three natural races of mankind.[119] In typical fashion, he analogized easily between humans and animals, claiming that "every practising [*sic*] physician has had occasion to remark how much more mulattoes are liable to scrofulous and phthisical [tuberculosis] diseases, and similar wasting complaints, than either the whites or blacks from whom they are descended; and we have no doubt but that a similar law holds in regard to Sheep when *species* are amalgamated."[120] The "amalgamation of *species*" even negated God's intelligent design: "Organs would be taken away from animals to whom they are invaluable, and conferred upon others to whom they would be an incumbrance. Propensities, which are the happiness of one species, would be torn from them to be imposed upon another to make them *miserable*."[121]

Browne believed that that the avoidance of such misery—and therefore the pursuit of species purity—was natural. "Among all animals, intelligent and instinctive," he wrote in *Trichologia Mammalium*, "there exists a *natural* abhorrence to the amalgamation of *species*." This "natural disgust planted in the minds of all animals to the mixture of species, seems to have been wisely pre-ordained, in order to *preserve* the purity and beauty of creation. . . . Without such a feeling [of disgust], the law of the harmony of species, throughout the immense varieties of created beings, which now people and beautify the earth, the air and the sea, would be utterly destroyed, and the whole animal commonwealth would be converted into a disgusting assemblage of unsightly monsters!"[122] Browne was confident that all races of humans shared this "natural feeling we have described," too, which was "not only proverbial among all European nations, but is evinced by Africans, in their own country," such as when "the negresses run[s] away in apparent fright and disgust by the sight of a *white* man."[123] Yet he expressed little curiosity about what might have caused the frequency of mixed ancestry he so disdained among the United States' Black population. There were the "rare cases of marriages between a white person and a negro," of which "every one of us must have been witness of the almost universal natural feeling of abhorrence of the community disgraced by such an outrage"—yet Browne seemed to imply that once removed from the African continent, African Americans were more easily able to "overcome . . . this natural abhorrence" that all mammals shared.[124] That Black Americans' mixed heritage was the product of a long history of sexual violence did not factor into his evaluation.

Browne argued that preserving pure species lines in sheep breeding was "the most important direction we have to give—it is the *golden rule*—the primatus principatus"—but why?[125] Why did it matter to Browne if American animals (and American people) were mixed or not? A letter he wrote to fellow Philadelphia attorney William Bradford Reed provides a clue. In this letter, Browne said of American sheep that "if we are to become one of the great wool-growing countries in the world, *we must found a permanent race*, possessing the good qualities of both parents, and not a continuous production of hybrids."[126] Browne saw his scientific research as wholly in service of this goal—the patriotic pursuit of greatness for the United States. Indeed, he chose the same epigraph for many of his books and for the custom paper on which he mounted his hair samples: "Ducit amor patriæ," or, *led by love of country*.[127] Browne believed that a thriving national agricultural economy depended on strong sheep, and strong sheep depended on controlled reproduction among male and female sheep from the same strong lineage. He analogized the same logic to humans, too. Browne's conceptualization of the body politic thus drew a direct line from species purity to national strength: if Americans could definitively identify different types of sheep—and, crucially, different races of people—species (and racial) purity could be preserved; this would make American livestock (and people) stronger, and therefore make the United States stronger, too. The lynchpin was identifying some kind of perfectly reliable evidence; Browne believed that strands of hair offered exactly that.

Hair and the Monogenesis / Polygenesis Debate

In the 1850s, Browne's obsession with species purity became part of a much larger scientific debate, as he increasingly saw the potential for his research to "shed new light" on an old question: "the ethnological problem of the unity of the human species."[128] Evaluating the hundreds of hair samples he had collected from living humans and mummified remains, Browne concluded that human not only belonged to three distinct species, but that each species' "ancestors have been its inhabitants for at least from 2,700 to 3,000 years—probably from the first creation of man."[129]

This claim placed Browne squarely in the middle of the most important debate in American racial science in the first half of the century: monogenesis versus polygenesis.[130] The monogenesis theory argued that all humans descended from a single origin: one Adam and one Eve. Prominent supporters of monogenesis included Charles Darwin, Johann Friedrich Blumenbach, and James Cowles Prichard. By contrast, polygenists believed that each racial group had descended separately since the very beginning of human existence. The polygenesis theory thus posited that rather than there being one *human species*, humans were instead divided into two or more separate species. Its supporters included many major figures in nineteenth-century American racial science, including Louis Agassiz, Samuel George Morton, George R. Gliddon, and Josiah C. Nott.[131] As Agassiz explained during an 1850 gathering of the American Association for the Advancement of Science in Charleston, South Carolina, he believed that "all the races of men . . . constituted one brotherhood" in their shared possession of "all the attributes of humanity," including "moral and intellectual powers, that raise them above the brutes." However, he stressed, "viewed zoologically, the several races of men were well marked and distinct," and "did not originate from a common centre, nor from a single pair."[132] Historian Walter Johnson has called polygenesis "one of the major foundations of much white supremacist and proslavery thought," and it is easy to see why: by denying any shared ancestry between white and Black Americans—between enslaver and the people they enslaved—proslavery rhetoricians and theorists flatly rejected any scientific basis for empathy, let alone equality, between racial groups.[133]

The connection between the monogenesis/polygenesis debate and the slavery debate was not lost on its contemporaries. Nott, one of the most prominent proponents of polygenesis in the United States, titled his 1850 speech on the subject, *An Essay on the Natural History of Mankind, Viewed in Connection with Negro Slavery.* He opened by acknowledging that "these investigations are assuming a peculiar interest in our country, from their connection with certain absorbing political questions now deeply agitating the American people, and shaking the very existence of our Government to its foundations."[134] Northerners, too, saw the political consequences of this scientific debate. In 1850, the New York City–based *United States Magazine and Democratic Review* predicted that "more lances will be broken in the war now raging among the learned on this subject [of monogenesis versus polygenesis], for the next quarter of a century, than at any former time" in part because of "the religious and political convulsions now agitating the civilized world, especially our own land, on the subject of pro and anti-slavery."[135]

However, it was not just its connections to broader debates about slavery that made monogenesis and polygenesis the subject of such popular discussion in the first half of the century. The debate also had the potential to contribute to scientific understandings of human history.[136] Nott acknowledged that, before the nineteenth century, most investigation into the "the Natural History of Mankind" had been theological. More recently, however, scientists had also begun to study this history, particularly since "the more enlightened feel assured that there can be no discrepancies between the Scriptures, properly interpreted, and the well-established truths of science." Among scientists, the key evidence for consideration was, as Nott wrote, "the deep-rooted intellectual and physical differences seen around us, in the White, Red, and Black Races." For this reason, scientific fields that focused on the study of the physical body—including ethnology, physiology, and anatomy—became the centerpiece of scientific investigation into human history.[137]

Polygenists, who became the dominant voice in the American debate over racial origins by the 1850s, focused their research on identifying body parts that they believed to be so distinct (and durably so) in humans from different racial groups that separate origins was the only reasonable conclusion. Scholars typically emphasize the importance of skulls to polygenic arguments, but less well known is that hair was also paramount to this research.[138] For example, in *Types of Mankind* (1854), the great magnum opus of American polygenesis, the authors included hair among the physical features that were especially immutable over centuries, and thus reliable evidence of what the authors called racial "*types*."[139] This is why, when Morton wrote in an 1837 letter that he was in search of "a few *heads* of Egyptian mummies" for use in his research on "the *varieties of the Human Race*," he requested that specimens should have "the hair preserved, if possible."[140] Like Morton, Browne was also very interested in acquiring hair samples from mummies—as he advertised on the back cover of *Trichographia Mammalium*—because of their potential to support his claim about the deep roots of racial division. Three years after placing that advertisement, Browne explained in *The Classification of Mankind* that he included the hair of six South American mummies in Class I alongside more contemporary samples to demonstrate "the antiquity and uniformity of this species of man."[141]

Browne's contemporaries understood the significance of his research because it could "bear directly and importantly on the question of the unity or diversity of the human species."[142] Indeed, the authors of *Types of Mankind* cited Browne's work to support their claim that hair affirmed the accuracy of polygenesis; the passage about hair ended with the footnote, "On the question of hair, consult the microscopic experiments of Mr. Peter A. Browne, in Proceed. Academy Natural Sciences, Philadelphia, Jan. and Feb. 1851; also Ibid. [Browne] in Morton's Notes on Hybridity, second Letter to Editors 'Charleston Med. Jour.,' 1851, p. 6."[143] Browne's entry into the polygenesis conversation coincided with the movement's highpoint: in the 1850s, polygenists dominated both the racial origin debate and the field of ethnology as a whole. Browne remained their most important source for hair evidence until 1860—the year that Browne died and the debate largely died too, as racial scientists turned their attention to pondering the potential consequences of the Civil War and abolition. Yet while he was alive, Browne saw his work as offering not merely *more* evidence in favor of polygenesis— but *the most definitive* evidence uncovered to date.

Trichology, Texture, and Race

When Dr. John Leonard Riddell cited Browne's research in his testimony in *Morrison v. White* in 1859, he summarized Browne's main thesis for the courtroom: if an expert examined a strand of hair from a person's head, the shape of a cross section from that strand definitively proved that person's racial identity. However, when Dr. Riddell *first* introduced Browne's research, he used a telling shorthand for the feature Browne deemed critical: "Peter A. Brown[e,] a distinguished Savant of Philadelphia[,] says that there is peculiar difference in the hair [—] *its texture & c*[—] of a person of African descent from that of a white person."[144] That Riddell conflated the shape of a single strand's cross section with the hair's texture was not a mistake or a misleading interpretation of Browne's research. It was a tell.

The appeal of hair as a marker of racial identity seemed to offer a solution to a problem that concerned many white Americans (including Browne) by the mid-nineteenth century: the problem of racial ambiguity. The social transformations already in process by midcentury—the growth of cities, the impersonality of market capitalism, the bustling crowds in theaters and lecture halls—created new possibilities for disguise and even transformation. As historian Allyson Hobbs has suggested, "racially ambiguous men and women, both free and enslaved, rushed into the openings created by this fluid, anonymous, and rapidly urbanizing world."[145] Despite the weight of racial determination popularly assigned to skin color, light skin could, as Hobbs writes, function "as a cloak" for enslaved people on the run—just like Alexina Morrison.[146] Indeed, the very existence of dozens of racial determination cases like Morrison's demonstrated the gravity of the situation: definitively determining a person's race could be the difference between imprisonment and liberty, or enslavement or freedom.

Browne believed that an accurate evaluation of the racial meanings conveyed by hair required expertise. For hair to correctly index a person's race required specific technologies (the microscope, trichometer, and discotome), specific training (scientific expertise), and specific media (strands of hair)—all of which the ordinary lay person did not have access to. This is why the *Morrison* case had to incorporate testimonies from so many experts. Yet, while ordinary people did not own trichometers or discotomes, they still derived racial meaning from hair's texture. Indeed, throughout the nineteenth century and into the twentieth, and in sources ranging from daily newspapers to sheet music to the court of law, Afro-textured hair was repeatedly treated as synonymous with African ancestry. This conflation of bodily feature and racial identity maintained a remarkable durability for Black and white Americans alike—one that persisted through abolition, Reconstruction, and Jim Crow.

Some sources mentioned kinky hair in concert with other bodily features, as in an 1865 critique of Black equality published on the front page in the Athens, Georgia newspaper *The Southern Watchman*, whose editor sneered that "the different races of man, like different coins at the mint, were stamped with their true value by the Almighty in the beginning." Black people's equality with white people would never occur "until you can take the kinks out of his wool, bleach his skin, change the shape of his head and foot and make his skull thinner."[147] Dark skin and kinky hair, in particular, were often elevated as paired definitional qualities of Blackness. In an inheritance case tried in Alabama in 1854, for example, the court ruled that a "white man, of fair skin" named Gustavus Florey who married a white woman, "also of fair skin," was suffering from insanity because he refused to admit that his son, Edward G. Florey—who had "the peculiar marks of the negro in his person" (he "was of dark skin" with "woolly or kinky hair")—was not his biological son. (The court affirmed that it was a "physiological fact, that a white man cannot be the father of a mulatto child by a white woman." Florey simply could not admit that his wife had had extramarital sex.)[148]

In addition to these examples where hair is just one of many racialized body parts, hair was sometimes elevated above *all* other bodily features as *the* paramount marker of Black identity. For example, in the popular minstrel song "When They Straighten All the Colored People's Hair" (1894), written and performed by the Black musician Gussie L. Davis, Davis explained that the kinkiness of Black people's hair stemmed from the Biblical story of Cain and Abel, singing in the third verse:

> Let me tell you how it happen',
> Cain and Abel got a scrappin',
> And a curse was put on Cain and all his race.
> *Then his hair began to kink, right away*, just only think,
> Then they stamped old Africa upon his face.[149]

In Davis's rendition of this infamous origin story of racial difference, Afro-textured hair becomes *the* original signifier of Black identity—prior to all other bodily differences.

Scientists and lay people alike repeatedly claimed that Afro-textured hair persisted in people of African descent—even if their African ancestry was very distant (what contemporaries might refer to as a large "admixture of white blood"), and *especially* when other bodily signifiers were ambiguous. For example, writing in *The Atlantic* in 1890, racial scientist Nathaniel Shaler explained that "in any large body of American negroes, we find a wide range of hue, some being relatively quite light colored," yet "the other African marks are very strong,—the hair closely kinked."[150] Nearly a half century later, a white interviewer for the Federal Writers' project's interviews with formerly enslaved people reinforced this same logic. Prior to recording interviewee Daniel Taylor's responses, the interviewer included this preface:

> In Uncle Daniel Taylor we find the unusual, fast disappearing type of negro ex-slave (it makes the sentimental white man feel a deep sadness in the passing of these gentle old souls, whose lives have been well spent in serving to the best of their ability). Uncle Dan is a light complected mulatto (octoroon) with a high and broad forehead (a noble brow) devoid of all negroid features, a heavy suit of silk like hair almost free of any kinks, a heavy suit of gray beard (*it is in the short kinky hair next to his throat that the negro stands out most prominently*) [and] a fine moustache which matches the snowy silkiness of his hair upon his head.[151]

Even though Taylor's skin was fair, and even though his head hair and mustache were soft and silky, it was the Afro-textured hair of his beard—nearly hidden from view, underneath his chin—that betrayed his Blackness.

Texture also turns out to be extremely important to the story of Browne's trichology. For all of his repeated proclamations that strand shape, specifically, was the most significant distinguishing features of strands of hair, partway through *Trichologia Mammalium* Browne admitted that strand shape and hair texture were, in fact, the same thing. In a section on "the Direction of Pile," Browne explained that "by direction we mean the course or path which a filament of pile pursues from the point where it pierces the epidermis to its apex"—in short, a hair's texture. There were three kinds of directions, Browne wrote: "the straight and lank," "the flowing or curling," and "the crisped or frizzled, which is generally spirally curled." Browne then explained the "Laws Relating to the Direction of Pile": "1. Hair that is cylindrical must necessarily hang straightly and lankly from the head. 2. Hair that is oval must inevitably flow or curl. 3. Wool that is eccentrically elliptical must always be crisped or frizzled, and sometimes curled."[152] The perfect three-part correspondence between racial group and hair strand shape extended, too, to hair texture. Indeed, Browne wrote, "these laws [of hair texture] being firmly established, we can judge of the *direction* of piles by its *shape*, and of the *shape* of pile by the *direction*"—the two characteristics so intertwined as to become synonymous.[153] Browne was thus saying the quiet part out loud: his entire scientific schema really just came down to texture.

Although Browne would vehemently deny it, it seems very possible that the strand shape evidence gleaned from the discotome and trichometer was probably just recapitulating textual difference. Browne claimed repeatedly that his tools stretched each strand of hair as straight as possible to ensure a perfect 90-degree cut. However, it seems quite plausible that strands of wavy, curly, or Afro-textured hair hair were *not*, in fact, stretched perfectly straight, and thus the slices he cut with the discotome were unintentionally cut on the bias, like scallions sliced with flourish to decorate a meal. Thus, when these tiny slices were viewed under a microscope, the very-straight hair frequent among Indigenous (and Asian) people appeared circular (because it actually *was* cut perpendicularly); the often-wavy hair of European-descended people appeared oval (because it was cut slightly at an angle), and the kinky hair of African-descended people appeared elliptical (because it was cut at an even greater angle).

Ultimately, what Browne was likely doing with individual strands of hair was merely reinforcing—with precision, quantification, and the reliability and trustworthiness of scientific expertise—a more popularly and broadly circulating belief: that, no matter if the skin color or other bodily features were ambiguous, kinky hair was the greatest bodily tell of Black identity. Browne was, in essence, announcing to the American public that, using his tools and expertise, he had confirmed that the differences they perceived visually between Black and white people's hair were accurate at the level of the *individual strand*—the hair's most biological quality of all.

PETER ARRELL BROWNE was, in the 1850s, the American scientific community's go-to expert for understanding the racial truths that hair promised to reveal. Yet the respect and confidence Browne received from his scientific peers did not always translate to the broader lay public, not all of whom were persuaded by his research methods or his conclusions. For example, in an 1854 article about Browne's involvement in the sensational trial of Eleazar Williams, the Richmond, Virginia, newspaper the *Daily Dispatch* ridiculed—in deeply racialized terms—what its editors saw as Browne's creepily rapacious appetite for hair samples. "This highly civilized and polished Philadelphian," the paper scoffed, "nourishes within his breast an appetite for scalps which would have reflected renown upon Red Jacket or Black Hawk. We have no doubt that his apartments are hung round with these tufted trophies of science, bequeathed to him perchance by the unfortunate convicts whom he has defended, and who left him as a last token of affection and gratitude, a lock of their hair."[154] The *Dispatch* contrasted the expert testimony by "four eminent physicians of Philadelphia," described as "learned advocates" and "acute logicians [armed] with the usual weapons of arguments and facts," with Browne, who "does not trouble himself with tedious investigation and comparison of testimony." Alluding to violent conflicts between Indigenous leaders and US Army generals, which white Americans often framed as a clash between barbarism and civility, the *Dispatch* accused Browne of "car[ing] about as much for the jargon of erudition uttered by the other disputants in the case, as Osceola or Billy Bowlegs cared for the rules laid down in [General Winfield] Scott's Infantry Tactics"—which is, to say, not at all.[155] To the *Dispatch*'s editors, Browne was not a scientific expert at all; he was just a blood-thirsty Indian on the hunt for scalps.

To Bela C. Perry, the Black hairdresser and practical dermatologist from Massachusetts, the problem with Browne's work was the speciousness of his hair-based racial classification system, which Perry dismissed as nothing more than a "fanciful theory." Were Browne's system to become widely adopted, Perry warned in 1865, it would cause "the lowering of the status of the *negro* races in the human family, since the hair of the negro more nearly resembles wool than that of the white man." Perry was not particularly worried, however, because "Mr. Browne is not a very sound philosopher."[156] Perry's comments were perceptive, even prescient: despite a small number of scattered attempts by anthropologists to identify racial correlations to hair strand shape in the twentieth and twenty-first centuries, trichological research like Browne's largely died with him.[157] In the decades that followed Browne's 1860 death, racial science raged on, but scientists became far less interested in the questions about racial origins—including monogenesis and polygenesis—that preoccupied Browne. Instead, after 1860 their focus shifted overwhelmingly to racial *futures*, especially the relationship between white and Black Americans in the aftermath of the Civil War and the abolition of slavery.[158] Even Browne's massive collection of hair samples was largely forgotten for over one hundred years. Browne deeded his hair collection to the Academy of Natural Sciences of Philadelphia, and it became part of the museum's collection upon his death. In 1976, when the museum moved to a new location, Browne's collection was almost thrown away. A chance encounter between curator Robert McCracken Peck and "three or four old, scuffed metal boxes, all marked for disposal," which Peck thankfully rescued, is the only reason we know about Browne's collection at all.[159]

What *was* lost to the historical record is the fate of Alexina Morrison—the enslaved woman from Louisiana who surrendered herself to the local jail claiming she was a white woman. After the third jury in *Morrison v. White* ruled in Morrison's favor in 1861, her enslaver James White appealed the case to the state supreme court for a second time. The court agreed to take the case in February 1862, but the Civil War intervened: within two weeks, Union troops had occupied the city of New Orleans, and the Supreme Court of Louisiana shut down. The case was again placed on the Court's docket on April 20, 1865—eleven days after the Confederate General Robert E. Lee surrendered—but it was, once again, postponed multiple times. The case remained on the court's delay docket for over a century, where cases called to trial but not submitted to the court are left in limbo. White died before the Supreme Court of Louisiana agreed to take the case for the second time, leaving his heirs to continue the legal fight. Morrison, however, disappeared completely from the historical record; no one knows what happened to her after 1862, though historian Ariela Gross speculates that "one way or the other, Morrison found her freedom in 1862 or 1863."[160]

Gross's confidence that Morrison found her way to freedom during the Civil War likely reflects Morrison's appearance. With her light skin, blue eyes, and blond hair, it is plausible to assume that Morrison passed as white and disappeared into the anonymity of ordinary American life. Indeed, from the moment she arrived at the Jefferson Parish Jail, William Dennison, the white jailer who received her, immediately perceived Morrison to be white. Dennison quickly became Morrison's primary advocate and protector: he invited her to live with his family in his home while she was awaiting trial, and even brought Morrison to social events frequented by white locals.[161] Dennison believed unwaveringly in Morrison's whiteness, and he believed that her physical appearance testified to this fact. Yet even he, Morrison's greatest champion, admitted that when it came to her hair, Morrison's appearance was unstable.

At Morrison's second trial, Dennison testified that when Morrison first arrived at the jail, "her hair was much darker than it appears now," and "appeared to have been colored to make it darker." Furthermore, her hair "seemed to him as if it had been attempted to be curled with the tongs," particularly since "her hair appeared to be growing straighter ever since."[162] Dennison was not merely relying on his memory of Morrison's initial appearance; in his testimony, Denison revealed that, when Morrison first surrendered herself in 1857, Dennison had cut off a piece of Morrison's hair—a lock of hair he still possessed. White's lawyers prodded Dennison about this lock of hair on cross examination; Dennison insisted that he had cut the lock of hair himself, that he "cut this hair the same day she came there [to the jail]," and that "he did this of his own accord and not at the instance [insistence] of any one."[163] Dennison did not explain what had compelled him to cut some of this young women's hair on the first day they met, and no further mention of the lock of hair appears in the trial transcripts. To preserve a lock of hair was not, itself, unusual in the nineteenth century, but most Americans kept hair from loved ones (or, in Browne's case, for use in scientific experimentation)—not new acquaintances, as Dennison had done.

The extant documents of Morrison's trial provide no additional clarity about Dennison's motivation on that day in 1857 when he first met the young blond runaway. Yet the way he viewed the hair is easier to suppose: like so many of his nineteenth-century contemporaries, Dennison likely saw Morrison embodied synecdochically in the hair shorn from her head. What is significant about this exchange, then, is just how unstable it revealed hair to be, and yet how unimportant this instability was for Dennison's assessment of Morrison's race. Dennison believed Morrison was white when he first met her in 1857, and he believed Morrison was white on the date of his testimony in 1859—even as the hair that grew from her head became lighter and straighter.[164] Dennison's testimony thus reveals an uncomfortable yet unavoidable fact about human hair—the very reason Browne was so insistent that microscopes, not the human eye, was the correct instrument to discern hair's truths: if hair was so trusted to transmit authentic and reliable information about immutable qualities like race, gender, and identity, then it could also be altered to change the very meaning it conveyed.

CHAPTER 4

HAIR FRAUD

THIS BOOK BEGAN WITH A passage translated from a French book of beauty secrets published in 1855—a lengthy taxonomy that outlined precise connections between character traits and specific hairstyles, colors, and textures. In the last four decades of the nineteenth century, more than fifty American newspapers and magazines published this taxonomy with minor tweaks and addendums. This passage, and *especially* its emphatic nationwide circulation across a wide range of popular media—from cheap local newspapers to middle-class magazines sold by subscription—made it clear that nineteenth-century Americans entrusted the hair they observed on a person's head or face to reveal that person's intrinsic characteristics. Yet, after listing a dozen correspondences between hair and character, and declaring that "the very way in which the hair flows is strongly indicative of the ruling passions and inclinations," almost all the newspapers and magazines concluded with a word of caution to their readers—one that seemed to turn the taxonomy on its head. "As long as girls will wear as much false hair as that naturally belonging to them," the warning said, "it would be puerile to attempt to read character or disposition in the fashion and character of the locks displayed."[1]

As the previous three chapters have shown, nineteenth-century Americans from different regions, racial and ethnic groups, and class backgrounds trusted hair to reveal the intrinsic, authentic truth about the person from whose body it grew. The growing emphasis on hair's biology—both its function as an integral part of the body and the reliability of meanings discerned from its biological features, such as strand shape—emerged during the eighteenth century and solidified in the nineteenth. So powerful were narratives of hair's biological meanings—especially as indexes of a person's racial and gender identity—that even certain forms of hairstyling, such as facial hair and head hair length, became naturalized as biologically inevitable. Hair, in many ways and many contexts, marked the boundaries of belonging in nineteenth-century America.

Yet at the same time, hair had one inescapable quality that challenged its reliability: unlike other parts of the body, hair can be easily changed. It can be dyed, cut, shaved, curled, straightened, augmented by a false hairpiece, or covered up entirely by a wig. Not all of hair's attributes were malleable, of course; as chapter 3 explained, Peter Browne focused his search for racial evidence on the shape of individual strands of hair precisely *because* this feature lay beyond human control, its salience accessible only to the expert and his microscope. Unlike strand shape, however, virtually all of hair's other characteristics—its texture, color, length, and abundance— can be changed. To be sure, some Americans believed that the head shape, too, was capable of change: according to some phrenologists, sustained mental cultivation could change the shape of the brain and thus the shape of the head. Since phrenological readings of head shape could be used to reinforce claims of Black inferiority, Black intellectuals and activists were particularly excited about this possibility for head shape change. However, to actually *achieve* head shape change—not just ponder its possibility—was far from easy: it required intense and repeated educational development, likely over many years. Even then, observable change—the kind a stranger could clock quickly—was not guaranteed.[2] Hair, on the other hand, could be changed by anyone, at any time, and without the need for specialized knowledge or tools—often, indeed, using products and techniques that ordinary people had at home or could purchase easily thanks to the nineteenth century's burgeoning consumer market. If hair allowed the public to discern a person's intrinsic self, it also permitted that person to change the way they were perceived with ease. If hair was so trustworthy, what happened, then, when the hair was a fraud?

Hair fraud had, indeed, been happening since the colonial period. Enslaved people, indentured servants, incarcerated people, teenagers, immigrants barred from legal entry, and even white women who wanted to serve in the military had long used alterations to their hairstyles—cutting, shaving, and dyeing their hair, or wearing a wig or false hairpiece—as a fundamental part of their disguises, whether they were trying to escape subjugation or simply go on an adventure. Crafting a convincing hair disguise enabled people in colonial North America and the United States to cross gender lines—even to pass as a different race. Crucially, however, these are not just stories about Black Americans passing as white, as popular conceptions of passing often imply. Rather, these are stories of creative and subversive play with the instability of bodily signifiers for white, Black, Indigenous, Spanish, Chinese, Mexican, and other racial and ethnic identities. In these stories, a convincing disguise was often contingent on getting the hair "right."

In the second half of the nineteenth century, with both hair's reliability and the significance of its biological meanings so firmly entrenched, social and political elites felt like the possibility for hair fraud was more alarming than ever. Hair disguises threatened the very foundation of the culture of hair: the narratives of hair's stability and legibility that many Americans— but especially the middle- and upper-class white Americans who held the most social and political power—trusted so fervently. Crucially, moreover, because hair's biological qualities (including those qualities now naturalized *as* biological, such as the amount of facial hair a man grew on his face) were understood to be particularly powerful indexes of racial and gender identity, hair fraud that crossed boundaries of race or gender posed the greatest social threat. In response to this alarm, American elites—and the political, carceral, and scientific institutions they led—tried to develop new kinds of mechanisms for detecting hair disguises, such as new forms of policing.

Ultimately, both the reality of hair fraud and the anxiety—and regulation—the fear of hair fraud inspired demonstrate the significance of the nineteenth century for the story of hair in American culture. Hair's styling always mattered—from the seventeenth-century Puritan leaders who scorned Christian men with long hair, to the late-nineteenth-century police detectives who saw the donning of a false beard as a sign of criminal intent. Yet once hair's biological qualities began to matter in such a big way in the nineteenth century, the importance of hair as an index of political subjecthood and social belonging—and thus the stakes of its disguise—became greater than ever.

The Art and Technology of Altering Hair

The information and tools required to alter human hair have existed in Europe and in North America for centuries. The Mojave tribe, for example, had long used the sticky black pitch from mesquite tree trunks to concoct a dark hair dye.[3] Nineteenth-century hair-care professionals also routinely cited the ancient origins of their craft. For example, Bela C. Perry explained that the ancient Greeks, Carthaginians, and Romans all purchased "large quantities of human hair" to create wigs, and that "they possessed the art of dyeing hair, and practiced it assiduously."[4] Even the newly professionalizing physician class drew on similarly lengthy timelines: An 1897 issue of the *Journal of the American Medical Association* claimed that the "oldest medical recipe" was, in fact, a hair tonic "prepared for an Egyptian queen" from 4000 BC, which "required dogs' paws and asses' hoofs to be boiled with dates in oil."[5]

In the seventeenth and eighteenth centuries, English colonists shared home remedies and consulted cookbooks, medical guidebooks, and household manuals to learn how to, for example, dye their hair or make it curlier.[6] Enslaved people sometimes used everyday goods or ad hoc technologies to alter their hair: coffee and axle grease could become black hair dye; a butter knife heated over a fire could become a curling iron; and lard, lye, and cooked potatoes could become hair straightener.[7] By the nineteenth century, such recipes and techniques continued to appear in guidebooks and etiquette manuals, but new technologies, the growth of the market economy, and a booming mass media made the possibilities for hair alterations greater than ever. An 1827 guidebook for servants described a recipe for a "safe liquid to turn red hair black," which combined black lead and ebony shavings.[8] Sarah Josepha Hale's popular guidebook *Mrs. Hale's Receipts for the Million* (1857) instructed readers that they could darken their eyebrows by mixing "an ounce of walnuts, an ounce of frankincense, an ounce of resin, and an ounce of mastic," burning it, capturing the powder released by the fumes, and mixing the powder with a little myrtle oil.[9] For Black Americans, hair straightening, too, was transformed by technology: although some Black city dwellers pressed their hair with a hot iron (the kind designed for clothing) as early as the 1820s, the invention of the hot comb in 1872—and especially its popularization in the 1900s and 1910s—significantly expanded the possibility for Black people, especially Black women, to wear their hair straight.[10]

As chapter 1 explored, wigs and false hair also had a long history in English North America.[11] During the nineteenth century, human hair—used to make wigs and other hairpieces—even became part of the emergent global market economy. While the periwigs worn by English citizens and colonists in the seventeenth and eighteenth centuries were mostly made from human hair from English heads, an international market for human hair began in the 1840s when the demand for false hairpieces in England outstripped domestic supply and the country began importing hair from France. The United States entered this market in the late 1850s, and from that time until the present, most of the wigs and hairpieces purchased in the United States have been made from imported hair, making human hair a valuable international commodity.[12] Most of the hair the United States imported in the second half of the nineteenth century came from French, German, or Italian heads; a smaller volume arrived from Russia, Norway, and Sweden.[13]

Wig-makers and other hair workers argued that the country of origin mattered because national differences affected hair quality: the highest quality hair, most agreed, came from poor European peasants—whose romanticized rural lifestyles left their hair pure and unadulterated—while the lowest quality hair came from Asia. Local newspapers claimed that hair imported from China was "rather coarse," so it was mostly "used in manufacturing low-grade theatrical wigs" rather than to create hairpieces for everyday use.[14] The disparagement of Chinese hair was also sometimes couched in the same kinds of anti-Chinese fears directed at Chinese immigrants, such as the claim that Chinese people—and thus Chinese hair—were inherently diseased. For example, the *San Francisco Call* once reported on a woman who bought a "genuine Chinese wig" to wear to a masquerade party; when she discovered she had leprosy on her forehead one week later, she blamed the wig.[15] These racial and ethnic dynamics in the human hair trade remained through the end of the century: By 1900, most hair—and the most valued hair—still came from Europe, and the most disparaged hair came from China.[16]

All of this imported human hair was put to use in the late nineteenth-century United States in the creation of false hairpieces (as well as wigs purchased by balding men). While most ordinary women at midcentury wore their hair simply parted at the center and pulled back from the face on either side—similar to the hairstyle Madame Clofullia wore in her photographic portrait (see fig. 2.7)—in the late 1860s white and Black women's fashionable hairstyles grew larger and more complicated, often demanding augmentation with false hair. Indeed, while advertisements for false hairpieces—including braids, chignons, curls, and puffs—could be found in American newspapers throughout the nineteenth century, the popularity of false hair (and the number of hairpieces purchased) grew in a major way in the 1860s, and increasingly, white women could purchase hairpieces from local shops or mail-order catalogs advertised in newspapers and magazines. Black periodicals, too, advertised false hair braids, bangs, and switches "made of kinky black hair"; the Indianapolis paper *The Freeman*, for example, suggested that readers mail their office a sample of their hair to ensure a perfect match with their own hair's color and texture.[17]

Many late-nineteenth-century women valued their false hairpieces, too, and wore them as part of their everyday attire—not always just for special occasions. In 1869, for example, a woman from Massachusetts named Elizabeth Warren Allen wrote to her sister Mary about a false hairpiece—probably, based on her description, false curls—that she wore regularly and required repair. Elizabeth told Mary that she had learned "there is someone in Keane [New Hampshire]"—where Mary lived—"who will fix my hair probably cheaper than at Boston," so Elizabeth thought that she "shall cut it off and send [it] to you" to be taken to the repair shop. Ten days later, Elizabeth wrote Mary again, asking her "if you receive my hair please get it done as speedily as possible"; Elizabeth "want[ed] it simply fixed so as to be able to coil it in as usual with what is left" of her natural hair.[18] For Elizabeth, false hair was already what *Scientific American* would later call "a necessity of the modern female existence."[19]

That false hairpieces became increasingly popular and accessible in the 1860s is part of a broader expansion in hair alteration. Indeed, while techniques for altering human hair may have existed for centuries, nineteenth-century conditions made it easier than ever to circulate and access the necessary information and raw material. By the second half of the century, the national market economy reached most people living in the United States; combined with the national postal system, which circulated catalogs and advertisements to potential customers across the country, Americans both urban and rural could purchase just about any hair product that existed in the country. Wigmakers in major cities like New York and New Orleans—who advertised that "persons at a distance can have Wigs made to order" if they mailed in their measurements and "a sample of hair"—could have their wigs "sent by Express to any part of the Union."[20]

Good-quality wigs were also available at different price points, making them relatively accessible for people of different occupations and social classes. An experienced New York wigmaker said that "the fastidious man of unlimited means" might buy "a new wig costing twenty-five dollars or thirty dollars as often as once a month," while a poorer man would purchase a wig but once a year.[21] Newspapers and magazines were bursting with advertisements for hair compounds, balms, pomades, and tonics that promised not just to cure a wide range of hair health ailments, but also to facilitate just about any change the customer desired. Parker's Hair Balsam, for example, claimed it "Never Fails to Restore the Youthful Color & Beauty to Grey Hair"; advertisements for Barry's Trichopherous, the hair specific discussed in chapter 3, declared it solved "those physical evils which refined civilization has brought in its train," including "bald heads and grey hairs."[22] Hair-care products designed for Afro-textured hair—such as Cheveline, Afro-American Scalp Food, and Nelson's Straightine—commercialized the hair-straightening process that many Black women had long pursued in more ad hoc ways at home, even though these lye-based straighteners were rarely effective and often injurious.[23] Even the freak show performers the Seven Sutherland Sisters capitalized on their famous long hair to sell their own tonic: the "Sutherland Sisters' Hair Grower!"[24] With just a catalog or newspaper, a post office box, and a small amount of money, virtually anyone in the country could get the tools they needed to radically change their hair.

Such radical alterations could, as in the case of fashionable women's hairstyles, be intentionally eye-catching—designed to showcase the hairpieces they contained. One magazine claimed in 1872 that "nineteen twentieths of all the women in the country who make any pretense to dress [well] wear false hair," and to "appear in society without supplementing their natural growth" would cause a fashionable woman to be "so hopelessly in the minority and so laughed at by all."[25] Yet false hairpieces—such as those designed for bald men—could also be completely undetectable. Indeed, as a Pittsburgh wigmaker explained in 1889, "the art of wig making is now so well understood that false hair cannot be detected." Nineteenth-century wigmakers strove for verisimilitude and undetectability, aiming to make each wig a naturalistic extension of the body—so realistic and so perfectly fit, in fact, that "even a barber would think the hair in them grew from the owner's head."[26] In the words of an 1870 encyclopedia, the purpose of a wig was to be so well made as "to imitate nature, and deceive the eye."[27]

The Power of Hair in Disguise

Hair's capability for transformation—and the ability of a good hair disguise to "deceive the eye"—had long appealed to people who, for a variety of reasons, wanted to pass in public with a different identity. Hair disguises—including both alterations to the hair on a person's head (a new cut, a different color) and the use of false hairpieces or wigs—were particularly appealing to people whose access to social and political power was limited, and who thus hoped to turn hair's potential for fraud to their advantage. Hair disguises helped young people run away from home, women serve in an all-male military, and, crucially, vulnerable people escape bondage, servitude, or violence. Indeed, as historian Tiya Miles has written, "hair was a medium through which captors and captives alike fought for corporeal as well as psychological control." This was especially true for enslaved people: Enslavers' claims to own the body (the *entire* body) of the people they enslaved meant, in a nineteenth-century framework, ownership of their hair, too. The stories of forcible haircuts for enslaved women, described in chapter 1, testify to this kind of coercive, often violent ownership. Yet at the same time, enslaved women (and men) pushed back against the totalizing effect of slavery by caring for their hair and claiming it as their own.[28] Hair's capacity for malleability thus offered the possibility of agency, too.

Hair frequently played a role in obfuscations of one's gender, race, or both. The way these stories were reported to the public and described by contemporaries vividly demonstrates just how significant hair was to strangers' assessments of a person's gender or race—more significant, in many cases, than other parts of the body or bodily adornments, such as clothing. The biological basis of hair's function as an external index of internal identities was emergent in the eighteenth century and firmly in place by the nineteenth, yet hair *styling* is what gave marginalized people the power to play with and even subvert the importance placed on biology—especially to cross the very gender and racial categories hair was entrusted to be an index for.

A change to the hair was rarely the only bodily alteration that Americans made as they took on new identities across gender and racial lines; changes to clothing, posture, gait, and even vocal tone were also often part of a nineteenth-century disguise. However, achieving a new hairstyle that could pass detection was *critical* to successfully disguising oneself in the nineteenth century. If the hair appeared *wrong* or *off* in some way, the disguise was almost certain to fail, particularly if it caught the eye of a suspicious stranger, police officer, or slave patroller. Convincing hair was thus the linchpin to a successful disguise.

Gender Passing

In both the late eighteenth and nineteenth centuries, some women dressed as men when they were trying to run away. Although extant sources rarely say so explicitly, it is reasonable to guess that the decision to pass as a man in public—which meant, by the nineteenth century, wearing short hair—may have been prompted by the relatively greater ease a man would have traveling unaccompanied in public spaces compared to a woman. The story of the mysterious disappearance of a twenty-four-year-old Vermont woman named Emma Sands—a mystery "of such all-absorbing interest" that it was reported on by newspapers as far away as Kansas and Louisiana—exemplifies this type of story.[29] On the evening of June 8, 1879, Sands went missing as she walked from Westford, Vermont—where she and her sister had been visiting a friend—back to her home in the nearby town of Essex. Local authorities initially assumed Sands had been murdered, but their only suspect was let go soon after his arrest owing to lack of evidence. Undeterred, large segments of the town scoured the woods for the body many were certain must be there. On June 13, with Sands's whereabouts still unknown, the *Press* reported an additional mystery—one that, at first, seemed unrelated: "On Tuesday morning a girl dressed in male attire was seen in this city, but disappeared before she could be arrested."[30] A few days later, the night watchman for the Central Vermont Railroad who spotted this person—whom the *Press* referred to as a "girl-boy"—identified her as Sands from a photograph.[31] Evidence continued to mount that Sands was, indeed, the "girl-boy," yet Sands's local community remained in disbelief: "No one in Westford, it may be added, believes that the girl in boy's clothes is Miss Sands"; it just seemed so unlikely that "a girl of irreproachable conduct and morals" would "start off on such a masquerading trip."[32]

The mystery of Sands's disappearance was finally solved on June 19, when, at three o'clock in the morning, a police officer and a railroad station agent found Sands as she traveled on a canalboat south of Whitehall, New York. Over the span of eleven days, she had traveled more than 125 miles by foot.[33] When the officers confronted her, Sands initially "stoutly maintained that she was not Emma Sands of Westford but 'Charlie Thompson of Rochester.'" Eventually, however, she cooperated with the officers. What the *Press* had once speculated was merely a harmless jaunt was reframed entirely: "It was at once evident that the unfortunate girl was insane, all her words and actions manifesting aberration of mind." Sands was brought back to Burlington and examined by a team of physicians, who concluded that "she is plainly insane." Newspaper accounts of this story did not suggest that her decision to cross-dress was evidence of mental instability—instead, it was the fact that she was completely unable to remember anything from before she disappeared "on that memorable Sunday night"; "everything in her history previous to that is a complete blank."[34] In August 1879, Sands was committed to an asylum in Brattleboro, Vermont—yet by 1883, she had recovered, married a man, and "gone West."[35]

Little else is known of Emma Sands, so it is impossible to confirm why she decided to run away, change her appearance, and take on the identity of Charlie Thompson. Extant sources cannot confirm whether she planned to continue her life as a man, or whether the disguise was merely a temporary measure intended to help her pass unmolested on trains and boats and in other public spaces—a task far easier for an unaccompanied white man than a white woman. What *is* evident, however, is what it took for Emma to pass as Charlie in public view: men's clothing and a short haircut. The day after her disappearance, the *Press* recounted, Sands purchased "two shirts, a pair of overalls, and a travelling bag" from a store in Burlington.[36] Then, *before* putting on her new clothing—and while still wearing a dress—Sands went to a barber shop and "had her hair cut, asking [the barber] to cut it like a boy's." According to witnesses, her reaction to the haircut was emotional: as the barber cut her hair, "she wept, saying she did not think she would feel so bad to have [her hair] cut off. The long locks she took with her, and went off down Church street, from which direction she came."[37]

The emotional reaction Sands had to the loss of her long hair echoes in other nineteenth-century stories of women passing as men. Indeed, a trip to the barber for a short haircut is a common trope in cross-dressing literature, especially narratives that describe the most well-documented reason that women dressed as men during the late eighteenth and nineteenth centuries: to serve in the military during wartime.[38] In these women's narratives, they and their editors were at pains to convey to the reader that their gender passing was only temporary and situational: presenting as a man was a means to an end, not a reflection of a desire to permanently live as a man.[39] For example, the "Publisher's Notice" that preceded one woman's narrative of Civil War service anticipated that some readers might "object to some of her disguises"; if so, "it may be sufficient to remind them it was from the purest motives and most praiseworthy patriotism, that she laid aside, for a time, her own costume, and assumed that of the opposite sex, enduring hardships, suffering untold privations, and hazarding her life for her adopted country"—she was born in Canada—"in its trying hour of need."[40] The editor of another cross-dressing narrative from the Civil War reassured the reader that the woman's motivation to disguise herself as a man was rooted in heteronormative feminine emotions: It was the grief she felt after the death of both of her children in 1860 that inspired her to serve.[41]

Martial cross-dressing narratives (both real and fictional) about women who served in the Revolutionary War, War of 1812, and Civil War trace the growing significance of hair as an index of gender over the course of the eighteenth and nineteenth centuries. In each of these stories—of Deborah Sampson, Lucy Brewer, Loreta Janeta Velazquez, and Sarah Emma Edmonds—a change to the hair is part of their transformation into a soldier who passes as a man. However, the significance of the hair to their disguise— and *especially* to the way each narrative *told the story* of their hair disguise— became greater over time. In the Revolutionary War narrative of Deborah Sampson, who took on the identity of Robert Shurtliff to fight for American independence, the first step of her transformation was not a haircut, but acquiring men's clothing. In his 1797 narrative of Sampson's life, *The Female Review*, author Herman Mann described how, while still debating whether she would join the Army, Sampson "privately dressed herself in a handsome suit of man's apparel and repaired to a prognosticator [fortune teller]." The fortune teller mistook Sampson for a man, "consider[ing] her as a blithe and honest young gentleman." Editor John Adams Vinton, who annotated a later edition of *The Female Review*, described how Sampson's new suit "became her so well, that even her mother, whom she visited in Plympton [her hometown] in this costume, did not know her." In contrast to the repeated descriptions of her clothing, *The Female Review* mentions that Sampson cut her hair just once, matter-of-factly, and without elaboration or discussion. It is left ambiguous whether the short haircut was crucial to Sampson's successful disguise or whether her new suit mattered the most, but the fact that some white men still wore long hair in the 1790s likely made her hair length of less significance than her clothing.[42]

Nearly twenty years later, narratives about Lucy Brewer's service in the War of 1812 also focused more on clothing than hair. However, they also revealed the growing significance of hair as an index of gender identity in

American culture, making clear that a successful disguise required a successful change to the hair. First published as a series of pamphlets sold in Boston between 1815 and 1818, *The Female Marine; or the Adventures of Lucy Brewer* is a collection of narratives about Brewer, a woman from rural Massachusetts who experiences a series of misfortunes and adventures. It is the most famous fictional account of a wartime gender transformation in the nineteenth century; historian Daniel Cohen suggests that, for a few years after its publication, the *Female Marine* narratives were "among the most widely circulated pamphlets in Boston."[43]

Unlike *The Female Review*, *The Female Marine* hid the identity of its male author, purporting to be Brewer's autobiographical recollections of her seduction, pregnancy, sex work, service as a sailor during the War of 1812, and eventual happy ending (in a heterosexual marriage). In these narratives, Brewer disguises herself as a man twice: once to escape from a Boston brothel and enlist in the marines; and once after her service had ended, when, after moving back into her parents' home, she decides she wants to travel again. Brewer's first experience in the guise of a man is described just briefly in the text, occupying less than a paragraph: Brewer simply puts on a man's suit, escapes the brothel, and walks on board the warship *Constitution* with a group of other recruits. In the *Constitution*'s all-male space, there was not "the least suspicion of my sex"; indeed, the narrator explains that during her three years in the service, "the whole time [she] succeeded in concealing my sex from all on board."[44] Thanks to the exigencies of war—and, significantly, a community composed entirely of strangers—Brewer was able to maintain her disguise quite easily. After returning to her parents' home and then deciding to travel once more, Brewer "again assumed my male habiliments [clothing]" and took a ride on a stagecoach—another exemplar of the world of strangers—to New York City.[45]

Brewer's disguise tactics changed, however, when she traveled to Boston weeks later, "a place where I had been so well known to many." Thus, "to guard myself well against every possibility of a detection, . . . I now took *extra pains* to disguise myself *in every possible way*": Brewer went "to a barber's shop, where my hair received a fashionable crop, and my head and shoulders a plentiful shower of powder." With her fresh haircut, Brewer "took a walk upon 'Change [Exchange, a Boston street], where, although surveyed by many from head to foot, no one, I am conscious, had the least suspicion of my sex. I several times passed through Cornhill, and many of the most public streets, and frequently met persons whom I well knew, but they did not appear to recognize me."[46] It is significant that this scene occurred more than three years after Brewer first passed as a man in public. Her trip to the barber shop was inspired by a newly urgent need to pass successfully caused by the fact that she was no longer among strangers. Putting on men's clothing was sufficient in a city where no one knew her, like Manhattan, but to truly pass as a man around people who *did* know her—including the very same Boston sex workers she had once lived among—Brewer needed to change her hair. It was having a fashionable short men's haircut that allowed her to fully and completely go undercover in her hometown.

By the mid-nineteenth century, as both men's hair length norms had solidified and hair had gained new significance as an index of intrinsic gender, clothing was no longer sufficient to disguise a woman as a male soldier, even among strangers. Unlike the fictional Lucy Brewer, the two most famous women to dress as men during the Civil War—Loretta Janeta Velazquez for the Confederacy, and Sarah Emma Edmonds for the Union—both changed their hair *as soon as* they went undercover, wrote extensively about the decision to change their hair, and made clear that hair disguises were paramount to their successful transformations.[47]

Loretta Janeta Velazquez described her service in the Confederate army in extensive detail in her memoir *The Woman in Battle: A Narrative of the Exploits, Adventures, and Travels of Madame Loreta Janeta Velazquez, Otherwise Known as Lieutenant Harry T. Buford, Confederate States Army* (1876). As the title suggests, gender transformation is central to this memoir. The text even includes two illustrated portraits of its subject: the frontispiece, which shows Velazquez "in Female Attire" (as the caption explains); and a second portrait of Velazquez in disguise as her alter ego, Confederate officer Harry T. Buford (see figs. 4.1a–b). The latter portrait, moreover, includes the sitter's signature, suggesting a transformation so complete as to wholly subsume her identity.

The first time Velazquez presented herself as a man—when her husband tried to dissuade her from going to the battlefield by exposing her to the coarse way men acted in homosocial spaces—she changed her hair in a temporary way: "Braiding my hair very close, I put on a man's wig, and a false mustache." Velazquez took pride in her male appearance, writing, "as I surveyed myself in the mirror I was immensely pleased with the figure I cut,

MADAM VELASQUEZ IN FEMALE ATTIRE.

4.1 Frontispiece (top) and interior illustration (bottom), both engraved by Rea, from *The Woman in Battle*. Velazquez's memoir of her time in disguise as a man while serving in the Confederate Army juxtaposes a portrait of herself "in female attire" (as the caption indicates) with a portrait of her male alter ego, Lieutenant Harry T. Buford.

CREDIT: Reproduced from Loreta Janeta Velazquez, *The Woman in Battle: A Narrative of the Exploits, Adventures, and Travels of Madame Loreta Janeta Velazquez, Otherwise Known as Lieutenant Harry J. Buford, Confederate States Army*, ed. C. J. Worthington (Hartford, CT: T. Belknap, 1876).

and fancied that I made quite as good looking a man as my husband."[48] After this successful outing—her husband's attempt to dissuade her was ineffective—Velazquez remained determined to enact a more long-term disguise, which required greater measures of physical transformation. To play the role of Lieutenant Buford, clothing was not enough; Velazquez wrote that her new uniform "transformed [her] into a man," but only "*so far as it was possible for clothing to transform me*."[49] For a complete transformation, her hair, too, had to change—a haircut was critical. In her exhaustive narrative, which runs more than six-hundred pages, Velazquez expressed regret at presenting as a man just once: "the only regret I had in making up my disguise, was the necessity for parting with my long and luxuriant hair. This gave me a real pang; but there was no help for it, and I submitted with as good a grace as I could muster."[50]

With her uniform and supplies purchased and a short haircut acquired, there was but one final item Velazquez required to complete her transformation: a fake mustache. Velazquez decided to don a fake mustache on the advice of a friend, who, "thinking that my disguise could be somewhat improved, and a more manly air given to my countenance, obtained a false mustache." (Indeed, as chapter 2 demonstrated, facial hair was common among American men by the Civil War.) Her friend then "carefully fastened the mustache to my upper lip with glue. This was a great improvement, and I scarcely knew myself when I looked in the glass."[51] Velazquez's disguise did not just convince herself—it was *so* convincing to fellow soldiers, she wrote, that a group of them boasted in front of her, "with very masculine positiveness, that no woman could deceive them" if she dressed up as a male soldier—"little suspecting that one was even then listening to them."[52] Her hair and especially her facial hair were crucial to her ability to successfully pass as a man.

Indeed, the first time Velazquez feared that her identity would be discovered was when the glass of buttermilk she was drinking appeared to loosen the glue on her fake mustache. Luckily for Velazquez, "my fright, after all, was causeless, for on examination I found that the hair was too firmly glued to my lip to be easily removed." This anecdote was so significant that it received its own section in Velazquez's narrative, entitled "My Mustache in Danger."[53] Moreover, multiple times during the narrative Velazquez described how she twisted her mustache during moments of doubt about her identity. For example, after being arrested, fined, and jailed in New Orleans on suspicion of being a woman, Velazquez quickly left the city. Later, she met up with a friend and fellow soldier who had recently been to New Orleans, and who had heard about the arrest. "To quiet any suspicions that might be lurking in his mind," Velazquez wrote, "I said, as I twisted my mustache, and put on all the swagger I was able, 'I am a queer-looking female, ain't I, major?'"—the mustache reinforcing the absurdity of the notion.[54] For Velazquez, false facial hair became one of the most important— if not *the* most important—visual cues of her masculine identity.

Racial Passing

The possibility of Civil War service that dressing as a man offered Southerner Loretta Janeta Velazquez also appealed to a Canadian-turned-northerner named Sarah Emma Edmonds, whose memoir *Nurse and Spy in the Union Army* (1865) described her eleven forays across enemy line to serve as a spy—"always with complete success and without detection"—four of which required her to take on a disguise that crossed racial, ethnic, or gender lines.[55] In total, Edmonds disguised herself as an Irish peddler woman, a white man from the border state of Kentucky, a Black woman, and a Black boy. Edmonds's narrative describes the mechanics of most of these disguises but briefly, mentioning that she wore a disguise but rarely elaborating on what it entailed.[56] The only disguise that received a detailed description was the one that required gender and racial transgression at once. To disguise herself as a Black boy, Edmonds listed the steps she took "to remodel, transform, and metamorphose" herself: she purchased a "a suit of contraband clothing, real plantation style," darkened her skin "as black as any African," and went to a barber to get her hair "sheared close to my head." Changing her hair was, indeed, crucial. Her disguise would not be convincing, she wrote, until she made one final change: "to complete my contraband costume, I required a wig of real negro wool."[57]

Edmonds's Afro-textured wig is rendered visually in the narrative, too. Captioned "Disguised as a Contraband" (see fig. 4.2a), the engraving shows Edmonds seated on the edge of a cart, dressed in a men's coat, shirt, pants, and shoes. Like two of the five Black working men in the background, Edmonds has a hat, but hers, crucially, is laid on her knee so that the reader can see the short, textured black wig she wears—a hairstyle that mirrors the three hatless Black men behind her. This visual parallel gives Edmonds's wig a naturalistic appearance—a naturalism that heightens the sensationalism

DISGUISED AS A CONTRABAND.—Page 113.

4.2 Frontispiece, engraved by George E. Perine (left); and "Disguised as a Contraband," engraved by R. O'Brien (right), from *Nurse and Spy in the Union Army*. Like Velazquez's, Edmonds's memoir of the disguises she wore during the Civil War juxtaposed her civilian female appearance with scenes of two of her disguises, both of which depict her as a Black person.

CREDIT: Reproduced from Sarah Emma Edmonds, *Nurse and Spy in the Union Army: Comprising the Adventures and Experiences of a Woman in Hospitals, Camps, and Battle-fields* (Hartford, CT: W. S. Williams & Co., 1865).

Engraved by Geo E Perine N.Y.

S. E. E. Edmonds

of the contrast this disguise presents with Edmonds's civilian appearance, shown in the engraving that serves as the narrative's frontispiece (see fig. 4.2b). Here, Edmonds—wearing a long dress and standing aside a horse, riding crop in hand—appears to be wearing her dark, wavy hair loose above her shoulders, the top covered by a decorative hat. This was a very uncommon style for adult white women in the 1860s, who almost always wore their hair up and styled when outside the home; Velazquez's frontispiece, for example, shows a common simple style for midcentury women: center parted and pulled securely to the back of the head (see fig. 4.1a).[58] That Edmonds made such an unusual choice for her portrait helped reinforce just how substantial her racial hair transformation really was.

Edmonds's wig was not merely different from the hair she grew naturally—it also proved crucial to successfully maintain her disguise as Black when another racial marker, her artificially darkened skin color, faltered. After a few days of successfully passing as a man, Edmonds noticed a Black boy looking at her "in a puzzled sort of manner." He turned to his friend and said, "'Jim, I'll be darned if that feller aint turnip' white; if he aint then I'm no nigger.'" Edmonds was startled by the remark, but as soon as she could get some privacy, she "took a look at my complexion by means of a small pocket looking-glass which I carried for that very purpose—and sure enough, as the negro had said, I was really turning white." The blackface makeup she had used was wearing off—and yet still, her true identity was not unmasked.[59] Crucially, even though Edwards had such light skin color, these two Black friends still believed she was Black because of her hair.

Just like Sarah Emma Edmonds's "wig of real negro wool," many people who disguised themselves across racial lines found an alteration to their hair to be important—even indispensable—for their facade to succeed. Since the eighteenth century, some enslaved people who fled their enslavement donned wigs in an effort to obfuscate their identity and pass as free. For example, a 1767 advertisement for David Gratenread indicated that he escaped with a "brown cut wig," boarded a boat, and "pretend[ed] to pass as a free man."[60] Similarly, Rochester and Phill, two "mulatto" men owned by different enslavers, were both described in the 1780s as frequently wearing "a false queue"; both owners feared that the enslaved man they were seeking "will, no doubt, attempt to pass as a free man."[61]

In addition to wearing a wig or false queue, some enslaved people altered the hair on their heads as they escaped from bondage in a similar effort to make themselves look less like the physical descriptions that circulated in newspaper advertisements. For example, a 1776 advertisement in a Pennsylvania newspaper described a man named Peter who "has remarkable hairy temple locks, unless cut off by shaving."[62] Similarly, an 1810 ad described a man named Billy, who ran away "wear[ing] a queue (which however he might cut off) and whiskers." Though Billy had "very black hair" that might have betrayed his African heritage, his enslaver specified that his hair was "not more curled than that of white men frequently is." It was no wonder, then, that the ad warned that Billy, who was also light-skinned, "will probably attempt to pass himself off as a free man."[63] In some cases, hair alterations could even facilitate a runaway's passing for Indigenous; an 1763 advertisement from Pennsylvania, for example, described how one man "had been seen with his Hair combed out straight" because he was going to try to "pass for an Indian."[64]

Enslaved women, too, could project a new kind of identity by changing their hair. For example, one 1774 advertisement described a twenty-two-year-old enslaved woman named Rachel who had run away from her master, John Jones. Jones listed the items of clothing Rachel was wearing when she escaped and indicated that she was about four-feet-eight inches tall—yet the only bodily feature the description included was her hair: "She has been brought up in the House, [and] combs her Hair long, endeavouring to impose herself on the Publick for a free Woman."[65] Jones thus believed that Rachel had manipulated her hair in an effort to make her external appearance seem consistent with that of a free woman—an impression she could likely bolster, once she began interacting with a stranger, with the social mores she learned by working in the white family's home; in this respect, these two facts about Rachel were mutually reinforcing. Yet it was her hair, Jones feared, that would allow Rachel to project an *initial* impression of freedom—an impression that would allow her to successfully run away and become just one more member of the American world of strangers.

In many stories of racial disguise both fictional and real, alterations to both the hair and the skin work together to facilitate a racial passing disguise. In Harriet Beecher Stowe's famous antislavery novel *Uncle Tom's Cabin* (1852), for example, an escaped enslaved man named George changes the color of both his skin and hair to evade detection. When George escapes from a plantation in Kentucky, his master advertises a reward for his capture in a handbill, which describes George as "a very light mulatto" with "brown curly hair" who "will probably try to pass for a white man." (His enslavement could also be read on his body, however; George was "deeply scarred on his back and shoulders; has been branded in his right hand with the letter H.")[66] After his escape, George disguises his appearance: "A little walnut bark has made my yellow skin a genteel brown, and I've dyed my hair black; so you see I don't answer to the advertisement at all.'"[67] George's disguise is so convincing that when he drives his buggy up to a group of men—some of whom he knows—the men perceive him to be just another stranger. The men do notice that George has black hair and brown skin; however, when read alongside other racially coded markers, such as his fine clothing and buggy, the group concludes that he must be a Spaniard.[68] (Ironically, although George's former master successfully guessed that George would attempt to pass as white after his escape—since Spanish was considered white or Caucasian in most influential racial classification systems—he may have been surprised to discover that George had actually *darkened* his hair and skin in order to pass!)[69]

Hair and skin did, indeed, often work in tandem in a racial disguise. Yet for nineteenth-century Americans who deeply understood the fundamental instability of racial categorization and the ambiguity of bodily signifiers, skin color was not enough to pass across racial lines or to confirm a person's authentic racial identity. For Black people seeking to pass as white, hair—*especially* hair texture—threatened to betray their disguise. As chapter 3 demonstrated, both scientific authorities and popular wisdom agreed that Afro-textured hair was the most important bodily marker of African descent. A wig, then, could cover the greatest racial tell of all.

Some advertisements for runaway enslaved people made this connection explicit. For example, an advertisement for David, a skilled hairdresser with a "yellowish Complexion," explained that "his Hair is *of the Negro Kind*, [and] he keeps it very high and well combed; but, as he wants to be free, I imagine he will cut it off, and get a Wig to alter and disguise himself."[70] Even more revealing is the advertisement for Stephen, a fifteen-year-old barber, who not only had skin "so near white, that he generally passes for a white boy"—he also had hair described by his enslaver as "straight and of a light color." On its face, this combination of features—light skin, light hair, *and* straight hair—suggests that Stephen would have little trouble passing for white. However, three weeks before he ran away, Stephen shaved his head, and "wore a wig when he went off" from his enslaver. Although the advertisement does not state so outright, the implication is clear: Stephen likely wore a wig to conceal any *hint* of texture in his newly grown-back hair—texture that would reveal his African ancestry and thus betray his assumed identity.[71]

For Chinese immigrants, altering the hair, too, offered the possibility of transformation. Treated poorly for their queues (as chapter 1 showed), barred from naturalized citizenship—and, after 1882, from legal immigration—

Chinese immigrants' status as Americans was extremely fraught in the nineteenth century. Yet the power of hair fraud seemed to offer a pathway to American belonging. For example, six months after President Arthur signed the Chinese Exclusion Act into law, an article in the *Philadelphia Press* described a Chinese immigrant named Lee Yoo who attempted to use a wig to transform himself into an American. Lee had reportedly "bought a wig for $15" to cover up his queue, "with the vain hope that his nationality might be disguised." The author asked Lee, who ran a laundry, why he wanted to "sink his Chinese characteristics as far as possible," and the answer was simple: to receive better treatment and therefore make a better living. Lee hoped that, with his new hairstyle, he could move to a new town, open a new laundry, and be perceived (and received) as an American just like his potential customers, who would no longer laugh or yell at him but simply let him clean their clothes. Lee claimed that as soon as he started wearing the wig, white people began to treat him better—just like an American man, he said—yet his disguise did not fool the *Press*'s reporter, who snickered that "nothing but his yellow face and unmistakable Mongolian physiognomy" gave away his true racial identity.[72] However, Lee's confidence that his wig *would* work was also borne of contemporary understandings that hair disguises usually *did* work.

Hair was such an important signal of identity by the late nineteenth century that getting the hair *right* often helped facilitate a successful disguise. Indeed, at the United States' southern border, other Chinese immigrants found that altering their hair *did* allow them to cross racial boundaries, and, in doing so, national borders. For example, a border smuggling operation run by a Chinese-Mexican man named José Chang disguised Chinese immigrants as Mexicans to help them enter the United States (via Mexico) during the exclusion era without arousing suspicion. To enact this disguise, Chang changed the immigrants' clothing and cut off their queues. As historian Erika Lee writes, one American immigration official "expressed with some amazement that it was 'exceedingly difficult to distinguish these Chinamen from Mexicans.'"[73] Their success—and Lee Yoo's failure—suggests that white people were less acutely observant of bodily differences between non-European-descended racial and ethnic groups than of their fellow white Americans, making a hair disguise far more likely to succeed than one that relied on clothing alone. (This, too, is part of the humor of George's racial disguise in *Uncle Tom's Cabin*.) Crucially, this was the power that made many kinds of hair fraud much more powerful as a tool for successful gender or racial passing than clothing (which could be removed) or artificial skin darkening (which would rub off or fade): most kinds of hair alterations would remain in place, at least for a little while. Hair indexed national belonging in the nineteenth century—and sometimes, hair fraud could undermine even federal immigration laws designed to keep the United States white.

The Threat of Hair in Disguise

Hair's essential capacity for alteration, the increased availability of technologies for altering the hair, and the many stories of people who used alterations to their hair to facilitate disguises made hair fraud feel foreboding to many elite Americans in the late nineteenth century. Indeed, hair's biological qualities had gained such strong significance by this time—understood to be such a reliable tell of a person's intrinsic character and identity, especially racial and gender identity—that both the threat of hair fraud and the consequences of a successful fraud felt grave.

The people most fearful of hair disguises were holders (and arbiters) of political and cultural power: white elites and the men and women in the emergent urban middle class, who felt uneasy about the ways in which their lives increasingly put them in contact with strangers. They worried that falsified hair disrupted their ability to accurately identify who was trustworthy and who was lying about their identity. There is evidence as early as the seventeenth century of religious leaders—often the same men who preached so vehemently against long hair for men—warning of the dangerous possibilities that hair fraud presented. For example, Puritan missionaries in the Massachusetts Bay Colony worried about affected conversion: Indigenous people who *claimed* conversion based on genuine faith, but were in fact only pretending in order to, as rhetoric scholar Jacqueline M. Henkel writes, "manage the English." One such example of affected conversion was a short haircut absent a complete conversion.[74] Elsewhere in the colony, Reverend Nicholas Noyes warned his congregation that periwigs "are many times used for Disguise by the worst of men, as by shaven crownd Popish Priests, Highway Robbers, etc."[75] Crucially, however, Noyes pointed out that even a person without criminal intentions could "disguiseth himself" by changing his hair. He hated periwigs because they "removeth one notable Distinction, or means of distinguishing one man from another." The effect was amplified if the man "keepeth diverse Perriwigs different from another in length, Colour, Culres [curls], or the like: sometime wearing one, sometimes another"; any man who did this was "strangely inconsistent with himself; and unlike to day, to what he was yesterday; and so less liable to be known."[76] Making sure that strangers were *known* was, indeed, extremely important to white middle-class and elite Americans, whose continued social and economic power hinged on legitimate business exchanges and other forms of legible social interaction, especially within the emergent market economy.

The increased accessibility of hair-altering technologies by the late nineteenth century bothered many white middle-class Americans because it fit squarely into a growing anxiety: that their increasingly fluid and anonymous world made is simply too easy for people to take on a false identity. As rapid increases to both immigration and rural-to-urban migration made urban populations swell, American cities seemed to offer opportunities for anonymity unmatched in the nation's history. Cities increasingly felt like they were composed entirely of strangers—and few stock characters were more associated with the dangers of strangers than the criminal, especially the confidence man, who gained the trust of an unsuspecting stranger, convinced them to give him their watch, and then disappeared with his prize in hand.[77] Yet as historian John F. Kasson has observed, the confidence man was not the only feared "urban imposter"; others included "pickpockets, shoplifters, 'sneak thieves' who depended upon stealth for their crimes, blackmailers, [and] forgers."[78] Large, fluid cities like New York, Chicago, and San Francisco seemed to offer a playground for disguise and impersonation— and hair, as a reliable index of who a person truly was, was also ripe for fraud.

Falsified Hair and Criminal Intent

In the second half of the nineteenth century, laypeople, scientific experts, and policing professionals increasingly worried that hair fraud could make crime easier to commit and arrest easier to evade. In his 1886 book *Professional Criminals of America*, detective Thomas Byrnes explained the threat of hair's malleability. Because a criminal "can grow or shave off a beard or mustache, [and] he can change the color of either," it was difficult to be certain that the person being arrested or put on trial was the correct man. As an example, Byrnes described the 1883 trial of a swindler who went by many aliases—whether he was the wanted James T. Watson or Al Wilson,

Charles H. Whittemore, or someone else entirely, was a central question at trial—which included conflicting testimony about the man's facial hair. While Byrnes described Watson as having "light brown whiskers and mustache," at trial "certain witnesses swore that the prisoner had worn a beard during November, and others swore that he wore only a mustache," leaving the jury with extremely unclear information as to whether the man in front of them was indeed swindler they were after.[79]

Even more so than a grown or shaved mustache, fake hairpieces—including wigs, fake beards, and false mustaches—were particularly worrisome because they could so quickly falsify a person's appearance, only to be reversed again as soon as the crime was complete. For example, Allan Pinkerton's 1884 memoir of his three-decade career as a New York City detective included exposés of common offenses he had observed, including the "Palace Car Thieves:" men who stole from passengers on sleeper cars. As part of his standard "mode of proceeding," the palace car thief would wear a large, bushy, fake beard, "which entirely conceals the lower part of his face"; if spotted by an awakened victim, he would quickly ditch the beard and hide in plain sight while police searched the train.[80] Stories of real-life crimes bore out the pattern Pinkerton posited: for example, State Rangers in Texas ambushed a group of wire cutters in 1886, killing one of the men, who "was disguised with false moustaches."[81] A bank robber named Billy Burke stole more than $10,000 from the Manufacturers' Bank in Cohoes, New York, while wearing a fake mustache, which police later discovered tucked in his clothing.[82]

Even more sensational was the story of Karl Hau, a German immigrant and law professor at George Washington University, who ordered a custom-made wig and beard to wear while he murdered his mother-in-law back in Germany—a story covered by more than one hundred newspapers across the United States in 1906 and 1907. Hau had lied to his wife about why he needed the false hairpieces, claiming that "he was going as a spy to Turkey and needed the wig and beard to protect him against attempts at assassination," but in truth these were criminal tools. After traveling to Germany with his family and then sending his wife and daughter ahead to London without him, Hau donned the false beard, traveled by train from Karlsruhe to his mother-in-law's home town of Baden-Baden, shot his mother-in-law in a post office, and then boarded the train again; at his trial, Hau admitted that he had "thrown [the beard] out of the [train] car window between

Baden-Baden and Karlsruhe."[83] Ironically, Kau's false beard ultimately drew *more* attention to him, not less, for "many persons at the Karlsruhe station had noticed that he wore a false beard and that he evidently was seeking to evade observation."[84]

As Karl Hau's failed use of a false beard suggests, by the second half of the nineteenth century wigs had become an incriminating accessory—a tip-off for policemen, detectives, and other suspicious observers of urban life that the stranger they were observing was doing something nefarious. One sensational story from 1860s Cincinnati—then the seventh-largest city in the country, with a large urban population of over 161,000—illustrates this dynamic.[85] One day in February 1867, two police detectives spotted a "very beautiful and elegantly dressed young lady," whose "clear, blonde face, large expressive and rather plaintive eyes, small, neatly cut mouth, with white and even teeth, and shapely nose" provoked, at first, a mere "passing glance of admiration" (or so the reporter for the *Cincinnati Commercial* claimed). Yet the woman had a "queer habit of raising her hand to her head, frequently," a head covered with "light, floss-like hair that hung in curls upon her shoulders—extraordinarily perfect curls"—that suggested "the idea of a wig!" The detectives quickly realized that but for the color of her hair and eyebrows, this woman matched the physical description of a criminal who had recently passed counterfeit money in their city. [86]

Satisfied that they had caught the suspect, the detectives took the woman to the police station, only to discover that she was not, in fact, the counterfeiter, but instead a woman attempting to conceal her identity for a much different reason: to hide an illegitimate pregnancy. The woman turned out to be from a small town outside Cincinnati; after she discovered that she was pregnant, the woman's mother helped her flee to the big city of Cincinnati, where she radically changed her hair in multiple ways: she dyed her eyebrows, cut off her hair, and donned a wig. These hair transformations wrought a transformation to the woman, too, turning her into "a lone woman who, in a city many miles away, *among strangers*, should give birth to a child." (The transformation was, however, temporary; she planned to return home as soon as her child was born, and had even held on to the four feet of shorn hair, which she carried in a large package.)[87] Like so many nineteenth-century hairpieces, the wig's natural appearance made her adoption of a temporary new identity all the easier. The reporter described the woman's wig as so exquisitely crafted, "not one cut of a thousand—*no one in fact*—would have had the slightest idea of a work of a peruquier [wigmaker] in making up her appearance . . . so neatly had the work been done."[88] Indeed, were it not for the woman's nervous habit of touching the wig, the detectives may not have noticed it at all.

The suspicious nature of wearing a wig—and the possibility that it signaled a broader inclination toward deceit—could even poison intimate relationships. Under the headline "Wig Deceived Her," the *Nashville American* reported on a broken engagement caused by a woman's discovery that her fiancé wore a wig. It was not the wig itself that upset her—it was the fact that her fiancé had hid it from her. The couple had started a savings account together with the agreement that "if the engagement was broken the money was to go to the one that proved true"; after ending the engagement, the woman filed a suit in court claiming she was entitled to the money because of her fiancé's "fraud and deceit"—his wig.[89]

The San Francisco False Beard Arrests of the 1890s

In cities across America, fake hair became increasingly associated with criminal intent. The way that fake hair intersected with white middle-class Americans' anxieties about modern urban life can be seen most acutely in a single unusual story: In the late 1880s and early 1890s, the San Francisco police arrested at least six people for the crime of wearing a false beard. According to the Chief of Police's end-of-the-year report, three people were arrested for wearing a false beard during the 1891–1892 fiscal year, and a fourth person in 1893–1894. In addition to these official records, local newspapers reported two additional men charged with wearing a false beard during the same period: S. S. Curtis in 1886 and David Marnell in 1887. (Curtis claimed that he was only intending to play a joke on a friend and was later released, while Marnell testified at his trial that he "was an amateur actor, and wore the beard on that account"; that Marnell was also wearing two pairs of pants, two vests, and "no less than four coats" when he was arrested made his false beard *really* look like evidence of intent to falsify his identity. Marnell was convicted.)[90] Of these six arrests, just two people were dismissed; the other four were convicted. Such a high conviction rate (67 percent) was not the norm for other crimes of falsified identity in San Francisco. For example, between 1886 and 1894, just seven of the fifty-three people arrested for "Personating an officer"—a mere 13 percent—were convicted of their crimes.[91] The surprising story of San Francisco's false beard arrests provides a window into three different concerns about identity in the modernizing United States: an anxiety about falsifiable identity, a concern about masked faces, and the emergence of the scientific study of criminality.

The false beard arrests in San Francisco reflected many middle-class white Americans' fear that the ease of assuming a falsified identity also made it easier to commit a crime. In addition to the six people arrested in San Francisco between 1850 and 1900 for wearing a false beard, dozens of people were arrested every year for other crimes related to false identity, including forgery, libel, impersonating a police officer or firefighter, or a crime called "False Pretenses (obtaining money or goods by)," which likely refers to a confidence trick. Between four and thirty-six people were also arrested every year after 1868 for "Burglars' Tools, carrying"—a category that included crowbars, brass knuckles, skeleton keys, and false hair.[92] Indeed, in the 1870s and 1880s, prominent detectives from cities beyond San Francisco described criminals who used wigs or false whiskers as one of the tools in their toolkit. Pinkerton, for example, described a notorious forger named William Ringgold Cooper who wrote forged checks and took on fake identities, including befriending and later forging the handwriting of British gentry in order to withdraw money from their accounts. Cooper sometimes donned "false whiskers" when conducting his criminal business, and once he was finally arrested in 1878, he was identified by two men he had hired to help him pass a forged check, as well as by "the barber who had made his false wig and whiskers."[93]

Similarly, detective Phillip Farley described how, after New York police arrested the notorious robber Dick Moore, "the house in which he had lived was searched, and an assortment of coats, wigs, hats, gowns, beards, *and other disguises* found."[94] There were even entries about wigs in the "Rogue's Lexicon" that George W. Matsell, the former Chief of Police for New York City, compiled in 1859; *caxon* was the word criminals used to refer to a wig, Matsell explained, and a *knob-thatcher* was a wigmaker.[95] The criminalization of wearing a false beard echoes this fear of falsifiable identity, and the way a false beard could easily serve as a criminal's tool.

A second urban concern intertwined with the false beard arrests in San Francisco was an unease about masked faces. Some cities even tried to outlaw masked faces altogether, though such laws proved difficult to design correctly. (In fact, over a century later, many US cities discovered they had long-dormant anti-masking laws on record that needed to be repealed or suspended when the COVID-19 pandemic made masking a public health necessity.)[96] For example, in 1885 the *Albany Law Journal* reported "an amusing example" that illustrated how hard it was to "write a statute so plain that some body will not misunderstand it":

> Section 453 of the Penal Code enacts that "An assemblage in any public house or other place of three or more persons disguised by having their faces painted, colored or concealed is unlawful." A man went to the theatre wearing a false beard. He had no companions in in[i]quity. But the police took him in and imprisoned him over night, and next morning he was fined $5. There is some doubt whether wearing a false beard is "concealing" the face. The phrase was probably aimed at masked balls. But at all events there was no "assemblage." The beard was so evidently false that the audience tittered, but that was no more "disorderly" in the man than it would be for a woman to wear a "Mother Hubbard" gown.[97]

The editor's analysis of this incident suggested that the arrest was absurd *not* because the man in question wore a false beard, but because he was so clearly not part of an assemblage. A false beard, the editor implied, may have in fact legally counted as "'concealing' the face." San Francisco's arrest records also show some arrests like this: three people were arrested in San Francisco for "Wearing a mask" between 1874 and 1876, and when David Marnell was convicted in 1887, the *Daily Alta California* reported that the charge for which he was found guilty was "wearing a mask."[98]

Although the specific item targeted by the Penal Code discussed in the *Albany Law Journal* article was a concealed face, it remains ambiguous whether the objectionable behavior in question was disguise itself, or the immoral behavior that could be *enabled* by wearing a disguise. Indeed, of all the issues that troubled San Francisco's long-standing police chief Patrick Crowley—who held the position for twenty-five years between the 1860s and 1890s—masquerade balls became a central preoccupation.[99] Crowley was far from alone in his disdain for masquerades. Many middle-class Americans and media made by and for the middle class, such as *Godey's Lady's Book*, saw masquerade balls as places of sexual promiscuity, deceptiveness, and frivolity.[100] Crowley made similar claims in his Chief of Police reports from 1892 until his retirement, in which he pleaded with the San Francisco Board of Supervisors to prohibit "bals masque, or masked balls"—a type of entertainment that was, at the time, licensed and regulated by the city. In an identical statement repeated in every end-of-year report, Crowley made his objections brief but clear: "They are scenes of debauchery, demoralizing to the youth of both sexes, and disgracing to the city."[101] For Crowley, masked balls were not a problem because they included disguises per se, but because masked balls had become, by the 1890s, common sites for what he believed to be immoral behavior. Thus, the San Francisco arrests for both masks and false beards echo these concerns about a form of entertainment some deemed morally reprehensible.

There is, however, one final way in which false beards, *specifically*, may have seemed threatening to local police, not as merely another example of fake identity or facial masking. In the criminological texts that began to circulate in the United States in the 1880s and 1890s—just as the San Francisco police force was arresting people for wearing a false beard—few physical features were more frequently discussed than the hair that grew from the head and the face. If a thin or patchy beard revealed criminal intent, as many criminology texts suggested, then wearing a false beard allowed a criminal to obfuscate the portion of his face that might otherwise reveal his nefarious intentions.

Hair and Criminology

Criminology, the scientific study of criminals and crime, was a new field of social scientific study that emerged in the late nineteenth century out of an anxiety about the urban criminal. In the final decades of the nineteenth century, middle-class white Americans—as well as the state institutions tasked with protected the citizenry, such as the police—argued that public safety required some mechanism to reliably identify criminals.[102] This was particularly true for the crimes of anonymity that felt newly threatening in a world of strangers, such as fraud, forgery, and counterfeiting.[103] As criminology scholar Simon Cole has written, "the criminal body" offered a solution: "Both good and evil, criminality and respectability, might inhabit a single body, but the body itself was stable and inescapable."[104]

Reading the body for criminal identity can proceed in two ways. The first is familiar to the twenty-first century: pinpointing individual people by their unique identifiers, such as fingerprints. A group of photographers, police clerks, detectives, and amateur anthropologists began working to develop techniques like this in the 1870s and 1880s. The most promising technologies of unique criminal identification were anthropometry (measurements of various portions of the human body) and dactyloscopy (classification of fingerprints). Both of these new sciences promised much easier and more effective categorization than photography, which police departments had used to preserve images of criminals since photography's inception in the mid-nineteenth century: French police took daguerreotypes of criminals as early as 1841, and the New York Police Department first displayed photographs of infamous criminals in a rogues' gallery in 1858.[105] Some medical and police investigators even tried to analyze strands of criminals' hair, but this technique did not become an accepted forensic science until the mid-twentieth century (though, in the last decade, the scientific validity of forensic hair analysis has been largely discredited).[106]

The second way nineteenth-century people attempted to read the criminal body, however, relied on singling out physical characteristics—including certain types of hair—that were believed to indicate inherent criminality. This type of corporeal analysis was known as criminal anthropology, and it was premised on what criminologist Nicole Hahn Rafter has called the "doctrine of the criminal as a physically anomalous human type."[107] Criminal anthropology began in Europe and first arrived in the United States through translated editions of, or references to, this European research. The first book on criminal anthropology to be published in the United States was *Anatomical Studies upon Brains of Criminals* (1881), an English translation of a German text written by Moriz Benedikt, a Hungarian neurologist who lived and studied medicine in Vienna.[108] Inspired by Franz Joseph Gall, the originator of phrenology, Benedikt dissected criminals' brains and determined that "the brains of criminals exhibit a deviation from the normal type."[109] However, despite being the first text accessible to English speakers in the United States, Benedikt's work did not have any significant impact on American thinking about criminals and criminology, and none of his other books were translated into English. Instead, it was another European physician, Cesare Lombroso from Italy, who became known as the father of criminology, and whose work most shaped criminology in the United States.[110]

Lombroso's key concept was the theory of the "born criminal," which asserted that specific physical or psychological features marked criminals' bodies and minds. In 1876 and 1893, respectively, he published his two most significant and influential books: *L'uomo delinquente* (*Criminal Man*) and

La donna delinquente, la prostitute e la donna normale (Criminal Woman, the Prostitute, and the Normal Woman). *Criminal Man* became the founding text of criminology in Europe and the United States, and was translated into French, German, Russian, and Spanish by 1899. Even though *Criminal Man* was not translated into English until 1911, American physicians, police officers, and social scientists learned about Lombroso's ideas through intermediaries, such as English physician and sexologist Havelock Ellis's influential book *The Criminal* (1890), which included summaries of Lombroso's research. As early as the 1890s, then, Lombrosian criminal anthropology became extremely influential in the United States.[111]

Lombroso's signature contribution was cataloging physical features that, his research suggested, had a higher probability of occurring in criminals than in what he deemed "the healthy population." One method Lombroso used to arrive at his conclusions about the connection between criminality and specific parts of the body was conducting statistical surveys. For the first edition of *Criminal Man*, for example, Lombroso counted the incidence of black, brown, blond, and red hair color among 390 criminals and 868 soldiers, controlling for region of origin. The resulting data table demonstrated that black hair was more common—and blond hair far less common—among the criminal group.[112] Indeed, hair and facial hair featured prominently in Lombroso's criminal typologies. For example, he wrote that "the criminal [man] is taller than the normal individual and even more so than the insane, with a broader chest [and] darker hair." They also had a distinct physiognomy: "Nearly all [male] criminals have jug ears, thick hair, thin beards, pronounced sinuses, protruding chins, and broad cheekbones."[113] Both male and female criminals were characterized by the thick, dark, and abundant hair on their heads, Lombroso claimed, and infrequent occurrence of balding; criminal men also had thin or scanty beards and were rarely gray-haired, while criminal women frequently had gray hair.[114] Lombroso even outlined connections between types of criminals and specific types of hair: thieves had "thick and close eyebrows"; pederasts (i.e., pedophiles) "are often distinguished by a feminine elegance of the hair"; arsonists had "an abundance of thick straight hair that is almost feminine"; "habitual murderers" had "crisply textured" hair; and sex workers had "fair and red hair."[115] Significantly, many of the hair traits that Lombroso linked to criminality—including "crisp hair" and "thin beards"—where the very same traits European and American racial scientists had long classified as biologically inherent on the bodies of African, Indigenous, and East Asian people. This was not a coincidence. As Lombroso wrote, "European criminals bore a strong racial resemblance to Australian aborigines and Mongols"; criminality, in other words, was atavistic. Lombroso's research thus linked criminality with the bodies of the people Europeans considered their racial inferiors.[116]

Lombroso's research promised that, with proper training and careful observation, experts could use features like hair color and texture to identify the most dangerous and inveterate criminals. While reading character and temperament in hair was something any observant lay person could do, identifying the physical markers of *criminality* was reserved for experts: physicians, scientists, police officers, and criminologists. Yet Lombroso's appeal in the United States extended far beyond experts: Whether they mentioned him by name or not, many American publications—including scholarly and professional, but also popular, periodicals—invoked Lombroso's arguments and data as they argued for a direct correspondence between the criminal and his body. An 1893 article on *Criminal Woman* published in *Popular Science*, for example, cited Lombroso's research on hair color among criminal women and sex workers.[117] Six years later, the *Kansas City Medical Index–Lancet* published a guide to "Criminals and their Characteristics" in which Dr. J. H. M'Cassy argued that "born criminals have invariably physical signs of degeneracy"—using Lombroso's framework though not his name. Dr. M'Cassy declared unequivocally that "in criminals, as a rule, the beard is scanty, the hair dark, abundant, long, and often woolly; baldness and gray hair are rare among them." (Dr. M'Cassy did not merely parrot all of Lombroso's research, however; he also added his own assertions to the taxonomy, declaring, for example, that criminal women who committed infanticide were likely to have hairy faces.)[118]

Like Peter Browne before him, Dr. M'Cassy believed that experts' privileged access to particular types of knowledge about hair could provide a patriotic public service, suggesting that a properly trained physician could protect the public from criminal activity, just as "he now protects our shores and municipalities from pestilence and infectious disease."[119] The criminal identification system envisioned by Lombroso and repeated (and expanded upon) by Americans like Dr. M'Cassy depended on physical signifiers that were stable and predictable. This is exactly why hair fraud seemed like such a threat: If distinctive dark or abundant hair could reliably identify born criminals by sight, something as simple as hair dye or a blond wig threatened to undermine the very foundation of the science.

BY THE END of the nineteenth century, the ability of ordinary Americans to alter their hair was higher than ever before. Hair dyes, hair removal depilatories, hair-care tools, hair specifics and tonics (which promised to cure baldness and gray hair and anything else that ailed a human head), false hairpieces, and wigs made of real human hair could be bought for cheap in local shops and mail-order catalogs. The possibility for transforming the hair seemed endless; wigmakers even advertised, in newspapers all across the country, false hairpieces they called "transformation wigs," or, simply, a "Transformation."[120] American elites, the likeliest to live in the nation's growing cities of strangers, feared the hair fraud that was so easily achieved. Hair was supposed to offer a legible, reliable, scientifically grounded index of a stranger's intrinsic qualities: their character, their gender, their race, their citizenship—even, by the end of the century, whether they were likely to commit a crime. Yet hair fraud threatened to undermine, even obliterate, all of this legibility; fear of this obliteration fueled the creation of institutional and carceral modes of detection and punishment.

The story of hair fraud demonstrates how hair's biological qualities—for all their supposed trustworthiness and reliability—could never fully subsume the destabilizing, subversive, and even liberatory possibilities that hair styling offered. As the twentieth century began, hair's meaning was about to shift once more—yet what would remain then, as it does to this day, was the uneasy coexistence of biology and styling at once. Indeed, as hair fraud reminds us, hair is, and was, biological; but it was *always* within the realm of culture, too.

CONCLUSION

IN THE FINAL WEEKS OF 1901, William A. Jones, the Commissioner for Indian Affairs in the Department of the Interior, sent a letter to the department's Indian agents, who governed Indigenous people living on reservations. In this letter, Jones outlined a series of "objectional and immoral practices" he wanted the agents to try to curtail on reservations, such as face painting, Indigenous dancing, and traditional forms of feasting.[1] But when, at the start of the new year, Jones started to hear rumblings that news of the letter had leaked far beyond his agency—including to white newspapers across the country—he discovered that no one was talking about the dancing or the feasting. They were talking, instead, about hair: they were *absolutely furious* that Jones had instructed his agents "to induce your male Indians to cut their hair."[2]

This was certainly not the first time that employees of the federal government had tried to control the hair-care practices of Indigenous people. Since 1879, the Carlisle Indian Industrial School—the first off-reservation boarding school for Indigenous children run by the US federal government, and the blueprint for over a dozen similar institutions—had tried to forcibly assimilate Indigenous children, and this Americanization process included compulsory haircuts. The school's founder, a Civil War veteran named Richard Henry Pratt, was convinced not only that Indigenous people in North America could be assimilated into the predominantly white United States, but that such assimilation was imperative to ensure Indigenous peoples' continued survival. Over its thirty-nine years of operation, Carlisle taught more than ten thousand students from dozens of tribes, including the Navajo, Lakota, Chippewa, Oneida, Seneca, Cherokee, and Cheyenne.[3] Pratt documented, publicized, and legitimized the school's attempts to assimilate these students through a series of photographs, which a local photographer took right when students arrived at Carlisle (labeled "before") and then again a few months or years later ("after"). Especially when paired together, such as the before-and-after portraits of a Navajo boy named Tom Torlino (see fig. C.1), these photographs dramatized the transformation they claimed to document—including transformations of the hair.

Indeed, one of the very first things a child experienced after arriving at Carlisle was a compulsory haircut.[4] Scholars uniformly note that boys with long hair received the normative short haircut associated with nineteenth-century white masculinity, but girls also recorded receiving short haircuts

TOM TORLINO—NAVAJO

As He Entered the School in 1882.   As He Appeared Three Years Later.

C.1 "Tom Torlino—Navajo" by John N. Choate. Choate photographed many Carlisle students, including Tom Torlino, when they arrived at Carlisle and a few months or years after they had attended the school; they were often paired together, as seen here, both in Choate's book of photographs from Carlisle and in promotional material circulated to donors and members of Congress.

CREDIT: Reproduced from John N. Choate, *Souvenir of the Carlisle Indian School* (1902), CIS-I-0039, Archives and Special Collections, Dickinson College, Carlisle, PA.

they did not want—in the 1880s, sometimes even the extremely short cut popular among white women during the "short hair craze" of 1885, as a circa 1885 portrait of seventeen Pueblo girls demonstrates (see fig. C.2). In a reminiscence of her days at a different boarding school written for the *Atlantic Monthly* in 1900, Gertrude Bonnin (Zitkala-Ša) recalled the devastation she felt when, on her very first day at the school, she learned that her hair would be cut short: "Our mothers had taught us that only unskilled warriors who were captured had their hair shingled by the enemy. Among our people, short hair was worn by mourners, and shingled hair by cowards." When it was time for her haircut, "I cried aloud, shaking my head all the while until I felt the cold blades of the scissors against my neck, and heard them gnaw off one of my thick braids. Then I lost my spirit."[5]

Compulsory haircuts like Bonnin's, their documentation in before-and-after photographs, and the widespread circulation of those photographs is,

C.2 "Seventeen female Pueblo students," photograph by John N. Choate, ca. 1885. The names of the girls seen in this photograph, each of whom wears a nearly identical short haircut (and four of whom hold blonde dolls), were not recorded on the photograph or archival records. The text written on the bottom of the print says, "Group of girl students at Indian School, Carlisle, Pa."

CREDIT: PC 2002.2, folder 5, Archives & Special Collections, Dickinson College, Carlisle, PA.

by now, a familiar story. Less familiar, however, is the way the Carlisle approach to Americanization-via-haircut became national—and applied to adult men, not just children—in 1901, when Jones sent the letter to his Indian agents. While Jones's insistence on short hair for Indigenous men on reservations was nothing new—echoing, as it did, the regulations governing hair length in the Massachusetts Bay Colony's seventeenth-century praying towns—what *was* new was the extremely negative response Jones's instructions received not just from Indigenous people, but also from white people. Crucially, the complete failure of the Bureau of Indian Affairs' attempt to use short hair as a vehicle for Indigenous Americanization demonstrates how ideas about hair were changing in the early days of the twentieth century.

Jones's letter to the Department of the Interior's Indian agents explained that "the wearing of long hair by the male population of your agency is not in keeping with the advancement they are making, or will soon be expected to make, in civilization. The wearing of short hair by the males will be a great step in advance, and will certainly hasten their progress toward civilization." Jones worried that "the returned male student"—back on the reservation after graduating from a school like Carlisle—"far too frequently goes back to the reservation and falls into the old customs of letting his hair grow long. He also paints profusely and adopts all the old habits and customs which his education in our industrial schools has tried to eradicate."[6] Jones thus framed long hair as a kind of slippery slope—the first step back toward savagery and away from the civilizing force that government officials were pursuing at Carlisle and the other schools it inspired. Jones was concurrently working on a change in reservation ration policy similar to the welfare-to-work policies of the 1990s, and, as he characterized it to the Secretary of the Interior in his annual report months later, he "realiz[ed] that the Indians could not continue to observe some savage customs and be industrious, too."[7]

After explaining why long hair on Indigenous men was a problem, Jones issued an order to the Indian agents: "You are therefore directed to induce your male Indians to cut their hair, and both sexes to stop painting." Jones anticipated that, while this order would be "an easy matter" for some Indigenous men on the reservations, "with others it will require considerable tact and perseverance on the part of yourself and your employees to successfully carry out these instructions." Jones suggested a solution: withhold rations, supplies, and jobs to those who do not comply. For employees and former boarding school students, whom Jones characterized in a follow up letter as "salaried servant[s] of the Government" and "the recipient[s] of boun-teous favors," respectively, noncompliance could have even more severe con-sequences: "If they become obstreperous about the matter[,] a short con-finement in the guardhouse at hard labor, with shorn locks, should furnish a cure." Jones reassured his agents that "certainly all the younger men should wear short hair, and it is believed by tact, perseverance, firmness, and with-drawal of supplies the agent can induce *all* to comply with this order."[8]

Some Indian agents reported that they were, indeed, able to carry out Jones's order without incident. For example, the agent assigned to Hopi territory, Charles E. Burton, reported in August 1902 that "gentle but firm pressure was brought to bear upon the Hopi, and every man cut his hair without much complaint, except a few at Shumopovi," one of the Hopi villages; "no force was used, but they were given to understand that they must yield and they did so." Burton added his support for the order as an effective tool for Americanization: "Their long hair is the last tie that binds them to their old customs of savagery, and the sooner it is cut, Gordian like, the better it will be for them."[9] (Although Burton was later accused by white journalist and activist Charles Lummis of violently bullying the Hopi into compliance, the Department of the Interior ultimately cleared Burton of wrongdoing.[10]) At the dawn of the twentieth century, Indian agents like Burton and Jones came to an unsurprising conclusion as they drew on a century of embodied hair knowledge: hair was the most powerful bodily index of a person's internal identity, and an Indigenous man could not be-come truly American until he had the short haircut of an American man.

However, Burton's reported ease in executing what had become known as "the short-hair order" belied just how controversial the order quickly be-came and how much resistance it inspired.[11] (Years later, under heavy criti-cism, Jones would claim that this order had the full support of President Theodore Roosevelt, "who takes a deep interest in the welfare and manage-ment of the red men."[12]) Many men on reservations did not acquiesce to having their hair cut short, such as a Cherokee man named Red Bird Smith, who, according to news reports, "said he wouldn't have his hair cut, no matter if the 'Great White Father' did order him to do so"; he then "per-suaded seven other Cherokees to join him."[13]

Some Indigenous leaders decided to pursue diplomatic avenues for re-sistance. The *Topeka State Journal* reported in January on its front page that

Chief White Eagle "will call a conference of all the Indian chiefs of Oklahoma and Indian Territory to discuss the order" and prepare to "go to Washington to confer with the president." Even Jones's agents were not uniformly supportive of the order: in February, a Laramie, Wyoming, newspaper noted that the local Indian agent assigned to the Shoshone reservation was currently traveling to the capital with six Shoshone to try to get the order revoked.[14] Some accounts evoked the specter of Indigenous violence in response to forcible assimilation, such a Montana newspaper's report that the agent assigned to the local Fort Belknap reservation had "a large police force at the agency [that was] entirely able to maintain order"; "an uprising would be quickly suppressed." Such fears of a potential uprising, the agent claimed, came from ranchers who lived along the border of the reservation: "these settlers have been alarmed for some time by the attitude of the Indians, who have been dancing for a week past"—a powerful allusion to the Ghost Dance performances that US Army soldiers used as justification for the Wounded Knee Massacre of 1890.[15]

It was not just Indigenous people and a few Indian agents who disliked the haircut order: Jones was shocked to discover public outcry in white newspapers across the country mere weeks after he sent out the letter. In late January, Jones even sent a follow up letter to his agents in response to "criticisms that have appeared in the newspapers and from information that has reached this office from other quarters," clarifying that he did not expect agents to *require* short haircuts so rashly or abruptly "as to give the Indians any cause for revolt"; instead, agents "should begin *gradually* and work steadily and tactfully till the end in view should be accomplished."[16] Jones could not understand why, out of all the practices he discussed in his December letter, "the press has noticed only that part which advocates the cutting of the hair."[17] And notice they had: dozens of newspapers across the country reacted to the haircut order with condemnation and ridicule. For example, the *Salt Lake Herald* sneered at the order because "there is no law which compels a white man to have his hair cut or a white woman to let her hair grow. These matters of personal appearance are left entirely to the individual most interested." The *Seattle Star* reported that the celebrity entertainer and frontiersman, Buffalo Bill Cody, "who himself wears long hair, thinks the way of wearing the hair should be left to the individual taste of the Indians." Both newspapers also pointed out the order's racist hypocrisy. The *Star* wrote that, since "Jones says in his order that short hair is an advancement in civilization," the Commissioner should "serve a copy on the supreme court judges, all of whom wear such hair as they have about as long as it will grow."[18] The *Herald* went a step further, suggesting—in a response dripping with sarcasm—that white men were not worthy of being held up as exemplars at all: "Possibly the secretary of the interior believes that the Indians will lose their strength with their hair; that, having made themselves so much like the white man, they will further imitate his winning ways. . . . Maybe at a distant date we'll have Indian gold brick agents, Indian bunko-steerers, Indian organizers of wildcat mining companies, and so on down the list of industries that are today peculiarly the white man's province."[19] What had white American culture become by the turn of the twentieth century but a corrupt capitalist landscape of scams, cons, and frauds?

Bathed in criticism from Indigenous people, some Indian agents, and the popular press—what Charles Lummis referred to in 1903 as "universal derision throughout the United States"—Jones and the Department of the Interior never strenuously enforced the haircut order.[20] The order gave Jones what one newspaper called an "undesirable notoriety," and he backed off calling it an order at all, telling an interviewer in 1903 that "there was never an order compelling them to cut their hair" (with the exception of employees and former boarding school students).[21] In his annual report to the Department of the Interior—which, upon publication in January 1903, caused a whole new raft of critical newspaper coverage—Jones wrote about the order at length, but only "because of the importance attached to it at the time by the public."[22]

In 1905, Jones was replaced by Francis E. Leupp as Commissioner of Indian Affairs. In an August 1905 interview, when Leupp was asked about "the effect of the so-called hair-cutting order," he responded firmly, "by no word or act of mine shall any Indian be compelled to cut his hair. Of course, hair cutting is urged as a matter of cleanliness, but I believe there are other and more important things to be done for the Indian than to compel him to have his long locks clipped." He compared forcible haircuts to young Christian children being forced to memorize a Bible passage as punishment for a wrongdoing: "Naturally, the small boy had a loathing for the good books from that time on and many Indians look upon hair cutting in the same light—a disgrace." Leupp ended his response by repeating his first comment to ensure there was no ambiguity: "There will be no forced hair cutting while I am commissioner of Indian affairs."[23]

That the Bureau of Indian Affairs completely failed to implement the haircut order vividly captures how ideas about hair were changing at the start of the twentieth century. The broadly shared sense—emergent in the eighteenth century and widespread by the nineteenth—that hair was a part of the body was beginning to wane, giving hairstyling renewed significance; hair's biological qualities still mattered, but they no longer enjoyed the kind of supremacy they had had in the nineteenth century. Yet unlike the way that hair's styling communicated social identity in the seventeenth century— and the often coercive way colonial religious and political leaders tried to enforce short hair for men—hairstyling in the twentieth century left open far greater possibilities for hair to communicate individual taste, aesthetics, and self-expression, just like clothing. Some of the public criticism of Jones's haircut order hinted at this shifting meaning. For example, the *Houston Daily Post* reported that John J. Fitzgerald, a congressman from New York, was "poking fun at the Indian commissioners' order," jokingly asking for "more information": "'I want to find out whether an Indian must wear a plug hat, white shirt, his hair pompadour and patent leather shoes before he can secure his rations,' says Mr. Fitzgerald. 'I don't think the latest order specifies whether the Indian must refer to his clothing as "pants," "breeches," or "trousers." Congress must settle this question.'"[24] Fitzgerald's jest thus compared haircut mandates to mandates for clothing and accessories. Autonomy over one's own hair remained vitally important to many Indigenous Americans—a form of self-sovereignty visible in the photographic portraits some Indigenous families, such as this Ho-Chunk family, commissioned at the turn of the twentieth century, when photography had become less expensive and more accessible than ever (see fig. C.3).[25]

Hair autonomy was also a form of self-sovereignty that white Americans increasingly recognized. For example, in 1905 the Superior Court of Riverside, California ruled in favor of Aqua His, a Yuma man who sued an Indian agent for five thousand dollars for forcibly cutting his hair under the haircut order. In his ruling, Judge Noyes declared that "the American Indian is a human being," and "it is not the law to cut an Indian's hair any more than it is to cut the hair of any other human being."[26] Charles Lummis celebrated the ruling as "an important as well as an honorable decision" and appealed to his white readers' sense of shared humanity:

> I don't know how you wear your hair, and you may not know how
> I wear mine; but we both know that we wear it as it happens to suit
> us. If any man or collection of men, or nation, or national law, were
> to step in and take you or me by the neck, hobble and gag us, and

C.3 "Studio Portrait of a Ho-Chunk Family," photograph by Charles Van Schaick, ca. 1903. This portrait shows a Ho-Chunk family who arranged to have their portrait taken at Van Schaick's studio in Black River Falls, Wisconsin: father George (Lyons) Lowe (AhHaZheeKah), mother Lena Nina Marie Decorah (Lyons) Lowe (AhHooSkaWinKah), and their three children: Lydia, Daniel, and Bessie Lowe.

chop our hair according to some plan agreed upon at a world congress in Paris—there would probably be something doing when we
were released from the clutches of the international barber. . . .
Aqua His had good long, thick hair. I would borrow $10,000, and
pay it, if I could cover my scalp with as full adornment. With primitive man, the hair is more significant than with a generation which
habitually gets baldheaded; but we need not spoof at that, for every
American woman has the same veneration for a fine head of hair. It
was, therefore, not only an insult to his individuality but to his religion, when a man who did not know enough to understand him
did him this violence.[27]

By the early twentieth century, hair was becoming a form of vital self-
expression. For federal institutions to try to force individuals to cut their
hair (outside of a military or carceral context) was not good governance—
it was a violation of individual rights.

IN THE FIRST quarter of the twentieth century, the social function of
hair changed dramatically. American people continued to go to hairdressers
and barber shops, advertise and purchase hair products, and, in some cases,
wear wigs and false hairpieces. The global human hair market that emerged
in the nineteenth century only continued to grow, and the expense and labor
of maintaining human hair—and the expectation that individuals *should* be
tending to their hair each day—continued apace. Yet the ability of hair to
reliably convey intrinsic information about Americans' identity and character—and the ability of onlookers to read this meaning on strangers'
bodies—had all but disappeared by the 1920s. Even the preservation and
collection of locks of hair, a practice nearly ubiquitous in nineteenth-century culture, started to seem odd, outmoded, or even repulsive. (The sole
exception still practiced in many American households is the lock of a baby's
hair, which typically marks an *occasion*—the first haircut—rather than func-
tioning, as it did in the nineteenth century, as a synecdochical bodily relic.)

In the first decades of the twentieth century, scientific and medical experts
began to rearticulate an understanding of hair that would have been familiar
to English colonists in the seventeenth and early eighteenth centuries,

explicitly defining hair as outside the boundaries of the body. In 1914, for example, Dr. Edwin F. Bowers wrote in the *New York Tribune*'s *Sunday Magazine* that hair was actually quite insignificant. Hair was "this mop of a material that has absolutely no physical or physiological use," Dr. Bowers wrote, "which toils not, neither does it spin, which is not sufficiently voluminous to keep one warm in winter or cool in summer, which isn't thick enough to overcome the direful effects of a carefully directed brickbat"— a piece of brick used as a weapon—"which is merely a perpetual source of labor and worry." Considering all of this uselessness, "the miracle is that folk put so much store by hair as they do; that, instead of rejoicing in the loss of it,—as the old man in Plato's dialogue rejoiced in the senile subsidence of the madness called 'love'—they bewail its passing."[28]

Anthropologists and ethnologists—who took over the search for racial difference in bodies from the nineteenth century's racial scientists like Samuel Morton, Josiah C. Nott, George Gliddon, and Peter Browne—similarly no longer included hair in their racial classification systems; eugenics, too, privileged inherited characteristics at the genetic level, not exterior features like hair strand shape. In his famous book *The American Negro* (1928), for example, anthropologist Melville J. Herskovits argued that the "American Negro"—a physical type distinct from the existing racial categories of African, Caucasian, and Mongoloid peoples—demonstrated a wide range of hair types. This internal variation ranged from "the tightly curled to that of Indian-like straightness."[29] Unlike nostril width, lip thickness, sitting height, or cephalic index (the ratio of head height to width), hair was not a contrastive feature. Therefore, Herkovits argued, hair was not useful for cataloging meaningful "differences in physical form" between racial groups.[30]

As hair became less trusted to reveal the truth about a person's identity, the hair taxonomies that had appeared so widely in American magazines and newspapers just a decade or two earlier disappeared as well, or were mentioned only with skepticism or sarcasm. This shift from proliferation to obscurity happened over a short time period, culminating around 1910. In 1890, *Ballou's Monthly Magazine* reported that "some clever individual has drawn up rules by which we may tell a person's character by the hair," and even in 1902 the *San Francisco Call* declared that "a woman may show her character more by her hair than by her eyes, nose, lips, or expression."[31] Yet by 1911, columnist Lillian Russell wrote unequivocally in the *Washington Post* that "temperament [is] not affected by hair." Indeed, "the fiery temper with which [red-haired women] are generally credited means nothing, as any person who is at all observant will note that temperaments among red-haired women vary from the angelic to the opposite extreme, much after the manner of their blonde and brunette sisters."[32] The nineteenth-century faith in the power of hair to communicate interior qualities like race or character faded significantly in the first decades of the twentieth century. Both hair that was attached to the body and hair that was severed from it largely lost its diagnostic and synecdochical power, a part of the body no longer.

Of course, hair continues to have meaning in the United States today. However, the way this meaning has been constructed in the twentieth and twenty-first centuries is different from the system of hair legibility that characterized the preceding century. Nineteenth-century Americans treated hair as a body part reliably capable of conveying intrinsic truths—especially through its *biological* qualities, such as its texture and strand shape. In other words, hair was understood to convey the aspects of the self that a person could not change or manipulate even if they wished to do so. These intrinsic truths included both the person's character strengths (or flaws) and crucial identity markers like gender and race. At the same time, people on the margins of social or political power sometimes exploited this presumption of reliability when they changed their hair in order to take on a new identity surreptitiously. Such changes to the hair were a means to a desired end, whether that was to run away from enslavement, to escape incarceration, or to begin a new kind of life. By the twentieth century, Americans largely stopped defining hair as a part of the body in the same manner. It is true that the salience of hair's biological qualities did not go away. For example, Afro-textured hair still matters in the regulation of Black hairstyles in many American institutions, and many people still dye their hair to mask the appearance of gray hair.[33] Yet, the biological explanations that nineteenth-century Americans grafted onto some hairstyles—such as long hair and facial hair—have largely faded, their sense of naturalized racial and gender meanings lost. Instead, hairstyling choices have largely become a medium for self-expression—*especially* for forms of self-expression that create stronger coherence between a person's interior sense of self and their exterior public-facing self, just like The Public Universal Friend did centuries ago. In the twenty-first century, hair has become a vehicle for expressing the wearer's own sense of their authentic cultural, religious, ethnic, racial, communal, gender, or other identity in ways that feel really *true*.

Stories of people celebrating their hair for helping them *feel like themselves* abound in contemporary life—in popular media and culture, but also among friends and families and within our communities. Some of these celebratory stories even center on the kinds of *changes* to the hair that would strike many nineteenth-century Americans as extremely suspicious, such as purchasing a very realistic wig. For example, some cancer patients who have lost their hair from chemotherapy select wigs that mirror their former hairstyles because the wigs offer a welcome restoration of identity amid the turmoil of cancer treatment. As television host Jill Martin put it in a 2023 social media post after being diagnosed with breast cancer, she was excited to buy a blond wig styled and colored to mimic the hair she had lost because "I want to feel like myself again."[34] So, too, can a new haircut facilitate a stronger connection between one's exterior and interior senses of self. In 2021, for example, author Aamina Khan interviewed a group of young queer people about the relationship between their identity and their hair for the magazine *Allure*, explaining that, for many queer Americans, hair can be "an affirmation to ourselves of what we know to be true." One interviewee, Cyrus Veyssi, described wearing their hair short as a child and teenager, even after coming out as queer. As an adult, Veyssi tried a new haircut— one that was still short on the sides but long and curly on top—and discovered how "it just gave me this androgynous kind of look that I hadn't always wanted. . . . I hadn't even embraced the intersections of my identity yet, but at that moment, I remember being like, 'This is the start of me wanting to perform my femininity,' and that haircut was really pivotal because it's the same haircut I have to this day." For Veyssi, their curls were intersectional: "The connection I have to my gender is very much based in my roots, and Persian roots are so focused on natural curls. Our curls are so historic and so cultural. So in that sense, my hair affirms my identity in all aspects the way that other forms of expression might not."[35]

Stories like these vividly illustrate just how much has changed in American hair discourse since the turn of the twentieth century. And yet, many traces of the nineteenth century remain. These traces are, in some ways, literal: the hundreds of samples of human hair, collected in the nineteenth century, that remain in American museums, archives, and other institutions. There are still twelve volumes of Peter Browne's human and animal hair in the Academy of Natural Sciences of Drexel University in Philadelphia; the Woodbury Collection at Harvard's Peabody Museum of Archaeology and

Ethnology includes hundreds of hair clippings from Indigenous people collected by anthropologist George Edward Woodbury, including hair from over seven hundred Indigenous children who attended the boarding schools run by the US government.[36] These locks, curls, and braids were collected in an era when the science of the body was deeply connected to the science of race—and even though hair no longer carries those meanings today, we are left to address the hair collected when it did. Indeed, it is the longevity of the severed hair itself—the very quality that made it worthy of special meaning to so many nineteenth-century people across different cultures— that creates the issue many archivists and curators are grappling with today: *What should we do with all this hair?* This issue became even more urgent in 2024 when the federal government clarified that the Native American Graves Protection and Repatriation Act, the law that mandates American institutions repatriate Indigenous cultural artifacts and human remains, defines human hair as human remains. Archives and museums are now compelled to return hair from Indigenous people to their descendants and tribal communities, to whom hair has long held important cultural and spiritual meaning.[37]

Even in our everyday lives, outside of archives and museums, we are still grappling with the legacy of the nineteenth century and its culture of hair. Indeed, some aspects of American hair culture today would actually feel familiar to nineteenth-century Americans. Some contemporary artists use human hair as a medium for creativity and artistic expression, imbuing strands with material (and sometimes emotional) worth.[38] American artist and craft worker Zen Hansen, for example, is teaching hairwork for the twenty-first century: under the title Hair Anthropology, Hansen sells customized hairwork jewelry, hairwork tools, instructional classes, and a guidebook for learning hair collecting and hairwork crafting.[39] Just as Hansen has reclaimed hairwork, so too have some Black Americans reclaimed the persistence of Afro-textured hair—once used by racial scientists as evidence of African descent in people of mixed ancestry—as a metaphor for Black resistance. As Lori L. Tharps has written, "[white supremacist] brainwashing worked on many Black people, but not all. But more importantly, it didn't work on the hair. Through multiple generations—even mixing White and Native American—Black hair refused to give up its distinctive kinks and coils."[40]

Hair is also still fraught in some of the ways that nineteenth-century Americans would recognize, for hair can still be weaponized to define the wearer as outside normative boundaries of gender, race, and nation. This is, in fact, one of nineteenth-century hair's greatest legacies: hair's biological qualities remain part of the way Americans conceptualize, treat, and police each other's hair. Women's facial hair is often still pathologized and condemned as it was when the Bearded Ladies and animal–women performed on stage. Moreover, since shifts in fashion norms have resulted in more of the body revealed in public, body hair is subject to cultural regulation, too, including hair grown on the legs, arms, torso, underarms, and pubic area. (Transfemme and genderqueer people are subject to even stricter surveillance about their body hair than cis women.[41]) Although research on body hair removal practices in the United States is frequently limited by demographics (just white women) or body region (just pubic hair care), surveys conducted since the 1980s suggest that as high as 80–95 percent of American women remove at least some of their body hair.[42] As critical and literary theorist Karín Lesnik-Oberstein writes in the introduction to the edited volume *The Last Taboo: Women and Body Hair* (2013)—the title itself indicative of the cultural unease women's body hair still inspires—women's body hair is largely absent from art, film, photography, and academic scholarship. Outside of medical or cosmetic study, "women's body hair is seen as, apparently, too ridiculous and trivial—or too monstrous—to be discussed at all."[43]

Hair worn by non-white Americans—especially Indigenous and Black men and women—is still subject to cultural and even legal regulation. Some schools and workplaces still classify natural Black hairstyles, such as locs, braids, twists, and Afros, as violations of dress codes or employee handbooks. In 2018, for example, two sixth-grade girls who attended a Catholic school in Gretna, Louisiana, were sent home from school for wearing box braids, which the school's principal said violated the school's requirement that "only the students' natural hair is permitted" because the braids included extensions. A judge's temporary restraining order allowed the girls to go back to school several days later; after the story gained extensive public attention, the school rescinded its policy.[44]

Yet pushback—and even structural change—is possible. In 2019, the Create a Respectful and Open Workplace for Natural Hair Act (or, CROWN Act), which prohibits discrimination on the basis of hair texture or style, became California state law. In the years since, a total of twenty-three states have passed the same or similar laws, and a federal CROWN Act passed the House in 2022; as of November 2024, it remains in committee in the Senate.[45] One of the CROWN Act's cosponsors and political champions is Congresswoman Cori Bush—the first Black woman to represent Missouri in the House of Representatives—for whom the Act is both political and personal. In a 2023 interview, Bush said that, on her first day in office at the Capitol, she "decided to just wear my hair straight," hoping that the style would allow her to care for her hair on her own because "I didn't have a hair stylist in Washington, D.C." yet. But wearing her hair straight did not feel right to Bush: "I didn't totally feel my authentic self." Asked by interviewer Brittany Luse what hairstyle would have felt more authentic, Bush replied, "Probably if I would have had my braids."[46] The ability to choose how one's own hair is styled *matters* in contemporary America, from local classrooms to the highest halls of political power.

Hair is biology, hair is culture; hair is personal, and it is political. Despite so many repeated efforts over the last four hundred years to do so, hair has never been fully controlled by regulatory apparatuses like science or policing or law. Indeed, what gives me hope are the stories of ordinary people who have seen that hair has power, but people have more—people who have understood their hair to be not destiny but possibility: the possibility to expand, even reimagine, the contours of an American body.

NOTES

INTRODUCTION

1 Séjour de Lorraine, *Les Secrets de la beauté du visage et du corps de l'homme et de la femme: Traité complet d'hygiene, de physiognomonie et d'embellissement* (Paris: Chez L'Auteur, 1855), hereafter *Secrets of Beauty*.

2 I found this passage (or an excerpt from it) in fifty-six American newspapers and magazines. See, for example, "How to Judge Character by the Hair," *Alton Telegraph* (IL), December 13, 1867 (the earliest US example I have found); "Signs of Character in the Hair," *American Phrenological Journal and Life Illustrated* 47, no. 2 (February 1868), 73; an untitled article in *Harper's Weekly* 14, no. 693 (April 9, 1870), 235; "Editor's Studies in Hygiene," *Herald of Health, Devoted to the Culture of Body and Mind* 23, no. 4 (April 1874): 173–175; "Hair as an Index of Character," *Monthly Journal of the Brotherhood of Locomotive Engineers* 7, no. 12 (December 1874), 626; "Hair and Temperament," *Daily Alta California*, February 4, 1882; and "Character Read by Hair," *Democrat* (Manchester, IA), September 3, 1902 (the latest US example I found).

Although the precise line of transmission from *Secrets of Beauty* to dozens of American periodicals is opaque, I suspect that the linchpin may have been an article published in the inaugural issue of the British trade magazine *The Hairdressers' Journal* in 1863, which translated *Secrets of Beauty*'s tenth chapter (which includes the oft-reprinted taxonomy) into English. See "Physiology of the Hair?," *The Hairdressers' Journal: Devoted to the Interest of the Profession* 1, no. 1 (March 1863): 4–6.

Just over half of the fifty-six US reprints correctly attributed the taxonomy to its original French-language source, *Les Secrets de la beauté du visage et du corps de l'homme et de la femme*. Although most of the remaining articles did not name their source material at all, starting in 1874 many articles incorrectly attributed the content to an English hairdresser named Edwin Creer. This error suggests another key step in the passage's transmission: English physician Andrew Wynters's essay "The Hair Markets of Europe and Fashions in Hair-Dressing," first published in the London periodical *Cassell's Magazine* (August 31, 1867), and later republished in its entirety in Wynter's book in *Peeps Into the Human Hive*, vol. 2 (London: Chapman and Hall, 1874). Wynter prefaced the quoted taxonomy by correctly attributing its source as *Secrets of Beauty*, and noting its quotation in one of Creer's books.

I suspect it was Wynter's essay—published less than four months before the first US example I have found—that facilitated the passage's movement from England to the United States, and from hair-care professionals to the broader reading public.

3   This particular sentence was not, in fact, from the original source material, *Secrets of Beauty*. Instead, it appears to be Wynter's commentary on the significance of the taxonomy, which first appeared in his 1867 article, "The Hair Markets of Europe." All but four of the US publications I found included Wynter's comments along the original French text, without indicating which material came from which source.

4   John H. Van Evrie, *Negroes and Negro "Slavery": The First an Inferior Race; The Latter Its Normal Condition* (1853; New York: Van Evrie, Horton & Co., 1861), 98.

5   Thomas Bogue, *A Treatise on the Structure, Color and Preservation of the Human Hair* (Philadelphia: J. W. Moore, 1841), 15; and H. T. Lovet, *Treatise on the Human Hair* (New York, 1854), 11 (emphasis added). As of 1839, Noah Webster's dictionary of American English indicated that barber surgery was no longer common nor medically acceptable. See Noah Webster, *An American Dictionary of the English Language,* stereotype edition, abridged from the original 1828 quarto edition (New York: N. & J. White, 1839), 72 and 813. Other examples of hair described as an *appendage* or haircuts as *bleeding* include: Peter A. Browne, *The Classification of Mankind, by the Hair and Wool of Their Heads. . . .* (Philadelphia: A. Hart, 1850), 4; George F. Storrs, *A Treatise on the Human Hair* (Philadelphia, 1850), 2; M. Lafayette Byrn, "The Art of Beautifying and Preserving the Hair," in *Knowledge in a Nut-Shell, or Repository of Valuable Information, and Universal Receipt Book for the People* (New York: published by the author, 1871), 248; and *Madame Viola, The Bearded Lady* (New York: Damon & Peets, [1878?]), 4.

6   The *New Oxford American Dictionary* defines *hair* as "any of the fine threadlike strands *growing from* the skin of humans, mammals, and some other animals." See "hair," in *New Oxford American Dictionary*, 3rd ed., ed. Angus Stevenson and Christine A. Lindberg (Oxford University Press, 2010), (emphasis added).

7   From 1800 to 1900, the percentage of Americans who lived in cities increased from 6 percent to 40 percent. See "Series A 57–72. Population in Urban and Rural Territory, by Size of Place: 1790 to 1970," in Chapter A, "Population," in *Historical Statistics of the United States, Colonial Times to 1970*, Part 1, bicentennial ed. (Washington, DC: The Census Library, 1975), 11–12, https://www2.census.gov/library/publications/1975/compendia/hist_stats_colonial-1970/hist_stats_colonial-1970p1-chA.pdf.

8   For the concept of a world of strangers, see Lyn H. Lofland, *A World of Strangers: Order and Action in Urban Public Spaces* (New York: Basic Books, 1973).

9   Karen Halttunen, *Confidence Men and Painted Women: A Study of Middle-Class Culture in America, 1830–1870* (New Haven, CT: Yale University Press, 1982), 34–35. Many historians have studied the sense of anxiety that permeated life in the nineteenth-century United States for so many of its inhabitants—especially, though not solely, middling white people—and the resulting interest in truth and deception.

See Halttunen, *Confidence Men and Painted Women*; James W. Cook, *The Arts of Deception: Playing with Fraud in the Age of Barnum* (Cambridge, MA: Harvard University Press, 2001); John F. Kasson, *Rudeness and Civility: Manners in Nineteenth-Century Urban America* (New York: Hill and Wang, 1990); Wendy Bellion, *Citizen Spectator: Art, Illusion, and Visual Perception in Early National America* (Chapel Hill: University of North Carolina Press, 2011); Neil Harris, *Humbug: The Art of P. T. Barnum* (Chicago: University of Chicago Press, 1973); Michael Leja, *Looking Askance: Skepticism and American Art from Eakins to Duchamp* (Berkeley: University of California Press, 2004); Stephen Mihm, *A Nation of Counterfeiters: Capitalists, Con Men, and the Making of the United States* (Cambridge, MA: Harvard University Press, 2007); and David M. Henkin, *City Reading: Written Words and Public Spaces in Antebellum New York* (New York: Columbia University Press, 1999), especially p. 28 for the concept of the instability of identity markers.

10   Halttunen, *Confidence Men and Painted Women*, 34.

11   Josh Lauer, "From Rumor to Written Record: Credit Reporting and the Invention of Financial Identity in Nineteenth-Century America," *Technology and Culture* 49, no. 2 (April 2008): 301–324, at 302–303.

12   For the function of popular entertainment and commercial amusements helped train Americans to discern truth from falsehood in the early republic and antebellum eras, see Bellion, *Citizen Spectator*; and Cook, *The Arts of Deception*.

13   Catherine Gallagher and Thomas W. Laqueur have argued that nineteenth-century transformations in the understanding of the body are linked to the contemporary emergence of modern politics, especially Enlightenment liberalism. Central to Enlightenment logic was the argument, articulated by Thomas Hobbes and others, that there was no basis in nature for any specific form of authority, such as kings over subjects, or masters over slaves. Under this new logic for social organization, there was no longer a natural justification for male–female relationships or the hierarchical relationships between racial groups. In response, European and American thinkers looked for bodily explanations to explain the real-life existence of men's domination of women, and European domination of non-white peoples. New interpretations of the human body thus became the foundation for the social order. See Gallagher and Laqueur, introduction to *The Making of the Modern Body: Sexuality and Society in the Nineteenth Century*, ed. Catherine Gallagher and Thomas W. Laqueur (Berkeley: University of California Press, 1987).

14   Stephanie M. H. Camp, "Black Is Beautiful: An American History," *Journal of Southern History* 81, no. 3 (August 2015): 675–690, at 676.

15   Physiognomy and phrenology have an extensive historiography. For the history, impact, and significance of these two fields in the United States, see, for example, John D. Davies, *Phrenology: Fad and Science—A 19th Century American Crusade* (New Haven, CT: Yale University Press, 1955); Madeline B. Stern, *Heads and Headlines: The Phrenological Fowlers* (Norman: University of Oklahoma Press, 1971); Arthur Wrobel, "Orthodoxy and Respectability in Nineteenth-Century Phrenology," *Journal of Popular Culture* 9, no. 1 (Summer 1975): 38–50; G. P. Brooks

and R. W. Johnson, "Contributions to the History of Psychology: XXIV. Johann Caspar Lavater's *Essays on Physiognomy*," *Psychological Reports* 46, no. 1 (February 1980): 3–20; Charles Colbert, *A Measure of Perfection: Phrenology and the Fine Arts in America* (Chapel Hill: University of North Carolina Press, 1997); Jan Todd, "Bigger Bodies, Better Brains: Phrenology and the Health Lift," in *Physical Culture and the Body Beautiful: Purposive Exercise in the Lives of American Women, 1800–1875* (Macon, GA: Mercer University Press, 1998), 173–210; Christopher J. Lukasik, *Discerning Characters: The Culture of Appearance in Early America* (Philadelphia: University of Pennsylvania Press, 2011); James Poskett, *Materials of the Mind: Phrenology, Race, and the Global History of Science, 1815–1920* (Chicago: University of Chicago Press, 2019); Courtney E. Thompson, *An Organ of Murder: Crime, Violence, and Phrenology in Nineteenth-Century America* (New Brunswick, NJ: Rutgers University Press, 2021); and Rachel Walker, *Beauty and the Brain: The Science of Human Nature in Early America* (Chicago: University of Chicago Press, 2022). For a world historical overview of efforts to read meaning in the physical body, see Christopher Rivers, "From Analogy to Causality: The History of Physiognomy before 1700," in *Face Value: Physiognomical Thought and the Legible Body in Marivaux, Lavater, Balzac, Gautier, and Zola* (Madison: University of Wisconsin Press, 1994), 18–32.

16   Walker, *Beauty and the Brain*, 19–20 and 46–47.

17   Sharon Block, *Colonial Complexions: Race and Bodies in Eighteenth-Century America* (Philadelphia: University of Pennsylvania Press, 2018), 10–13; and Susan Scott Parrish, *American Curiosity: Cultures of Natural History in the Colonial British Atlantic World* (Chapel Hill: University of North Carolina Press, published for Omohundro Institute of Early American History & Culture, 2006), 77–79.

18   Walker, *Beauty and the Brain*, 19 and 46–47.

19   Jill Burke, *How to Be a Renaissance Woman: The Untold History of Beauty and Female Creativity* (New York: Pegasus Books, 2024), 188.

20   Anu Korhonen, "Strange Things Out of Hair: Baldness and Masculinity in Early Modern England," *Sixteenth Century Journal* 41, no. 2 (Summer 2010): 371–391, at 377n19; and Parrish, *American Curiosity*, 79.

21   William Prynne, *The unlovelinesse, of love-lockes* (1628), 20, 29–30, https://quod.lib.umich.edu/e/eebo/A10199.0001.001/1:3?rgn=div1;view=fulltext.

22   James Howell, *Epistolæ Ho-Elianæ. Familiar Letters, Domestick and Foreign*, vol. 1, 7th ed. (1645; London: T.G., 1705), 44 (emphasis added).

23   Kathleen M. Brown, *Undoing Slavery: Bodies, Race, and Rights in the Age of Abolition* (Philadelphia: University of Pennsylvania Press, 2023), 45–47; and Parrish, *American Curiosity*, 77–79.

24   James Axtell, *The Invasion Within: The Contest of Cultures in Colonial North America* (New York: Oxford University Press, 1985), 171–172.

25   Mairin Odle, *Under the Skin: Tattoos, Scalps, and the Contested Language of Bodies in Early America* (Philadelphia: University of Pennsylvania Press, 2023), 73. Importantly, Odle demonstrates that the historical memory of scalping as

synonymous with Indigeneity, which English sources established by the eighteenth century, erases the role scalp bounties played in hastening and deepening the dispossession of Indigenous tribes (8).

26   "Whiskers, OR. . . . A CLEAN SHAVE," *Daily Picayune* (New Orleans), August 8, 1843 (emphasis in the original). Although the original article was unsigned, it was reprinted—with attribution—three years later in a collected volume of the author's articles: Dennis Corcoran, *Pickings from the Portfolio of the Reporter of the New Orleans "Picayune"* (Philadelphia: T. K. & P. G. Collins, 1846), 3.

27   Etymology for "trichology" (noun), *Oxford English Dictionary* (first published in 1914; not yet revised), https://www.oed.com/dictionary/trichology_n?tab =etymology#17820888.

28   *Trichology* comes from the root *tricho-* which means "hair, in many terms of botany, zoology, etc." See *Oxford English Dictionary,* s.v. "tricho-, combining form," https://www.oed.com/dictionary/tricho_combform1?tab=etymology.

29   Archaeologists Andrew T. Chamberlain and Michael Parker Pearson have written of bodily decay that "hair is often the best surviving material, as it consists largely of the structural protein keratin which is strong and insoluble. Intact hair is sometimes preserved together with bones and teeth after the rest of the body has disappeared." However, hair does not last forever nor in all archaeological conditions, though there is scant research on the precise timescales for decay in various environments. See Chamberlain and Pearson, *Earthly Remains: The History and Science of Preserved Human Bodies* (New York: Oxford University Press, 2001), 18; Andrew S. Wilson et al., "Towards an Understanding of the Interaction of Hair with the Depositional Environment," *Chungara: Revista de Antropología Chilena* [The journal of Chilean anthropology] 33, no. 2 (June–December 2001): 293–296, at 293; and Thomas W. Laqueur, *The Work of the Dead: A Cultural History of Mortal Remains* (Princeton, NJ: Princeton University Press, 2015), 3. Reverend Nicholas Noyes claimed in his 1700 essay that the severed hair used to construct periwigs was "always withering and decaying," and required "artificial Oyle and Perfumes, to keep it from Putrefaction," but there is no evidence that this assessment is correct. See Worthington Chauncey Ford, "Samuel Sewall and Nicholas Noyes on Wigs," in *Publications of the Colonial Society of Massachusetts,* vol. 20, *Transactions 1917–1919,* February Meeting, 1918 (Boston: printed by society, 1920): 109–156, at 126.

30   Margaret E. Smiley, hair album, private collection of Sheryl Jaeger, Eclectibles, Tolland, CT, viewed February 7, 2015.

31   Mark Campbell, *Self-Instructor in the Art of Hair Work, Dressing Hair, Making Curls, Switches, Braids, and Hair Jewelry of Every Description* (New York: printed by author, 1867), 264.

32   Charles Ball, *Slavery in the United States . . .* (New York: John S. Taylor, 1837), 31–32.

33   "A Lock of Hair," *Godey's Lady's Book,* May 1855, 471. The quoted passage was attributed to the English essayist Leigh Hunt.

34   Mary Cole to her husband, June 16, 1812, in John W. Kirn, *A Genuine Sketch of the Trial of Mary Cole, for the Willful Murder of Her Mother, Agnes Thuers* (New Jersey, 1812), 9.

35   Religious historian Samuel Morris Brown suggests one additional way that severed hair held special meaning for Mormons and other Christians awaiting the resurrection: "Bones would await the resurrection in their graves, facing the rising sun, while hair, partaking of the adamant immortality of the skeleton, was a portable memorial that could remain on the person of a survivor." See Brown, *In Heaven as It Is on Earth: Joseph Smith and the Early Mormon Conquest of Death* (New York: Oxford University Press, 2012), 65.

36   O. S. and L. N. Fowler, *The Illustrated Self-Instructor in Phrenology and Physiology, with One Hundred Engravings, and a Chart of the Character* (New York: Fowler and Wells, 1857), 31, https://www.gutenberg.org/cache/epub/33223/pg33223 -images.html.

37   Walker, *Beauty and the Brain*, 46 and 177–181.

38   Two books that helped me conceptualize and articulate this framework are Barbara Young Welke, *Law and the Borders of Belonging in the Long Nineteenth Century United States* (New York: Cambridge University Press, 2012); and Alison Piepmeier, *Out in Public: Configurations of Women's Bodies in Nineteenth-Century America* (Chapel Hill: University of North Carolina Press, 2004), esp. ch. 4.

39   Ingrid Banks, *Hair Matters: Beauty, Power, and Black Women's Consciousness* (New York: New York University Press, 2000), 4.

40   Examples of anthropological or ethnographic studies of hair include the following: Charles Berg, *The Unconscious Significance of Hair* (London: George Allen & Unwin, 1951); Edmund Leach, "Magical Hair," *Journal of the Royal Anthropological Institute of Great Britain and Ireland* 88, no. 2 (July–December 1958): 147–164; C. R. Hallpike, "Social Hair," *Man* 4, no. 2 (1969): 256–264; Raymond Firth, "Hair as Private Asset and Public Symbol," in *Symbols: Public and Private* (Ithaca, NY: Cornell University Press, 1973), 262–298; P. Hershman, "Hair, Sex and Dirt," *Man* 9 (1974): 274–298; Gananath Obeyesekere, *Medusa's Hair: An Essay on Personal Symbols and Religious Experience* (Chicago: University of Chicago Press, 1981); Anthony Synnott, "Shame and Glory: A Sociology of Hair," *British Journal of Sociology* 38, no. 3 (1987): 381–413; Jeannette Marie Mageo, "Hairdos and Don'ts: Hair Symbolism and Sexual History in Samoa," *Man* 29, no. 2 (June 1994): 407–432 (also published in *Frontiers: A Journal of Women's Studies* 17, no. 2 (1996): 138–167); Alf Hiltebeitel and Barbara D. Miller, eds., *Hair: Its Power and Meaning in Asian Cultures* (Albany: SUNY Press, 1998); Roy Sieber and Frank Herreman, eds., *Hair in African Art and Culture* (New York: Museum for African Art, 2000); Elizabeth C. Hirschman, "Hair as Attribute, Hair as Symbol, Hair as Self," *Gender and Consumer Behavior* 6 (2002): 355–366; Rose Weitz, *Rapunzel's Daughters: What Women's Hair Tells Us About Women's Lives* (New York: Farrar, Straus and Giroux, 2004); and Emma Tarlo, *Entanglement: The Secret Lives of Hair* (London: Oneworld, 2017), 201.

Some studies focus on hair symbolism specifically in biblical texts or early Christian religious practice. See, for example, Roberta Miliken, *Ambiguous Locks: An Iconography of Hair in Medieval Art and Literature* (Jefferson, NC: McFarland, 2012); Susan Niditch, *"My Brother Esau Is a Hairy Man": Hair and Identity in Ancient Israel* (Oxford: Oxford University Press, 2008); Gregory Mobley, "The Wild Man in the Bible and the Ancient Near East," *Journal of Biblical Literature* 116 (1997): 217–233; and Saul Olyan, "What Do Shaving Rites Accomplish and What Do They Signal in Biblical Ritual Contexts?," *Journal of Biblical Literature* 117 (1998): 611–622.

41   See, for example, Wendy Cooper, *Hair: Sex Society Symbolism* (New York: Stein and Day, 1971); Diane Simon, *Hair: Public, Political, Extremely Personal* (New York: St. Martin's Press, 2000); Robin Bryer, *The History of Hair: Fashion and Fantasy Down the Ages* (London: Philip Wilson, 2000); Caroline Cox and Lee Widdows, *Hair and Fashion* (London: V&A, 2005); Geraldine Biddle-Perry and Sarah Cheang, *Hair: Styling, Culture, and Fashion* (Oxford: Berg, 2008); Jacky Colliss Harvey, *Red: A History of the Redhead* (New York: Black Dog & Leventhal Publishers, 2015); and Kurt Stenn, *Hair: A Human History* (New York: Pegasus Books, 2016).

Such popular histories of hair also frequently lack citations. Although Henry Latimer Seaver's essay "Hair and Holiness," published in *Proceedings of the Massachusetts Historical Society* 68 (Oct. 1944–May 1947): 3–20, is well cited and draws on many primary source examples, it suffers from many of the same problems as the popular genre. Seaver tends to flatten historical context and change over time in favor of cataloging examples of hair and wig incidents in early European history. Three useful popular history reference books are Richard Corson, *Fashions in Hair: The First Five Thousand Years* (London: Peter Owen, 1984); Marian I. Doyle, *An Illustrated History of Hairstyles, 1830–1930* (Atglen, PA: Schiffer, 2003); and Victoria Sherrow, *Encyclopedia of Hair: A Cultural History* (Westport, CT: Greenwood, 2006).

42   See, for example, Robert Bartlett, "Symbolic Meaning of Hair in the Middle Ages," *Transactions of the Royal Historical Society* 4 (1994): 43–60; Frank Dikötter, "Hairy Barbarians, Furry Primates, and Wild Men: Medical Science and Cultural Representations of Hair in China," in Hiltebeitel and Miller, *Hair*, 50–74; Weikun Cheng, "Politics of the Queue: Agitation and Resistance in the Beginning and End of Qing China," in Hiltebeitel and Miller, *Hair*, 123–142; Afsaneh Najmabadi, *Women with Mustaches and Men without Beards: Gender and Sexual Anxieties of Iranian Modernity* (Berkeley: University of California Press, 2005); Shane White and Graham White, "Slave Hair and African American Culture in the Eighteenth and Nineteenth Centuries," *Journal of Southern History* 61, no. 1 (February 1995): 45–76; Willie Morrow, *400 Years Without a Comb* (San Diego: Morrow's Unlimited, Inc., 1973); Gael Graham, "Flaunting the Freak Flag: *Karr v. Schmidt* and the Great Hair Debate in American High Schools, 1965–1975," *Journal of American History* 91, no. 2 (September 2004): 522–543; Rebecca Herzig, *Plucked: A History of Hair Removal* (New York: NYU Press, 2015); Rebecca Herzig, "The Woman Beneath the Hair: Treating Hypertrichosis, 1870–1930," *NWSA Journal* 12, no. 3 (2000): 50–66; and

Kimberly A. Hamlin, "The 'Case of the Bearded Woman': Hypertrichosis and the Construction of Gender in the Age of Darwin," *American Quarterly* 63, no. 4 (December 2011): 955–981. See also *Eighteenth-Century Studies* 38, no. 1 (Fall 2004), which was a special issue focused on hair in an eighteenth-century context. In particular, Angela Rosenthal's opening essay resonates with many of the central ideas in this book, including its insistence that hair has been underemphasized in existing scholarship about the body. Angela Rosenthal, "Raising Hair," in "Hair," ed. Angela Rosenthal, special issue, *Eighteenth-Century Studies* 38, no. 1 (Fall 2004): 1–16.

Galia Ofek's *Representations of Hair in Victorian Literature and Culture* (Farnham, UK: Ashgate, 2009) has perhaps the most in common with this book because it examines representations of hair in nineteenth-century Britain. Ofek focuses particularly on the way that specific hair colors and styles worn by women were broadly understood to comprise a kind of "hair code" (x) in British society, and how this code reflected contemporary anxieties about the changing role of women.

43   Hair studies—in reference to humanistic and social scientific work, not biological or medical study of the body—is a recent term that captures interdisciplinary scholarship and cultural criticism on hair. Two books that self-identify as within this field of inquiry are Sarah Mesle, *Tangled* (Boston: Beacon, 2025); and Elizabeth L. Block, *Beyond Vanity: The History and Power of Hairdressing* (Cambridge, MA: MIT Press, 2024). Mesle also writes hair studies articles for the *Los Angeles Review of Books* that focus on film, television, and celebrity culture, including "Mare's Hair" (June 10, 2021), https://avidly.lareviewofbooks.org/2021/06/10/mares-hair/.

44   Banks, *Hair Matters*, 4. Banks's call for the power of personal stories echoes in the dance-theater performance *Hair & Other Stories* by the ensemble Urban Bush Women, which turns up the lights in the theater and turns the performance's questions of hair, beauty, and Black identity directly on the audience. See *Hair & Other Stories*, dir. and chor. Chanon Judson and Mame Diarra Speis, Zellerbach Playhouse, Berkeley, CA, December 1, 2023.

45   Banks, *Hair Matters*, 10.

46   Jasmine Nichole Cobb, *New Growth: The Art and Texture of Black Hair* (Durham, NC: Duke University Press, 2023), 1. See also Camp, "Black Is Beautiful."

47   Book-length examinations of Madam C. J. Walker include A'Lelia Bundles, *On Her Ground: The Life and Times of Madam C. J. Walker* (New York: Scribner, 2001), which was also the inspiration for the Netflix series *Self Made* (2020); Beverly Lowry, *Her Dream of Dreams: The Rise and Triumph of Madam C. J. Walker* (New York: Alfred A. Knopf, 2003); P. J. Graham, *Madam C. J. Walker: Entrepreneur and Self-Made Millionaire* (New York: Cavendish Square, 2019); Erica L. Ball, *Madam C. J. Walker: The Making of an American Icon* (Lanham, MD: Rowman and Littlefield, 2021); and Tyrone McKinley Freeman, *Madam C. J. Walker's Gospel of Giving: Black Women's Philanthropy during Jim Crow* (Urbana: University of Illinois Press, 2021).

48   bell hooks, "Straightening Our Hair," in *Tenderheaded: A Comb-Bending Collection of Hair Stories*, ed. Juliette Harris and Pamela Johnson (New York:

Pocket Books, 2001), 111–112. See also Noliwe M. Rooks, *Hair Raising: Beauty, Culture, and African American Women* (New Brunswick, NJ: Rutgers University Press, 1996), 3.

49 hooks, "Straightening Our Hair," 115.

50 Banks, *Hair Matters*, 17; and hooks, "Straightening Our Hair," 114–115.

51 Cobb, *New Growth*, 9.

52 hooks, "Straightening Our Hair," 114–115.

53 Some of the Black feminist scholarship on hair that most informs this book include the following: Rooks, *Hair Raising*; Banks, *Hair Matters*; hooks, "Straightening Our Hair"; Ayana Byrd and Lori Tharp, *Hair Story: Untangling the Roots of Black Hair in America* (New York: St. Martin's Press, 2001); Ima Ebong, ed., *Black Hair: Art, Style, and Culture* (New York: Universe, 2001); Lanita Jacobs-Huey, *From the Kitchen to the Parlor: Language and Becoming in African American Women's Hair Care* (Oxford: Oxford University Press, 2006); Tameka N. Ellington and Joseph L. Underwood, eds., *Textures: The History and Art of Black Hair* (Kent, OH: Kent State University Museum, 2020); Emma Dabiri, *Twisted: The Tangled History of Black Hair Culture* (New York: Harper Perennial, 2020); Cobb, *New Growth*; Lyzette Wanzer, ed., *Trauma, Tresses, & Truth: Untangling Our Hair through Personal Narratives* (Chicago: Chicago Review Press, 2023); and Tameka N. Ellington, ed., *Black Hair in a White World* (Kent, OH: Kent State University Museum, 2023).

54 Despite its wide popularity in the United States, hair work and the broader practice of hair collection has been mostly relegated to the arena of antiquarian fascination, and scholarly analysis has been limited. The main references for the subject of American hair work are Helen Sheumaker, "'This Lock You See': Nineteenth-Century Hair Work as the Commodified Self," *Fashion Theory: The Journal of Dress, Body & Culture* 1, no. 4 (1997): 421–445; and Helen Sheumaker, *Love Entwined: The Curious History of Hairwork in America* (Philadelphia: University of Pennsylvania Press, 2007). Sheumaker's research is extremely valuable for scholars interested in a starting point on the subject. However, her work focuses heavily on finished pieces of hair work exchanged in formal or informal market economies, thus emphasizing the practices of white middle-class people with sufficient money and time to make or purchase such objects. Other publications on the subject include mostly graduate theses and dissertations, offering the possibility of exciting work to come in the future. See, for example, Jennifer Reeder, "'To Do Something Extraordinary': Mormon Women and the Creation of a Useable Past" (PhD diss., George Mason University, 2013); Rachel Robertson Harmeyer, "'The Hair as Remembrancer': Hairwork and the Technology of Memory" (MA thesis, University of Houston, 2013); Lauren Clark, "A (Hair) Work of Memory: Mattanna Fairchild's Decorative Memorial Works in the Post War South" (MA thesis, George Mason University, 2015); and Keith Beutler, *George Washington's Hair: How Early American Remembered the Founders* (Charlottesville: University of Virginia Press, 2021).

Finally, some historians have included severed hair as one example of a broader interest in relic collecting or remembrance practices in the nineteenth-century

United States and Europe. For the United States, see Geoffrey Batchen, *Forget Me Not: Photography and Remembrance* (New York: Princeton Architectural Press, 2004); and Teresa Barnett, *Sacred Relics: Pieces of the Past in Nineteenth-Century America* (Chicago: University of Chicago Press, 2013). For England and France, see Judith Pascoe, *The Hummingbird Cabinet: A Rare and Curious History of Romantic Collectors* (Ithaca, NY: Cornell University Press, 2006).

55 "Life Cut Short: Hamilton's Hair and the Art of Mourning Jewelry," New-York Historical Society, accessed November 11, 2024, https://www.nyhistory .org/exhibitions/life-cut-short-hamiltons-hair-and-art-mourning-jewelry; and Ellen P. Gilbert, [Victorian hair-work album of Gilbert and Armitage families of Pennsylvania], [ca. 1863], Graphic Arts Bound Volumes 087, American Antiquarian Society, Worcester, MA.

56 Lucy Chase to [unknown recipient], [1869?], in *Dear Ones at Home: Letters from Contraband Camps*, ed. Henry Lee Swint (Nashville: Vanderbilt University Press, 1966), 252–253.

57 For femininity in the nineteenth century, see, for example, Carroll Smith-Rosenberg and Charles Rosenberg, "The Female Animal: Medical and Biological Views of Woman and Her Role in Nineteenth-Century America," *Journal of American History* 60, no. 2 (September 1, 1973): 332–356; Smith-Rosenberg, *Disorderly Conduct: Visions of Gender in Victorian America* (New York: Knopf, 1985); Gregory Kent Stanley, *The Rise and Fall of the Sportswoman: Women's Health, Fitness, and Athletics, 1860–1940* (New York: P. Lang, 1996); Beverly Gordon, "Woman's Domestic Body: The Conceptual Conflation of Women and Interiors in the Industrial Age," *Winterthur Portfolio* 31, no. 4 (1996): 281–301; Jan Todd, *Physical Culture and the Body Beautiful: Purposive Exercise in the Lives of American Women, 1800–1870* (Macon, GA: Mercer University Press, 1998); Piepmeier, *Out in Public*; Kathy Peiss, *Hope in a Jar: The Making of America's Beauty Culture* (New York: Metropolitan Books, 1998; Philadelphia: University of Pennsylvania Press, 2011); and Nora Doyle, *Maternal Bodies: Redefining Motherhood in Early America* (Chapel Hill: University of North Carolina Press, 2018). For masculinity in the nineteenth century, see Gail Bederman, *Manliness and Civilization: A Cultural History of Gender and Race in the United States, 1880–1917* (Chicago: University of Chicago Press, 1995); Michael Zakim, *Ready-Made Democracy: A History of Men's Dress in the American Republic, 1760–1860* (Chicago: University of Chicago Press, 2003); Melissa N. Stein, *Measuring Manhood: Race and the Science of Masculinity, 1830–1934* (Minneapolis: University of Minnesota Press, 2015); Amy S. Greenberg, *Manifest Manhood and the Antebellum American Empire* (New York: Cambridge University Press, 2005); Kristin L. Hoganson, *Fight for American Manhood* (New Haven, CT: Yale University Press, 1998); Timothy R. Buckner and Peter Caster, eds., *Fathers, Preachers, Rebels, Men: Black Masculinity in U.S. History and Literature, 1820–1945* (Columbus: Ohio State University Press, 2011); E. Anthony Rotundo, *American Manhood* (New York: Basic Books, 1993); and Michael S. Kimmel, *Manhood in America: A Cultural History*, 2nd ed. (New York: Oxford University Press, 2006). Finally,

recent scholars have done important work in documenting people whose gender identities fell outside this binary, including genderqueer and trans people. See, for example, Alice Domurat Dregar, *Hermaphrodites and the Medical Invention of Sex* (Cambridge, MA: Harvard University Press, 1998); Elizabeth Reis, "Impossible Hermaphrodites: Intersex in America, 1620–1960," *Journal of American History* (September 2005): 411–441; and Jen Manion, *Female Husbands: A Trans History* (New York: Cambridge University Press, 2020).

58   See Daphne Brooks, *Bodies in Dissent: Spectacular Performances of Race and Freedom, 1850–1910* (Durham, NC: Duke University Press, 2007); Kyla Wazana Tompkins, *Racial Indigestion: Eating Bodies in the Nineteenth Century* (New York: NYU Press, 2012); Deirdre Cooper Owens, *Medical Bondage: Race, Gender, and the Origins of American Gynecology* (Athens: University of Georgia Press, 2017); Rana A. Hogarth, *Medicalizing Blackness: Making Racial Difference in the Atlantic World, 1780–1840* (Chapel Hill: University of North Carolina Press, 2017); Christopher Willoughby, "His Native, Hot Country: Racial Science and Environment in Antebellum American Medical Thought," *Journal of the History of Medicine and Allied Sciences* 72, no. 3 (July 2017): 328–351; Mark Smith, *How Race Is Made: Slavery, Segregation and the Senses* (Chapel Hill: University of North Carolina Press, 2007); Amy Louise Wood, *Lynching and Spectacle: Witnessing Racial Violence in America, 1890–1940* (Chapel Hill: University of North Carolina Press, 2009); Samuel J. Redman, *Bone Rooms: From Scientific Racism to Human Prehistory in Museums* (Cambridge, MA: Harvard University Press, 2016); and Kyla Schuller, *The Biopolitics of Feeling: Race, Sex, and Science in the Nineteenth Century* (Durham, NC: Duke University Press, 2017). Although it focuses on the eighteenth (rather than the nineteenth) century, Block's *Colonial Complexions* is also an extremely important part of this literature.

59   See Jennifer Terry, ed., *Deviant Bodies: Critical Perspectives on Difference in Science and Popular Culture* (Bloomington: Indiana University Press, 1995); Rosemarie Garland-Thomson, *Extraordinary Bodies: Figuring Physical Disability in American Culture and Literature* (New York: Columbia University Press, 1997); Susan Schweik, *The Ugly Laws: Disability in Public* (New York: New York University Press, 2009); Welke, *Law and the Borders of Belonging in the Long Nineteenth Century United States*; Dea H. Boster, *African-American Slavery and Disability: Bodies, Property, and Power in the Antebellum South, 1800–1860* (New York: Routledge, 2013); Sarah Handley-Cousins, *Bodies in Blue: Disability in the Civil War North* (Athens: University of Georgia Press, 2019); Jenifer L. Barclay, *The Mark of Slavery: Disability, Race, and Gender in Antebellum America* (Urbana: University of Illinois Press, 2021); and Sarah E. Chinn, *Disability, the Body, and Radical Intellectuals in the Literature of the Civil War and Reconstruction* (New York: Cambridge University Press, 2024).

60   For the bodies of the dead, see Michael Sappol, *A Traffic in Dead Bodies: Anatomy and Embodied Social Identity in Nineteenth-Century America* (Princeton, NJ: Princeton University Press, 2002); Franny Nudelman, *John Brown's Body:*

Slavery, Violence, and the Culture of War (Chapel Hill: University of North Caro-
lina Press, 2004); Drew Gilpin Faust, *This Republic of Suffering: Death and the
American Civil War* (New York: Alfred A. Knopf, 2008); and Laqueur, *The Work of
the Dead*. For the history of specific senses, see Mark Smith, *How Race Is Made:
Slavery, Segregation and the Senses* (Chapel Hill: University of North Carolina
Press, 2007); Amy Louise Wood, *Lynching and Spectacle: Witnessing Racial Violence
in America, 1890–1940* (Chapel Hill: University of North Carolina Press, 2009);
Schuller, *The Biopolitics of Feeling*; and Melanie A. Kiechle, *Smell Detectives: An
Olfactory History of Nineteenth-Century America* (Seattle: University of Washington
Press, 2017).

61   See Regina Markell Morantz, "Making Women Modern: Middle Class
Women and Health Reform in 19th Century America," *Journal of Social History* 10,
no. 4 (1977): 490–507; Stephen Nissenbaum, *Sex, Diet, and Debility in Jacksonian
America: Sylvester Graham and Health Reform* (Westport, CT: Greenwood Press,
1980); James C. Whorton, *Crusaders for Fitness: The History of American Health
Reformers* (Princeton, NJ: Princeton University Press, 1982); Kathleen M. Brown,
Foul Bodies: Cleanliness in Early America (New Haven, CT: Yale University Press,
2009); Karen Sánchez-Eppler, *Touching Liberty: Abolition, Feminism, and the Poli-
tics of the Body* (Berkeley: University of California Press, 1993); Sara DuBow, "Dis-
covering Fetal Life, 1870s–1920s," in DuBow, *Ourselves Unborn: A History of the
Fetus in America* (New York: Oxford University Press, 2010), 10–36; James B. Salazar,
Bodies of Reform: The Rhetoric of Character in Gilded Age America (New York: New
York University Press, 2010); and Kathleen M. Brown, *Undoing Slavery: Bodies,
Race, and Rights in the Age of Abolition* (Philadelphia: University of Pennsylvania
Press, 2023). DuBow's book, for example, shows how movements as varied as anti-
abortionists, eugenicists, and euthenists all drafted the fetal body into the elabora-
tion of their activism.

62   See Anson Rabinbach, *The Human Motor: Energy, Fatigue, and the Ori-
gins of Modernity* (Berkeley: University of California Press, 1992); and Carolyn
Sorisio, *Fleshing Out America: Race, Gender, and the Politics of the Body in American
Literature, 1833–1879* (Athens: University of Georgia Press, 2002). Dubow's *Ourselves Unborn* also considers how fetal bodies became symbolic of the body politic.
So too does Sánchez-Eppler's *Touching Liberty* consider the human body as em-
blematic of the values of the body politic. Finally, Maurizio Valsania, *Jefferson's
Body: A Corporeal Biography* (Charlottesville: University of Virginia Press, 2017),
while idiosyncratic, alludes similarly to the resonance between the body and the
body politic.

63   My use of "historical body" here is informed by Brown, *Undoing Slavery*.

64   American Medical Association, "About," *AMA*, https://www.ama-assn.org
/about; American Association for the Advancement of Science, "Mission and History," *AAAS*, https://www.aaas.org/mission; American Bar Association, "ABA Timeline," *ABA*, https://www.americanbar.org/about_the_aba/timeline/; and American
Historical Association, "Brief History of the AHA," *AHA*, https://www.historians
.org/about/aha-history/brief-history-of-the-aha/.

65   Ronald L. Numbers, *Darwinism Comes to America* (Cambridge, MA: Harvard University Press, 1998), 30.

66   An early example of a historian and archivist explaining the possibilities posed by archival digitization is John H. Whaley Jr, "Digitizing History," *American Archivist* 57, no. 4 (Fall 1994): 660–672.

67   Many scholars have documented and analyzed the limitations of the archive as a site of historical knowledge production. See, for example, Ula Y. Taylor, "Women in the Documents: Thoughts on Uncovering the Personal, Political, and Professional," *Journal of Women's History* 20, no. 1 (2008): 187–196; Nupur Chaudhuri, Sherry J. Katz, and Mary Elizabeth Perry, eds., *Contesting Archives: Finding Women in the Sources* (Urbana: University of Illinois Press, 2010); Marisa Fuentes, *Dispossessed Lives: Enslaved Women, Violence, and the Archive* (Philadelphia: University of Pennsylvania Press, 2016); and Saidiya Hartman, *Wayward Lives, Beautiful Experiments: Intimate Histories of Riotous Black Girls, Troublesome Women, and Queer Radicals* (New York: Norton, 2019).

68   For the history and significance of body hair from a humanistic perspective, see Karín Lesnik-Oberstein, ed., *The Last Taboo: Women and Body Hair* (Manchester: Manchester University Press, 2006); Christine Hope, "Caucasian Female Body Hair and American Culture," *Journal of American Culture* 5, no. 1 (Spring 1982): 93–99; Kirsten Hansen, "Hair or Bare? The History of American Women and Hair Removal, 1914–1934" (BA thesis, Barnard College, 2007); Herzig, *Plucked*; Breanne Fahs, *Unshaved: Resistance and Revolution in Women's Body Hair Politics* (Seattle: University of Washington Press, 2022); and Burke, *How to Be a Renaissance Woman,* ch. 9.

69   The lives and labors of hair-care industry workers—including barbers, hairdressers, wigmakers, professional hair workers, human hair importers, and hair-care product entrepreneurs—will not be discussed in depth in this book. For the history of Black barbers, see William Johnson, *William Johnson's Natchez: The Ante-Bellum Diary of a Free Negro,* ed. William Ransom Hogan and Edwin Adam Davis (Baton Rouge: Louisiana State University Press, 2000 [1951]); Douglas W. Bristol, Jr., *Knights of the Razor: Black Barbers in Slavery and Freedom* (Baltimore, MD: Johns Hopkins University Press, 2009); Quincy T. Mills, *Cutting Along the Color Lines: Black Barbers and Barber Shops in America* (Philadelphia: University of Pennsylvania Press, 2013); and Sean Trainor, "The Rise and Fall of the American Barber Shop: African-American Barbers and the End of Clean-Shavenness," in "Groomed for Power: A Cultural Economy of the Male Body in Nineteenth-Century America" (PhD diss., Pennsylvania State University, 2015), 28–73. For beauty shops, see Julie Willett, *Permanent Waves: The Making of the American Beauty Shop* (New York: New York University Press, 2000); Julia Kirk Blackwelder, *Styling Jim Crow: African American Beauty Training During Segregation* (College Station: Texas A&M University Press, 2003); Tiffany M. Gill, *Beauty Shop Politics: African American Women's Activism in the Beauty Industry* (Urbana: University of Illinois Press, 2010); and Blain Roberts, *Pageants, Parlors, and Pretty Women: Race and Beauty in the Twentieth-Century South* (Chapel Hill: University of North Carolina Press, 2016). Finally, for the

white women laborers who produced the hair-work objects popular in the nineteenth century, see Sheumaker, *Love Entwined*.

70 I am indebted to Gail Bederman's *Manliness and Civilization* for elaborating this type of organizing mechanism in her introduction.

71 The term *enfreakment* was first used by David Hevey, *The Creatures Time Forgot: Photography and Disability Imagery* (New York: Routledge, 1992). Many current freak show scholars, who recognize that *freak* (like so many other categories of identity) is culturally constructed, use *enfreakment* it to mean *the process of turning a person or category of people into a freak*.

72 Rose Weitz, *Rapunzel's Daughters: What Women's Hair Tells Us About Women's Lives* (New York: Farrar, Straus and Giroux, 2004), xiii–xiv.

1. LONG HAIR

1 In China, under the Manchu rule of the Qing Dynasty (which began in 1644), men of Han ethnicity were compelled to wear the queue as a symbol of their loyalty to the emperor. Prescribing and policing male appearance had long been a central way that Chinese rulers both marked cultural differences between themselves and neighboring communities and reinforced and reproduced their authority. See Weikun Cheng, "Politics of the Queue: Agitation and Resistance in the Beginning and End of Qing China," in *Hair: Its Power and Meaning in Asian Cultures*, ed. Alf Hiltebeitel and Barbara D. Miller (Albany: State University of New York Press, 1998), 123–125. I am grateful to Daniel Friedman for his help with sources on the queue in China.

2 Thomas M. Cooley, "Ho Ah Kow v. Matthew Nunan," *American Law Register* 27, no. 11 (1879): 676–689; and "Cutting Their Queues: Five Chinese Prisoners Suffer a Great Indignity in San Francisco," *New York Times*, June 12, 1876, 7.

3 *Periwig* is an obsolete form of *wig*. *Periwig* derives from *peruke*, a French loanword that, in the fifteenth century, meant "a natural head of hair." By the sixteenth century, its generally accepted meaning became instead "a skullcap covered with hair as to imitate the natural head of hair." *Periwig* is effectively the same word as *peruke*, but with a different vowel after the initial syllable: the [u] in *peruke* (/pəruk/) became the first [ɪ] in *periwig* (/pɛrɪwɪg/). See *Oxford English Dictionary*, s.v. "periwig, *n.*" and "peruke, *n.*," December 2023, http://www.oed.com/view/Entry/141111?rskey=B7fPW2&result=1&isAdvanced=false#eid and http://www.oed.com/view/Entry/141644?rskey=nR5wSI&result=1&isAdvanced=false#eid.

4 Both the gendered parameters of American political citizenship and the racialization of American masculinity have been ably established by many scholars. For gender and citizenship see, for example, Mark E. Kann, *A Republic of Men: The American Founders, Gendered Language, and Patriarchal Politics* (New York: NYU Press, 1998); Linda Kerber, *Women of the Republic: Intellect and Ideology in Revolutionary America* (Chapel Hill: University of North Carolina Press, 1980); E. Anthony

Rotundo, *American Manhood: Transformations in Masculinity from the Revolution to the Modern Era* (New York: Basic Books 1993); Michael S. Kimmel, *Manhood in America: A Cultural History* (Oxford: Oxford University Press, 2006); and Rosemarie Zagarri, *Revolutionary Backlash: Women and Politics in Early American Republic* (Philadelphia: University of Pennsylvania Press, 2011). For whiteness and masculinity see, for example, Amy S. Greenberg, *Manifest Manhood and the Antebellum American Empire* (Cambridge: Cambridge University Press, 2005); Kristin L. Hoganson, *Fighting for American Manhood: How Gender Politics Provoked the Spanish-American and Philippine-American Wars* (New Haven, CT: Yale University Press, 1998); Gail Bederman, *Manliness and Civilization: A Cultural History of Gender and Race in the United States, 1880–1917* (New Haven, CT: Yale University Press, 1995); and Timothy R. Buckner and Peter Caster, eds., *Fathers, Preachers, Rebels, Men: Black Masculinity in U.S. History and Literature, 1820–1945* (Columbus: The Ohio State University Press, 2011).

5   Kathleen M. Brown's examination of body care (including hair care) in the seventeenth and eighteenth centuries makes frequent mention of barbers and cleaning practices in the English colonies and early United States. See Brown, *Foul Bodies: Cleanliness in Early America* (New Haven, CT: Yale University Press, 2009).

6   Carmen M. Cusack, *Hair and Justice: Sociolegal Significance of Hair in Criminal Justice, Constitutional Law, and Public Policy* (Springfield, IL: Charles C. Thomas, 2015), 110–111; Peggy Doty, "Constitutional Law: The Right to Wear a Traditional Indian Hair Style—Recognition of a Heritage," in *Native American Cultural and Religious Freedoms,* ed. John R. Wunder (New York: Garland, 1999; repr. New York: Routledge, 2013), 85–100, at 85–86; and Ashley Lomboy, "My Son's Hair Is Part of a Thousand-Year-Old Tribal Culture. His School Called It a 'Fad,'" News and Commentary, ACLU, March 22, 2023, https://www.aclu.org/news/racial-justice/my-sons-hair-is-part-of-a-thousand-year-old-tribal-culture-his-school-called-it-a-fad.

7   Richard Corson, *Fashions in Hair: The First Five Thousand Years* (London: Peter Ownes, 1984), 215 and 264.

8   Richard Godbeer, "Perversions of Anatomy, Anatomies of Perversion: The Periwig Controversy in Colonial Massachusetts," *Proceedings of the Massachusetts Historical Society* 109 (1997): 1–23, at 2–3.

9   Corson, *Fashions in Hair,* 275–277.

10   English colonists and early Americans (including George Washington) often used the word *queue* to refer to their periwig or own-hair ponytails. However, by the mid-nineteenth century, *queue* referred almost exclusively to the hairstyle worn by Chinese men. For descriptions of Washington's hairstyle that used the word *queue*, see, for example, "Ten Common Misconceptions about George Washington," *Mount Vernon* (accessed September 7, 2023), https://www.mountvernon.org/george-washington/facts/myths/ten-misconceptions-about-washington; and Maris Fessenden, "How George Washington Did His Hair," *Smithsonian Magazine,* June 9, 2015, https://www.smithsonianmag.com/smart-news/how-george-washington-did-his-hair-180955547/.

11   Corson, *Fashions in Hair,* 275–290.

12   J. M. Austin, "Sketches of Fashion's Eccentricities," *Universalist and Ladies Repository* 6, no. 8 (January 1838): 389.

13   Devereux Jarratt, *The Life of Reverend Devereux Jarratt, Written by Himself* (Baltimore, MD: Warner & Hanna, 1806), reprinted as "A Virginia Minister" in *Remarkable Providences: Readings in Early American History,* rev. ed., ed. John Demos (Boston: Northeastern University Press, 1991), 103–122 (emphasis in the original). The word *genteel,* Richard L. Bushman has shown, was attached to many objects, people, and behaviors. Genteel periwigs were worn by people riding on genteel saddles, expressing themselves through genteel speech, and carefully practicing genteel posture. See Richard L. Bushman, *The Refinement of America: Persons, Houses, Cities* (New York: Vintage, 1993), 60–61.

14   Gaye Wilson, "Wigs," *Monticello,* updated July 1999, https://www.monticello.org/research-education/thomas-jefferson-encyclopedia/wigs/; and Shane White and Graham White, *Stylin': African American Expressive Culture from the Beginnings to the Zoot Suit* (Ithaca, NY: Cornell University Press, 1998), 50.

15   Some enslaved people wore wigs each day for other reasons: an 1811 runaway slave advertisement described one enslaved man who wore wigs or a handkerchief everyday "in consequence of some defect on his head." See *Richmond Enquirer* (VA), February 7, 1811, republished in Daniel Meaders, *Advertisements for Runaway Slaves in Virginia, 1801–1820* (New York: Garland, 1997), 159.

16   White and White, *Stylin',* 50.

17   *Pennsylvania Gazette,* November 29, 1750. See also Rev. Joseph B. Pelt, "Collections Relating to Fashion and Dress in New England. —*(Continued),*" *Daily Courant* (Hartford, CT), November 5, 1838; and John Donald Duncan, "Servitude and Slavery in Colonial South Carolina, 1670–1776" (PhD diss., Emory University, 1972), 241. The use of wigs as part of a disguise for runaways (as well as for criminals) will be discussed in detail in chapter 4.

18   Jarratt, *Life of Reverend Devereux Jarratt,* 109; and Karin Calvert, "The Function of Fashion in Eighteenth-Century America," in *Of Consuming Interests: The Style of Life in the Eighteenth Century,* ed. Cary Carson, Ronald Hoffman, and Peter J. Albert (Charlottesville: University of Virginia Press, 1994), 265.

19   *Pennsylvania Gazette,* December 18, 1750 (emphasis added).

20   Dr. Alexander Hamilton, *Hamilton's Itinerarium. . . .,* ed. Albert Bushnell Hart (Saint Louis, MO: privately printed, 1907), 111–113.

21   Calvert, "The Function of Fashion," 265. Wearing one's own hair in the style of a periwig was also one way to keep up with contemporary fashions on the cheap—without the cost of a stylish wig. See Corson, *Fashions in Hair,* 224.

22   [Advertisement for Jack], *Connecticut Courant,* October 27, 1783, in Freedom on the Move (digital archive by Cornell University, the University of Alabama, the University of New Orleans, University of Kentucky, and the Ohio State University), https://fotm.link/a/8cc55d57-9465-442e-a8d6-1840fe0429bd; and [Advertisement for Harry], *The New-York Gazette: or, The Weekly Post-Boy,* July 4, 1773,

Freedom on the Move, https://fotm.link/a/0fd3d519-453e-4e78-b1c5-55ff19673737. Runaway advertisements are the most extensive and detailed textual record scholars have of what enslaved Americans looked like; however, because runaway advertisements were created by white people, they must be interpreted with care. See Shane White and Graham White, "Slave Hair and African American Culture in the Eighteenth and Nineteenth Centuries," *Journal of Southern History* 61, no. 1 (February 1995): 45–76, at 49; and White and White, *Stylin'*, 43–44. For an extensive examination of bodily descriptions in runaway advertisements from the eighteenth century, see Sharon Block, *Colonial Complexions: Race and Bodies in Eighteenth-Century America* (Philadelphia: University of Pennsylvania Press, 2018).

23 White and White, *Stylin'*, 17 and 45–46. It is unclear from surviving records if Alic was enslaved or a servant. White and White refer to Alic as "a black servant" (45). The Maryland Center for History and Culture, which holds this object in its collection, refers to Alic as "an African American slave or servant of Bathurst Jones (1760–1810) of Hanover Town, Virginia." Benjamin Henry LaTrobe, *Alic . . .* , watercolor on paper, November 3, 1797, object ID 1960.108.1.3.12, Maryland Center for History and Culture, https://www.mdhistory.org/resources/alic-a-faithful-and-humorous-old-servant-belonging-to-mr-bathurst-jones-of-hanover/.

24 White and White, "Slave Hair and African American Culture," 50; White and White, *Stylin'*, 41–45; and Bruce M. Tyler, "Black Hairstyles, Appearance, Conduct, and Cultural Democracy," *Western Journal of Black Studies* 14, no. 4 (Winter 1990): 235–250, at 235.

25 White and White, "Slave Hair and African American Culture," 48–49.

26 White and White, *Stylin'*, 41; Ayana Byrd and Lori Tharp, *Hair Story: Untangling the Roots of Black Hair in America* (New York: St. Martin's Press, 2001), 12–13; and Willie Morrow, *400 Years Without a Comb* (San Diego: Morrow's Unlimited, Inc., 1973), 19. In place of traditional African-style combs, some enslaved people combed their hair with a metal-toothed tool intended for separating wool fiber.

27 White and White, *Stylin'*, 51.

28 Corson, *Fashions in Hair*, 205.

29 Corson, *Fashions in Hair*, 228 and 328; and Bela C. Perry, *Human Hair, and the Cutaneous Diseases Which Affect It: Together with Essays on Acne, Sycosis, and Chloasma,* 2nd ed. (New York: James Miller, 1866), 29–32.

30 Corson, *Fashions in Hair*, 171–172. Although advertisements for runaway enslaved people are one of the primary databases historians have for evaluating the hair, clothing, and other bodily features of enslaved people, enslaved women are extremely underrepresented in runaway advertisements, and thus evidence of enslaved women's hairstyles is also less abundant. See White and White, "Slave Hair and African American Culture," 53.

31 Paul Benjamin Moyer, *The Public Universal Friend: Jemima Wilkinson and Religious Enthusiasm in Revolutionary America* (Ithaca, NY: Cornell University Press, 2015), 2–3. Moyer's extensive research has not uncovered any evidence that Wilkinson harbored interest in living as a man or presenting in a masculine way

before 1776; "thus it appears that whatever change Wilkinson experienced upon her rebirth as a heavenly prophet was driven by spiritual factors rather than some long-term struggle over her gender identity" (8).

32   As Moyer acknowledges, pronouns present a linguistic challenge to anyone who writes about the Friend. Moyer decided to conform to the way Friend's disciples themselves referred to the Friend, which was with the masculine pronouns "he" and "him," though Moyer maintains the feminine "she" and "her" when discussing "contemporary commentators who denied the legitimacy of Wilkinson's claims and continued to view her as a designating or deluded woman" (9). In my own writing, I have attempted to acknowledge the Friend's agender identity by refraining from using pronouns and instead using "the Friend," repetitive though it may be.

33   *Freeman's Journal*, February 14, 1787; and Moyer, *Public Universal Friend,* 3–9 and 90–93.

34   Jacob Cox Parsons, *Extracts from the Diary of Jacob Hiltzeimer of Philadelphia, 1765–1798* (Philadelphia: Wm. F. Fell, 1893), 145; Alice Morse Earle, *Colonial Dames and Good Wives* (Boston: Houghton, Mifflin, & Company, 1895), 177–178; and Moyer, *Public Universal Friend,* 95.

35   A common story used to illustrate colonial periwig critique is Samuel Sewall and Nicholas Noyes's disagreement in 1701, which is discussed later in this chapter. See, for example, Worthington Chauncey Ford, "Samuel Sewall and Nicholas Noyes on Wigs," in *Publications of the Colonial Society of Massachusetts*, vol. 20, *Transactions 1917–1919,* February Meeting, 1918 (Boston: printed by society, 1920): 109–156, at 114–115; and Godbeer, "Perversions of Anatomy," 1–2.

36   William Prynne, *The unlovelinesse, of love-lockes* (1628), 14, https://quod .lib.umich.edu/e/eebo/A10199.0001.001/1:3?rgn=div1;view=fulltext.

37   A compilation of "extracts from sermons supposed to have been preached by Rev. Michael Wigglesworth of Malden" were reprinted as Wigglesworth, "On the Wearing of the Hair," in *New England Historical & Genealogical Register*, vol. 1, ed. William Cogswell (Boston: Samuel G. Drake, 1847), 369. See also the June 1, 1669, entry about a Wigglesworth sermon on hair in Margaret Smith, *Leaves from Margaret Smiths' Journal. . . .* (Boston: Ticknor, Reed, and Fields, 1849), 208–211.

38   This translation is from the Geneva Bible, which was the version preferred by Puritans (emphasis added). See Naseeb Shaheen, "Misconceptions about the Geneva Bible," *Studies in Bibliography* 37 (1984): 156–158.

39   Thomas Hutchinson, *The History of the Massachusetts Bay Colony*, vol. 1, 2nd ed. (London: privately printed, 1765), 151–152.

40   The proclamation letter was reprinted in Hutchinson, *History of the Massachusetts Bay Colony*, 151–152. Some sources (such as Seaver) refer to this proclamation as a Harvard College order, which seems to be because it was copied into the college's records for that year. See Godbeer, "Perversions of Anatomy," 8.

Although Endecott's proclamation included no explicit language suggesting that these guidelines were legally binding or punishable, many later sources referred to this 1649 letter as constituting an official law against long hair on men. See, for example, Francis S. Drake, *The Town of Roxbury.* . . . (Roxbury, MA: printed by author, 1878), 54; and "The Parson's Periwig," *Connecticut Courant*, February 22, 1802.

41 *A Copy of the Laws of Harvard College, 1655, with an introduction by Samuel A. Green, M.D.* (Cambridge, MA: Press of John Wilson and Son, 1876), 6, https://quod.lib.umich.edu/m/moa/abj6548.0001.001/. See also Godbeer, "Perversions of Anatomy," 8.

42 James Axtell, *The Invasion Within: The Contest of Cultures in Colonial North America* (New York: Oxford University Press, 1985), 174–175; and Karen Ordahl Kupperman, "Presentment of Civility: English Reading of American Self-Presentation in the Early Years of Colonization," *William and Mary Quarterly* 54, no. 1 (January 1997): 205–207.

43 Thomas Shepard, *The Clear Sun-shine of the Gospel Breaking Forth upon the Indians in New-England* (London: R. Cotes, 1647), 5; Ann Marie Plane, *Colonial Intimacies: Indian Marriage in Early New England* (Ithaca, NY: Cornell University Press, 2000), 50; Axtell, *Invasion Within*, 170; and R. Todd Romero, *Making War and Minting Christians: Masculinity, Religion, and Colonialism in Early New England* (Amherst: University of Massachusetts Press, 2011), 110.

44 Axtell, *Invasion Within*, 171–172.

45 Axtell, *Invasion Within*, 171–172.

46 John Eliot, *Tears of repentance: or, A Further narrative of the progress of the Gospel amongst the Indians in New-England: Setting forth, not only their present state and condition, but sundry confessions of sin by diverse of the said Indians, wrought upon by the saving power of the gospel; together with the manifestation of their faith and hope in Jesus Christ, and the work of grace upon their hearts* (London: Peter Cole, 1653), 18–19, https://name.umdl.umich.edu/A84357.0001.001; Daniel K. Richter, *Facing East from Indian Country: A Native History of Early America* (Cambridge, MA: Harvard University Press, 2003), 111–115; and Jacqueline M. Henkel, "Represented Authenticity: Native Voices in Seventeenth-Century Conversion Narratives," *New England Quarterly* 87, no. 1 (March 2014): 5–45, at 6–8.

47 Eliot, *Tears of Repentance*, 18–19; and Richter, *Facing East from Indian Country*, 111–115.

48 Henkel calls this passage on Monesquassun's hair "a kind of odd prelude to his climactic statement of confession." See Henkel, "Represented Authenticity," 39.

49 Mairin Odle, *Under the Skin: Tattoos, Scalps, and the Contested Language of Bodies in Early America* (Philadelphia: University of Pennsylvania Press, 2023), 73 and 147n29.

50 Convers Francis, *The Life of John Eliot, Apostle to the Indians* (Boston: Hilliard, Gray, and Co., 1836), 8 and 219–220; Drake, *Town of Roxbury*, 188; and Pelt, "Collections Relating to Fashion and Dress in New England." I searched the *Oxford English Dictionary*, other dictionaries, and the Internet more broadly in an effort to discover the meaning of *protexity*, but I had no success: every relevant result was merely a repetition of Eliot's quote.

51   Francis, *Life of John Eliot,* 322–323 and 335.

52   Nathaniel B. Shurtleff, ed., "Att an Adjournment of the Genll Court of October, held at Boston, the 3d of November 1675," in *Records of the Governor and Company of Massachusetts Bay in New England,* vol. 5 (Boston: William White, 1854), 58–63; and Eric Foner, *Give Me Liberty! An American History,* vol. 1, Seagull Edition (New York: Norton, 2005), 89.

53   Shurtleff, "Att an Adjournment of the Genll Court," 58.

54   Shurtleff, "Att an Adjournment of the Genll Court," 58–59; and James Axtell, *The European and the Indian: Essays in the Ethnohistory of Colonial North America* (New York: Oxford University Press, 2006), 60.

55   Ford, "Samuel Sewall and Nicholas Noyes on Wigs," 126.

56   Ford, "Samuel Sewall and Nicholas Noyes on Wigs," 121.

57   It seems likely that Noyes's essay was not widely published or circulated in his lifetime. Every citation to this essay that I have identified actually originates with its publication in the 1920 edition of the transactions of the Colonial Society of Massachusetts. Society member Worthington Chauncey Ford had found Sewall's handwritten transcription of Noyes's manuscript in the former's oft-cited diary. There, Sewell dated it "January 15th, 1702–03," although historian John Demos has since dated it to 1700. See Ford, "Samuel Sewall and Nicholas Noyes on Wigs," 109–128; and Nicholas Noyes, "An Essay Against Periwigs," in *Remarkable Providences: Readings in Early American History,* rev. ed., ed. John Demos (Boston: Northeastern University Press, 1991), 253–261 (emphasis added).

58   Citing Noyes's essay, Karin Calvert argues that "the new fashion [of wearing periwigs] met with opposition at first, not because of the expense or implicit vanity, but because the best periwigs were made of women's hair" (Calvert, "The Function of Fashion," 263). However, Noyes is the only writer I have found who objected to periwigs on this ground.

59   Ford, "Samuel Sewall and Nicholas Noyes on Wigs," 121. Anticipating an objection, Noyes reminded his readers that even when Jacob wore a wig in the Bible, his wig was made "with Goat's hair, and not with womens" (120).

60   Noyes, "An Essay Against Periwigs," 125.

61   Noyes, "An Essay Against Periwigs," 125–126.

62   Worthington Chauncey Ford was first person to bring this story to historians' attention, reporting on it to fellow members of the Colonial Society of Massachusetts in 1918. Ford had a difficult time understanding why Sewall hated periwigs, noting that Sewall was not "a bigoted adherent to puritan views"; he did not generally condemn costly clothing and accessories, and it was difficult to imagine him condemning periwigs on aesthetic grounds alone. Sewall's actions were likely unintelligible to Ford because of Ford's own historical context: by the time he read Sewall's diary in the 1910s, American culture had largely stopped defining hair as a part of the body—a necessary precondition for understanding Sewall's assertion about hair's spiritual significance. See Ford, "Samuel Sewall and Nicholas Noyes on Wigs," 114–115; and Godbeer "Perversions of Anatomy."

63 John Calvin, *Institutes of the Christian Religion*, trans. John Allen, 6th American ed., vol. 1 (Philadelphia: Presbyterian Board of Publication, 1813), 645–650.

64 Samuel Sewall, *Diary of Samuel Sewall, 1624–1729*, vol. 2, *1699–1700–1714*, in *Collections of the Massachusetts Historical Society*, 5th ser., vol. 6 (Boston: printed by society, 1879), 114–115.

65 Sewall, *Diary of Samuel Sewall*, 2:36–37.

66 Sewall, *Diary of Samuel Sewall*, 2:114–115.

67 Wamditanka, "A Sioux Story of the War: Chief Big Eagle's Story of the Sioux Outbreak of 1862," *Minnesota Historical Society Collections* 6 (1894): 382–391, at 385; and H. Glenn Penny, *Kindred by Choice: Germans and American Indians Since 1800* (Chapel Hill: University of North Carolina Press, 2013), 82.

68 Corson, *Fashions in Hair*, 398; Pelt, "Collections Relating to Fashion and Dress in New England"; and Donald R. Hickey, "The United States Army versus Long Hair: The Trials of Colonial Thomas Butler, 1801–1805," *Pennsylvania Magazine of History and Biography* 101, no. 4 (October 1977): 462–474, at 462. The exception to the rejection of wigs were bald men, who continued to purchase wigs throughout the nineteenth century. These wigs, however, were short and deliberately crafted to look like hair grown from the head—the exact opposite intended effect of the seventeenth- and eighteenth-century periwig. For example, an 1806 advertisement for an ornamental hair maker in Boston offered that "the young Gentleman and the aged Sire can be accommodated with Wigs suitable to their ages, which are such a perfect imitation of Nature, as to baffle the nicest Investigation." See Belcher and Armstrong, "No. 11 (to be continued weekly.) of the Emerald. For July 12, 1806" (Boston: Belcher & Armstrong, 1806), American Antiquarian Society, Worcester, MA.

69 John Whitcomb and Claire Whitcomb, *Real Life at the White House: Two Hundred Years of Daily Life at America's Most Famous Residence* (New York: Routledge, 2002), 37.

70 Jen Manion has documented many stories of female husbands—people assigned female at birth who lived their lives as men—in the United States between 1830 and 1910. In some of these stories, a short haircut was part of the process of transition, which echoes the growing uniformity of short hair for men by 1830. Moreover, newspaper exposés also sometimes cited a female husband's long hair (or absence of facial hair) as evidence that they had been assigned female at birth; these accounts resonate with the larger system of hair culture that was emerging in this period—that hair was biological tell of a person's intrinsic identity, and the naturalization of short hair and facial hair for men, and long hair and bare faces for women. See Jen Manion, *Female Husbands: A Trans History* (New York: Cambridge University Press, 2020), 259–260.

71 White and White, *Stylin'*, 52–55. White and White speculate that the decline of elaborate, often lengthy hairstyles among enslaved men may also be related to generational changes in the enslaved population as the Atlantic slave trade dwindled (52). See also White and White, "Slave Hair and African American Culture," 66.

72   Ashton Gonzalez, *Visualizing Equality: African American Rights and Visual Culture in the Nineteenth Century* (Chapel Hill: University of North Carolina Press, 2020), 58–59; Charles Edwards Lester, *Chains and Freedom: or, The Life and Adventures of Peter Wheeler, A Colored Man Yet Living* (New York: E. S. Arnold & Co., 1839), https://www.gutenberg.org/files/61074/61074-h/61074-h.htm; and White and White, *Stylin'*, 55. Fashion historian Marian I. Doyle affirms the uniformity of short hair for men from 1830 through the end of the century, though she points out that long hair did remain socially acceptable for some men with specific occupations (such as artists and musicians), on the frontier, or in rarified performance spaces, such as Wild West shows. See Marian I. Doyle, *An Illustrated History of Hairstyles, 1830–1930* (Atglen, PA: Schiffer, 2003), 97.

73   Hickey, "The United States Army versus Long Hair," 466–467. Three months after the short hair order, Wilkinson issued a second order that prohibited soldiers from wearing facial hair. Because beard wearing was already extremely uncommon in 1801, the facial hair order was uncontroversial.

74   Hickey, "The United States Army versus Long Hair," 464–469. Butler's court martial also pertained to a claim of neglecting his duties because, one year earlier, he had failed to report to a new post as quickly as Wilkinson thought he should have. The judges in his first trial acquitted him of this charge.

75   Hickey, "The United States Army versus Long Hair," 469–473.

76   Hickey, "The United States Army versus Long Hair," 473.

77   "Col. Butler's Defense," *Louisiana Gazette,* January 3, 1806, reprinted in Hickey, "The United States Army versus Long Hair," 467 (emphasis added).

78   David Hackett Fischer is the main proponent of the explanation that the decline of the periwig was part of changing ideas about age; periwigs, he argues, flattered older bodies by hiding the wearer's natural hair (or lack thereof), whereas natural hair emphasized youthful appearances instead. See David Hackett Fischer, *Growing Old in America* (Oxford: Oxford University Press, 1979), 47 and 86–87. For the explanation rooted in American independence, see, for example, William Pencak, "'Faithful Portraits of our Hearts': Images of the Jay Family, 1725–1814," *Early American Studies* 7, no. 1 (Spring 2009): 82–108, at 95; and Calvert, "The Function of Fashion," 252–283.

79   Kate Haulman, *Politics of Fashion in Eighteenth-Century America* (Chapel Hill: University of North Carolina Press, 2011), 156. For the ways in which the consumer revolution in England shaped consumption in English North America, see Calvert, "The Function of Fashion."

80   See Calvert, "The Function of Fashion," 263–270; Lynn Festa, "Personal Effects: Wigs and Possessive Individualism in the Long Eighteenth Century," *Eighteenth-Century Life* 29, no. 2 (Spring 2005): 47–90; and Michael Kwass, "Big Hair: A Wig History of Consumption in Eighteenth-Century France," *American Historical Review* 111, no. 3 (June 2006): 631–659.

81   Kann, *A Republic of Men,* 5–11.

82   Kann, *A Republic of Men,* 12–15. Kann calls these competing ideals republican manhood and self-made manhood, respectively.

83 Kann, *A Republic of Men*, 12–13.

84 "Letter to the Editor," *Connecticut Courant,* March 21, 1796.

85 John Jay to John Adams, March 1783, quoted in Pencak, "'Faithful Portraits of our Hearts,'" 99. Pencak confirms that Jay did begin wearing a wig in the mid-1790s, but at the time he wrote this letter he did not (95).

86 "Letter to the Editor," *Connecticut Courant,* March 21, 1796.

87 For more on the enslaved labor that helped maintain periwigs and long hair for men in the late eighteenth century, see Laura J. Galke, "Tressed for Success: Male Hair Care and Wig Hair Curlers at George Washington's Childhood Home," *Winterthur Portfolio* 52, no. 2–3 (Summer/Autumn 2018): 85–135.

88 George F. Storrs, *A Treatise on the Human Hair; with directions for preserving it in a state of health, and remarks relative to the treatment of children's hair; and important testimonies of the properties of Storrs' Chemical Hair Invigorator; invented and prepared by George F. Storrs; Philadelphia* (Philadelphia: [publisher unknown], 1850), 3, American Antiquarian Society, Worcester, MA. See also Edward Phalon, *Treatise on the Hair* (New York: [unknown], 1847), 6, American Antiquarian Society, Worcester, MA.

89 Lynn Festa cites the Council of Rouen in 1096 as the earliest documented instance of the church denouncing long hair on men by citing 1 Corinthians. See Festa, "Personal Effects," 60.

90 In the nineteenth century, perhaps the only other body part that similarly delineated the racial and gendered boundaries of beauty was the buttocks. Many scholars have, for example, examined the long cultural legacy of Saartjie (Sarah) Baartman, a Khoikhoi woman who was displayed in English and French universities and popular entertainment venues as the "Hottentot Venus" from 1810 to 1815. The part of Baartman's body that garnered the greatest curiosity and scientific interest was her buttocks, which was larger than European norms. As Janell Hobson explains, "the Hottentot Venus came to symbolic both the presumed ugliness and heightened sexuality of the African race during her era" (1). However, I argue that the hair was *more capable* of carrying the racial and gendered boundaries of beauty in the nineteenth century because of its omnipresence in ordinary life: unlike the buttocks, which was visible in that century only in extraordinary or rarified settings (such as freak shows), hair was everywhere.

For more on Baartman's legacy and the buttocks' intersectional associations with women's beauty, see, for example, Janell Hobson, *Venus in the Dark: Blackness and Beauty in Popular Culture*, 2nd ed. (New York: Routledge, 2018); Sabrina Strings, *Fearing the Black Body: The Racial Origins of Fat Phobia* (New York: New York University Press, 2019); and Heather Radke, *Butts: A Backstory* (New York: Avid Reader Press, 2022).

91 Thomas Bogue, *A Treatise on the Structure, Color and Preservation of the Human Hair* (Philadelphia: J. W. Moore, 1841), 48–50 (emphasis added).

92 Peter A. Browne, *Trichologia Mammalium* (Philadelphia: Jones, 1853), 101.

93 "A Series of Papers on the Hair: Chapter I," *Godey's Lady's Book and Magazine* 50, no. 1 (January 1855), 31.

94   "Proper Management of the Hair," *Journal of Health* 1, no. 18 (May 26, 1830): 279–280 (emphasis in the original); reprinted in the *Connecticut Courant*, August 10, 1830.

95   Bogue, *Treatise on the Structure*, 7, 49, and 79.

96   Mrs. A. Walker, *Female Beauty, as Preserved an Improved by Regiment, Cleanliness and Dress; and Especially by the Adaptation, Colour and Arrangement of Dress, as Variously Influencing the Forms, Complexion, and Expression of Each Individual, and Rendering Cosmetic Impositions Unnecessary*, American ed. (New York: Scofield and Voorhies, 1840), 245. I have read one letter by a woman describing a short haircut prescribed to her by her physician, though the ailment it was intended to cure was left unmentioned. The letter writer, Carolyn, fretted to her grandmother that no one would recognize her "since all my hair was cut off . . . I look & feel very queer with it short, & secretly wish many times that I had it again, but Dr. Greene knows best." See Caroline Lynette Burr Oberlin to Caroline Burr Grant, December 22, 1890, box 4, folder 10, Grant–Burr Family Papers, American Antiquarian Society, Worcester, MA.

97   *First Annual Report of Oneida Association: Exhibiting its History, Principles, and Transactions to Jan. 1, 1849* (Oneida Reserve: Leonard & Company, 1849), 8–9 (emphasis added).

98   *First Annual Report of Oneida Association* 9. See also Laura Ping, "Short Hair and Short Dresses: The Oneida Community and Reforming Women's Fashion," lecture, Oneida Community Mansion House, April 7, 2022, Oneida, NY, 1:07:29, https://youtu.be/GUdakLt9U7A?si=YyPtIvEMBmZiL86U.

99   There *is* evidence of a brief fad for short hair among white women in 1884 and 1885, which the popular press referred to as the "short hair craze." Although its origins are murky, the style may have been in imitation of the hairstyle favored by Rose Cleveland, sister of then-president Grover Cleveland who functioned as de facto first lady for the first year of his presidency. For a discussion of the fad and Cleveland's role in spurring it, see, for example, "Parting with Their Hair," *Evening Star* (Washington, DC), August 29, 1885, 6.

100   "The Hair," *Young Ladies' Journal*, January 1, 1867, 845; in "The Hair," *Godey's Lady's Book and Magazine*, May 1867, 464. Both of these texts quoted the same source material, which was cited by the *Journal* as merely "a little book, entitled 'The Human Hair: Its Management in Health and Disease,' by Felix Sultana, the Royal Perfumer, of 23, Poulty, London." I was unable to locate the original source.

101   Seth Pancoast, *The Ladies' Medical Guide: A Complete Instructor and Counsellor, Embracing A Full and Exhaustive Account of the Structure and Functions of the Reproductive Organs; the Diseases of Females and Children, with Their Causes, Symptoms and Treatment; the Toilet considered in reference to Female Health, Beauty and Longevity, etc., etc., etc. With an appendix containing Startling Facts in Plain Words for Mothers and the Young* (Philadelphia: Hubbard Bros., 1875), 478 and 480.

102   Pancoast, *Ladies' Medical Guide*, 473.

103   Pancoast, *Ladies' Medical Guide*, 480 (emphasis in the original).

104   Doyle, *Illustrated History of Hairstyles.* It was not socially acceptable for an adult woman to wear her hair completely down and loose in public until the twentieth century.

105   *The Habits of Good Society: A Handbook for Ladies and Gentlemen* (New York: Carleton, 1865), 94 (emphasis added) and 137.

106   An example of a source that urged women to use their hair to enhance their features (rather than follow trends) is "A Series of Papers on the Hair. Chapter V: Modes of Wearing the Hair," *Godey's Lady's Book and Magazine* 50, no. 5 (May 1855): 435–437.

107   "Human Hair and Its Substitutes," *Scientific American* 26, no. 18 (April 27, 1872): 276.

108   "The Art of Hair-Dressing," *Hartford Courant,* November 1, 1894, 6.

109   Nell Irvin Painter, *The History of White People* (New York: Norton, 2010), 59–63.

110   Stephanie M. H. Camp, "Black Is Beautiful: An American History," *Journal of Southern History* 81, no. 3 (August 2015), 682. See also Painter, *History of White People,* 71.

111   M. H. Freeman, "The Educational Wants of the Free Colored People," *Anglo-African Magazine* 1, no. 4 (April 1859): 116–119, https://hdl.handle.net/2027 /uc1.32106005410862. Freeman's list of harmful hair alterations also included a reference to wigs: "Sometimes the natural hair is shaved off, and its place supplied by a straight wig, thus presenting the ludicrous anomaly of Indian [i.e., Indigenous] hair over negro features" (117). This is the only such reference to Black people wearing the kinds of wigs discussed in chapter 4 (those that strove for verisimilitude, in contrast to the periwig) I have found in my research—the overwhelming majority of which suggests that this type of wig wearing did not become common for Black women until the twentieth century. I cannot account for Freeman's assertion here but to posit that it might be a unique or even hypothetical example, rather than evidence of a broad cultural practice in the nineteenth century.

112   "The Boston Massacre, March 5, 1770. Commemorative Festival in Faneuil Hall," *The Liberator* (Boston, MA), March 12, 1858, 2. (The reference to "Great laughter" was part of *The Liberator's* reporting!)

113   "The Boston Massacre, March 5, 1770. Commemorative Festival in Faneuil."

114   Tiya Miles, *All That She Carried: The Journey of Ashley's Sack, A Black Family Keepsake* (New York: Penguin Random House, 2021), 110–114; Stephanie M. H. Camp, *Closer to Freedom: Enslaved Women and Everyday Resistance in the Plantation South* (Chapel Hill: University of North Carolina Press, 2004), 84; and White and White, "Slave Hair and African American Culture," 73.

115   Byrd and Tharp, *Hair Story,* 16; and Camp, *Closer to Freedom,* 84.

116   The Library Company of Philadelphia has a full set of Clay's illustration in its archives, many of which are available digitally: "Life in Philadelphia Collection," The Library Company of Philadelphia, https://digital.librarycompany.org

/islandora/object/Islandora%3ALINP1. Many scholars have analyzed Clay's cartoons for the way they caricature and lampoon Black urbanites, their bodies, and their supposed pretensions of middle-class respectability. See, for example, White and White, *Stylin'*; Gary B. Nash, *Forging Freedom: The Formation of Philadelphia's Black Community, 1720–1840* (Cambridge, MA: Harvard University Press, 1988); Jasmine Nichole Cobb, "'Look! A Negress': Public Women, Private Horrors, and the White Ontology of the Gaze," in Cobb, *Picture Freedom: Remaking Black Visuality in the Early Nineteenth Century* (New York: New York University Press, 2015), 111–147; and Linzy Brekke-Aloise, "'A Very Pretty Business': Fashion and Consumer Culture in Antebellum America," *Winterthur Portfolio* 48, no. 2/3 (Summer/Autumn 2014).

117 See Cobb, *Picture Freedom;* and Gonzalez, *Visualizing Equality.*

118 Gonzalez, *Visualizing Equality*, 223–225.

119 I first encountered this portrait of Mattie Allen in Gonzalez, *Visualizing Equality*, 228–229. I am grateful to Gonzalez for both sharing this photograph and for his insights on the way this portrait portrays Black femininity.

120 John Van Evrie, *The Six Species of Men* (New York: Van Evrie, Horton & Co., 1866), reprinted in *Popular American Literature of the Nineteenth Century*, ed. Paul Gutjahr (New York: Oxford University Press, 2001), 764. Van Evrie's complete dismissal of light hair in people of African descent reveals his complicated ideological relationship with mixed people and his disregard for white sexual violence against Black people. See chapter 2 for a fuller examination of Van Evrie's perspective on hair and white supremacy.

121 John Van Evrie, *White Supremacy and Negro Subordination; or, Negroes a Subordinate Race, and (So-called) Slavery Its Normal Condition* (New York: Van Evrie, Horton & Co., 1868), 98–100.

122 Van Evrie, *White Supremacy and Negro Subordination*, 98–100.

123 Harriet Jacobs, *Incidents in the Life of a Slave Girl: Written by Herself* (Boston: "Published for the Author," 1861), 118, https://docsouth.unc.edu/fpn/jacobs/jacobs .html; and Miles, *All That She Carried*, 113.

124 White and White, *Stylin'*, 55–56; and Miles, *All That She Carried*, 110–114.

125 This story of James Brittain's interview is included in White and White, *Stylin'*, 55–56; White and White, "Slave Hair and African American Culture," 68; and Miles, *All That She Carried*, 114.

126 "A Series of Papers on the Hair: Chapter IV," *Godey's Lady's Book and Magazine* 50, no. 4 (April 1855): 342.

127 The Page Act, the United States' first restrictive immigration law, forbid immigration of East Asian people who were unfree laborers as well as any woman intending (or likely) to perform sex work. The Chinese Exclusion Act expanded the excludable categories to include *all* Chinese laborers, leaving exceptions only for specific professions like teachers, students, diplomats, and merchants. See Page Act, 18 Stat. 477 (1875); and Chinese Exclusion Act, 22 Stat. 58 (1882).

128 Richard Samuel West, *The San Francisco Wasp: An Illustrated History* (Northampton, MA: Periodyssey, 2004), 12; Philip P. Choy, Lorraine Dong, and

Marlon K. Hom, eds., *Coming Man: 19th Century American Perceptions of the Chinese* (Seattle: University of Washington Press, 1994), 19; and Roger Olmsted, "The Chinese Must Go!," *California Historical Quarterly* 50, no. 3 (Sept. 1971): 286. See also Erika Lee, *America for Americans: A History of Xenophobia in the United States* (New York: Basic Books, 2019).

129   West, *San Francisco Wasp*, 12.

130   Erika Lee, *At America's Gates: Chinese Immigration During the Exclusion Era, 1882–1943* (Chapel Hill: University of North Carolina Press, 2003), 25–26.

131   Karen Leong, "'A Distant and Antagonistic Race': Constructions of Chinese Manhood in the Exclusionist Debates," in *Across the Great Divide: Cultures of Manhood in the American West*, ed. Laura McCall, Matthew Basso, and Dee Garceau (New York: Routledge, 2000), 133; and Lee, *At America's Gates*, 26–27. See also Beth Lew-Williams, *The Chinese Must Go: Violence, Exclusion, and the Making of the Alien in America* (Cambridge, MA: Harvard University Press, 2018).

132   "The Chinaman Again," *Pacific Rural Press*, November 9, 1901, 292. I appreciate Erika Lee's book *At America's Gates* for pointing me to this article.

133   West, *San Francisco Wasp*, 27 and 63; and Kenneth M. Johnson, *The Sting of the Wasp: Political and Satirical Cartoons from the Truculent Early San Francisco Weekly* (San Francisco: Book Club of California, 1967), 6 and 15.

134   "That Balky Team of Ours," *San Francisco Illustrated Wasp*, February 9, 1878, 434.

135   For more on political cartoonists' illustration techniques when depicting humans, and their implications, see Thomas Milton Kemnitz, "The Cartoon as a Historical Source," *Journal of Interdisciplinary History* 4, no. 1 (Summer 1973): 81–93, at 82–83; and Lawrence H. Streicher, "On a Theory of Political Caricature," *Comparative Studies in Society and History* 9, no. 4 (July 1967): 427–445, at 432.

136   President Arthur vetoed the first version of the act not because he opposed exclusion, but because the proposed length of the exclusion period, twenty years, seemed too long to him. He signed the second version, which established an exclusion period of ten years instead. See Chester A. Arthur, "Veto of the Chinese Exclusion Act," speech delivered to the Senate on April 4, 1882, https://millercenter.org/the-presidency/presidential-speeches/april-4-1882-veto-chinese-exclusion-act.

137   Lee, *At America's Gates*, 166.

138   Browne, *Trichologia Mammmalium*, 101.

139   I am grateful to Joseph Nejad-Duong for helping me think through this point.

2. FACIAL HAIR

1   Sean Trainor, "Groomed for Power: A Cultural Economy of the Male Body in Nineteenth-Century America" (PhD diss., Pennsylvania State University, 2015), 4–7. One of Trainor's most valuable insights is that, starting in the 1850s, the word

beard was corporeally capacious because its primary cultural meaning was ideological, not physical. As Trainor explains, "The *essential* definition of the beard resided, not in the physical pattern of grooming it designated, but rather in the gendered meanings with which it was associated," thanks in large part to the extensive writing by "pro-beard polemicists" who cemented the beard's associations with manhood in the mid-1850s (7 and 11). As we will see, however, the values encoded in the mid-nineteenth-century beard were not only gendered but also racialized. Still, as Trainor acknowledges, even though *beard* and *hair on the chin* were not synonymous, nineteenth-century Americans did distinguish between different facial hair configurations in some contexts.

2   The only two barefaced presidents during this bearded era were Andrew Johnson (who was not elected) and William McKinley (whose opponent in both the 1896 and 1900 elections, William Jennings Bryan, was also barefaced). I am grateful to my research assistant Christina James who confirmed the data on presidential facial hair referenced in this chapter during her summer research project in 2012.

3   A small historiography on facial hair in the United States has emerged in the past decade. See Trainor, "Groomed for Power"; Christopher Oldstone-Moore, *Of Beards and Men: The Revealing History of Facial Hair* (Chicago: University of Chicago Press, 2016); Sharon Twickler, "Combing Masculine Identity in the Age of the Moustache, 1860–1900," in *New Perspectives on the History of Facial Hair: Framing the Face,* ed. Jennifer Evans and Alun Withey (Cham, Switzerland: Palgrave Macmillan, 2018), 149–168; and Peter Ferry, *Beards and Masculinity in American Literature* (New York: Routledge, 2020).

4   Hollister Noble, "Beardless Man Is Facing a Dreary Existence," *New York Times Magazine,* March 21, 1926, 2.

5   Sean Trainor's research corroborates my conclusion that Clofullia was the first Bearded Lady in an American freak show. See Trainor, "Fair Bosom/Black Beard: Facial Hair, Gender Determination, and the Strange Career of Madame Clofullia, 'Bearded Lady,'" *Early American Studies* 12, no. 3 (Fall 2014): 548–575, at 550.

6   I am using *performance* here in the way it is used by Judith Butler: to signal not falsehood, but the active and repeated enactment of an identity. See Butler, *Gender Trouble: Feminism and the Subversion of Identity* (New York: Routledge, 1990).

7   Londa Schiebinger, *Nature's Body: Gender and the Making of Modern Science* (New Brunswick, NJ: Rutgers University Press, 2004), 120–125.

8   Trainor, "Groomed for Power," 34.

9   Richard Corson, *Fashions in Hair: The First Five Thousand Years* (London: Peter Owen, 1984), 302–303.

10   In my extensive research on the history of the American freak show, I have not seen any examples of hairy African-descended people who performed in the "animal people" mode, which is why I identify this group of performers as East Asian and Indigenous rather than more broadly as women of color. Robert Bogdan's

study *Freak Show: Presenting Human Oddities for Amusement and Profit* (Chicago: University of Chicago Press, 1988) does not mention any examples of Black women performing in this mode, either, although many African-descended women portrayed archetypes that he calls "cannibals and savages" (176).

11   Corson, *Fashions in Hair*, 220 and 302–325; Allan D. Peterkin, *One Thousand Beards: A Cultural History of Facial Hair* (Vancouver: Arsenal Pulp, 2001), 27–36; Edwin Valentine Mitchell, *Concerning Beards* (New York: Dodd, Mead, and Company, 1930), 67 and 74; and Lewis Gannett, "American Hair: Its Rises and Falls," *New Yorker*, October 15, 1938, 32–44.

12   Trainor, "Groomed for Power," 1; see also Paul E. Johnson and Sean Wilentz, *The Kingdom of Matthias: A Story of Sex and Salvation in 19th-Century America* (New York: Oxford University Press, 1994).

13   "Persecuted Joseph Palmer," *Boston Daily Globe*, December 14, 1884; Stewart Holbrook, "The Beard of Joseph Palmer," in *The Bear Book II: Further Readings in the History and Evolution of a Gay Male Subculture*, ed. Les Wright (New York: Harrington Park Press, 2001), 95–104; Corson, *Fashions in Hair*, 403; and Mitchell, *Concerning Beards*, 75.

14   Reginald Reynolds, *Beards: Their Social Standing, Religious Involvement, Decorative Possibilities, and Value and Defence through the Ages* (Garden City, NY: Doubleday, 1949), 267–275; and Corson, *Fashions in Hair*, 302.

15   For example, when Louis XIII became the King of France in 1610 at the young age of eight, beards became unfashionable. Beards likewise fell out of fashion in Spain when King Philip V was unable to grow one of his own. See Mitchell, *Concerning Beards*, 68; Trichocosmos (pseud.), *Notes Historical, Aesthetical, Ethnological, Physiological, Anecdotal, and Tonsorial on the Hair and Beard* (London, Read & Co., [1850?]), 35; and *The Encyclopædia Britannica, A Dictionary of Arts, Sciences, and General Literature*, 9th ed., vol. 3 (Edinburgh: Adam and Charles Black, 1875), under "beard."

16   "Art. II—The Beard," *Westminster Review* (July 1854): 27; and "The Mustache Movement," *The Favourite* 1 (1854): 46.

17   "Persecuted Joseph Palmer"; Naton Leslie, "John Brown's Grave," *North American Review* 287, no. 3/4 (May–August 2002): 74–77, at 77. Information about John Hovendon, *The Last Moments of John Brown* (1882–1884) from The Metropolitan Museum of Art's virtual exhibit label about the painting, https://www.met museum.org/art/collection/search/11160.

18   Although scholarship on nineteenth-century beards tends to focus on white men, Shane White and Graham White claim that "beards became common among whites as well as blacks" by midcentury. See White and White, "Slave Hair and African American Culture in the Eighteenth and Nineteenth Centuries," *Journal of Southern History* 61, no. 1 (February 1995): 45–76, at 58.

19   Christopher Oldstone-Moore, "The Beard Movement in Victorian Britain," *Victorian Studies* 48, no. 1 (2005): 7–34, at 7. Examples of sources that retell the

Crimean War story include "Illustrated History of Beards," *Emerson's Magazine and Putnam's Weekly* 6, no. 45 (1858): 251; Reynolds, *Beards,* 279–281; Mitchell, *Concerning Beards,* 42–43; and Corson, *Fashions in Hair,* 405.

20   See, for example, Trainor, "Groomed for Power," 125.

21   Unlike women, who gathered information about fashion and hairstyles directly from magazines like *Godey's Lady's Book,* men's fashion was mediated by tailors, who viewed fashion plates in trade magazines and shaped the clothing they made for men accordingly. Fashion scholar Valerie Steele posits that tailors may have functioned as more general fashion advisors to nineteenth-century men, and fashion plates corroborate the facial hair timeline of textual sources. See Valerie Steele, *Paris Fashion: A Cultural History* (New York: Oxford University Press, 1988), 116; Joan L. Severa, *Dressed for the Photographer: Ordinary Americans and Fashion, 1840–1900* (Kent, OH: Kent State University Press, 1995), 25; Michael Zakim, *Ready-Made Democracy: A History of Men's Dress in the American Republic, 1760–1860* (Chicago: University of Chicago Press, 2003), 194–198; and James Laver, *Fashions and Fashion Plates, 1800–1900* (New York: Penguin, 1943), 33–44.

22   Trainor, "Groomed for Power," 29 and 35.

23   Trainor, "Groomed for Power," 36.

24   As Jen Manion has documented in their history of female husbands in the United States between 1830 and 1910, some newspaper exposés cited a female husband's absence of facial hair as evidence that they had been assigned female at birth. These stories illustrate the way that beards (or their absence) did not just become extremely popular for men by midcentury, but were also framed as biological evidence of a person's intrinsic identity. See Jen Manion, *Female Husbands: A Trans History* (New York: Cambridge University Press, 2020), 259–260.

25   Mary P. Ryan, *Women in Public: Between Banners and Ballots, 1825–1880* (Baltimore, MD: Johns Hopkins University Press, 1990), 3–4; and Oldstone-Moore, "The Beard Movement in Victorian Britain."

26   Nicholas L. Syrett's study of white fraternities and nineteenth-century masculinity helped me conceptualize this claim about the codification of male appearance. Syrett argues that, even though exclusion was central to how fraternity men defined their masculinity since the first fraternities were founded in the 1820s, fraternity men had no need to explicitly codify the terms of this exclusion along racial, religious, and gender lines until their universities began admitting Black, Jewish, Catholic, and women students in the second half of the century. See Syrett, *The Company He Keeps: A History of White College Fraternities* (Chapel Hill: University of North Carolina Press, 2009), 171–173.

27   Jacques Antoine Dulaure, *Pogonologia: Or a Philosophical and Historical Essay on Beards* (London: R. Thorn, 1786), iii–iv and 29, https://www.gutenberg.org/files/59006/59006-h/59006-h.htm; and J. Rennie, *The Art of Preserving the Hair; On Philosophical Principles: Including an Account of the Diseases to Which it is Liable,* "New Edition" (London: Septimus Prowett, 1826), 245–246.

28   Trainor, "Groomed for Power," 17, 113–116, and 150–152.

29 Trainor, "Groomed for Power," 34 and 163; and "Why Do Men Shave?," *Grand River Times* (Grand Haven, MI), December 28, 1853, 4. The value of $350 to $1,000 in contemporary currency is about $15,000 to $41,000. For relative value calculations here and throughout this book, I used the tool Measuring Worth, which was created by economist Samuel H. Williamson for economic historians: https://www.measuringworth.com/calculators/uscompare/.

30 John Shoebridge Williams, *An Address to the Officers and Citizens of the United States, Recommending a Manifestation in Favor of the Bible. To which is appended a synopsis of the spiritual experience of the medium. With reasons for not shaving the beard* (Baltimore, MD: Sherwood & Co., 1854); and Bret E. Carroll, "'I Must Have My House in Order': The Victorian Fatherhood of John Shoebridge Williams," *Journal of Family History* 24, no. 3 (July 1999): 275–304, at 275.

31 "The Beard," *Texas State Gazette* (Austin, TX), April 7, 1855, 3.

32 "Illustrated History of Beards" 251.

33 Will Fisher, "The Renaissance Beard: Masculinity in Early Modern England," *Renaissance Quarterly* 54, no. 1 (2001): 155–187, at 173–175.

34 See, for example, "Shaving the Face," *Daily Express* (Petersburg, VA), January 6, 1855, 2; "The Beard Question," *Andover Advertiser* (MA), January 20, 1855, 1; and "Shaving the Face," *Southern Banner* (Athens, GA), February 8, 1855, 1. Even publishers overseas commented on Dr. Sanborn's musings; see, for example, "The Beard," *The Lamp* 8, no. 19 (May 12, 1855): 319, which was a London-based literary, arts, and science journal.

35 E. Sanborn, "Evil Effects of Shaving the Beard," *Boston Medical and Surgical Journal* 51, no. 20 (December 1854): 398–399.

36 Sanborn, "Evil Effects," 399.

37 Sanborn, "Evil Effects," 400.

38 Williams, *An Address . . .* (1854), emphasis in the original. "Male man" sound duplicative to modern ears, but Williams likely meant *male* to refer to gender (not a woman) and *man* to refer to age (not a boy).

39 Trichocosmos, *Notes Historical, Aesthetical,* 29.

40 Trichocosmos, *Notes Historical, Aesthetical,* 18.

41 "Illustrated History of Beards," 254; and Trichocosmos, *Notes Historical, Aesthetical,* 13.

42 For example, see Trichocosmos, *Notes Historical, Aesthetical,* 18 and 21–22; "Illustrated History of Beards," 256 and 260; and B[ela] C. Perry, *Human Hair, and the Cutaneous Diseases Which Affect It: Together with Essays on Acne, Sycosis, and Chloasma,* 2nd ed. (1865; New York: James Miller, 1866), 21. Perry was a Black barber from New Bedford, Massachusetts, one of the only examples of a Black author in the hair science discourse discussed in chapter 3.

43 "Illustrated History of Beards," 262 (emphasis added).

44 Williams, "An Address to the Officers . . ." (1854).

45 "Wearing the Beard," *Northern Islander* (St. James, MI), September 21, 1854, 2.

46   "Illustrated History of Beards," 262 (emphasis added); and "Wearing the Beard," *Northern Islander* (St. James, MI), September 21, 1854, 2.

47   Helen Marie Weber, "Our Dress," *The Lily,* May 1851, 38.

48   Contemporary writers and modern scholars recognize that nineteenth-century women's rights activists argued that women were both similar to men *and* different from men, and that neither line of reasoning negated the validity of the other. See Nancy Cott, *The Grounding of Modern Feminism* (New Haven, CT: Yale University Press, 1987), 19–20.

49   Horace Bushnell, *Women's Suffrage: The Reform Against Nature* (New York: Charles Scribner, 1869), 50–51 (emphasis added).

50   George A. Dondero, "Why Lincoln Wore a Beard," *Journal of the Illinois State Historical Society* 24, no. 2 (July 1931): 321–325; and "With Malice toward None: The Abraham Lincoln Bicentennial Exhibition," Library of Congress, online companion to exhibition held February 12–May 10, 2009, https://www.loc.gov/exhibits /lincoln/candidate-lincoln.html#obj4.

51   Two of the muscular Christianity's most ardent supporters penned detailed tracts about Jesus in the first two decades of the twentieth century, and both paid particular attention to artists' depictions of Jesus's face. See G. Stanley Hall, *Jesus, The Christ, in Light of Psychology* (Garden City, NY: Doubleday, Page, and Company, 1917); and William E. Barton, *Jesus of Nazareth: The Story of His Life and Scenes of His Ministry* (Boston: The Pilgrim Press, 1903). For muscular Christianity in the United States, see Clifford Putney, *Muscular Christianity: Manhood and Sports in Protestant America, 1880–1920* (Cambridge, MA: Harvard University Press, 2001); and Stephen Prothero, *American Jesus: How the Son of God Became a National Icon* (New York: Farrar, Straus, and Giroux, 2003).

52   "HEROES: Uncle Sam," *Time,* May 11, 1931, 18; and Morton Keller, *The Art and Politics of Thomas Nast* (New York: Oxford University Press, 1968), vii, 7, 44, and 58. The earliest example of a bearded Uncle Sam drawn by Nast that I could find was published in 1866.

53   Louis Dalrymple, "School Begins," *Puck* 44, no. 1142 (January 25, 1899), https://www.loc.gov/pictures/item/2012647459/.

54   Kristin L. Hoganson, *Fighting for American Manhood: How Gender Politics Provoked the Spanish-American and Philippine-American Wars* (New Haven, CT: Yale University Press, 1998), 91–93. For more on shifting norms of American masculinity at the turn of the twentieth century and the growing cultural dominance of this kind of assertive and aggressive masculinity, see Gail Bederman, *Manliness and Civilization: A Cultural History of Gender and Race in the United States, 1880– 1917* (Chicago: University of Chicago Press, 1995).

55   *Cartoons of the War of 1898, with Spain, from Leading Foreign and American Press* (Chicago: Belford, Middlebrook & Co., 1898).

56   Hoganson, *Fighting for American Manhood,* 91.

57   Josiah C. Nott and George R. Gliddon, ed., *Types of Mankind. . . .* (Philadelphia: Lippincott, Grambo & Co., 1854), 432–433. *Types of Mankind* was written

in tribute to Samuel George Morton, the era's most influential (and recently deceased) American racial scientist, who was a mentor to most of the book's authors (including editors Nott and Gliddon).

58   Josiah C. Nott and George R. Gliddon, *Indigenous Races of the Earth* (Philadelphia: J. B. Lippincott, 1857), 620.

59   John Smith, *The Generall Historie of Virginia, New-England, and the Summer Isles: With the Names of the Adventurers, Planters, and Governours from Their First Beginning An: 1584. To This Present 1624* (London: I. D. and I. H. for Michael Sparkes, 1624), 29–30, https://docsouth.unc.edu/southlit/smith/smith.html; and Kathleen M. Brown, *Foul Bodies: Cleanliness in Early America* (New Haven, CT: Yale University Press, 2009), 54.

60   Thomas Jefferson, *Notes on the State of Virginia* (Philadelphia: Prichard and Hall, 1788), 65, https://docsouth.unc.edu/southlit/jefferson/jefferson.html.

61   Perry, *Human Hair*, 23.

62   Nott and Gliddon, *Indigenous Races of the Earth,* 280 and 282.

63   Nott and Gliddon, *Indigenous Races of the Earth,* 280 (emphasis added).

64   Samuel George Morton, *Crania Americana; or, A Comparative View of the Skulls of Various Aboriginal Nations of North and South America* (Philadelphia: J. Dobson, 1839), 5–6 and 67. Morton *did* acknowledge that beard-wearing norms could vary from tribe to tribe, noting that ethnologist Henry Schoolcraft "mentions beards as common among the Potowatomies" (68).

65   Sanborn, "Evil Effects," 399.

66   Charles Hamilton Smith, *The Natural History of the Human Species* ([Edinburgh, 1848]; Boston: Gould & Lincoln, 1852), ix–x and 858–859. A slightly different rendering of the tripartite titles appears on a triangular-shaped chart in the Boston edition: "Woolly-Haired or Tropical Type," "Mongolic or Beardless Type," and "Caucasian or Bearded Type" (222).

67   Smith, *The Natural History of the Human Species,* 359–360.

68   Smith, *The Natural History of the Human Species,* 224.

69   Donald Yacovone, *Teaching White Supremacy: America's Democratic Ordeal and the Forging of Our National Identity* (New York: Pantheon, 2022), 40; and James Lander, *Lincoln and Darwin: Shared Visions of Race, Science, and Religion* (Carbondale: Southern Illinois University Press, 2010), 98. I first encountered Van Evrie in Melissa N. Stein, *Measuring Manhood: Race and the Science of Masculinity, 1830–1934* (Minneapolis: University of Minnesota Press, 2015), ch. 2. Stein argues that, during the Civil War and Reconstruction period, American ethnologists became preoccupied with the future of race relations in the United States (rather than racial origins, as the previous generation of race scientists emphasized), and their conceptions of racial difference were deeply informed by their conceptions of idealized manhood and womanhood.

70   Yacovone, *Teaching White Supremacy*, 40; and Michael E. Woods, "Popularizing Proslavery: John Van Evrie and the Mass Marketing of Proslavery Ideology," *Journal of the Civil War Era*, May 26, 2020, https://www.journalofthecivilwarera

.org/2020/05/popularizing-proslavery-john-van-evrie-and-the-mass-marketing-of
-proslavery-ideology/.

71   Woods, "Popularizing Proslavery"; and John Van Evrie, preface, *White Supremacy and Negro Subordination; or, Negroes a Subordinate Race, and (so-called) Slavery Its Normal Condition* (New York: Van Evrie, Horton & Co., 1868), vii.

72   John H. Van Evrie, *Negroes and Negro "Slavery:" The First An Inferior Race; The Latter Its Normal Condition* (1853; New York: Van Evrie, Horton & Co., 1861), 101–103, https://www.gutenberg.org/cache/epub/61063/pg61063-images.html; and Stein, *Measuring Manhood*, 89 and 132. See also Lander, *Lincoln and Darwin*, 98.

73   Yacovone, *Teaching White Supremacy*, 40; and Woods, "Popularizing Proslavery." Yacovone argues that Van Evrie's influence "has been either overlooked or grossly underestimated by most modern historians and remains unknown to the wider public." As a result, he argues, historians have largely "failed to understand how much he helped shape modern white supremacist ideology, even in the South" (41).

74   Van Evrie, *The Six Species of Men* (New York: Van Evrie, Horton & Co., 1866), reprinted in *Popular American Literature of the Nineteenth Century*, ed. Paul Gutjahr (New York: Oxford University Press, 2001), 754.

75   Van Evrie, *Six Species of Men*, 756–764.

76   Van Evrie, *Six Species of Men*, 759–761 (emphasis in the original).

77   Van Evrie, *Six Species of Men*, 762 and 764 (emphasis added).

78   Van Evrie, *Six Species of Men*, 764.

79   Shane White and Graham White, *Stylin': African American Expressive Culture from Its Beginnings to the Zoot Suit* (Ithaca, NY: Cornell University Press, 1998), 47; and Corson, *Fashions in Hair*, 402.

80   All of the advertisements described here are from the collection The Geography of Slavery in Virginia (archive by Tom Costa and the Rector and Visitors of the University of Virginia), http://www2.vcdh.virginia.edu/gos. The advertisement for Tony was from *Virginia Gazette* (Parks), Williamsburg, May 18 to May 25, 1739; London was from *Virginia Gazette (Hunter)*, Williamsburg, December 12, 1755; Peres was from the *Maryland Gazette (Green)*, Annapolis, August 20, 1761; Harry is from *Virginia Gazette* (Purdie & Dixon), Williamsburg, December 3, 1767; and Africa is from *Norfolk Herald* (Willett and O'Connor), Norfolk, July 9, 1796.

81   This illustration is also analyzed in Martha Jones, *Vanguard: How Black Women Broke Barriers, Won the Vote, and Insisted on Equality for All* (New York: Basic Books, 2020), ch. 9, EBSCOhost.

82   Willie Morrow, *400 Years without a Comb* (San Diego: Morrow's Unlimited, Inc., 1973), 97–101; and Currier & Ives, "The first colored senators and representatives—in the 41st and 42nd Congress of the United States" (1872), Prints and Photographs Division, Library of Congress, https://lccn.loc.gov/98501907.

83   Joseph Hoover, "Heroes of the Colored Race" (Philadelphia, 1881), Prints and Photographs Division, Library of Congress, https://lccn.loc.gov/00651114.

84   John Stauffer, Zoe Trodd, and Celeste-Marie Bernier, Introduction, *Picturing Frederick Douglass: An Illustrated Biography of the Nineteenth Century's Most Photographed American* (New York: Liveright Publishing Corporation, 2015), ix.

85 Frederick Douglass, "A Tribute for the Negro," *North Star,* April 7, 1849, quoted in Stauffer, Trodd, and Bernier, Introduction, *Picturing Frederick Douglass,* xv. On Douglass's wariness about artistic representations of Black portraits, see also Rachel E. Walker, *Beauty and the Brain: The Science of Human Nature in Early America* (Chicago: University of Chicago Press, 2022), 166–167.

86 Frederick Douglass, "Lecture on Pictures," December 3, 1861, Boston, MA, reprinted in Stauffer, Trodd, and Bernier, *Picturing Frederick Douglass,* 127.

87 Henry Louis Gates, Jr., "Epilogue: Frederick Douglass's Camera Obscura: Representing the Anti-Slave 'Clothed and in Their Own Form,'" in Stauffer, Trodd, and Bernier, *Picturing Frederick Douglass,* 209.

88 I based this summary on an evaluation of the 158 portraits that appear in Stauffer, Trodd, and Bernier's *Picturing Frederick Douglass* (just two of the extant 160 portraits are missing from the archive); see 179–196.

89 For more on Douglass's hair, and especially the significance of its texture in photographic portraits, see Jasmine Nichole Cobb, "New Growth: Black Hair and Liberation," in *New Growth: The Art and Texture of Black Hair* (Durham, NC: Duke University Press, 2023), 1–4.

90 Stauffer, Trodd, and Bernier, *Picturing Frederick Douglass,* 2–5; and Douglass, *Narrative of the Life of Frederick Douglass, an American Slave* (Boston: Anti-Slavery Office, 1849), Library of Congress, Rare Book and Special Collections Division, https://lccn.loc.gov/82225385.

91 I based this claim on Douglass's facial hair on the 158 portraits that appear in Stauffer, Trodd, and Bernier's *Picturing Frederick Douglass.* Even Douglass's plaster death mask, created by sculptor Ulric Dunbar the day after his death, features his full beard and mustache. See "Frederick Douglass Death Mask," *Frederick Douglass National Historic Site,* National Park Service, https://www.nps.gov/museum/exhibits/douglass/exb/visionary/FRDO240_deathMask.html.

92 My examination of the extant photographic archive suggests that the only portraits after September 1873 that show Douglass without a full beard, mustache, and side-whiskers are five portraits taken in January 1874, which show Douglass with a clean-shaven chin while the rest of his facial hair growth remains. See Stauffer, Trodd, and Bernier, *Picturing Frederick Douglass,* 187–188.

93 Van Evrie's responses was published in the *Day Book* and reprinted in Douglass, "The Day Book—The Pathfinder—and Douglass," *Frederick Douglass's Paper* (Rochester, NY), June 17, 1853, 2, https://lccn.loc.gov/sn84026366.

94 Van Evrie, *The Six Species of Men,* 764; and Frederick Douglass, "Is the Negro a White Man?—Dr. Van Evrie and the New York Day-Book," *Frederick Douglass' Paper* (Rochester, NY), September 14, 1855, 2, https://lccn.loc.gov/sn84026366.

95 Douglass, "Is the Negro a White Man?" (emphasis in the original).

96 Frederick Douglass, "The Day Book on the Negro's Beard," *Frederick Douglass's Paper* (Rochester, NY), February 1, 1856, 2 (emphasis in the original), https://lccn.loc.gov/sn84026366.

97 Terminal hair indicates dark, blunt hair, such as that which forms eyebrows or mustaches. It contrasts with the soft, downy hair that covers most of the

human body. See P. Kynaston Thomas and D. G. Ferriman, "Variation in Facial and Pubic Hair Growth in White Women," *American Journal of Physical Anthropology* 15, no. 2 (June 1957): 171–180.

Scholarship on women's facial hair has grown over the past two decades. Useful studies include: Trainor, "Fair Bosom/Black Beard"; Sherry Velasco, "Women with Beards in Early Modern Spain," in *The Last Taboo: Women and Body Hair*, ed. Karín Lesnik-Oberstein (Manchester: Manchester University Press, 2006), 181–190; Mark Albert Johnston, "Bearded Women in Early Modern England," *Studies in English Literature, 1500–1900* 47, no. 1 (Winter 2007): 1–28; Mark Albert Johnston, "Re-evaluating Bearded Women," in *Beard Fetish in Early Modern England: Sex, Gender, and Registers of Value* (New York: Routledge, 2011), 159–212; Kimberly A. Hamlin, "The 'Case of the Bearded Woman': Hypertrichosis and the Construction of Gender in the Age of Darwin," *American Quarterly* 63, no. 4 (December 2011): 955–981; and Rebecca M. Herzig, *Plucked: A History of Hair Removal* (New York: New York University Press, 2015).

98 Herzig, *Plucked,* 35–49.

99 J. G. Wood, "De Monstris," *Transatlantic Magazine* 5, no. 12 (May 1872): 551.

100 George M. Gould and Walter L. Pyle, *Anomalies and Curiosities of Medicine* (Philadelphia: W. B. Saunders, 1896), 228.

101 For the history of the American freak show and its most significant figures, see, for example, Robert Bogdan, *Freak Show: Presenting Human Oddities for Amusement and Profit* (Chicago: University of Chicago Press, 1988); Rachel Adams, *Sideshow U.S.A.: Freaks and the American Cultural Imagination* (Chicago: University of Chicago Press, 2001); Rosemarie Garland-Thomson, ed., *Freakery: Cultural Spectacles of the Extraordinary Body* (New York: New York University Press, 1996); Neil Harris, *Humbug: The Art of P. T. Barnum* (Chicago: University of Chicago Press, 1973); Bluford Adams, *E Pluribus Barnum: The Great Showman and the Making of U.S. Popular Culture* (Minneapolis: University of Minnesota Press, 1997); Benjamin Reiss, *The Showman and the Slave: Race, Death, and Memory in Barnum's America* (Cambridge, MA: Harvard University Press, 2001); James W. Cook, *The Arts of Deception: Playing with Fraud in the Age of Barnum* (Cambridge, MA: Harvard University Press, 2001); and Trainor, "Fair Bosom/Black Beard." Two of the earliest books in the field of freak show studies are Frederick Drimmer, *Very Special People: The Struggles, Loves, and Triumphs of Human Oddities* (New York: Amjon, 1973); and Leslie Fiedler, *Freaks: Myths and Images of the Secret Self* (New York: Simon & Schuster, 1978).

102 Bogdan, *Freak Show,* 25–26. The nineteenth century was not the first time people had gathered to view unusual bodies. For example, in the eighteenth century, English citizens and colonists could view human (or animal) curiosities that traveled with a manager from town to town, appearing in fairs, taverns, or rented spaces. The innovation of the freak show was less of content than of scale: showmen presented groups of people together, and spectators paid a single entrance fee to see them. Performers typically stood on a raised stage that physically separated them from the audience.

103   On this cultural resonance, see Clare Sears, "'A Dress Not Belonging to His or Her Sex': Cross-dressing Law in San Francisco, 1860–1900" (PhD diss., University of California, Santa Cruz, 2005), esp. 191–192.

104   For the significance of the Circassian Beauty archetype to nineteenth-century understandings of race and slavery, see Linda Frost, *Never One Nation: Freaks, Savages, and Whiteness in U.S. Popular Culture, 1850–1877* (Minneapolis: University of Minnesota Press, 2005), esp. ch. 3: "The White Gaze and the Spectacle of Slavery;" and Sarah Lewis, *The Unseen Truth: When Race and Sight Changed America* (Cambridge, MA: Harvard University Press, 2024).

105   Gould and Pyle, *Anomalies and Curiosities of Medicine,* 230.

106   An international study of the incidence of conjoined twins published in 2011 found an incidence of 1.47 per 100,000 births. See O. M. Mutchinick et al., "Conjoined Twins: A Worldwide Collaborative Epidemiological Study of the International Clearinghouse for Birth Defects Surveillance and Research," *American Journal of Medical Genetics, Part C, Seminars in Medical Genetics* 157, no. 4 (2011): 274–287, at 274.

107   Bogdan, *Freak Show,* 224. Particularly vehement on this point is James W. Cook, who has written that "every single one" of Barnum's human oddities was an embodied disruption of the "normative boundaries" between binary categories. See Cook, *Arts of Deception,* 121.

108   Fanny Fern, "Barnum's Museum," in *Shadows and Sunbeams* (London, W. S. Orr, 1854), 289.

109   Drimmer, *Very Special People,* 123.

110   James W. Cook, Introduction to Phineas T. Barnum, *The Colossal P.T. Barnum Reader: Nothing Else Like It in the Universe,* ed. James W. Cook (Urbana: University of Illinois Press, 2005), 2; and Cook, *Arts of Deception,* 94.

111   Cook, *Arts of Deception,* 121–122.

112   Joseph Mitchell, "Lady Olga," *New Yorker,* August 3, 1940, 20.

113   Freak show performer autobiographies and biographies are a fraught historical source. Leslie Fiedler has argued that the autobiographies were "invariably ghost-written, a part of the act rather than a way of seeing beyond it." The nature of these texts, which were typically printed as inexpensive pamphlets and sold at shows to promote the acts they described, predispose them to hyperbole and fabrication. However, few other sources remain today that would provide an alternative, or more verifiable, source of information about the famous Bearded Ladies. Whether or not the pamphlets are accurate, their value is the way in which they crafted the Bearded Ladies' personas and back stories to suit the needs of the audience and the goals of the freak show proprietor. See Fiedler, *Freaks,* 274.

114   "How the Boys Kept the Fourth of July," *New York Times,* July 7, 1853; and Josephine Boisdechêne Clofullia Ghio, *Life of the Celebrated Bearded Lady, Madame Clofullia and Her Infant Esau* (New York: Courrier Des États-Unis, 1856), 16–17.

115   Ghio, *Life of the Celebrated Bearded Lady,* 4–9; and W. D. Chowne, "A Remarkable Case of Hirsute Growth in a Female," *The Lancet* 2, no. 1 (July 1852): 45–47.

116   Ghio, *Life of the Celebrated Bearded Lady,* 9–15; and Chowne, "Remarkable Case of Hirsute Growth," 46.

117   Ghio, *Life of the Celebrated Bearded Lady,* 14–16.

118   Trainor, "Fair Bosom/Black Beard," 574–575.

119   *Madame Viola, The Bearded Lady* (New York: Damon & Peets, [1878?]), 9–11; and Louis A. Duhring, "Case of a Bearded Woman," *Archives of Dermatology* 3 (April 1877): 193–200.

120   *Madame Viola, The Bearded Lady* 14–16; and J. S. Ingram, *Centennial Exposition Described and Illustrated* (Philadelphia: Hubbard Bros., 1876), 18.

121   *Madame Viola, The Bearded Lady,* 16; and "Globe Dime Museum," *New York Dispatch* (October 12, 1884), 5. Viola is also mentioned briefly in the 1886 book about electrolysis, but only as a bearded woman who had been on exhibition "during the past ten years." See George Henry Fox, *The Use of Electricity in the Removal of Superfluous Hair and the Treatment of Various Facial Blemishes* (Detroit: George S. Davis, 1886), 8.

122   Erin Naomi Burrows, "By the Hair of Her Chin: A Critical Biography of Bearded Lady Jane Barnell" (MA thesis, Sarah Lawrence College, 2009), 2; and Mitchell, "Lady Olga," 20.

123   Mitchell, "Lady Olga," 24–25.

124   Mitchell, "Lady Olga," 20 and 24–26.

125   Mitchell, "Lady Olga," 20.

126   Mitchell, "Lady Olga," 20.

127   Mitchell, "Lady Olga," 20–23; and "Death Certificate for Olga Oboyle," July 21, 1945, Historical Vital Records, New York City Municipal Archives, https://a860-historicalvitalrecords.nyc.gov/view/7296780. Barnell's modern biographer, Erin Naomi Burrows, found no trace of Lady Olga after 1940, not even her obituary, as of 2009. Digitization of Manhattan death certificates in the years since enabled me to identify her location and date of death. See Burrows, "By the Hair of Her Chin," 87.

128   Neil Harris proposed the concept of the "operational aesthetic" to describe a mode of presentation in which the audience's enjoyment comes from figuring out how the presentation was constructed, whether or not it is authentic, and where the fault lines between authenticity and forgery lay. See Harris, *Humbug,* ch. 3. For more on the decide-for-yourself experience of attending a freak show, see Cook, *Arts of Deception,* 27–29.

129   Ghio, *Life of the Celebrated Bearded Lady,* 14–20; and Chowne, "Remarkable Case of Hirsute Growth in a Female," 46.

130   "A Bearded Woman," *Boston Medical and Surgical Journal* 49, no. 26 (January 25, 1854), 526–527.

131   "The Bearded Lady of Geneva," *Gleason's Pictorial Drawing-Room Companion,* April 23, 1853, 268; Ghio, *Life of the Celebrated Bearded Lady,* 19–20; and "The Bearded Woman and Child," *Southern Medical and Surgical Journal* 12, no. 2 (February 1856): 125. The claim that Barnum likely arranged this stunt himself comes from Harris, *Humbug,* 67.

132 "The Bearded Woman and Child."

133 Duhring, "Case of a Bearded Woman," 199. One exception to the scientific press's emphasis on Bearded Ladies' overwhelming femininity was the Fowlers' and Wells' *American Phrenological Journal*, which published a detailed evaluation of Clofullia's "phrenological character" in 1853. The article concluded that "her Phrenological and Physiological organization indicates a predominance of the masculine element of mind" (40). See "Josephine Fortune Clofullia," *American Phrenological Journal and Repository of Science, Literature, and General Intelligence* 18, no. 2 (August 1853): 39–40.

134 This kind of democratic decide-for-yourself way of looking echoed in nineteenth-century popular culture more broadly. See, for example, Cook, *Arts of Deception*; Wendy Bellion, *Citizen Spectator: Art, Illusion, and Visual Perception in Early National America* (Chapel Hill: University of North Carolina Press, 2011); and Michael Leja, *Looking Askance: Skepticism and American Art from Eakins to Duchamp* (Berkeley: University of California Press, 2004).

135 Chowne, "Remarkable Case of Hirsute Growth in a Female," 46; and Sears, "'A Dress Not Belonging to His or Her Sex,'" 3. Sears points out that although these laws aimed to police and eliminate problematic bodies while the freak show paraded them in public view, the freak show ultimately "reinscribed the boundary between normative and deviant corporeality that the law strove to police" (182).

136 Chowne, "Remarkable Case of Hirsute Growth in a Female," 46; Duhring, "Case of a Bearded Woman," 194–195 and 199; and "Case of a Bearded Woman," *The Lancet* 1, no. 66 (January 1853): 66.

137 Ghio, *Life of the Celebrated Bearded Lady,* 8 and 14.

138 Mitchell, "Lady Olga," 20.

139 For more on the hairstyles and clothing that were popular among ordinary American women in the 1850s, see Severa, *Dressed for the Photographer,* 84–184 (pp. 132–133 were particularly useful for interpreting the Easterly photograph).

140 Ghio, *Life of the Celebrated Bearded Lady*, 9; and Bogdan, *Freak Show,* 224. Joanne Meyerowitz demonstrates that since the nineteenth century and continuing to the present, the "default logic" with regards to sex, gender, and sexuality is that "a female is naturally and normally a feminine person who desires men." Joanne Meyerowitz, *How Sex Changed: A History of Transsexuality in the United States* (Cambridge, MA: Harvard University Press, 2002), 4.

141 Burrows, "By the Hair of Her Chin," 42. Having her beard cut in the latest styles for men helped Lady Olga further conflate the masculine and feminine; while her beard matched those of the men in the audience, her dress likely matched those of the women in the audience. See Mitchell, "Lady Olga," 20.

142 In the 1970s, sexologists and feminists began to make the now-familiar argument that *sex* and *gender* should be considered separately; although the former was determined by biology, they argued, the latter was culturally constructed. More recently, scholars like Judith Butler, Thomas Laqueur, Anne Fausto-Sterling, and Sandra Eder have taken this idea a step further, arguing that sex, too, is culturally

constructed. Moreover, research and activism by transgender and gender noncon-forming people and scholars have completely reimagined the relationship between gender identity and the physical body. For more on sex, gender, and the body, see Butler, *Gender Trouble*; Thomas W. Laqueur, *Making Sex: Body and Gender from the Greeks to Freud* (Cambridge, MA: Harvard University Press, 1990); Susan Struker, ed., *The Transgender Issue* (Durham, NC: Duke University Press, 1998); Anne Fausto-Sterling, *Sexing the Body: Gender Politics and the Construction of Sexuality* (New York: Basic Books, 2000); Sarah S. Richardson, *Sex Itself: The Search for Male and Female in the Human Genome* (Chicago: University of Chicago Press, 2013); Sandra Eder, *How the Clinic Made Gender* (Chicago: University of Chicago Press, 2022); and Caster Semenya, *The Race to Be Myself* (New York: Norton, 2023). For the use of Madame Clofullia as a lens onto nineteenth-century concepts of gender and sex, see Trainor, "Fair Bosom/Black Beard."

143 None of the medical examinations of nineteenth-century Bearded La-dies that I reviewed in my research suggested that the bearded woman under ex-amination was a man in disguise; all affirmed that she was, indeed, a woman who simply grew a beard. Some physicians diagnosed women who performed as Bearded Ladies with *hypertrichosis,* a medical term first used in the late nineteenth century to describe people with hair growth on the face or body that was unusual in its location, thickness, or quantity. Today, excessive hair growth—particularly in women—would likely instead be diagnosed as *hirsutism.* For hirsutism in modern medical literature, see, for example, David Ferriman and J. D. Gallwey, "Clinical Assessment of Body Hair Growth in Women," *Journal of Clinical Endo-crinology & Metabolism* 21, no. 11 (November 1961): 1440–1447; Catherine Marin DeUrgarte et al., "Degree of Facial and Body Terminal Hair Growth in Unselected Black and White Women: Toward a Populational Definition of Hirsutism," *Journal of Clinical Endocrinology & Metabolism* 91, no. 4 (April 2006): 1345–1350; and Kathryn A. Martin et al., "Evaluation and Treatment of Hirsutism in Pre-menopausal Women: An Endocrine Society Clinical Practice Guideline," *Journal of Clinical Endocrinology and Metabolism* 103, no. 4 (April 2018): 1233–1257. For the origins of hypertrichosis in the nineteenth century, see Rebecca Herzig, "The Woman Beneath the Hair: Treating Hypertrichosis, 1870–1930," *NWSA Journal* 12, no. 3 (2000): 50–66.

144 For more on McKoy, see, for example, Sarah E. Gold, "Millie-Christine McKoy and the American Freak Show: Race, Gender, and Freedom in the Post-bellum Era, 1851–1912," *Berkeley Undergraduate Journal* 23, no. 1 (2010); Ellen Sam-uels, "Examining Millie and Christine McKoy: Where Enslavement and Enfreak-ment Meet," *Signs* 37, no. 1 (Autumn 2011); and Joanne Martell, *Millie-Christine: Fearfully and Wonderfully Made* (Durham, NC: Blair, 2000).

145 Jones, *Vanguard*, introduction.

146 "The Bearded Lady of Geneva," 268. Newspapers published in other cities reprinted this story, such as *People's Press* (Winston-Salem, NC), May 14, 1853. *Herod* refers to Herod the Great, a Biblical King of Judea who ordered the death of all male children in Bethlehem because he was afraid of losing his throne to the newborn

Jesus; this incident is known as the Massacre of the Innocents. A possible interpretation of this metaphor is that by wearing facial hair, the Bearded Lady was subverting men's authority or power, thus killing men symbolically. See *Smith's Bible Dictionary* [1884], s.v. "Herod," by William Smith, last modified 2005, http://www.ccel.org/ccel/smith_w/bibledict.html? term=herod.

147   "Bearded Lady of Geneva," 268.

148   "Men and Women," *New York Times*, September 6, 1853, 4 (emphasis in the original).

149   Fern, "Barnum's Museum," 289; and Joyce W. Warren, *Fanny Fern: An Independent Woman* (New Brunswick, NJ: Rutgers University Press, 1992), 2.

150   Historian Sean Trainor has argued that Madame Clofullia's public reception in the 1850s was significantly different from the way later Bearded Ladies were discussed: Clofullia's womanhood was rarely questioned or probed (with the exception of the physicians who conducted physical examinations of her body), and it was with relative infrequency that writers spoke disparagingly of Clofullia or used her to critique feminist political struggles. Trainor cites the *Gleason's* article I discuss as an exception to the rule—one of a small number of publications that printed "hostile comments" about Clofullia. While I am indebted to Trainor's exceptional and detailed analysis of Clofullia's freak show career, I see more continuity than change in the use of Bearded Ladies (including Clofullia) as a point of reference to critique other women who pushed for more social and political power. See Trainor, "Fair Bosom/Black Beard."

151   Bushnell, *Women's Suffrage,* 49 and 56.

152   *Madame Viola, The Bearded Lady,* 4.

153   *Madame Viola, The Bearded Lady,* 4–5.

154   This cartoon by A.S. Daggy was published in *Life*, February 9, 1911, 315.

155   See, for example, *The Emporia [KS] News,* March 25, 1870, 2; and Rudolf Cronau, *Woman Triumphant: The Story of Her Struggles for Freedom, Education and Political Rights* (New York: R. Cronau, 1916), 259.

156   Noble, "Beardless Man Is Facing a Dreary Existence."

157   Herzig, "The Woman Beneath the Hair," 50–66, at 52 and 57–59; and Herzig, *Plucked,* 77.

158   Duhring, "Case of a Bearded Woman," 200 (emphasis added).

159   George Henry Fox, "The Permanent Removal of Hair by Electrolysis," *Independent Practitioner* 3, no. 4 (April 1882): 241.

160   Bogdan, *Freak Show,* 226–229. While I have identified one advertisement that used the aggrandized title "The Bearded Princess" included in the text, Annie Jones was more often advertised as simply "Miss Annie Jones, The Bearded Lady" or "Bearded Girl." See advertisement for Sackett & Wiggins' Mammoth Dime Museum, Menagerie and Theatorium, *Telegram-Herald* (Grand Rapids, MI), July 4, 1886, 2.

161   Burrows, "By the Hair of Her Chin," 40–42.

162   Some scholars have classified freak show performers like Julia Pastrana and Krao as within the category of Bearded Ladies; Kimberly A. Hamlin, for

example, refers to both women as "bearded ladies of color." Hamlin, "The 'Case of the Bearded Woman,'" 956. However, there is a meaningful—and I would even argue categorial—difference between the Bearded Lady (capitalized) archetype, in which white-presenting performers like Clofullia and Olga appeared consistently, and the appellation *bearded lady* (in lower case) which sometimes (and inconsistently) appeared among a list of identifiers for dark skinned performers. Krao's *New York Times* obituary, for example, refers to her as "Krao Farini, the 'Bearded Lady,' 'Missing Link' and 'Ape-woman' of the Ringling Brothers and Barnum & Bailey Circus;" see "Circus Folk Mourn 'Best-Liked Freak,'" *New York Times,* April 19, 1926, 7. See also Hamlin "The 'Case of the Bearded Woman,'" 972; and *Home Journal* (Winchester, TN), June 14, 1860, 1.

163 Janet Browne and Sharon Messenger, "Victorian Spectacle: Julia Pastrana, The Bearded and Hairy Female," *Endeavour* 27, no. 4 (2003): 155–159; Hamlin, "The 'Case of the Bearded Woman,'" 972; and Rosemarie Garland-Thomson, "Julia Pastrana, the 'Extraordinary Lady,'" *ALTER* 11, no. 1 (January–March 2017), 36. For more on the connections between beauty and race, see Nell Irvin Painter, *The History of White People* (New York: Norton, 2011). For more on the implications of the word *nondescript* as freak show nomenclature, see James W. Cook, "Describing the Nondescript," in *The Arts of Deception: Playing with Fraud in the Age of Barnum* (Cambridge, MA: Harvard University Press, 2001), 119–162.

164 "Bear Woman," *Semi-Weekly Standard* (Raleigh, NC), February 9, 1856, 3, "The Bear Woman," *Daily American Organ* (Washington, DC), January 12, 1856, 3; "Abnormal Growth of Hair," *Ottawa Free Trader* (IL), February 19, 1887, 3; J. T. B., "Continuation from Leipsic," *Edgefield Advertiser* (SC), June 2, 1858, 2; and Bottle G. Jones, "Communicated," *The Weekly Comet* (Baton Rouge, LA), February 25, 1855, 2.

165 Charles Wilson, "An Artist Finds a Dignified Ending for an Ugly Story," *New York Times,* February 11, 2013; Bess Lovejoy, "Julia Pastrana: A 'Monster to the Whole World," *Public Domain Review,* November 26, 2014, https://publicdomain review.org/essay/julia-pastrana-a-monster-to-the-whole-world/; and Beth Lovejoy, "Julia Pastrana's Long Journey Home: A Conversation with Laura Anderson Barbata," *The Order of the Good Death,* December 21, 2017, https://www.orderofthe gooddeath.com/article/julia-pastranas-long-journey-home-a-conversation-with-laura -anderson-barbata/. Pastrana's infant son predeceased her shortly after his birth, and his body, too, was embalmed and displayed alongside his mother's for over a century. However, when the Oslo police recovered the bodies from a carnival's warehouse in the late 1970s—following vandalism by local teenagers—the baby's body was "damaged beyond repair" and "ended up in the trash," which is why Pastrana alone was repatriated in 2013. See Lovejoy, "Julia Pastrana: A 'Monster to the Whole World.'"

166 J. Z. Laurence, "A Short Account of the Bearded and Hairy Female Now Being Exhibited at the Regent-Gallery," *The Lancet* 10, no. 1767 (July 11, 1857), 48 (emphasis in the original).

167 "A Bearded Woman," 526–527; "The Bearded Woman and Child," 125; "Case of a Bearded Woman," *The Lancet,* 66; and Laurence, "A Short Account of the Bearded and Hairy Female," 48.

168   Nicholas Márquez-Grant, "What Happened to the Body of Julia Pastrana (1834–1860)? Addressing Ethical Issues and Human Remains," *Forensic Science International: Reports* 2 (2020), art. 100103, p. 1.

169   "The Bear Woman," *Richmond Indiana Palladium,* June 14, 1855, 1.

170   "A Strange Creature," *Silver State* (Unionville, NV), January 25, 1883, 1; and "Krao, the 'Human Monkey,'" *Scientific American* 48, no. 6 (February 10, 1883), 89. Some sources refer to Krao as "Krao Farini," however the last name Farini was imposed by her kidnapper. Most scholars refer to her by first name in their scholarship, and I have decided to do this same. See, for example, Hamlin, "The 'Case of the Bearded Woman."

171   *The San Francisco Illustrated Wasp,* April 14, 1883, cover; "John S. Gray in Custody," *Sacramento Daily Record-Union,* April 5, 1883, 1; and "The Capture of Gray," *Sacramento Daily Record-Union,* April 6, 1883, 1.

172   "Circus Folk Mourn 'Best-Liked Freak,'" *New York Times,* April 19, 1926, 7; and Hamlin, "The 'Case of the Bearded Woman,'" 972.

173   Herzig, *Plucked,* 64.

174   Advertisement in *Pittsburgh Dispatch,* March 6, 1892, 20.

175   Advertisement in *Pittsburgh Dispatch,* March 6, 1892, 20.

176   Lindsey B. Churchill, "What Is It? Difference, Darwin, and the Victorian Freak Show," in *Darwin in American Cultures,* ed. Patrick B. Sharp and Jeannette Eileen Jones (New York: Routledge, 2010), 136.

177   "Circus Folk Mourn 'Best-Liked Freak'"; Churchill, "What Is It?," 136; and Jane Goodall, *Performance and Evolution in the Age of Darwin* (New York: Routledge, 2002), 78.

178   Noble, "Beardless Man Is Facing a Dreary Existence," 134.

179   Russell B. Adams Jr., *King C. Gillette: The Man and His Wonderful Shaving Device* (Boston: Little, Brown, 1978), 6.

180   Jackson Lears, *Fables of Abundance: A Cultural History of Advertising in America* (New York: Basic Books, 1994), 163–174; and Oldstone-Moore, *Of Beards and Men,* 213–234.

181   Edwin F. Bowers, MD, "The Menace of Whiskers," *McClure's Magazine,* March 1916, 90; Nancy J. Tomes, *The Gospel of Germs: Men, Women and the Microbe in American Life* (Cambridge, MA: Harvard University Press, 1998), 158–159; and Tomes, "American Attitudes toward the Germ Theory of Disease: Phyllis Allen Richmond Revisited," *Journal of the History of Medicine and Allied Sciences* 52, no. 1 (January 1997): 17–50, at 47–48.

3. HAIR SCIENCE

1   Motion for a Suspensive Appeal, February 11, 1862, *Morrison v. White,* Louisiana Supreme Court case 442, 16 La. Ann. 100 (1861), Supreme Court of Louisiana Collection, Earl K. Long Library, University of New Orleans, New Orleans, LA; Ariela Gross, *What Blood Won't Tell: A History of Race on Trial in America*

(Cambridge, MA: Harvard University Press, 2009), 2; and Walter Johnson, "The Slave Trader, the White Slave, and the Politics of Racial Determination in the 1850s," *Journal of American History* 87, no. 1 (June 2000): 13–38, at 36. Two historians have studied Morrison's case at length: Ariela Gross and Walter Johnson. Although I would argue that neither places sufficient emphasis on the role of hair, my understanding of this complex case is deeply indebted to their exhaustive research. See Ariela Gross, "Litigating Whiteness: Trials of Racial Determination in the Nineteenth-Century South," *Yale Law Journal* 108, no. 1 (October 1998): 109–188; Johnson, "The Slave Trader"; and Gross, *What Blood Won't Tell*.

2   The precedent that allowed racial identity to stand in for slave status— that is, the legal presumption that white people were free, and Black people were enslaved—was *Hudgins v. Wright*, which was tried in Virginia in 1806. See *Hudgins v. Wright*, 11 Va. 134 (1806).

3   Racial determination cases occurred when a state law's application hinged on the accused's racial identity. In addition to cases like Morrison's about legality of enslavement, some states in the South had criminal statutes that forbid Black people from, for example, carrying guns, inheriting property, or testifying as witnesses. See Gross, "Litigating Whiteness," 120–121.

4   I arrived at this claim by analyzing all of the affidavits and witness testimony from the trial transcript, which was prepared by the Supreme Court of Louisiana in 1862 as it was preparing to hear the case for the second time. A total of thirty-three testimonies across the three trials referred to Morrison's physical appearance as their evidence of her accurate racial identity: four on White's behalf declared Morrison was Black, and the remaining twenty-nine on Morrison's behalf declared she was white. The seven witnesses who used Morrison's body as racial evidence in the first trial cited her eyes, complexion, cheeks, lips, and teeth. In the second and third trials, by contrast, 63 percent of the witnesses to rely on Morrison's physical appearance (seven out of eleven) cited her hair; other testimony referred to her eyes, complexion, cheeks, lips, nose, ears, head or face, breasts, back, legs or feet, arms or hands, or nails. See testimony of J. B. Clawson, Fritz Fulner, S. N. Cannon, John D. Kemper, W. J. Martin, Hon. B. A. Breaux, and Mr. R. Preston, September 22, 1858; Testimony of S. N. Cannon and P. C. Perret, May 18, 1859; Testimony of P. E. Laresche, Seaman Hopkins, H. L. Clinch, Dr. Brickell, Thos D. Harper, and J. L. Riddell, May 19, 1859; and Testimony of G. A. Breaux, Dr. Samuel Choppin, and S. Castera, May 21, 1859, *Morrison v. White*.

5   At the time, Riddell was a professor of chemistry at the Medical College of Louisiana (which became Tulane University). An important and influential member of New Orleans's scientific community, he served as the president of the New Orleans Academy of Science and was a founding member of the American Association for the Advancement of Science (AAAS). See Hubert Skinner and Karlem Reiss, "John Leonard Riddell: From Rensselaer to New Orleans (1827–1865)," *Earth Sciences History* 4, no. 1 (1985): 75–80; Ralph W. Dexter, "The Early Career of John L. Riddell as a Science Lecturer in the 19th Century," *Ohio Journal of Science* 88, no. 5

(December 1988): 184–188; and Everett F. Bleiler, "John Leonhard Riddell, Pioneer," *Science Fiction Studies* 36, no. 2 (July 2009): 284–286.

6   Testimony of J. L. Riddell, May 19, 1859, *Morrison v. White*. Such physical examinations of Black people's hair occurred in many mid-nineteenth-century courtrooms. The Black San Francisco newspaper *Pacific Appeal* even mocked the prevalence of hair evidence in the state's courtrooms, calling it "hairology." See Lynn M. Hudson, *West of Jim Crow: The Fight against California's Color Line* (Urbana: University of Illinois Press, 2020), 37; and "Mockery of Justice," *Pacfiic Appeal*, April 5, 1862, 2–3.

7   Rebecca Herzig refers to *Trichologia Mammalium* as a "well circulated 1853 treatise" and "Lecture on Hair, Wool, and Sheep Breeding" as a "widely reprinted lecture." See Herzig, *Plucked: A History of Hair Removal* (New York: NYU Press, 2015), 31–32; Peter A. Browne, *Trichologia Mammalium; or, A Treatise on the Organization, Properties and Uses of Hair and Wool; together with an Essay upon the Raising and Breeding of Sheep* (Philadelphia: J. H. Jones, 1853); and [Browne], "Lecture on Hair, Wool and Sheep Breeding," *Southern Planter* 11, no. 4 (April 1851): 1–6.

8   John Van Evrie, *The Six Species of Men* (New York: Van Evrie, Horton & Co., 1866), reprinted in *Popular American Literature of the Nineteenth Century*, ed. Paul Gutjahr (New York: Oxford University Press, 2001), 764. The quoted passage does not reference Browne by name, but it is nearly identical to a similar passage in his earlier book, which did explicitly cite Browne as the source. John H. Van Evrie, *Negroes and Negro "Slavery:" The First an Inferior Race; The Latter Its Normal Condition* (1853; New York: Van Evrie, Horton & Co., 1861), 99.

9   Julia Schickore, *The Microscope and the Eye: A History of Reflections, 1740–1870* (Chicago: University of Chicago Press, 2007), 242.

10   "Woolly knots" is quoted from Thomas Bogue, *Treatise on the Structure, Color, and Preservation of the Human Hair* (Philadelphia: J. W. Moore, 1841), 28; and Seth Pancoast, *The Ladies' Medical Guide: A Complete Instructor and Counsellor, Embracing a Full and Exhaustive Account of the Structure and Functions of the Reproductive Organs; the Diseases of Females and Children, with Their Causes, Symptoms and Treatment; the Toilet Considered in Reference to Female Health, Beauty, and Longevity, etc., etc., etc.* (Philadelphia: Hubbard Bros., 1875), 468–469.

11   Peter A. Browne, *The Classification of Mankind, by the Hair and Wool of Their Heads, with the Nomenclature of Human Hybrids* (Philadelphia: J. H. Jones, 1852), 6. Twentieth- and twenty-first-century research does not corroborate Browne's claims. There are a small number of US studies by anthropologists that examined correlations between hair strand shape and race, and while some studies identified specific hair strand measurements that tended to cluster depending on the person's racial heritage, they also found significant variation within racial groups. Hair strand shape, therefore, is not contrastive according to race. See Donald G. Vernall, "A Study of the Size and Shape of Cross Sections of Hair from Four Races of Men," *American Journal of Physical Anthropology* 19, no. 4 (December 1961): 345–350; Daniel Hrdy, "Quantitative Hair Form Variation in Seven Populations," *American Journal of*

Physical Anthropology 39, no. 1 (July 1973): 7–17; and Sanda L. Kock, Mark D. Shriver, and Nina G. Jablonski, "Variation in Human Hair Ultrastructure among Three Biogeographic Populations," *Journal of Structural Biology* 205, no. 1 (January 2019): 60–66.

12   Blumenbach, *On the Natural Variety of Mankind* (1775), in *The Anthropological Treatises of Johann Friedrich Blumenbach, Late Professor at Göttingen and Court Physician to the King of Great Britain,* ed. and trans. Thomas Bendyshe (London: Longman, Green, Longman, Roberts, & Green, 1865).

13   Samuel George Morton, *Crania Americana; or, A Comparative View of the Skulls of Various Aboriginal Nations of North and South America* (Philadelphia: J. Dobson, 1839), 3–7.

14   Molly Rogers, *Delia's Tears: Race, Science, and Photography in Nineteenth-Century America* (New Haven, CT: Yale University Press, 2010), 58.

15   Samuel J. Redman, *Bone Rooms: From Scientific Racism to Human Prehistory in Museums* (Cambridge, MA: Harvard University Press, 2016), 23–26.

16   Morton, *Crania Americana*, 166–167.

17   Redman, *Bone Rooms*, 25.

18   Redman, *Bone Rooms*, 25.

19   Morton, *Crania Americana*, v (emphasis on "authentic" added, emphasis on "skulls of all nations" in the original).

20   Rachel E. Walker, *Beauty and the Brain: The Science of Human Nature in Early America* (Chicago: University of Chicago Press, 2022), 168.

21   Walker, *Beauty and the Brain*, 167–168.

22   See, for example: V[air] Clirehugh, *A Treatise on the Anatomy and Physiology of the Skin and Hair, as applied to the causes, treatment and prevention of baldness and grey hair; the removal of scurf, dandriff, etc.* (New York: "Corner of Broadway and Fulton Street," [1838–1842?]); Bogue, *Treatise on the Structure, Color*; Edward Phalon, *Treatise on the Hair* (New York, 1847), Pams. P534 Trea 1847, American Antiquarian Society, Worcester, MA; George F. Storrs, *A Treatise on the Human Hair; with directions for preserving it in a state of health, and remarks relative to the treatment of children's hair; and important testimonies of the properties of Storrs' Chemical Hair Invigorator; invented and prepared by George F. Storrs; Philadelphia* (Philadelphia: [publisher unknown], 1850), Backlog 19P 3200, American Antiquarian Society, Worcester, MA; Alexander C. Barry, *A Treatise on the Human Hair, and the formation of the skin; with Directions for Preserving them in a State of Health. With remarks relative to the treatment of children's hair, and important testimonies of the properties of the tricopherous or medicated compound, which has been patronized and adopted by the most eminent of the faculty* (New York: John A. Gray, 1852); H. T. Lovet, *Treatise on the Human Hair* (New York, 1854), G566 L898 T854, American Antiquarian Society, Worcester, MA; Bela C. Perry, *A Treatise on the Human Hair, and Its Diseases* (New Bedford, MA: Charles Taber & Co., 1859), available through National Library of Medicine Digital Collections, https://collections.nlm.nih.gov/bookviewer?PID=nlm:nlmuid-67460160R-bk; and Sarah A. Chevalier, *Treatise on the Hair* (New York: printed by author, 1868).

23   Clirehugh, *Treatise on the Anatomy and Physiology*; and *Longworth's American Almanac, New-York Register and City Directory of the Sixty-First Year of American Independence* (New-York: Thomas Longworth, 1836), 161. Clirehugh's *A Treatise on the Anatomy and Physiology* is the earliest example of a scientific hair treatise in the American Antiquarian Society's extensive collection of early American ephemera. (AAS archivists estimated its date of publication as between 1838 and 1842.) Clirehigh called his specific Tricopherous, but the name ultimately became popularly associated with his rival, Alexander C. Barry. Barry was originally Clirehugh's assistant hair cutter before he was fired; soon thereafter, he began selling his own specific. Clirehugh was so enraged by Barry's betrayal that he took out advertisements warning consumers of this counterfeit product, and even brought a lawsuit against Barry that reached the Supreme Court of New York in 1849. See "Counterfeit of Barry's Tricopherous" (advertisement), *New-York Tribune*, October 6, 1842; "To Prevent Baldness and Grey Hair, Tricopherous, Or, Medicated Compound" (advertisement), *Evening Post* (New York), January 7, 1840; "Daring Attempt to Imitate Clirehugh's Tricopherous!" (advertisement), *Evening Post* (New York), December 11, 1841; "Supreme Court of New York," *American Law Journal* 2 (January 1850): 328; and *The New York Mercantile Union Business Directory* (New York: S. French, L. C. & H. L. Pratt, et al., 1850), 302.

24   For Leonard's credentials, see the cover of C. Henri Leonard, *The Hair; Its Growth, Care, Diseases, and Treatment* (Detroit: The Illustrated Medical Journal Co., 1879). For Barry's biography, see Victoria Sherrow, *Encyclopedia of Hair: A Cultural History* (Westport, CT: Greenwood, 2006), 175. For Perry's credentials, see B[ela] C. Perry, *Human Hair, and the Cutaneous Diseases Which Affect It: Together with Essays on Acne, Sycosis, and Chloasma*, 2nd ed. (1865; New York: James Miller, 1866); and Perry, *Treatise on the Human Hair.*

25   Chevalier, *Treatise on the Hair.* I was unable to find any extant evidence that Chevalier attended medical school; virtually all sources about her are advertisements for (or otherwise related to) her hair specific.

26   Lovet, *Treatise on the Human Hair*, 2; "Chevalier's Life for the Hair," *New York Times*, March 5, 1864, 7 (emphasis in the original); and Michael Sappol, *A Traffic in Dead Bodies: Anatomy and Embodied Social Identity in Nineteenth-Century America* (Princeton, NJ: Princeton University Press, 2002), 151. For the use of specialized medical vocabulary, see, for example, Clirehugh, *Treatise on the Anatomy and Physiology*, 1–7.

27   Perry, *Treatise on the Human Hair*, v–vi.

28   Barry, *A Treatise on the Human Hair*, 1; and Sherrow, *Encyclopedia of Hair*, 175.

29   Chevalier, *Treatise on the Hair*, 16.

30   M. Benjamin, "Dangerous Cosmetics," *New Remedies: An Illustrated Monthly Trade Journal of Materia Medica, Pharmacy, and Therapeutics* 7, no. 11 (November 1878): 326.

31   Noah Webster, *An American Dictionary of the English Language*, stereotype edition (New York: N. & J. White, 1839), s.v. "specific, *n.*" (emphasis in the original).

32   In its first 1820s editions, Webster's American English dictionary defined *science* as "knowledge, or certain knowledge; the comprehension of understanding of truth or facts by the mind." See Webster, s.v. "science."

33   Sappol, *Traffic in Dead Bodies,* 150–151.

34   Clirehugh, *Treatise on the Anatomy and Physiology,* 1.

35   Bogue, *Treatise on the Structure, Color,* 10–13. A solar microscope projected the microscopic image onto the wall of a darkened room, allowing multiple people to view the image at the same time. See Schickore, *Microscope and the Eye,* 36.

36   Pancoast, *Ladies' Medical Guide,* 463–464 (emphasis in the original).

37   Pancoast, *Ladies' Medical Guide,* 463–464.

38   Bogue, *Treatise on the Structure, Color,* viii.

39   Schickore, *Microscope and the Eye,* 1–5 and 242.

40   *Chambers' Encyclopaedia: A Dictionary of Universal Knowledge for the People,* vol. 5 (Philadelphia: J.B. Lippincott & Co., 1872), s.v. "hair."

41   Bogue, *Treatise on the Structure, Color,* 28.

42   Pancoast, *Ladies' Medical Guide,* 468–469.

43   Pancoast, *Ladies' Medical Guide,* 468–469. Madison Grant, *The Passing of the Great Race: Or, the Racial Bias in European History* (New York: C. Scribner, 1916) divided Europe into three hierarchical racial groups according to latitude: the Nordics, Alpines, and Mediterraneans.

44   For the trustworthiness (or untrustworthiness) of the eye in the nineteenth century, see Wendy Bellion, *Citizen Spectator: Art, Illusion, and Visual Perception in Early National America* (Chapel Hill: University of North Carolina Press, 2011); and Michael Leja, *Looking Askance: Skepticism and American Art from Eakins to Duchamp* (Berkeley: University of California Press, 2004).

45   Curator Robert McCracken Peck raised Browne's contemporary visibility with the publication of *Specimens of Hair.* The book's extensive collection of full-color photographs of many of Browne's specimens makes the collection more accessible than ever before. Peck also indicates that Browne created the word *trichology* himself. See Peck, *Specimens of Hair: The Curious Collection of Peter A. Browne* (New York: Blast Books, 2018), 26.

46   Peter A. Browne to [William Maclure], ANSP President, March 10, 1818, box 2, folder 19, Official Correspondence File, Academy of Natural Sciences of Drexel University, Philadelphia, PA; *Aurora General Advertiser* (Philadelphia), January 27, 1804, 2; Peter A. Browne, "The Hair and Wool of the Different Species of Man," *United States Magazine and Democratic Review* 27 (November 1850): 451–456; A. L., "On the Unity of the Human Race," *Southern Quarterly Review* 20 (October 1854): 273–304; "Mission and History," The Franklin Institute, Philadelphia, n.d., https://www.fi.edu/about-us/mission-history; and "About the APS," *American Philosophical Society,* n.d., https://amphilsoc.org/about. On Philadelphia as a major center for racial science in the nineteenth century, see Kathleen M. Brown, *Undoing Slavery: Bodies, Race, and Rights in the Age of Abolition* (Philadelphia: University of Pennsylvania Press, 2023), 19.

47 "Publisher's Notice," *Southern Literary Messenger* 1, no. 1 (August 1834): 1; Jonathan Daniel Wells, introduction to Benjamin Blake Minor, *The Southern Literary Messenger, 1834–1864* (Columbia: University of South Carolina Press, 2007), xi; and William Robert Taylor, *Cavalier and Yankee: The Old South and American National Character* (New York: Oxford University Press, 1993), 199.

48 In the early 1800s Browne placed many advertisements in local Philadelphia newspapers advertising himself as "Attorney at Law." See, for example, *United States Gazette* (Philadelphia), March 29, 1804, 4. The latest publication I identified that referred to Browne representing a client in court was in 1859, in reference to Browne's representation of George F. Alberti, who was notorious among Philadelphia's abolitionist community for, under the auspices of the Fugitive Slave Act, kidnapping both runaway enslaved people and free people of color. Browne authored an impassioned defense of his client in 1851. See "Our Philadelphia Correspondence," *National Anti-Slavery Standard* (New York), February 19, 1859, 2; and *A Review of the Trial, Conviction, and Sentence, of George F. Alberti, for Kidnapping* (Philadelphia, 1851).

49 "Editorial Remarks," *Southern Literary Magazine* 1, no. 4 (December 1834): 191; and "Editorial Remarks," *Southern Literary Messenger* 1, no. 2 (October 1834): 63.

50 "New Test of Sanity," *North-Carolinian* (Fayetteville, NC), June 21, 1851, 1; "Have We a Bourbon Among Us?," *Daily Dispatch* (Richmond, VA), April 28, 1854, 2; "The Hair Theory of Peter Browne," *Anti-Slavery Bugle* (New-Lisbon, OH), June 3, 1854, 4; and Abel Stevens, ed., "Scientific Items," *National Magazine* 5, no. 1 (July 1854): 96.

51 "Medical Jurisprudence: A New Physiological Test of Insanity," *American Law Journal* 11, no. 1 (July 1851): 2; and Frank Fox, "Quaker, Shaker, Rabbi: Warder Cresson, The Story of a Philadelphia Mystic," *Pennsylvania Magazine of History and Biography* 95 (April 1971), 176–177.

52 Peter A. Browne, "On Raising and Breeding Swine for the Bristle," *The Plough, the Loom, and the Anvil* 3, no. 6 (December 1850): 372–374; and Peter A. Browne, "The Rocky Mountain Goat Recommended to Be Domesticated and Added to Our Wool-Bearing Animals," *The Plough, the Loom, and the Anvil* 3, no. 3 (September 1850): 195–196.

53 Peter A. Browne, *The Classification of Mankind, by the Hair and Wool of Their Heads, with an Answer to Dr. Prichard's Assertion, that 'The covering of the head of the negro is hair, properly so termed, and not wool' Read Before the American Ethnological Society, November 3, 1849* (Philadelphia: A. Hart, 1850), 4. The *Oxford English Dictionary* defines *tegument* as "the natural covering of the body, or of some part or organ, of an animal or plant; a skin, coat, shell, husk, or the like"; Webster's 1838 edition defined the word as "a cover or covering." See *Oxford English Dictionary*, s.v. "tegument, *n.*," http://www.oed.com/view/Entry/198617?redirectedFrom=tegument #eid; and Noah Webster, *An American Dictionary of the English Language. . . .*, 15th ed. (New York: N. & J. White, 1838), s.v. "tegument."

54 Richard Veit, "Mastodons, Mound Builders, and Montroville Wilson Dickeson—Pioneering American Archaeologist," *Expedition Magazine* 41, no. 3

(November 1999), https://www.penn.museum/sites/expedition/mastodons-mound
-builders-and-montroville-wilson-dickeson-pioneering-american-archaeologist/.

55   Peter A. Browne and Montroville W. Dickeson, *Trichographia Mammalium; or, Descriptions and Drawings of the Hairs of Mammalia, with the Aid of the Microscope* (Philadelphia: J. H. Jones, 1848), back cover.

56   Browne, "The Rocky Mountain Goat"; and Browne, "On Raising and Breeding Swine."

57   Browne, *Trichologia Mammalium*, iv.

58   Browne and Dickeson, *Trichographia Mammalium*, back cover.

59   Browne, *Trichologia Mammalium*, iv (emphasis in the original).

60   Browne, *Trichologia Mammalium*, iv.

61   Browne and Dickeson, *Trichographica Mammalium*.

62   "Death of Dr. Louis Mandl," *Medical Times and Gazette* (London), July 16, 1881, 75.

63   Browne, *Trichologia Mammalium*, 53 (emphasis in the original).

64   Peter A. Browne to Samuel George Morton, June 29, 1851, box 2, folder 19, Official Correspondence File, Academy of Natural Sciences of Drexel University, Philadelphia, PA.

65   Although rare today, *pile* was popularly used in nineteenth-century scientific texts to refer to hair. Webster's dictionary defined the noun *pile* as "*properly*, a hair; the fibre of wool, cotton, and the like; the nap, the fine, hairy substance of the surface of cloth." See Webster, s.v. "pile, *n*."
Browne, *Classification of Mankind* (1852), 3; and Rebecca Herzig, "Situated Technology: Meanings," in *Gender and Technology: A Reader,* ed. Nina E. Lerman, Ruth Oldenziel, and Arwen P. Mohun (Baltimore, MD: Johns Hopkins University Press, 2003), 75. There are multiple scientific instruments called the *discotome*, including a device to remove gunpowder embedded in soldiers' faces and a device to relieve pain and pressure caused by a herniated disc. See B. A. Watson, "Gunpowder Disfigurements," *St. Louis Medical and Surgical Journal* 35, no. 3 (September 1878): 145–148; and Association of Surgical Technologists, *Surgical Technology for the Surgical Technologist: A Positive Care Approach*, 4th ed. (Clifton Park, NY: Delmar Cengage Learning, 2014), 1179.

66   Browne, *Trichologia Mammalium*, iv and 52–53.

67   Browne, *Trichologia Mammalium*, iv; and Peck, *Specimens of Hair*, 45.

68   I viewed examples of Browne's hair sample collection in volumes 9–12, boxes 4–6, Peter Arrell Browne Papers, Academy of Natural Sciences of Drexel University, Philadelphia, PA. (At the time of my visit, volumes 1–8 were closed for research, so I could not confirm if these volumes also used the same custom paper.)

69   Browne, *Trichologia Mammalium*, 32.

70   Peck, *Specimens of Hair*, 84. Browne concluded that Pastrana's hair was cylindrical in shape (affirming her indigeneity), but lamented that he was unable to examine hair from her beard.

71   Browne and Dickeson, *Trichographia Mammalium*, back cover.

72   Robert McCracken Peck, "George Washington's Brush with Immortality: The Hair Relics of a Sainted Hero," *Magazine Antiques* 182, no. 4 (July/August 2015): 124–131, at 129; Gretchen Worden, *Mutter Museum of the College of Physicians of Philadelphia* (New York: Blast Books, 2002), 132–133; "Presidential Hair," Academy of Natural Sciences of Drexel University, https://ansp.org/exhibits/online-exhibits /presidential-hair/; and Browne, *Trichologia Mammalium,* 59.

73   Janet Golden and Lynn Weiner, "Reading Baby Books: Medicine, Marketing, Money and the Lives of American Infants," *Journal of Social History* 44, no. 3 (Spring 2011): 667–687; and Helen Sheumaker, *Love Entwined: The Curious History of Hairwork in* America (Philadelphia: University of Pennsylvania Press, 2007).

74   Peck, *Specimens of Hair,* 101.

75   Browne, *Trichologia Mammalium,* 56.

76   Browne, *Trichologia Mammalium,* 60.

77   *Pennsylvania Packet,* July 22, 1776, reprinted in Don H. Hagist, *Wives, Slaves, and Servant Girls: Advertisements for Female Runaways in American Newspapers, 1770–1783* (Yardley, PA: Westholme, 2016), 94–95.

78   Webster, s.v. "wool," 2nd def. (The first definition pertains to the covering of sheep and other similar animals.) See also Sharon Block, *Colonial Complexions: Race and Bodies in Eighteenth-Century America* (Philadelphia: University of Pennsylvania Press, 2018), 77–78.

79   John Campbell, *Negro-Mania: Being an examination of the falsely assumed equality of the various races of men.* . . . (Philadelphia: Campbell & Power, 1851), 6; and Melissa N. Stein, *Measuring Manhood: Race and the Science of Masculinity, 1830–1934* (Minneapolis: University of Minnesota Press, 2015), 27.

80   Campbell, *Negro-Mania,* 8–10.

81   Wilford Woodruff, *Wilford Woodruff's Journal, 1833–1898,* vol. 2, ed. Scott G. Kenney (Midvale, UT: Signature Books, 1983–1985), entry from August 19, 1860.

82   "Africans at Home," *Southern Quarterly Review* 26, no. 19 (July 1854): 70 and 73; and William M. Moss, "Vindicator of Southern Intellect and Institutions: The *Southern Quarterly Review,*" *Southern Literary Journal* 13, no. 1 (Fall 1980): 72–108, at 72.

83   "Africans at Home," 76.

84   "Africans at Home," 82.

85   "Africans at Home," 77 (emphasis in the original). In the United States, too, the word *hair* could refer to animals. Nineteenth-century publications sometimes referred to *horsehair*—hair from a horse's mane or, more often, tail—simply as *hair*, such as in reference to horsehair used as mattress stuffing ("hair mattresses") or as broom bristles ("hair brooms"). See *Thirteenth Annual Report of the Commissioner of Labor: Hand and Machine Labor,* vol. 2, *General Table* (Washington, DC: Government Printing Office, 1899), 1316; and "The Bedroom and General Cleaning," *Kitchen Garden* 1, no. 3 (February 1884): 22.

86   A. L., "On the Unity of the Human Race," 299 (emphasis in the original). Surprisingly, given his ideological alignment with, and citations to, Browne's

work, Van Evrie rejected the hair-versus-wool distinction, writing that "the popular notion that it is 'wool' that covers the head of the negro, instead of hair, is fallacious. It is *hair*." See Van Evrie, *Six Species of Men*, 764 (emphasis in the original).

87   Browne, *Classification of Mankind* (1850), 19–20 (emphasis in the original).

88   Volume 11, box 6, Peter Arrell Browne Papers, Academy of Natural Sciences of Drexel University, Philadelphia, PA (emphasis added).

89   Browne, *Trichologia Mammalium*, 51 (emphasis in the original).

90   For the development of pro-slavery scholarship in the decades preceding the Civil War, see, for example, Larry E. Tise, *Proslavery: A History of the Defense of Slavery in America, 1701–1840* (Athens: University of Georgia Press, 1988); Jeffrey Robert Young, ed., *Proslavery and Sectional Thought in the Early South, 1740–1829: An Anthology* (Columbia: University of South Carolina Press, 2006); Charles F. Irons, *The Origins of Proslavery Christianity: White and Black Evangelicals in Colonial and Antebellum Virginia* (Chapel Hill: University of North Carolina Press, 2008); and Lacy K. Ford, *Deliver Us from Evil: The Slavery Question in the Old South* (New York: Oxford University Press, 2009).

91   Browne makes brief reference to facial hair in *Trichologia Mammalium*. In two sections of the book, he quoted or cited other writers' descriptions of beard fashions in different parts of the world and unusual stories of extraordinary facial hair growth. However, Browne merely relays these stories with comment or addition, demonstrating how little he cared for anecdote. See *Trichologia Mammalium*, 30–31 and 94–95.

92   Browne to Morton, June 29, 1851, Academy of Natural Sciences of Drexel University.

93   Browne, *Classification of Mankind* (1850), 6.

94   Johann Gottfried von Blumenbach, *De Generis Humani Varietate Nativa* [On the natural variety of mankind], 3rd ed. (Gottingæ, Germany: Vandenhoek et Ruprecht, 1795), reprinted in Blumenbach, *Anthropological Treatises*, 264–266.

95   Browne, *Classification of Mankind* (1852), 4–5. In a different published version of his taxonomy, Browne also includes a second Chinese person—"Asjunk, of Canton"—in his discussion of American Indians' hair. See Browne, "Examination and Description of the Hair of the Head of the North American Indians. . . .," in *Information Respecting the History, Condition, and Prospects of the Indian Tribes of the United States. . . .*, ed. Henry Schoolcraft (Philadelphia: Lippincott, Grambo & Company, 1853), 376.

96   Browne, *Trichologia Mammalium*, 63. Browne was not the only person to make such a conflation: just three years after the initial publication of *The Classification of Mankind* (1850), this same logic—possibly even Browne's own research—proved crucial to the California Supreme Court case *People v. Hall*. In 1853, George Hall was arrested for murder after killing a Chinese miner named Ling Sing during a robbery. Hall's attorney tried to get the other miners' testimony excluded from the trial, claiming that California's Criminal Practice Act of 1850 prohibited Chinese people from testifying against white people. The judge disagreed: while the Act excluded Black, mulatto, and Indigenous people from testifying against white

people, it made no mention of Chinese people. Hall's attorney appealed to the State Supreme Court, claiming that the law's authors *accidentally* omitted Chinese people but intended to exclude testimony from *all* non-white people. Chief Justice Hugh C. Murray agreed. In a revised version of the act passed in 1854, Judge Murray categorized Chinese people *as* Indigenous, writing that it was "the remarkable resemblance in eyes, *beard, hair,* and other peculiarities" that caused many scientists categoize Indigenous North American and Asian people together within the "three distinct types of the human species." See *People v. Hall,* 4 Cal 399 (1854), 400, https://casetext.com/case/people-v-hall-2243; and Donald Michael Bottoms, Jr., "'An Aristocracy of Color': Race and Reconstruction in Post-Gold Rush California" (PhD diss., University of California Los Angeles, 2005), 28–29. I appreciate Natalie Novoa for bringing *People v. Hall* to my attention.

97   Browne, *Trichologia Mammalium,* 67.

98   Isabelle Charmantier, "Black Lives in the Linnean Society Collections: Amelia Newsham," News, *Linnean Society of London,* October 19, 2020, https://www.linnean.org/news/2020/10/19/black-lives-in-the-linnean-society-collections-amelia-newsham.

99   James Cowles Prichard, *Researches into the Physical History of Man* (London: Printed for John and Arthur Arch, Cornhill; and B. and H. Barry, Bristol, 1813), 165–167.

100   Peter A. Browne, "A Microscopic examination and description of some of the Piles of the head of Albinos," in *Proceedings of the American Association for the Advancement of Science. Third Meeting, Held at Charleston, S. C. March, 1850* (Charleston, SC: Steam-Power Press of Walker and James, 1850): 108 (emphasis in the original).

101   Browne, "A Microscopic examination and description," 113. Browne explained that he had "no pile of an American Indian Albino," although other scientists had reported seeing albinism among Indigenous people.

102   Browne, "A Microscopic examination and description," 113–114.

103   Samuel Morton has also been accused of distorting the cranial measurements he declared to be proof both that polygenesis was correct and that the group of people he called Caucasian were the most intelligent of all races; whether these distortions were intentional or unintentional is unclear. See Redman, *Bone Rooms,* 24–25.

104   Browne, *Classification of Mankind* (1850), 4.

105   Browne, *Classification of Mankind* (1852), 4–6.

106   Browne, *Trichologia Mammalium,* 59.

107   Josiah C. Nott, *An Essay on the Natural History of Mankind, Viewed in Connection with Negro Slavery, Delivered before the Southern Rights Association, 14th December 1850* (Mobile, AL: Dade, Thompson, & Co., 1851), 4 (emphasis in the original).

108   Browne, *Classification of Mankind* (1850), 7 (emphasis in original).

109   *A Review of Peter A. Browne's Treatise on Hair and Wool* ([publisher unknown], [1850?]), 7 (emphasis in the original), Sc Rare+F 12-45, Schomburg Center

for Research in Black Culture – Manuscripts & Archives, The New York Public Library, New York, NY.

110   Browne, *A Lecture on the Oregon Territory* (Philadelphia: United States Book and Printing Office, 1843), 3 (emphasis in the original).

111   Browne, *Lecture on the Oregon Territory*, 10.

112   Browne, *Review of the Trial*, 9 (emphasis in the original).

113   Browne, *Review of the Trial*, 20–21 (emphasis in the original).

114   *Aurora General Advertiser* (Philadelphia, PA), October 9, 1804, 4. Although Pennsylvania outlawed slavery two years before Browne was born and there is no evidence he was an enslaver, it is clear from this advertisement that he personally benefited from unfree Black labor.

115   Browne, *Review of the Trial*, 21 (emphasis in the original).

116   Browne, *Trichologia Mammalium*, 67 (emphasis in the original).

117   Browne, *Trichologia Mammalium*, 73. Browne did allow that there were some exceptions: "sometimes, however, where the constitutional energy of one parent outweighs that of the other, only one species of pile will be found" (73).

118   "Have We a Bourbon Among Us?," 2.

119   Browne, *Trichologia Mammalium*, 170 (emphasis in the original).

120   Browne, *Trichologia Mammalium*, 168 (emphasis in the original). Modern medical research does not find a higher incidence of tuberculosis among people with mixed racial ancestry. See "TB and Black or African American Persons," Centers for Disease Control and Prevention, April 2024, https://www.cdc.gov/tb/health -equity/black-or-african-american-persons.html?CDC_AAref_Val=https://www.cdc .gov/tb/topic/populations/tbinafricanamericans/default.htm.

121   Browne, *Trichologia Mammalium*, 165 and 167 (emphasis in the original).

122   Browne, *Trichologia Mammalium*, 167 (emphasis in the original).

123   Browne, *Trichologia Mammalium*, 166 (emphasis in the original).

124   Browne, *Trichologia Mammalium*, 155–156.

125   Browne, *Trichologia Mammalium*, 158.

126   Peter A. Browne, "On Wool.—From W. F. Van Amringe, Esquire, to P. A. Browne, Esq., LL.D.," *The Plough, the Loom, and the Anvil* 3, no. IV (October 1851), 251 (emphasis in the original).

127   See, for example, Browne, *An Inquiry into the Expediency of Altering and Amending the Naturalization Law of the United States, Respectfully Addressed to the American People* (Philadelphia: Barrett & Jones, 1846); Browne, *Trichologia Mammalium*; and vols. 9–12, boxes 4–6, Peter Arrell Browne Papers, Academy of Natural Sciences of Drexel University.

128   Browne, *Trichologia Mammalium*, iv.

129   Browne, *Trichologia Mammalium*, 66.

130   Stein, *Measuring Manhood*, 32–33. Stein's survey of seventy-seven antebellum racial science publications found that one-quarter of texts focused on racial origins, specifically the polygenesis versus monogenesis question. No other theme was more highly represented in her sample.

131 For more on polygenesis and monogenesis in the nineteenth century, see Bruce Dain, *A Hideous Monster of the Minds: American Race Theory in the Early Republic* (Cambridge, MA: Harvard University Press, 2002), esp. chs. 2 and 7; William Stanton, *The Leopard's Spots: Scientific Attitudes toward Race in America, 1815–1859* (Chicago: University of Chicago Press, 1960); Thomas Gossett, *Race: The History of an Idea in America* (Dallas, TX: Southern Methodist University Press, 1963); George M. Frederickson, *The Black Image in the White Mind: The Debate over Afro-American Character and Destiny, 1817–1914* (New York: Harper & Row, 1971); and Reginald Horsman, *Josiah Nott of Mobile: Southerner, Physician, and Racial Theorist* (Baton Rouge: Louisiana State University, 1987). Walter Johnson offers a useful survey of the relevant literature on this subject; see Johnson, "The Slave Trader," 27.

132 *Proceedings of the American Association for the Advancement of Science. Third Meeting, Held at Charleston, S. C., March, 1850* (Charleston, SC: Steam-Power Press of Walker and James, 1850), 107.

133 Johnson, "The Slave Trader," 27.

134 Nott, *An Essay on the Natural History of Mankind*, 3.

135 "Natural History of Man," *United States Magazine and Democratic Review* 27 (November 1850), 41.

136 "Natural History of Man."

137 Nott, *An Essay on the Natural History of Mankind*, 3; and A. L., "On the Unity of the Human Race," 303.

138 See, for example, Dain, *Hideous Monster of the Minds*.

139 Josiah C. Nott and George R. Gliddon, ed., *Types of Mankind. . . .* (Philadelphia: Lippincott, Grambo & Co., 1854), 97 (emphasis in the original).

140 Nott and Gliddon, *Types of Mankind*, xxxv (emphasis in the original).

141 Browne, *Classification of Mankind* (1852), 4–6; and Browne, *Trichologia Mammalium*, 59.

142 Browne, "Hair and Wool of the Different Species of Man," 452.

143 Nott and Gliddon, *Types of Mankind*, 97 and 717n44; Redman, *Bone Rooms*, 23; and Caroline Winterer, *The Mirror of Antiquity: American Women and the Classical Tradition, 1750–1900* (Ithaca, NY: Cornell University Press, 2009), 182.

144 Testimony of J. L. Riddell, May 19, 1859, *Morrison v. White* (emphasis added).

145 Allyson Hobbs, *A Chosen Exile: A History of Racial Passing in American Life* (Cambridge, MA: Harvard University Press, 2014), 34.

146 Hobbs, *Chosen Exile*, 29.

147 "Negro Equality," *Southern Watchman* (Athens, GA), June 14, 1865.

148 *Florey's Executors vs. Florey* (1854), in J. W. Shepherd, *Reports of Cases Argued and Determined in the Supreme Court of Alabama, during a part of June Term, 1853, and the whole of January Term, 1854* (Montgomery: Cowan & Martin, 1854), 241–248. By ruling that Gustavus was suffering from an "insane delusion," his will—which left his entire estate to his only child, Edward G.—was rendered void.

149   Gussie L. Davis (lyrics and music), "When They Straighten All the Colored People's Hair," Spaulding & Gray, New York, 1894 (emphasis added).

150   Nathaniel Shaler, "Science and the African Problem," *The Atlantic,* July 1890, 41.

151   Daniel Taylor, Federal Writers' Project: Slave Narrative Project, vol. 1, *Alabama,* Aarons–Young, 367, https://www.loc.gov/item/mesn010 (emphasis added).

152   Browne, *Trichologia Mammalium,* 57–58 (emphasis in the original).

153   Browne, *Trichologia Mammalium,* 58 (emphasis in the original).

154   "Have We a Bourbon Among Us?," 2.

155   "Have We a Bourbon Among Us?," 2.

156   Perry, *Human Hair, and the Cutaneous Diseases,* 64.

157   I have only found one nineteenth-century source that recapitulated Browne's research after his death. Leonard, *The Hair: Its Growth, Care, Diseases, and Treatment* (1879) describes a three-part hair strand shape taxonomy—virtually identical to Browne's and, I suspect, plagiarized from him—without attribution. In the nearly 150 years since, I have found a very small number of studies that sought to connect hair strand shape with race, none of which reference (nor corroborate) Browne's research. See Vernall, "A Study of the Size and Shape"; Hrdy, "Quantitative Hair Form Variation"; and Kock, Shriver, and Jablonski, "Variation in Human Hair Ultrastructure."

158   Stein, *Measuring Manhood,* 91–92.

159   Peck, *Specimens of Hair,* 9–11.

160   Motion for a Suspensive Appeal, February 11, 1862, *Morrison v. White;* and Gross, *What Blood Won't Tell,* 2.

161   Petition for Change in Venue, September 22, 1858, Judgment on Prayer for Change of Venue, September 22, 1858, and Testimony of Wm Denison, May 19, 1859, *Morrison v. White.* Dennison's house was attached to the jail.

162   Testimony of Wm Denison, May 19, 1859, *Morrison v. White.*

163   Testimony of Wm Denison, May 19, 1859, *Morrison v. White.*

164   Testimony of Wm Denison, May 19, 1859, *Morrison v. White.* Dennison's testimony is an outlier among the witnesses who testified on Morrison's behalf across her three trials: he was the only plaintiff witness not to mention Morrison's physical features or appearance as evidence for her whiteness; instead, Dennison said that he knew she was white because "during the whole time witness had the girl near him, she always behaved herself well as a White girl should do." It is possible that hair evidence may not have been compelling to Dennison even if it had been more stable, but it is also possible that its very *instability* is what made Dennison look elsewhere for evidence of Morrison's whiteness.

4. HAIR FRAUD

1   Séjour de Lorraine, *Les Secrets de la beauté du visage et du corps de l'homme et de la femme: Traité complet d'hygiene, de physiognomonie et d'embellissement* (Paris:

Chez L'Auteur, 1855), hereafter *Secrets of Beauty*. This quote comes not from the original taxonomy in *Secrets of Beauty*, but Andrew Wynter's commentary on the taxonomy's significance, first published as Andrew Wynter, "The Hair Markets of Europe and Fashions in Hair-Dressing," *Cassell's Magazine,* August 31, 1867, and later republished in its entirety in Wynter, *Peeps into the Human Hive,* vol. 2 (London: Chapman and Hall, 1874). All but four of the US publications I examined included Wynter's comments along the original French text.

2   Rachel E. Walker, *Beauty and the Brain: The Science of Human Nature in Early America* (Chicago: University of Chicago Press, 2022), 177–181.

3   Barry M. Pretzker, "Mojave," in *A Native American Encyclopedia: History, Culture, and Peoples* (Oxford: Oxford University Press, 2000), 46–49; and Janice Emily Bowers, *Flowers and Shrubs of the Mojave Desert* (Tucson, AZ: Southwest Parks and Monuments Association, 1999), 36.

4   Bela C. Perry, *Human Hair, and the Cutaneous Diseases Which Affect It: Together with Essays on Acne, Sycosis, and Chloasma,* 2nd ed. (1865; New York: James Miller, 1866), 13–14.

5   Henry Alfred Robbins, "Hair and Its Anomalies," *Journal of the American Medical Association* 34, no. 19 (May 12, 1900): 1169–1172.

6   Kathy Peiss, *Hope in a Jar: The Making of America's Beauty Culture* (Philadelphia: University of Pennsylvania Press, 1998), 12–14.

7   Ayana Byrd and Lori Tharp, *Hair Story: Untangling the Roots of Black Hair in America* (New York: St. Martin's Press, 2001), 17; and Willie Morrow, *400 Years Without a Comb* (San Diego: Morrow's Unlimited, Inc., 1973), 62–66.

8   Robert Roberts, *The House Servant's Directory,* 2nd ed. (Boston: Munroe and Francis, 1828), iii and 117, https://archive.org/details/houseservantsdir00robe /page/n7/mode/2up.

9   Sarah Josepha Hale, *Mrs. Hale's Receipts for the Million* (Philadelphia: T. B. Peterson, 1857), 130–131.

10   Bruce M. Tyler, "Black Hairstyles, Appearance, Conduct, and Cultural Democracy," *Western Journal of Black Studies* 14, no. 4 (Winter 1990): 235–250, at 235; and Tameka N. Ellington and Joseph L. Underwood, eds., *Textures: The History and Art of Black Hair* (Kent, OH: Kent State University Museum, 2020), 72. The inventor of the hot comb remains contested. Although many sources (including Tyler) attributed its invention to Madam C. J. Walker, more recent evidence indicates that Walker popularized, but did not originate, this technology. Ellington and Underwood identify François Marcel Grateau from France as the correct inventor.

11   Wigs have also long been part of some religious traditions: Many Orthodox Jewish women wear wigs, called *sheitels,* to cover their hair after they are married. For the practice of hair covering (including *sheitels*) in Jewish American communities, see, for example, Amy K. Milligan, *Hair, Headwear, and Orthodox Jewish Women: Kallah's Choice* (Lanham, MD: Lexington, 2014); and Lynee Schrieber, ed., *Hide and Seek: Jewish Women and Hair Covering* (New York: Urim Publications, 2003).

12   Richard Corson, *Fashions in Hair: The First Five Thousand Years* (London: Peter Ownes, 1984), 215.

13   Mark Campbell, *Self-Instructor in the Art of Hair Work, Dressing Hair, Making Curls, Switches, Braids, and Hair Jewelry of Every Description* (New York: M. Campbell, 1867), 260–263; "Where the Ladies' False Hair Comes From," *Daily American* (Nashville, TN), June 24, 1877; *Chambers's Encyclopædia: A Dictionary of Universal Knowledge for the People, Illustrated,* vol. 5 (Philadelphia: J.B. Lippincott & Co., 1870), c.v. "hair manufactures"; "The Trade in False Hair," *Scientific American* 39, no. 22 (November 30, 1878): 2415; and "Human Hair and Its Substitutes," *Scientific American* 26, no. 18 (April 27, 1872): 276.

14   "Men Who Wear Wigs," *Pittsburgh Dispatch,* January 6, 1889; "Human Hair and Its Substitutes"; "Wigs and Wig-Making," *Barber County Index* (KS), March 20, 1889; "Hair for Wigs," *True Northerner* (Paw Paw, MI), March 25, 1886; "Hair for Wigs," *Abbeville Messenger* (SC), May 11, 1886; and "Hair for Wigs," *Orange County Observer* (NC), July 17, 1886.

15   "Girl Gets Leprosy from a Chinese Wig. Tragic Result of Realism at Fancy Dress Ball," *San Francisco Call,* July 2, 1911.

16   Ariel E. V. Dunn, "The Art of Wigmaking," *Billboard* 38, no. 52 (December 25, 1926): 15 and 87.

17   "City Happenings—Personal," *The Freeman* (Indianapolis, IN), January 26, 1895, 8; advertisement for T. W. Taylor in *The Freeman* (Indianapolis, IN), August 24, 1910, 3; Marian Doyle, *An Illustrated History of Hairstyles, 1830–1930* (Atglen, PA: Schiffer, 2003), 5–9; and Corson, *Fashions in Hair,* 532–559. It wasn't until the twentieth century that wigs became a major part of Black women's hair-care routines. See Bruce, "Black Hairstyles," 242–243.

18   Elizabeth Waterhouse Allen to Mary Ware Allen Johnson, February 26, 1869, and March 7, 1869, box 1, folder 15, Allen–Johnson Family Papers, 1759–1992, American Antiquarian Society, Worcester, MA; and "Human Hair," *New York Times,* August 3, 1866.

19   "The Trade in False Hair." Very few sources describe false hairpieces worn by women to cover bald or thinning spots. A rare example comes from *Scientific American,* which described women who used added false "switches" to their natural hair—a fact that was desperately kept secret from everyone except "her most intimate lady friends." See "Human Hair and Its Substitutes."

20   Edward Phalon, *Treatise on the Hair* (New York, 1847), back cover; *Times–Picayune* (New Orleans, LA), December 5, 1847; and Campbell, *Self-Instructor in the Art of Hair Work,* 267.

21   The interview with this wigmaker was republished in many newspapers. See, for example, "Wigs and Wig-Making," *The Times* (Clay Center, KS), January 31, 1889; "Wigs and Wig-Making," *Witchita (KS) Daily Eagle,* February 7, 1889; "Wigs and Wig-Making," *Belvidere (IL) Standard,* February 13, 1889; "Wig Making," *Falcon* (Elizabeth City, NC), February 15, 1889; "Wigs and Wig-Making," *Reno (NV) Gazette-Journal,* March 7, 1889; "Wigs and Wig-Making," *Barber County (KS) Index,* March 20, 1889;

"Wigs and Wig-Making," *Decatur Herald* (IL), March 31, 1889; "Wigs and Wig-Making," *Chetopa Advance* (KS), May 31, 1889; "Wigs and Wig-Making," *Alabama Enquirer,* May 29, 1890; and "Wigs and Wig-Making," *Perrysburg Journal* (OH), August 9, 1890. The value of a $25–$30 wig in 1889 is equivalent to $854–$1,020 in 2023.

22 Hiscox & Co., "Parker's Hair Balsam. 'How to preserve the hair,' is a question that troubles many who, through age, disease, or neglect are growing bald, or whose hair is turning gray. . . . Parker's ginger tonic. A medicine that should be in every family. . . . Hiscox & Co. . . . New York. . . . ," trade card (New York: [1870–1900]), Ephemera Late Trade Pers 0079, American Antiquarian Society, Worcester, MA; and "Professor Alex. C. Barry's Trichopherous, or Medicated Compound," *Spirit of the Times,* July 30, 1853, 287.

23 Advertisements from *The Freeman* (Indianapolis, IN), October 15, 1892, 3; December 22, 1900, 2; and November 16, 1912, 3; and Byrd and Tharp, *Hair Story,* 23.

24 S. B. Wright & Co., "'A woman's crowning glory is her hair.' Sutherland Sisters' Hair Grower! Will grow hair. . . . S.B. Wright & Co., agents . . . [illegible] Everlasting Cologne . . . S.B. Wright & Co., manufacturers . . . Boston, Mass. . . . ," (Boston, [1870–1900]), Ephemera Late Trade Pers 0088 American Antiquarian Society, Worcester, MA.

25 "Human Hair and Its Substitutes."

26 "Men Who Wear Wigs," *Pittsburgh Dispatch*, January 6, 1889.

27 *Chambers's Encyclopædia: A Dictionary of Universal Knowledge for the People, Illustrated,* vol. 5 (Philadelphia: J. B. Lippincott & Co., 1870), s.v. "hair manufactures."

28 Tiya Miles, *All That She Carried: The Journey of Ashley's Sack, a Black Family Keepsake* (New York: Penguin Random House, 2021), 115.

29 "Emma Sands," *Burlington Free Press* (VT), June 18, 1879. For reportage in faraway states, see, for example, "Crime and Casualty," *Atlanta Constitution*, June 19, 1879; "A Vermont Mystery," *Times-Picayune* (New Orleans, LA), June 21, 1879; and "A Mystery in Vermont," *Coffeyville Weekly Journal* (KS), June 28, 1879.

30 "Foul Play Suspected," *Burlington Daily Free Press and Times* (VT), June 11, 1879; and "That Missing Girl," *Burlington Daily Free Press and Times* (VT), June 13, 1879. Neither the state of Vermont nor any local municipality had a law prohibiting cross-dressing during the 1870s, so it is unclear why the article presumed the girl would have been arrested. See Clare Sears, "'A Dress Not Belonging to His or Her Sex': Cross-dressing Law in San Francisco, 1860–1900" (PhD diss., University of California, Santa Cruz, 2005), 215–216.

31 "That Missing Girl," *Burlington Daily Free Press and Times* (VT), June 14, 1879.

32 "The Missing Girl," *Burlington Daily Free Press and Times* (VT), June 16, 1879.

33 "At Last," *Burlington Daily Free Press and Times* (VT), June 19 and June 20, 1879; "Miss Sands," *Burlington Daily Free Press and Time* (VT), June 27, 1879.

34 "At Last," *Burlington Daily Free Press and Times* (VT), June 20, 1879.

35   *Burlington Daily Free Press and Times* (VT), August 9, 1879; and "Essex Junction," *Burlington Daily Free Press and Times* (VT), April 24, 1883. These two articles were the last mentions of Emma Sands in any Vermont newspaper. Her name is sufficiently common to make it extremely difficult to track Sands's move west; the same holds true for her potential alter ego, Charlie Thompson.

36   "The Missing Girl."

37   "Missing Miss Sands," *Burlington Daily Free Press and Times* (VT), June 17, 1879. After the haircut, Sands tried to sell her hair at another Burlington shop; she was later identified by the shopgirl who served her.

38   Historian Daniel A. Cohen estimates that "dozens, if not hundreds or even thousands, of disguised women" served in North American armies in the eighteenth and nineteenth centuries. See Cohen, Introduction, *The Female Marine and Related Works: Narratives of Cross-Dressing and Urban Vice in America's Early Republic* (Amherst: University of Massachusetts Press, 1997), 9.

39   Such emphatic denunciations may have been intended to contrast these women's stories with the sensational stories published contemporaneously in the popular press about female husbands: people assigned female at birth who lived their lives as men. See Jen Manion, *Female Husbands: A Trans History* (New York: Cambridge University Press, 2020).

40   "Publisher's Notice" in Sarah Emma Edmonds, *Nurse and Spy in the Union Army: Comprising the Adventures and Experiences of a Woman in Hospitals, Camps, and Battle-Fields* (Hartford, CT: W.S. Williams & Co., 1865), 6.

41   Loreta Janeta Velazquez, *The Woman in Battle: Narrative of the Exploits, Adventures, and Travels of Madame Loreta Janeta Velazquez, Otherwise Known as Lieutenant Harry T. Buford, Confederate States Army* (Richmond, VA: Dustin, Gilman & Co., 1876), 37 and 50–51.

42   Citizen of Massachusetts [Herman Mann], *The Female Review . . .* (Dedham, MA: Nathaniel and Benjamin Heaton, 1797; repr., John Adams Vinton, ed., Tarrytown, NY: William Abbatt, 1916), 83–84 (emphasis added).

43   Cohen, Introduction to *The Female Marine and Related Works*, 1–6; and Daniel A. Cohen, "'The Female Marine' in an Era of Good Feelings: Crossdressing and the 'Genius' of Nathaniel Coverly Jr.," *Proceedings of the American Antiquarian Society* 103 (1994): 359–393, at 365.

44   Cohen, ed., *Female Marine and Related Works,* 84.

45   Cohen, ed., *Female Marine and Related Works,* 85.

46   Cohen, ed., *Female Marine and Related Works,* 90 (emphasis added).

47   Cohen, introduction to *Female Marine and Related Works,* 9.

48   Velazquez, *Woman in Battle,* 53.

49   Velazquez, *Woman in Battle,* 63 (emphasis added).

50   Velazquez, *Woman in Battle,* 63.

51   Velazquez, *Woman in Battle,* 68–69.

52   Velazquez, *Woman in Battle,* 60.

53 Velazquez, *Woman in Battle*, 77–78.

54 Velazquez, *Woman in Battle*, 178–182 and 198. New Orleans had passed a municipal law in 1856 that prohibited the wearing of a mask or disguise in public. This law did not explicitly prohibit cross-dressing—unlike laws against cross-dressing passed in thirty-four US cities between 1848 and 1900—but in its enforcement the New Orleans law sometimes also targeted cross-dressing. See Sears, "'A Dress Not Belonging to His or Her Sex,'" 3–4 and 216; and William N. Eskridge Jr., "Law and the Construction of the Closet: American Regulation of Same-Sex Intimacy, 1880–1846," *Iowa Law Review* 82 (1997): 1007–1136, at 1040–1041.

55 "Publishers' Notice," in Edmonds, *Nurse and Spy in the Union Army*, 5.

56 Edmonds, *Nurse and Spy in the Union Army*, 154, 262, and 312–316.

57 Edmonds, *Nurse and Spy in the Union Army*, 18 and 105–107.

58 Doyle, *Illustrated History of Hairstyles*, 17–45.

59 Edmonds, *Nurse and Spy in the Union Army*, 116.

60 [Advertisement for David Gratenread,] *Virginia Gazette*, May 7, 1767, in The Geography of Slavery in Virginia (archive by Tom Costa and the Rector and Visitors of the University of Virginia), http://www2.vcdh.virginia.edu/gos.

61 [Advertisement for Rochester,] *Virginia Herald and Fredericksburg Advertiser*, June 19, 1788, in The Geography of Slavery in Virginia; and [Advertisement for Phill,] *Virginia Gazette and Weekly Advertiser*, September 4, 1784, in The Geography of Slavery in Virginia. That some runaways altered their hair to pass as white during their escape does not imply that they intended to pass permanently; such racial disguises may have been instrumental and temporary. See Allyson Hobbs, *A Chosen Exile: A History of Racial Passing in America* (Cambridge, MA: Harvard University Press, 2016), 29.

62 *Pennsylvania Packet*, July 22, 1776, reprinted in Don H. Hagist, *Wives, Slaves, and Servant Girls: Advertisements for Female Runaways in American Newspapers, 1770–1783* (Yardley, PA: Westholme, 2016), 95.

63 *The Richmond Enquirer*, November 30, 1810, republished in *Advertisements for Runaway Slaves in Virginia, 1801–1820*, ed. Daniel Meaders (New York: Garland, 1997), 147.

64 *Pennsylvania Gazette*, November 10, 1763, in Sharon Block, *Colonial Complexions: Race and Bodies in Eighteenth-Century America* (Philadelphia: University of Pennsylvania Press, 2018), 79.

65 *Virginia Gazette*, February 10, 1774, reprinted in Hagist, *Wives, Slaves, and Servant Girls*, 50.

66 Harriet Beecher Stowe, *Uncle Tom's Cabin, Or, Life Among the Lowly*, vol. 1 (Boston: John P. Jewett & Company, 1852), 157–158.

67 Stowe, *Uncle Tom's Cabin*, 161.

68 Stowe, *Uncle Tom's Cabin*, 159 (emphasis added).

69 See, for example, Johann Friedrich Blumenbach, *De Generis Humani Varietate Nativa* [On the natural variety of mankind], 3rd ed. (Gottingæ, Germany: Vandenhoek et Ruprecht, 1795), repr. in Blumenbach, *The Anthropological Treatises*

of Johann Friedrich Blumenbach . . . ., ed. and trans. Thomas Bendyshe (London: Longman, Green, Longman, Roberts, & Green, 1865), 264–265.

70   *Virginia Gazette*, November 5, 1772, in The Geography of Slavery in Virginia.

71   *Virginia Gazette and General Advertiser* (Davis), Richmond, VA, November 9, 1796, in The Geography of Slavery in Virginia.

72   "Why Lee Yoo Bought a Wig," *Hartford Daily Courant* (CT), reprinted from the *Philadelphia Press*, November 27, 1882.

73   Erika Lee, *At America's Gates: Chinese Immigration during the Exclusion Era, 1882–1943* (Chapel Hill: University of North Carolina Press, 2003), 161–162.

74   Jacqueline M. Henkel, "Represented Authenticity: Native Voices in Seventeenth-Century Conversion Narratives," *New England Quarterly* 87, no. 1 (March 2014): 5–45, at 32.

75   Worthington Chauncey Ford, "Samuel Sewall and Nicholas Noyes on Wigs," in *Publications of the Colonial Society of Massachusetts*, vol. 20, *Transactions 1917–1919* (Boston: printed by society, 1920), 120.

76   Ford, "Samuel Sewall and Nicholas Noyes on Wigs," 120.

77   For the Confidence Man character in nineteenth-century culture, see Karen Halttunen, *Confidence Men and Painted Women: A Study of Middle-Class Culture in America, 1830–1870* (New Haven, CT: Yale University Press, 1982).

78   John F. Kasson, *Rudeness and Civility: Manners in Nineteenth-Century Urban America* (New York: Hill and Wang, 1990), 105–106.

79   Thomas Byrnes, *Professional Criminals of America* (New York: Cassell, 1886), 53 and 280–282.

80   Allan Pinkerton, *Thirty Years a Detective: A Thorough and Comprehensive Exposé of Criminal Practices of All Grades and Classes. Containing Numerous Episodes of Personal Experience in the Detection of Criminals, and Covering a Period of Thirty Years' Active Detective Life* (New York: G.W. Carleton, 1884), 152–157.

81   "A Fight with Fence Cutters," *Times–Democrat* (New Orleans, LA), November 11, 1886.

82   Byrnes, *Professional Criminals of America*, 234–235.

83   "Hau Defies Court," *Washington Post*, July 18, 1907.

84   "Hau Defies Court"; and "The Case of Karl Hau," *New York Times*, July 17, 1907.

85   US Census Bureau, "Population of the 100 Largest Urban Places: 1860," 1998, https://www2.census.gov/library/working-papers/1998/demographics/pop-twps 0027/tab09.txt.

86   "The Story of a Wig," *Republican Banner* (Nashville, TN), February 20, 1867.

87   "The Story of a Wig" (emphasis added).

88   "The Story of a Wig" (emphasis added).

89   "Wig Deceived Her," *Nashville American* (TN), March 21, 1901.

90   "Arrested in Disguise," *San Francisco Chronicle*, January 14, 1886; "An Obscene Masker," *San Francisco Chronicle*, May 26, 1887; and "A Wretch Properly Punished," *Daily Alta California*, May 28, 1887. It is unclear why these two arrests were not included in the official city records.

91   *San Francisco Municipal Reports, 1859–1960* to *1899–1900*, published by Order of the Board of Supervisors, San Francisco; see Bancroft Library, University of California, Berkeley. While none of the forty-two Chief of Police reports I evaluated specify the crime for which these people were arrested and San Francisco's ordinance books have no laws prohibiting false beards or covered faces, it is likely that those arrested had run afoul of a state law instead: California Penal Code, section 185, amended in 1873 or 1874, which made it a misdemeanor to "wear any mask, false whiskers, or any personal disguise (whether complete or partial)" either for the purpose of committing a crime, or escaping after arrest or conviction. See CA Penal Code § [185.] (2021); *San Francisco Municipal Reports, Ordinances and joint resolutions of the city of San Francisco: Together with a list of the officers of the city and county, and rules and orders of the Common Council* (San Francisco: Monson & Valentine, 1854); *General Orders of the Board of Supervisors, Providing regulations for the government of the City and County of San Francisco* (San Francisco: Cosmopolitan Print. Co, 1869); and *General Orders of the Board of Supervisors providing regulation for the government of the city and county of San Francisco. Also, ordinances of Park commissioners* (San Francisco: P. J. Thomas, 1884).

92   *San Francisco Municipal Reports.*

93   Pinkerton, *Thirty Years a Detective,* 432–436.

94   Philip Farley, *Criminals of America; or, Tales of the Lives of Thieves. Enabling Every One to Be His Own Detective. With Portraits, Making a Complete Rogues' Gallery* (New York, 1876), 318 (emphasis added).

95   George W. Matsell, *Vocabulum; or, The Rogue's Lexicon* (New-York: George W. Matsell & Co., 1859), iii, 18, and 40.

96   Thomas Fuller, "Before the Pandemic, Many States Had Anti-mask Laws on the Books. Repealing Them Could Be a Challenge," *New York Times,* June 5, 2021. Some cities' anti-masking laws were twentieth-century responses to Ku Klux Klan gatherings, not the urban disorder that triggered most of the nineteenth-century iterations discussed here.

97   "Current Topics," *Albany Law Journal,* January 17, 1885, 40. A Mother Hubbard gown was a loose dress with a square yoke often worn at home in the nineteenth century while housekeeping or doing farm labor. However, wearing a Mother Hubbard in public was unusual and likely to provoke ridicule, as the quoted passage suggests. Although some municipalities criminalized wearing Mother Hubbards in public in the 1880s, San Francisco did not. See Helvenston Gray, "Searching for Mother Hubbard: Function and Fashion in Nineteenth-Century Dress," *Winterthur Portfolio* 48, no. 1 (Spring 2014): 29–74, at 49–50.

98   *San Francisco Municipal Reports*; *General Orders of the Board of Supervisors* (1869); *General Orders of the Board of Supervisors* (1884); and "A Wretch Properly Punished," *Daily Alta California*, May 28, 1887.

99   John Garvey, *San Francisco Police Department* (San Francisco: Arcadia, 2004), 11.

100   Halttunen, *Confidence Men and Painted Women*, 66–67; and Mary P. Ryan, *Women in Public: Between Banners and Ballots, 1825–1880* (Baltimore, MD: Johns Hopkins University Press, 1990), 81.

101   The same pleading language was repeated in each yearly report form 1891–1892 to 1895–1896, Crowley's final report as Chief of Police. See *San Francisco Municipal Reports*.

102   For a summary of the anxiety around criminal identification in the late nineteenth century, see Simon A. Cole, *Suspect Identities: A History of Fingerprinting and Criminal Identification* (Cambridge, MA: Harvard University Press, 2001), 1–3.

103   Cole, *Suspect Identities*, 21; and Tamara Plakins Thornton, *Handwriting in America: A Cultural History* (New Haven, CT: Yale University Press, 1996), 110–116.

104   Cole, *Suspect Identities*, 2.

105   Cole, *Suspect Identities*, 20 and 32–34.

106   In 2015, the Justice Department and the FBI admitted that there is insufficient scientific basis for the forensic hair analysis used in hundreds of trials in which FBI agents provided expert testimony, and that this testimony routinely overstated the reliability of hair evidence in a way that benefited the prosecution. See Spencer S. Hsu, "Convicted Defendants Left Uninformed of Forensic Flaws Found by Justice Dept.," *Washington Post*, April 16, 2012; Hsu, "FBI Admits Flaws in Hair Analysis over Decades," *Washington Post*, April 18, 2015; and Cole, *Suspect Identities*, 291–293.

107   Nicole Hahn Rafter, "Criminal Anthropology in the United States," *Criminology* 30, no. 4 (1992): 525–546, at 525.

108   Moriz Benedikt, *Anatomical Studies upon Brains of Criminals*, trans. E. P. Fowler (New York: William Wood, 1881).

109   Benedikt, *Anatomical Studies*, 157; and Rafter, "Criminal Anthropology," 528.

110   Rafter, "Criminal Anthropology," 529.

111   Portions of *La donna delinquente* were translated into English as *The Female Offender* in 1895, but this translation was but a shadow of the original; it omitted all discussion of "la donna normale," most of the material on sex workers and almost all references to women criminal's sexuality. In addition to Ellis's book, American elites learned about Lombroso's ideas through the introductions Lombroso wrote to English-language books on criminology, or through a single article Lombroso published in English in a New York journal in 1895. See Nicole Hahn Rafter and Mary Gibson, "Introduction," to Cesare Lombroso and Guglielmo Ferrero, *Criminal Woman, the Prostitute, and the Normal Woman*, trans. Nicole Hahn Rafter and Mary Gibson (Durham, NC: Duke University Press, 2004), 4; Rafter, "Criminal Anthropology," 528–530; Jennifer Devore, "The Rise and Fall of the American Institute of Criminal Law and Criminology," *Journal of Criminal Law and*

Criminology 100, no. 1 (Winter 2010): 9–18; Arthur MacDonald, *Criminology, with an Introduction by Dr. Cesare Lombroso* (New York: Funk & Wagnalls, 1893); August Drahms, *The Criminal: His Personnel and Environment, A Scientific Study, with an Introduction by Cesare Lombroso* (New York: Macmillan, 1900); and Cesare Lombroso, "Criminal Anthropology: Its Origins and Application," *The Forum* 20 (September 1895): 33–49.

112   Cesare Lombroso, *Criminal Man*, ed. and trans. Mary Gibson and Nicole Hahn Rafter (Durham, NC: Duke University Press, 2006), 54.

113   Lombroso, *Criminal Man*, 52 and 56.

114   Lombroso, *Criminal Man,* 52 and 55; and Lombroso, *Criminal Woman,* 126. Lombroso did not discuss facial hair on criminal women at any length. He mentioned that some criminal women exhibited "early appearance of facial hair" and "downiness," but noted that "these traits appear frequently in normal women," too. See Lombroso and Ferrero, *Criminal Woman,* 53.

115   Lombroso, *Criminal Man*, 51; and Lombroso and Ferrero, *Criminal Woman*, 126.

116   Lombroso, *Criminal Man*, 57; and Gibson and Rafter, introduction to *Criminal Man*, 7.

117   Helen Zimmern, "Criminal Women," *Popular Science Monthly,* December 1893, 220.

118   J. H. M'Cassy, "Criminals and Their Characteristics," *Kansas City Medical Index–Lancet* 20, no. 10 (October 1899): 640–643.

119   M'Cassy, "Criminals and Their Characteristics," 640–643.

120   See, for example, *Brooklyn Daily Eagle*, June 9, 1901; *Anaconda Standard* (MT), October 24, 1901; *Atlanta Constitution*, December 13, 1903; *Delaware County Daily Times* (PA), July 1, 1912; *Oakland Tribune* (CA), June 24, 1914; and *Lead Daily Call* (SD), August 5, 1914.

CONCLUSION

1   W. A. Jones to E. A. Hitchcock, February 19, 1902, reprinted in *Annual Report of the Commissioner of Indian Affairs to the Secretary of the Interior for the Fiscal Year Ended June 30, 1902* (Washington, DC: Government Printing Office, 1902), 14.

2   Jones to Hitchcock, 13–14.

3   Lonna Malmsheimer, "'Imitation White Man': Images of Transformation at Carlisle Indian School," *Studies in Visual Communication* 11, no. 4 (1985): 54–75, at 55; Cristina Stanciu, *The Making and Unmaking of Americans: Indians and Immigrants in American Literature and Culture, 1879–1924* (New Haven, CT: Yale University Press, 2023), 81 and 99; and Eric Margolis, "Looking at Discipline, Looking at Labour: Photographic Representations of Indian Boarding Schools," *Visual Studies* 19, no. 1 (2004): 72–96, at 73–74. The list of tribal affiliations included here

comes from the student records digitized as part of Dickinson College's Carlisle Indian School Digital Resource Center, https://carlisleindian.dickinson.edu/index .php/student_records.

4   Malmsheimer, "Imitation White Man," 54 and 58; Hayes Peter Mauro, *The Art of Americanization at Carlisle* (Albuquerque: University of New Mexico Press, 2011), 5; Margolis, "Looking at Discipline, Looking at Labour," 78; and Stanciu, *Making and Unmaking*, 94.

5   Gertrude Bonnin (Yankton Sioux), "School Days of an Indian Girl, 1900," in *Reconstructing Native American Writings in the Boarding School Press*, ed. Jacqueline Emery (Lincoln: University of Nebraska Press, 2017), 255–257.

6   Jones to Hitchcock, 13.

7   "The Contemporary Press," *Evening Times* (Washington, DC), February 4, 1902, 4.

8   Jones to Hitchcock, 13–14.

9   "Report of School Superintendent in Charge of Moqui," in *Annual Reports of the Department of the Interior for the Fiscal Year Ended June 30, 1902. Indian Affairs. Part 1: Report of the Commissioner, and Appendixes* (Washington, DC: Government Printing Office, 1903), 153. The phrase "Gordian like" is a reference to a proverb from Ancient Greece: when Alexander the Great reached the city of Gordium, he encountered the chariot once owned by the founder of the city, Gordius, which was tied to a pole with a very complex knot. Alexander was told that only the conqueror of Asia would be able to untie the knot—and so he found a way to undo the knot forcefully, and faster: to cut through it with his sword. The phrase "cutting the Gordian knot" later became synonymous with "a bold solution to a complicated problem." See "Gordian knot," *Encyclopedia Britannica*, updated June 26, 2024, https://www.britannica.com/topic/Gordian-knot.

10   "Burton Investigation," *Coconino Sun* (Flagstaff, AZ), November 21, 1903, 1–2 and 5. See also Charles Lummis, *Bullying the Moqui*, ed. Robert Easton and Mackenzie Brown (Prescott, AZ: Prescott College Press, 1968).

11   In his own reports Jones uses the former term, writing in his annual report, for example, that "this is what is known as the 'short-hair' order." See Jones to Hitchcock, 14. In local newspapers, some articles also used "short-hair order" while others called it the "haircut order" or "hair-cut order."

12   "Poor Lo Petted Too Much," *Omaha Daily Bee*, October 7, 1903, 7.

13   "'Barbering' the Indian," *Salt Lake Herald* (UT), March 18, 1902, 4.

14   "Indians Resent Reforms," *Topeka State Journal*, January 24, 1902, last edition, 1; and "Indians Don't Like Hair-Cutting Order," *Laramie Republican* (WY), February 25, 1902, 3.

15   "No Trouble Feared," *Kalispell Bee* (MT), January 22, 1902, 1. For more on the Ghost Dance and the Wounded Knee Massacre, see Louis Warren, *God's Red Son: The Ghost Dance Religion and the Making of Modern America* (New York: Basic Books, 2017).

16   Jones to Hitchcock, 14 (emphasis added).

17   Jones to Hitchcock, 14. Jones's characterization of the newspapers' responses is not entirely correct: much of the initial reporting of the order in January–March 1902 *did* reference its mandates around face painting; some, though fewer, referenced dancing and feasting, too. However, by April 1902, the reporting I have found largely focused on the haircut mandate alone.

18   "'Barbering' the Indian"; and "What Bill Cody Says," *Seattle Star,* March 8, 1902, 5.

19   "'Barbering' the Indian."

20   Lummis, *Bullying the Moqui,* 17–18.

21   "Indians Getting Too Wealthy," *Press* (Stafford Springs, CT), April 9, 1903, 1; and "Poor Lo Petted Too Much."

22   *Annual Report of the Commissioner of Indian Affairs to the Secretary of the Interior for the Fiscal Year Ended June 30, 1902* (Washington, DC: Government Printing Office, 1902), 13.

23   W. W. Jermane, "Best Indians Now Independent," *Minneapolis Journal,* August 30, 1905, 5.

24   "Points About People," *Houston Daily Post,* February 19, 1902, 3.

25   I am grateful to Amy Lonetree to bringing to my attention the Wisconsin Historical Society's vast collection of Ho-Chunk portrait photographs. More than three hundred of these photographs (as well as an introductory essay by Lonetree) are reprinted in Tom Jones, Michael Schmudlach, Matthew Daniel Mason, Amy Lonetree, and George A. Greendeer, *People of the Big Voice: Photographs of Ho-Chunk Families by Charle Van Schaick, 1879–1942* (Wisconsin Historical Society Press, 2011).

26   The full text of the ruling was reprinted in "A Man and His Hair," *Out West* 23, no. 4 (October 1905), 371, https://archive.org/details/outwestland23archrich.

27   Charles Lummis, "In the Lion's Den," *Out West* 22, no. 6 (June 1905): 424–425, https://www.google.com/books/edition/Out_West_Magazine/a24LAQA AIAAJ?hl=en&gbpv=1&pg=PA363&printsec=frontcover.

28   Edwin F. Bowers, "Hair and Heads," *New York Tribune*, Sunday Magazine, October 18, 1914.

29   Melville J. Herskovits, *The American Negro: A Study in Racial Crossing* (New York: Alfred A. Knopf, 1928), 19.

30   Herskovits, *American Negro,* 11.

31   "Reading Character by the Hair," *Ballou's Monthly Magazine* 71, no. 4 (April 1890): 278; and "Beauty Quest," *San Francisco Call*, February 23, 1902.

32   Lillian Russell, "'Titian Was Not the Only Man to Admire Auburn Tresses' says Lillian Russell," *Washington Herald*, October 29, 1911.

33   Ría Tabacco Mar, "Why Are Black People Still Punished for Their Hair?" *New York Times,* August 29, 2018; and "Hair Color/Dye Market in the U.S.—Statistics and Facts," *Statista,* updated February 15, 2014, https://www.statista.com/topics /6216/hair-color-dye-market-in-the-us/#topicOverview.

34   Charna Flam, "Jill Martin Shares Emotional Videos While Trying on Wigs After Chemo Hair Loss: 'I'm Dressing Up as Myself,'" *People*, December 28, 2023, https://people.com/jill-martin-shares-emotional-videos-while-trying-wigs-after-chemo -hair-loss-8420541.

35   Aamina Khan, "How I Found a Queer Haircut That Finally Felt Like Home," *Allure*, June 28, 2021, https://www.allure.com/story/gay-queer-haircut-trans -androgynous-hair.

36   Finding aid for Peter Arrell Browne Papers, Academy of Natural Sciences of Drexel University, accessed September 27, 2024, https://archivalcollections.drexel .edu/repositories/3/resources/856; and "Addressing the Woodbury Collection," *Peabody Museum of Archaeology & Ethnology*, accessed October 28, 2024, https://pea body.harvard.edu/woodbury-collection. When I visited the Academy of Natural Sciences of Drexel University in September 2024, only four of the twelve volumes of Browne's hair collection were available for researchers to access. Volumes 1–8, the volumes that contain human hair, were closed to research as the archival staff reevaluated its stewardship of human remains. The finding aid for the Peter Arrell Browne papers indicated this closure; I confirmed its cause in conversation with archivist Jessica Lydon and librarian Briana Giasullo on September 27, 2024.

37   Interior Department, Rule, "Native American Graves Protection and Repatriation Act Systematic Processes for Disposition or Repatriation of Native American Human Remains, Funerary Objects, Sacred Objects, and Objects of Cultural Patrimony," *Federal Register* 88, no. 238 (December 13, 2023): 86452, https://www .federalregister.gov/d/2023-27040; and Rosa Cartagena, "Philadelphia Museums Hold Strands of Hair from Indigenous People: That May Soon Change," *Philadelphia Inquirer*, May 18, 2024, https://www.inquirer.com/arts/nagpra-philadelphia -museum-mutter-penn-academy-natural-sciences-20240518.html.

38   Hettie Judah, "Mona Hatoum's Hair: Interweaving Strands, and the Artist's Work," *Interwoven: The Fabric of Things*, http://kvadratinterwoven.com/mona -hatoums-hair.

39   Zen Hansen, *Hair Anthropology*, accessed May 21, 2024, https://www .hairanthropology.com/.

40   Lori L. Tharps, "Black Hair Is . . . ," in *Textures: The History and Art of Black Hair*, ed. Tameka N. Ellington and Joseph L. Underwood (Kent, OH: Kent State University Museum, 2020), 20. See also Willie Morrow, *400 Years Without a Comb* (San Diego: Morrow's Unlimited, Inc., 1973), 15. Morrow was a barber and Black hair care and history expert who is credited for creating and selling the first mass-produced afro pick in the 1960s. See Clay Risen, "Willie Lee Morrow, Barber Who Popularized the Afro Pick, Dies at 82," *New York Times*, July 6, 2022.

41   Alok Vaid-Menon (@alokvmenon), "on the other size of shame, BODY HAIR IS BEAUTIFUL," Instagram, August 28, 2021, https://www.instagram .com/p/CTH7QO5F2oI.

42   Christine Hope, "Caucasian Female Body Hair and American Culture," *Journal of American Culture* 5, no. 1 (1982): 93–99, at 93; Susan A. Basow, "The

Hairless Ideal: Women and Their Body Hair," *Psychology of Women Quarterly* 15, no. 1 (March 1991): 83–96; Karín Lesnik-Oberstein, "The Last Taboo: Women, Body Hair, and Feminism," in *The Last Taboo: Women and Body Hair,* ed. Karín Lesnik-Oberstein (Manchester: Manchester University Press, 2013), 14n1; and Andrea L. DeMaria and Abbey B. Berenson, "Prevalence and Correlates of Pubic Hair Grooming among Low-income Hispanic, Black, and White Women," *Body Image* 10, no. 2 (March 2013): 226–231.

43 Lesnik-Oberstein, "The Last Taboo: Women, Body Hair, and Feminism," 1–2. The Spring/Summer 2024 fashion show for French design house Maison Margiela showed sheer dresses through which the models' merkins—pubic toupees made from human hair sewn onto silk tulle—were visible. See Chloe Mac Donnell, "The Latest High-fashion Accessory? Say Hello to the Merkin," *The Guardian,* February 2, 2024.

44 Mar, "Why Are Black People Still Punished for Their Hair?"; "Judge Allows Girls in 'Braided-Hair Extension' Dispute to Return to School for Now," *WWLTV,* August 23, 2018, https://www.wwltv.com/article/news/local/judge-allows -girls-in-braided-hair-extension-dispute-to-return-to-school-for-now/289-587037071; Julia Jacobo, "6th Grader Asked to Leave Private School over Rule Banning Hair Extensions, Family Says," ABC News, August 21, 2018, https://abcnews.go.com/US /6th-grader-asked-leave-private-school-rule-banning/story?id=57311484; and Jacqueline Laurean Yates, "Mickey Guyton's 'Love My Hair' Is Based on This Inspiring 14-Year-Old," *Good Morning America,* November 22, 2021, https://www.good morningamerica.com/style/story/mickey-guytons-love-hair-based-inspiring-14-year -81285800.

45 H.R.2116—Creating a Respectful and Open World for Natural Hair Act of 2022, 117th Congress, https://www.congress.gov/bill/117th-congress/house-bill /2116/text; and "About," *The CROWN Act,* https://www.thecrownact.com/about.

46 Congress.gov, "Cosponsors—H.R.2116—117th Congress (2021–2022): Creating a Respectful and Open World for Natural Hair Act of 2022," March 21, 2022, https://www.congress.gov/bill/117th-congress/house-bill/2116/cosponsors; and "Curls and Courage with Michaela Angela Davis and Rep. Cori Bush," *It's Been a Minute,* January 13, 2023, https://www.npr.org/transcripts/1148394231.

ACKNOWLEDGMENTS

I have been working on this book in one way or another since my first year of graduate school in 2010. It is as old as both of my children combined, and to finally see it come to life in print feels like the fulfillment of my own childhood dream: When I was eight years old, I announced to my parents that I was going to be a writer when I grew up. While I have written many things in the thirty years since, this is my first book. I am so grateful to the many colleagues, teachers, friends, and family who have supported me generously and patiently as I accomplished this dream.

The staff at Harvard University Press have been instrumental to the creation and completion of this book. Thank you to Sharmila Sen for seeing the potential in this book, even when it was just a proposal in the Press's inbox. Sending off a proposal can feel like throwing paperwork into a black hole, but she believed in *Whiskerology* from the very beginning and stuck with me until the very end. I am also grateful that Sharmila brought on a second editor to support this project: Emily Silk. This book became better than I ever thought it could be because of Emily. Thank you to Emily for her unfailing optimism, infectious enthusiasm, and incredibly incisive editing. I could not have imagined a better experience as a first-time author than the one we had together. Thank you also to the other HUP staff who helped bring this book to life: Jillian Quigley, Susan Karani Virtanen, Stephanie Vyce, and Gabriele Wilson. Thank you to Pablo Delcan for the cover artwork, and to Gabriele Wilson for the beautiful jacket design.

Even though much of the research I conducted for this project was digital, I was also the beneficiary of the tremendous knowledge and generosity of archivists, curators, and library staff on both coasts. Thank you to Lee Anne Titanagos at the Bancroft Library at University of California, Berkeley; Teresa Johnson and Russell Johnson at the Louise M. Darling Biomedical Library at the University of California, Los Angeles; Lauren Hewes, Thomas Knoles, Kimberly Pelkey, and Nan Wolverton at the American Antiquarian

Society; and Jessica Lydon and Briana Giasullo at the Academy of Natural Sciences at Drexel University.

This project began as a dissertation I completed in the University of California, Berkeley's History Department, where I received financial support in the form of the Rosalie M. Stern Fellowship, a Berkeley Connect fellowship, and a Student Mentoring and Research Teams fellowship. The History Department was my intellectual home for nearly fifteen years, from 2005 (when I took my first undergraduate lecture course) through my two years as visiting faculty. For the last six years, I have found a new home in the Program in American Studies, which has provided incredible support, community, and friendship. As a non-tenure-track academic, I do not take for granted the amount of research support (both intellectual and financial) that I have received as I worked on this book. Thank you to this remarkable community of interdisciplinary faculty of which I am lucky to be part: Mark Brilliant, Michael Mark Cohen, Alexander Benjamin Craghead, Margaretta Lovell, David H. Miller, Kathy Moran, Christine Palmer, Andy Shanken, and Shannon Steen. And my thanks to Laura Spautz for supporting our faculty and students alike.

Research is what drew me to academia, but teaching is what made me stay. I am especially grateful to my own teachers: Lars Trupe, my tenth grade AP World History teacher, who first planted the seed; Robin Einhorn, who inspired me to become a historian; Waldo E. Martin, who helped me develop my scholarly voice; and David Henkin, who taught me how to *be* a historian. Even when my career path was uncertain, David always believed this project could become a book. I am lucky to have been the recipient of his excellent advice and mentorship for the last fifteen years; so much of who I am as a teacher and scholar is thanks to him.

Thank you to my research assistants who helped me with this book: Christina James, Natalie Fulton, and Riley Knott. And my thanks to my incredible students, whose curiosity, tenacity, and deep wells of empathy inspire me every semester. I am especially grateful to the students who took American Studies H110 with me in Spring 2024, when I was deep into my revisions for this book. Traces of our weekly conversations about the making and unmaking of the American body are all over this book. Thank you to Diana Choi, Katie Latta, Megan Lee, Brittany Postle, Kelthie Truong, and Hope Waggoner.

I am enormously grateful to all the colleagues and friends who have talked with me about this project (and even sent me leads during their own archival travels) over the past decade. Thank you to Ryan Acton, Rachel Barrett Martin, Cassandra Berman, Chris Casey, Andra Chastain, James Cook, Brian DeLay, Sandra Eder, Maggie Elmore, Adrianne Francisco, Diana Greenwold, Paulina Hartono, Rebecca Herman, Andrea Horbinski, Trevor Jackson, Stephanie E. Jones-Rogers, Danny Kelly, Mary Klann, Tom Laqueur, Kim Nalley, Joseph Nejad-Duong, Natalie Novoa, Christopher Oldstone-Moore, Lindsey Passenger Wieck, Caitlin Rosenthal, Brendan Shanahan, Ronit Stahl, Julie Stein, Jessica Stewart, Sarah Stoller, Sean Trainor, and Felicia Viator. Thank you especially to Daniel Friedman, Erica Lee, Natalie Mendoza, Rachel B. Reinhard, Julia Shatz, and Zoe Silverman—my favorite people to talk to about teaching—and to the wonderful women who have made the Western Association of Women Historians my intellectual home away from home: Kate Flach, Laura Ping, Jennifer Robin Terry, Patricia Schechter, Pamela Stewart, Ula Taylor, and Jennifer Thigpen.

Lastly, I want to thank my friends and family, who believed that I could write this book, even when it took years longer than expected. Thank you to my beloved Book Club (Kelsey Blegen, Irene Pasma, Tanya Pham, Becca Rasmussen, and Lisa Rosete) for always cheering me on. Thank you to Hiking Club and to the second generation of Hiking Club babies. Thank you to the Dixon family for all the hikes and good talks. My thanks to the Fockele family and the commune we will one day create together. And thank you to Kelly Campbell; let's write the next book together.

I would never have made it this far in my education had it not been for the foundation built by my parents, Dan and Patty Gold, who gave me the intellectual curiosity and confidence that has allowed me to turn my love of writing, research, and teaching into a career. Thank you to my in-laws, Dennis and Linda McBride, my cousins, and my siblings, Sam Rotengold, Becca Gold, Ariela Rotengold, Graham Davis, and Kaitlin McBride, for loving me (and letting me stop to read all the historical plaques). Thank you to my children, Louis and Rosalie. When I was on a book deadline and holed up in my office for an entire Saturday, Louis and Rosalie slipped cards under the door (with candy inside, for sustenance), and made me a sign for my desk that said, "Go Mom! Finish your book!! Finish your book!!!" They have been more encouraging, generous, and patient with the hours I spent writing this book than any nine- or six-year-old has the right to be. Finally, thank you to my husband, James McBride, for being my partner in the truest sense of the word, and for *always* believing that I could do this. I am the luckiest of all to have you.

INDEX

Page numbers in *italics* refer to illustrations.